IMAGES, POWER, AND POLITICS

Figurative Aspects of
Esarhaddon's Babylonian Policy

Stele found at Zincirli (ancient Sam'al) in north Syria representing Esarhaddon
as conqueror of the Westlands, an image which contrasts with the
benevolent image of the ruler presented by his inscriptions for Babylon.
(Staatliche Museen zu Berlin, Vorderasiatisches Museum)

Images, Power, and Politics

Figurative Aspects of
Esarhaddon's Babylonian Policy

BARBARA NEVLING PORTER

AMERICAN PHILOSOPHICAL SOCIETY
Independence Square · Philadelphia
1993

MEMOIRS OF THE
AMERICAN PHILOSOPHICAL SOCIETY
HELD AT PHILADELPHIA
FOR PROMOTING USEFUL KNOWLEDGE
VOLUME 208

Jacket Illustration:

Esarhaddon holding on a leash Baal of Tyre and Ušanaḫuru, crown prince of Egypt.
VA 2708. J. Börker-Klähn, *Altvorderasiatische Bildstelen und vergleichbare Felsreliefs*, Baghdader Forschungen 4 (1982), Fig. 219.

Library of Congress Card No.: 92-85335
International Standard Book No.: 0-87169-208-2
USISSN: 0065-9738

To
M.H.P.

Contents

Plates, Maps, and Plans

SOURCES

The drawing appearing on the DUSTCOVER is by J. Börker-Klähn, *Altvorderasiatische Bildstelen und vergleichbare Felsreliefs*, Baghdader Forschungen 4 (1982), Fig. 219.

The photographs used are reproduced by courtesy of: FRONTISPIECE, Staatliche Museen zu Berlin, Vorderasiatisches Museum; PLATE ONE, page 9, Musée du Louvre; PLATE TWO, page 85, The Pierpont Morgan Library, New York; PLATE THREE and PLATE FOUR, pages 88 and 89, The Trustees of the British Museum.

The topographic coordinates of the maps are from the Central Intelligence Agency's World Data Bank II, as reformatted for micro-computer use by Fred Pospeschil and Antonio Riveria, with additional detail from the relevant Tactical Pilotage Charts available from the U.S. Government Defense Mapping Agency. Locations of ancient cities are drawn from Albert R. Al-Haik, *Key Lists of Archaeological Excavations in Iraq, 1842–1965*, edited by Henry Field and Edith M. Laird (Coconut Grove, Florida: Field Research Projects, 1968); Albert R. Al-Haik, *Key Lists of Archaeological Excavations in Iraq: II, 1966–1971*, edited by Henry Field and Edith M. Laird (Coconut Grove, Florida: Field Research Projects, 1971); Richard S. Ellis, *A Bibliography of Mesopotamian Archaeological Sites* (Wiesbaden: Harrassowitz, 1972); Simo Parpola, *The Correspondence of Sargon II, Part I: Letters from Assyria and the West*, State Archives of Assyria, I (Helsinki: Helsinki University Press, 1987), end-pocket map, "The Assyrian Empire"; and Ran Zadok, *Répertoire Géographique des Textes Cunéiformes VIII: Geographical Names According to New- and Late-Babylonian Texts*, Beihefte zum Tübinger Atlas des Vorderen Orients, ed. Wolfgang Röllig (Wiesbaden: Dr. Ludwig Reichert Verlag, 1985). The maps and plans were prepared by Michael H. Porter, of the Cartographic Division of the Cumberland Mainland and Islands Trust, to whom I offer my grateful thanks for his skill and patience.

The plans of Babylon and the temples Esagila and Etemenanki are adapted from the site plans of Friedrich Wetzel, published in Friedrich Wetzel, *Die Stadtmauern von Babylon*, WVDOG, 48 (Leipzig: J.C. Hinrichs, 1930) and in Friedrich Wetzel and F.H. Weissbach, *Das Hauptheiligtum des Marduk in Babylon, Esagila und Etemenanki*, WVDOG, 59 (Leipzig: J.C. Hinrichs, 1938).

Acknowledgments

WITHOUT THE HELP OF MANY PEOPLE OVER THE YEARS, this study would never have reached completion. I owe them thanks for innumerable suggestions and improvements; the flaws that remain are my own. I am grateful to James D. Muhly and James B. Pritchard for advice and warm support in the years when this study was first taking shape as a doctoral dissertation, and I am especially indebted to Tzvi Abusch, who supervised the dissertation in its final years and was an unfailing source of encouragement and perceptive advice. Among the friends and colleagues who have taken the time to offer comments, criticism, encouragement or prodding as the book evolved, I am particularly grateful to William W. Hallo, Sara A. Immerwahr, Robert C. Hunt, Louis D. Levine, Simo Parpola, Julian Reade, and Hayim Tadmor. J.A. Brinkman and Irene J. Winter read the manuscript in its final stages and showered me with helpful suggestions and comments; I am indebted to both of them.

I would like to thank the Chebeague Island Library and its librarian, Martha Hamilton, for years of efficient interlibrary loan service. I am indebted to William W. Hallo, curator of the Yale Babylonian Collection, for granting me access to materials in the collection and for making me warmly welcome there, and to Paul-Alain Beaulieu and Ulla Kasten for cheerfully helping me to find my way around it. For their gracious help and for permission to publish photographs of objects in the collections of their museums, I would like to thank E. Klengel and the Vorderasiatisches Museum of the Staatliche Museen zu Berlin; Edith Porada and the Pierpont Morgan Library, New York; C.B.F. Walker and the Trustees of the British Museum; and Annie Caubet and the Département des Antiquités Orientales of the Musée du Louvre. I would like also to thank my editor, Carole N. Le Faivre of the American Philosophical Society, for her tactful and efficient help.

I owe special thanks to my three children, Stephen B. Porter, Anne K. Porter, and Seth H. Porter, for their affectionate encouragement of a mother who has been "doing Esarhaddon" for most of their lives. Above all, I want to thank my husband, Michael H. Porter; without his help and patience, this book could never have been written.

Note on the Texts

IN THIS STUDY, PASSAGES FROM ESARHADDON'S ROYAL inscriptions have been identified by the title assigned the text in Riekele Borger's edition of the inscriptions (*Die Inschriften Asarhaddons, Königs von Assyrien* [Graz: 1956]) and are based on the Akkadian texts established there, supplemented or revised as necessary to incorporate new material published after Borger's edition appeared. Such new material is cited in the accompanying footnotes, and is also listed separately in Appendix III. Esarhaddon inscriptions recognized and published after Borger's 1956 edition have been assigned titles according to Borger's system. The translations of Esarhaddon's inscriptions which appear here, although they owe much to Borger's translations and commentary, are my own.

Inscriptions of kings other than Esarhaddon are quoted from the translation in the edition cited in each instance. Most letters are quoted from the translations of Simo Parpola in his *Letters from Assyrian Scholars*, as noted.

In accordance with Assyriological convention, parentheses within a passage translated from Akkadian mark comments added by the translator to make the translation clearer. Brackets mark the translator's suggested restorations of broken passages in the text. Roman numerals indicate column numbers, and Arabic numerals indicate line numbers of a given text.

The transliteration of personal names and place names in the Neo-Assyrian period is problematic, since it is often unclear from the Akkadian how contemporaries would have pronounced a given name, and since the Akkadian writing of names is sometimes inconsistent. To make it possible for readers, particularly non-specialists, to recognize the person or place being discussed as one already known from previous studies, I have so far as possible adopted the form of the name that appears in a standard reference work, rather than imposing a consistent pattern of transliteration; personal names which appear in Assyrian letters have thus been cited in the form adopted by Simo Parpola in *Letters to Assyrian Scholars*, and names of Aramean tribes, in the form used by J.A. Brinkman in *A Political History of Post-Kassite Babylonia*. For other proper names, I have used a normalized form reflecting current Assyriological practice, rather than one reflecting a plene writing of that name in Assyrian texts—again, because these forms are more likely to be readily recognizable from earlier studies. For some Akkadian names, such as Sennacherib, or Nineveh, a conventional English form already exists, usually derived from the form in which the word appears in Biblical or Classical sources; in such cases, I have used the English version of the name, without diacritical marks.

List of Abbreviations

In the case of abbreviated references in the list below, see the bibliography under the respective authors for a full citation.

AB	Assyriologische Bibliothek
ABL	Robert Harper, *Assyrian and Babylonian Letters*
AfO	*Archiv für Orientforschung*
AHw	Wolfram von Soden, *Akkadisches Handwörterbuch*
AJSL	*American Journal of Semitic Languages and Literatures*
ANET	James B. Pritchard, ed., *Ancient Near Eastern Texts.*
AOAT	Alter Orient und Altes Testament
App.	Appendix
AS	Assyriological Studies (University of Chicago)
Asarh.	Riekele Borger, *Die Inschriften Asarhaddons, Königs von Assyrien*
Bd.	Band
BiOr	*Bibliotheca Orientalis* (Nederlands Instituut voor het Nabije Oosten)
BM	Initial letters of British Museum identification numbers
Bu	British Museum identification numbers, object purchased by E.A. Wallis Budge
CAD	A. Leo Oppenheim, J.A. Brinkman, et al., ed., *The Assyrian Dictionary of the Oriental Institute of the University of Chicago*
Ch.	chapter
Chr.	Babylonian Chronicle text, published in A.K. Grayson, *Assyrian and Babylonian Chronicles*
col.	column
CT	*Cuneiform Texts from Babylonian Tablets . . . in the British Museum.* For *CT* 15, see bibliography under King; for 44, under Pinches; for 53, under Parpola; and for 54, under Dietrich.
cyl.	cylinder
diss.	dissertation
Ep.	"Episode" or "Episoden," Borger's designation for a section of an inscription or group of inscriptions
frt.	fragment
Gbr	"Gottesbrief" or "letter to a god" inscription of Esarhaddon in Borger's labeling system

HUCA	*Hebrew Union College Annual*
JAOS	*Journal of the American Oriental Society*
JCS	*Journal of Cuneiform Studies*
JNES	*Journal of Near Eastern Studies*
K	Kouyunjik or Kuyunjik, part of the ruins of Nineveh; initial letter of British Museum registration number of objects said to have been found there (sometimes in error)
KAH I	Leopold Messerschmidt, *Keilschrifttexte aus Aššur historischen Inhalts*, I, WVDOG 16
KAH II	Otto Schroeder, *Keilschrifttexte aus Aššur historischen Inhalts*, II, WVDOG 37
KAR II	Erich Ebeling, *Keilschrifttexte aus Aššur religiösen Inhalts*, WVDOG 34
l. or ll.	line or lines
LAS	designates an Assyrian letter published by Simo Parpola in *Letters from Assyrian Scholars to the Kings Esarhaddon and Assurbanipal, Part 1: Texts*
Letters, IIa	Simo Parpola, *Letters from Assyrian Scholars to the Kings Esarhaddon and Assurbanipal, Part II A: Introduction and Appendixes* (1971)
Letters, IIb	Simo Parpola, *Letters from Assyrian Scholars to the Kings Esarhaddon and Assurbanipal, Part II: Commentary and Appendices* (1983)
MAH	initial letters of identification number for objects in the Musée d'Art et d'Histoire, Geneva
MDOG	*Mitteilungen der Deutschen Orient-Gesellschaft*
Mnm	monument; designates text inscribed on a monument or cliff in Borger's labeling system
Nin.	Nineveh; in Borger's labeling system designates text dealing primarily with Nineveh
n.	note
obv.	obverse, or front, of a tablet
OIP, 2	Daniel David Luckenbill, *The Annals of Sennacherib*
Or.	*Orientalia* (new series)
pl.	plate
PN	personal name
R	Henry C. Rawlinson, *The Cuneiform Inscriptions of Western Asia:* IR=vol. I, *A Selection from the Historical Inscriptions of Chaldea, Assyria, and Babylonia* (1861); IIIR=vol. III, *A Selection from the Miscellaneous Inscriptions of Assyria* (1870); IVR=vol. IV, *A Selection from the Miscellaneous Inscriptions of Assyria* (1875)
RA	*Révue d'assyriologie et d'archéologie orientale*
rpt.	reprint
rs.	reverse, or back, of a tablet
RLA	*Reallexikon der Assyriologie*, E. Ebeling, et al., ed.

Rm	initial letters of British Museum identification numbers for objects excavated by Hormuzd Rassam
(s.)	singular
Smlt.	"Sammeltext," Borger's designation (pp. 93–95) for a summarizing inscription of Esarhaddon
TCS	Texts from Cuneiform Sources
VAT	initial letters of identification numbers for clay tablets belonging to the Staatliche Museen zu Berlin, Vorderasiatische Abteilung
WO	*Die Welt des Orients*
WVDOG	Wissenschaftliche Veröffentlichungen der Deutschen Orient-Gesellschaft
YBC	initial letters of identification numbers of objects in the Yale Babylonian Collection, Yale University, New Haven, Connecticut
ZA	*Zeitschrift für Assyriologie und vorderasiatische Archäologie*

CHAPTER ONE

Introduction

THE KINGS OF ASSYRIA ACQUIRED IN THEIR own day a reputation for ruthlessness which they were careful to encourage, depicting themselves in royal inscriptions and public monuments as merciless fighters and as rulers who punished any attempt to resist by torturing rebel leaders and pillaging cities. This image, powerfully presented, had the dual effect of reassuring the Assyrians of their own power and at the same time reminding their subjects of the high price of resistance. Bitter references in Biblical texts to the Israelites' experiences at the hands of their Assyrian conquerors lend credence to this picture and have helped keep the memory of Assyrian ruthlessness alive into modern times. Even today, the poet Byron's description of the Assyrian king Sennacherib, who "came down like the wolf on the fold," is the phrase by which the Assyrians are most often remembered. Although the Assyrians' reputation for violence is well deserved, a close look at their handling of Babylonia suggests that coercion through violence was only one aspect of Assyrian rule; the effectiveness of the Assyrians' own propaganda of violence has to a large extent prevented subsequent generations from recognizing their equally skillful use of the peaceful arts of government to control conquered populations.

This book is intended in part as a corrective to this common perception of the Assyrians as rulers. It focuses on Assyrians' use of peaceful means to maintain control over the conquered nation of Babylonia during the reign of Esarhaddon, king of Assyria in the early seventh century BC, a time when Assyria was still the controlling imperial power in the Middle East. Documentary evidence from Esarhaddon's reign suggests that he was not only a successful military leader but an effective diplomat, as well, who succeeded in controlling the chronically rebellious Babylonians largely by developing a public relations program designed to encourage their acceptance of Assyrian rule. Esarhaddon's approach to Babylonia is an example of Assyrian political control exercised less through terror and intimidation than through a shrewd and intelligent responsiveness to the needs of the people he governed. In the chapters that follow, as we trace Esarhaddon's tumultuous rise to power and his successful efforts to stabilize his position by establishing peace in Babylonia, a new and more complex model of how the Assyrians ruled their empire emerges, one in which the political skills of the kings of Assyria can be seen to play a major role.[1]

When Esarhaddon came to the throne late in the year 681,[2] Assyria had been for some time the dominant power in the Near East, controlling an empire stretching from the Persian Gulf to the borders of Egypt. Suffering from a chronic illness, Esarhaddon was to rule that empire for only eleven years until his death in the year 669—a short and difficult reign. From the beginning, when he seized control of Assyria in the midst of the civil war that followed his father's murder, Esarhaddon was under pressure from conflicting factions within Assyria. Outside the homeland, he faced recurrent threats of rebellion from already conquered nations and threats of attack from nations beyond the empire's borders.

In spite of these difficulties, Esarhaddon governed Assyria and her empire with more success than he has sometimes been credited with; he brought a quick end to the civil war of 681, carried out an ambitious building program in both Assyria and Babylonia, waged successful campaigns in Mannea, Šubria, and Phoenicia, conquered Assyria's longtime rival Egypt, and managed to engineer the peaceful transfer of power to his sons at his death, a series of achievements that make him one of the more successful Neo-Assyrian kings.

Perhaps the most impressive of his achievements, however, was his success in controlling the chronically rebellious Babylonians with a minimum of military intervention; the era of relatively peaceful relations between the two states which he created was to continue throughout his reign and for almost seventeen years after his death. Considering the state of Assyrian–Babylonian relations at the time of Esarhaddon's accession, this period of relative harmony was a remarkable achievement. Assyria had been conducting intermittent campaigns in Babylonia since the thirteenth century, finally imposing direct Assyrian rule on the Babylonians in the reign of the Assyrian king Tiglath-

---

[1] In an essay on Assyrian treaties and loyalty oaths, Simo Parpola comments that the Assyrians' extensive use of such documents as tools of foreign diplomacy suggests "that Assyria was something more than just the crude military power which it is pictured as in the schoolbooks" (Simo Parpola and Kazuko Watanabe, *Neo-Assyrian Treaties and Loyalty Oaths*, SAA, II [Helsinki: 1988], xxv). Esarhaddon's techniques for controlling Babylonia illustrate another aspect of the Assyrians' political skills.

[2] For dates of Mesopotamian rulers, I have generally followed J.A. Brinkman, "Mesopotamian Chronology of the Historical Period," in A. Leo Oppenheim, *Ancient Mesopotamia: Portrait of a Dead Civilization* (Chicago: 1964), 335–347. All ancient dates cited here fall in the period before the Christian era (BC), unless otherwise noted. The Assyrian year overlaps two years of the modern Julian calendar, since its beginning was timed to coincide with the vernal equinox, part way through the month of March. Strictly speaking, then, Esarhaddon ascended the throne of Assyria in Julian year 680, since he took the throne in Addāru (Feb./March), which was the last month of the Assyrian year but in the Julian calendar was already the second month of the following year. In the interests of simplicity, however, dates cited here will reflect the year as the Assyrians conceived it, e.g., "681" rather than the more precise "681/80," except in the few cases where a more exact date is significant.

Pileser III, in the eighth century. The Babylonians, however, had remained stubbornly resistant to Assyrian rule; Esarhaddon's predecessors, despite repeated campaigns against Babylonia, had found themselves unable to rule Babylonia for more than short periods of time before being confronted by yet another revolt. In the time of Esarhaddon's father Sennacherib, the destructive cycle of Babylonian revolts and Assyrian punitive campaigns reached a climax. After confronting a series of Babylonian uprisings, Sennacherib finally attacked the venerable city of Babylon itself, reportedly looting it, deporting its citizens, and diverting a canal to flood the remains. Although Sennacherib's accounts may exaggerate the extent of the damage he inflicted, they are evidence of the intense hostility that had developed by this time on both sides.

Esarhaddon's efforts to establish peace between the two states in the following years confronted an animosity rooted in these years of conflict and not easily dispelled. It is not surprising that reports from Esarhaddon's reign attest to continued tension and occasional outbreaks of violence on both sides despite the king's efforts to effect a reconciliation.[3] The anti-Assyrian feeling in Babylonia is reflected, for example, in a letter to Esarhaddon which reports that citizens of the city of Babylon had "set up a wail (and) protested" at the Assyrian governor's imposition of heavy taxes and would probably be accused by him of pelting his messengers with lumps of clay.[4] From the Assyrian side, a similar hostility is evident in a letter to Esarhaddon from one of his advisers suggesting that the next candidate for substitute king (a person chosen at a time of unfavorable omens to take upon himself the king's impending

---

[3] Wolfram von Soden has argued that Esarhaddon was much under the control of his astrologers and haruspices, implying that he was thus not the main source of many of the policy decisions of his administration. He argues, for example, "Die Briefe bezeugen uns ferner, wie gross der persönliche Einfluss bestimmter Astrologen und Priester auf den offenbar nicht immer einer klaren Linie folgenden König war" (Wolfram von Soden, *Herrscher im Alten Orient* [Berlin, Göttingen, Heidelberg: 1954], 125). Simo Parpola has since argued persuasively that both astrologers and haruspices were bound by professional standards which prevented them from freely interpreting omens to favor their own political agendas and that there is in any case considerable evidence that the king maintained his independence from these advisers, challenging their interpretations on technical grounds with a skill that shows him well able to evaluate the reports he received, and also at times simply rejecting their advice (Simo Parpola, *Letters from Assyrian Scholars to the Kings Esarhaddon and Assurbanipal, Part IIA: Introduction and Appendixes*, Diss. Helsinki 1971; hereafter, *Letters*, IIa). While it is difficult to establish the roles of various Assyrian kings and their advisers in formulating public policy, it seems likely that the king in most cases played some role—possibly the dominant role—in such decisions. It is thus reasonable to refer to Esarhaddon, or to Esarhaddon and his advisers, as the source of the policies whose outlines we can trace in his royal inscriptions. In the final analysis, however, it is not of particular significance whether it was Esarhaddon himself or one or another of his advisers who was in the main responsible for devising the Babylonian policy of his reign; my interest is in tracing and describing that policy throughout his administration, whatever its source.

[4] Letter no. 276 in Simo Parpola, *Letters from Assyrian Scholars to the Kings Esarhaddon and Assurbanipal, Part I: Texts*, AOAT, 5/1, hereafter, "LAS." I have translated "governor" here rather than "commandant" to suggest the broader responsibilities of a *šākin ṭēmi*.

misfortune and perhaps death) should be chosen from among the Babylonians, remarking, "[the king my lord] knows the Babylonians . . .; (these) plotters should be affli[cted]."[5]

The hostile feelings such letters reveal periodically erupted in hostile actions as well. From Babylonia there are numerous accusations of plotting to overthrow the Assyrian government. While some of these accusations may have been made by people trying to even up old scores or seek advancement, several of the accusations have a convincing ring. One report, for instance, claims that during the turmoil at the beginning of the reign, a group of Babylonians offered money to the king of Elam in the hope of hiring troops to help in a planned revolt against Assyria.[6] It is a plausible story, since Elam had regularly helped Babylonia in past revolts, and since the accusation is supported by statements from two Babylonian witnesses. Equally convincing are the accusations leveled against a man named Ṣallāju, which are so frequent and so detailed, and come from so many sources, that it is hard to avoid the conclusion that he was actively plotting against Assyria. One of the more explicit accusations reports that Ṣallāju had inquired about three leaders of Babylonia, "speaking about upheaval of the country," and concluding, "'Seize the fortified places one after another!'"[7] Such reports of treason and plotting in Babylonia were a common topic of letters to the king and attest to the magnitude of the problem Esarhaddon confronted in attempting to establish lasting peace between the two states.

It is a sign of his remarkable success in this undertaking that none of the plotting in Babylonia produced an uprising under Esarhaddon's rule, in marked contrast to earlier reigns. We learn of the plots from Esarhaddon's reign precisely because they were discovered in the planning stages and reported to the Assyrian authorities, who interfered before any action could take place.[8] In several cases we are told explicitly that the plotters had been de-

---

[5] LAS 185. The king's irritation with one group of Babylonians is reflected in the letter ABL 403, where he addresses them as "the Non-Babylonians" and quotes a proverb reflecting his exasperation at their ingratitude for his help.

[6] This conspiracy, led by a certain Nabû-aḫḫē-iddina, is described in an anonymous report, VAT 4923, published by Ernst Weidner, "Hochverrat gegen Asarhaddon," 5–9.

[7] LAS 30. A man named Ṣallāju was also implicated in the earlier plot to murder Sennacherib; see the letter published by Simo Parpola, "The Murderer of Sennacherib," in *Death in Mesopotamia*, Mesopotamia, 8, ed. Bendt Alster (Copenhagen: 1980), 171–182. Ṣallāju is also implicated in plots against Assyria in the letters ABL 223, 327, 416, 540, 702, 1255, and *CT* 54, nos. 22 and 527.

[8] Examples of Babylonian plots that were nipped in the bud include the conspiracy led by Nabû-aḫḫē-iddina (see note 6, above) and a later conspiracy involving Bēl-ēṭir, Šamaš-zēra-iqīša and Aplāyu, reported to Šamaš-šumu-ukīn (Simo Parpola, "A Letter from Šamaš-šumu-ukīn to Esarhaddon," 21–34). Although Manfried Dietrich has argued in *Die Aramäer Südbabyloniens in der Sargonidenzeit (700–648)*, 16, 25, 29–30 and 39 ff., that Ṣallāju actually led a revolt against Assyria, there is in fact no clear evidence of anything but plotting. For problems in Dietrich's handling of the evidence about Ṣallāju, see the review by John A. Brinkman, "Notes on Arameans and Chaldeans in Southern Babylonia in the Early Seventh Century BC," 317–318. Dietrich's claims that a

nounced by other Babylonians, suggesting that Babylonian opposition to Assyrian rule had become less than unanimous.[9]

Since the chapters that follow focus on the strategies Esarhaddon uses to effect a partial reconciliation of the Babylonians to Assyrian rule, it is worth taking a moment at the outset to make it clear that he does succeed in this very difficult undertaking—a point that has not always been clear to commentators on his reign. In the first months of his reign, he did, to be sure, dispatch an Assyrian army into Babylonia to relieve the siege of Ur, part of an uprising set off by his father's sudden death and the subsequent civil war in Assyria, but the rebels fled Babylonia before a confrontation with the advancing Assyrian forces could occur.

After this initial incident, we know of only three situations during the reign in which the Assyrians intervened with a show of force, all three incidents apparently of minor importance. In 678, the Assyrians removed from office the governor based in the Babylonian city of Nippur along with a leader of the Bīt-Dakkūri tribe settled in that area; both men were taken to Assyria and executed, an action reinforced by a punitive raid on Bīt-Dakkūri territory by Assyrian troops. The reason the texts offer for this raid is that the Bīt-Dakkūri leader had seized land belonging to inhabitants of Babylon and Borsippa; the governor, although his role is not explained, may have been suspected of collaborating in the project. Three years later, in 675, there was evidently further trouble in Nippur; the city's new governor and another Bīt-Dakkūri leader were removed to Assyria and probably executed. In this case, the texts give no explanation for the Assyrians' intervention; Pamela D. Gerardi has suggested that the incident may represent a failed Elamite-Babylonian alliance against Assyria, the Elamite aspect of which con-

---

man named Sāsî led a revolt in Nippur in 675 (pp. 50–56) seem to me equally unconvincing. The letter K. 1353 (*CT* 54, no. 22), which Dietrich cites, reports that someone "gives (or will give) to Sāsî and Sallāju" certain valuables (rs., ll. 5–6) and shortly thereafter refers to a revolt that had occurred (*sīḫi epšu*, rs., l. 8), but makes no claim that the two men were involved in it. The letter ABL 1217, which Dietrich also cites, accuses Sāsî of disloyalty to the king and reports that he was named in an oracle which predicted the fall of Sennacherib's line, but provides no evidence of treasonous action by Sāsî, nor of any attempt to revolt. For further discussion, see Brinkman, 312–315. There is ample evidence of plotting in Esarhaddon's reign, but no evidence of actual rebellion. The omen texts cited as evidence of a revolt against Esarhaddon by Jörgen Alexander Knudtzon, *Assyrische Gebete an den Sonnengott für Staat und königliches Haus aus der zeit Asarhaddons und Asurbanipals*, p. 12 and nos. 108–131, should probably be understood as routine security checks made before appointing particular persons to office.

[9] Nabû-aḫḫē-iddina's plot, for example, was reported to the Assyrians by the Babylonian major-domo of the household of one of the plotters and also by the local Babylonian scribe the plotters had employed to write the letter (Weidner, "Hochverrat," 5–9). The plot reported in the letter BM 135586 (Parpola, "Letter from Šamaš-šumu-ukīn," 21–34) was also betrayed to the Assyrian authorities by Babylonians. Reports from Babylonians were probably, of necessity, the Assyrians' main source of information about Babylonian plots.

sisted of a raid on Babylonian territory earlier in the same year.[10] The third
incident, which took place a year later, in 674, was an attack by Assyrian troops
on the Chaldean city of Ša-amīlē in southern Babylonia.[11] All three incidents
suggest that the leaders of the Chaldean tribes and the city of Nippur were
trying to form a coalition against the Assyrians but were finding little support
for their efforts. None of the reports in either Babylonian or Assyrian sources
suggest that anything as serious as an uprising had occurred; all three incidents
appear to have been Assyrian police actions in response to minor disturbances.

Esarhaddon's reign differs significantly from that of his father and grandfather in that outbreaks of violence between the two states were, in fact, so
minor. During his reign, Esarhaddon succeeded in establishing a period of relatively peaceful relations between the two nations that was to last for almost
thirty years and did so without invading Babylonia—a remarkable success
achieved against high odds and one that marks him as a ruler of considerable
political skill.

The change in Assyrian-Babylonian relations that occurred in Esarhaddon's reign was the product of many factors. The military and political situation in Babylonia at the time of Esarhaddon's accession, the effectiveness of
the administrative structure Esarhaddon adopted for Babylonia, and the abilities and personalities of the king's administrators and of the king himself, for
example, each contributed in substantial ways to the success of his rule in Babylonia. Of central importance, however, was Esarhaddon's use of images and
symbols associated with kingship and nation as tools to help him develop support for his rule of Babylonia. It is this aspect of his rule which will concern
us in the pages that follow. A central characteristic of Esarhaddon's policy
toward Babylonia, one that has not yet been widely recognized, is his success
in winning the Babylonians' acceptance for his rule not only by conferring
on them tangible benefits, such as building projects and freedom to trade, but
also by focusing on what might be characterized as the symbolic and figurative
aspects of political life, the symbols and images that help to shape a people's
concepts of their own political situation and identity.

In an essay discussing the forces that bring political communities into
being and hold them together, Michael Walzer emphasizes the extent to
which nations are mental constructs; in his words, "The state is invisible; it
must be personified before it can be seen, symbolized before it can be loved,
imagined before it can be conceived."[12] Esarhaddon, I will argue, deliberately

---

[10] Pamela D. Gerardi, "Assurbanipal's Elamite Campaigns: A Literary and Political Study," 12.

[11] The first two incidents are reported in the Babylonian Chronicles (Chr. 1, iv 1–2 and iv
14–15, and Chr. 14, ll. 10–11 and 19) and in Esarhaddon's inscriptions (Nin. A and B, Ep. 12); the
third, in Chr. 14, l. 20. For debates about the location of Ša-amīlē, see A. Kirk Grayson, *Assyrian
and Babylonian Chronicles*, 219.

[12] Michael Walzer, "On the Role of Symbolism in Political Thought," 194.

concerned himself with the images that shaped Babylonians' and Assyrians' idea of their states. In the early years, his statements and activities in Babylonia seem designed to present Esarhaddon to the Babylonians not so much as an individual ruler, but rather as a type, a personification of the Babylonian concept of kingship, a traditional emblem of their identity as a nation. Through symbolic action (the performance of the Babylonian royal ritual of basket-bearing), through figuratively charged language (the adoption of traditional Babylonian royal titles which not only reflected practical political realities but also represented each successive Babylonian king as the personification of ancient Babylonian traditions of rule), and finally through the rhetoric of his texts for Babylonia and the image of the king they presented, Esarhaddon presented himself publicly in Babylonia as the very type of a Babylonian ruler. In his inscriptions for Babylonia, I will argue, Esarhaddon is presented less as an individual who happens to rule than as kingship personified—even more significantly for an Assyrian ruler, as *Babylonian* kingship personified. In his inscriptions for Assyria and in his public actions there, however, he presents in contrast the *persona* of a typical Assyrian ruler.

Later, in the second half of his reign, the emphasis of his inscriptions changes, focusing greater attention on the image of the Babylonians and Assyrians as nations, presenting to both states a new and expanded image of themselves as essentially one united community sharing common concerns, albeit under Assyrian rule. To encourage acceptance of this changed national image, Esarhaddon also introduces in the final years of the reign a project involving the restoration of the cult statue of the Babylonians' chief god Marduk; he uses the transformed figure of the god Marduk to draw the Assyrians and Babylonians into a closer relationship to one another, a relationship now personified by the god Marduk himself. In the chapters that follow we trace and examine Esarhaddon's use of these figurative aspects of political life—first the *persona* of the king and later the image of the nation and the magnetic power of the god Marduk—to encourage allegiance to an expanded concept of nation which would include both Babylonia and Assyria as a single, united political and cultural community under Assyrian rule. The power of symbols and images to change the concept of kingship and of nation in Assyria and Babylonia, in short, is Esarhaddon's chief tool in his governance of Babylonia; he uses the figurative and symbolic aspects of the political life of both states to draw them into a closer relationship.

The evidence for these activities appears chiefly in the royal inscriptions, since it is these texts that presented the king's public image and public messages to the nations he ruled. Fortunately, a revised modern edition of these documents, *Die Inschriften Asarhaddons Königs von Assyrien*, published in 1956 by Riekele Borger, has resolved many of the philological problems that hindered earlier studies of Esarhaddon's reign; in his admirable edition, Borger collects the widely scattered inscriptions from Esarhaddon's reign and provides reliable Akkadian texts and translations, as well as extensive philological commentary for each document,[13] paving the way for a thorough reassessment of Esarhaddon's reign. Borger's publication of the royal inscriptions was followed by badly needed new editions of much of the official correspondence from Esarhaddon's reign, prepared by Simo Parpola[14] and Manfried Dietrich,[15] and by a revised edition of the Babylonian Chronicles, including those covering Esarhaddon's reign, prepared by A. Kirk Grayson.[16]

The philological advances these editions represent have been complemented by further archeological investigation, as well, most notably the Iraqi excavation of a small section of Esarhaddon's palace at Nineveh and the British excavation of Esarhaddon's palaces at Nimrud (ancient Calaḫ),[17] providing further material evidence for Esarhaddon's reign. Despite the contributions of these projects, however, visual images of Esarhaddon as king are almost entirely lacking to us, in part because his principal palace at Nineveh lies beneath the mosque of Nebi Yunus, and only a small part of it has been excavated. The surviving visual representations of Esarhaddon are limited to representations of the king on three nearly identical stelae found in conquered cities to the west of the Assyrian homeland, one badly fragmented rock carving that is one of a series of ancient representations of kings carved on cliffs at the mouth of the Nahr el-Kelb in Lebanon (again a western, non-Assyrian setting) and finally one image of the king with his mother, embossed on a strip of metal whose original provenance is unknown. With the exception of this last piece, about whose provenance we can only speculate, our evidence for the visual iconography of kingship in Esarhaddon's reign is confined to these four images of a conquering king presented to audiences in the Assyrian provinces of the west. Of the visual iconography of his reign in Assyria itself, or that directed at Babylonia, there is as yet no trace. Despite recent archeological discoveries of significant Esarhaddon materials, our study

[13] Riekele [more correctly, Rykle] Borger, *Die Inschriften Asarhaddons Königs von Assyrien*, AfO, Beiheft 9, hereafter *Asarh*. For a discussion of this edition and of the other documentary evidence for Esarhaddon's reign, see Appendix I: "Introduction to the Documentary Sources."

[14] Simo Parpola, *Letters from Assyrian Scholars to the Kings Esarhaddon and Assurbanipal, Part I: Texts*, AOAT, 5/1, hereafter, LAS, and *Part II: Commentary and Appendices*, AOAT, 5/2, hereafter *Letters*, IIb. An earlier version of the commentary in this second volume was published in 1971 under the title, *Letters from Assyrian Scholars to the Kings Esarhaddon and Assurbanipal, Part II A: Introduction and Appendixes*, hereafter *Letters*, IIa. Parpola has also published a cuneiform edition of the previously unpublished Assyrian letters, *Cuneiform Texts from Babylonian Tablets in the British Museum, Part 53: Neo-Assyrian Letters from the Kuyunjik Collection*.

[15] Manfried Dietrich published the cuneiform texts of the previously unpublished Babylonian letters to Neo-Assyrian kings under the title *Cuneiform Texts from Babylonian Tablets in the British Museum, Part 54: Neo-Babylonian Letters from the Kuyunjik Collection*. For further bibliography, see Appendix I under "Letters."

[16] *Assyrian and Babylonian Chronicles*, Texts from Cuneiform Sources, V.

[17] For a discussion of the results of these excavations, see Chapter IV, below.

PLATE ONE

Fragment of an inscribed bronze plaque showing Esarhaddon followed by his
mother Naqi'a, who is identified by name on her upper arm (AO 20185;
Musée du Louvre, Antiquités Orientales, © R.M.N.)

of the images of king and nation projected by Esarhaddon in Assyria and Babylonia and their role in his Babylonian policy must of necessity focus on documentary evidence alone.

Fortunately, the documentary evidence is rich and has been further supplemented by recent discoveries. One of the most significant of these was the
discovery at Calaḫ of a set of documents recording oaths imposed on certain
eastern vassals of Assyria, requiring them to support Esarhaddon's arrangements for the succession to the thrones of Assyria and Babylonia. These texts
were originally published by D.J. Wiseman in 1958 under the title, *The Vassal-
Treaties of Esarhaddon*, and have since been published in a revised edition with
commentary prepared by Kazuko Watanabe, and in a revised translation prepared jointly by Watanabe and Simo Parpola.[18] Although up-to-date editions
are still needed for several groups of documents from the reign, in particular
the liver omen texts and the remaining letters, these philological and archeological advances have made it possible to begin a much-needed reexamina-
tion of Esarhaddon's reign and of his successful government of Babylonia.

Esarhaddon's extensive efforts to gain public support for his policies were
in part necessitated by the uncertainty of his position in Assyria as he began
his reign. They were also a response to the complex political situation that
had developed in Babylonia. We begin our investigation of Esarhaddon's
public relations efforts in the two nations by tracing his tumultuous rise to
power in Assyria and its effect on his political position there. We then turn
our attention to the complex political and military situation which confronted
him in Babylonia at the time of his accession.

With these preliminaries completed, we can then begin to examine the
elements of the program Esarhaddon developed to create public support for
his Babylonian policy, tracing the development of that program throughout
his reign. We start by examining the extensive program of building projects
Esarhaddon sponsored in Babylonia and Assyria to give concrete evidence of
his benevolent concern for both nations.

In Babylonia, one effect of Esarhaddon's sponsorship of temple building
projects was to present him publicly in a role usually reserved for Babylonian
kings alone. Esarhaddon's efforts to reinforce this image of himself in Babylonia by adopting Babylonian royal titles, performing Babylonian royal ritual,
and presenting himself in royal inscriptions as an essentially Babylonian king,
is the topic of the fifth chapter, which also traces Esarhaddon's simultaneous
efforts to reassure the Assyrians of his continuing commitment to them and

---

[18] Wiseman's edition was published in *Iraq*, 20 (1958), part 1. The revised edition by Kazuko
Watanabe is entitled, *Die adê-Vereidigung anlässlich der Thronfolgeregelung Asarhaddons*, Baghdader Mitteilungen, Beiheft 3 (Berlin: 1987), and the jointly prepared transliteration and translation is included
in Simo Parpola and Kazuko Watanabe, ed., *Neo-Assyrian Treaties and Loyalty Oaths*, State Archives
of Assyria, II, 28–58.

their traditions by presenting a consistently Assyrian royal *persona* in the home-land. Esarhaddon's program to create public support for his Babylonian policy underwent significant changes as the reign progressed; in the final chapter, we examine the changing national images of Babylonia and Assyria presented in royal inscriptions, the growing importance of those images as elements in Esarhaddon's program of public relations, and the restoration and return of Marduk's statue as the final elements in Esarhaddon's efforts to draw Assyria and Babylonia closer together in the final years of his reign.

CHAPTER TWO

The Years of Preparation

ALTHOUGH THIS STUDY WILL FOCUS PRIMARILY on Babylonia, the forces that shaped Esarhaddon's Babylonian policy had their roots partly in Assyria, and it is there that any study of his Babylonian policy must begin. When Esarhaddon took the throne of Assyria late in the year 681, the most pressing problem confronting him was simply survival. Esarhaddon took the throne by force during an uprising after his father's death, and it was necessary that he make immediate efforts to secure his position in Assyria if he was not to fall victim himself to a second uprising. The need became even more pressing when he began almost immediately to initiate a Babylonian policy that Assyrians were likely to find unpalatable. To strengthen his position in Assyria and achieve some modicum of security, Esarhaddon developed over the years an elaborate program of public relations designed to present him in his homeland as an unequivocally Assyrian king whose primary loyalty was to Assyria, however extensive his attentions to Babylonia. This public relations program, as we will see, involved public appearances by the king, written (and probably verbal) messages, and an extensive program of public works.

These efforts to win Assyrian support were necessary not only because of Esarhaddon's somewhat controversial Babylonian policy—the problem that has most often captured the attention of historians interested in his reign—but also because of the insecurity of Esarhaddon's initial political position, a legacy of his early years. Although the chain of events that brought him to power is not always clear—it must be reconstructed from evidence which is often sparser than we would like—the available evidence suggests that Esarhaddon was not his father's initial choice as heir, that even after he was chosen heir he fell from favor and found it expedient to leave Assyria for his own safety, and that he took the throne in the end by force, seizing it from his warring brothers after the murder of his father.

The struggles that brought him to the throne made Esarhaddon's position in Assyria at the beginning of his reign precarious. So long as any brothers remained alive, Esarhaddon faced the possibility of assassination or renewed uprisings at any time. To survive, he needed to win, and keep, the support of the Assyrian power elite. It seems likely that Esarhaddon's careful attention to Assyrian public opinion throughout his reign was in part a calculated response to the uncertainties created by his tumultuous rise to power.

Unfortunately, it is difficult to trace the events of that rise to power in any detail. Only a few official accounts survive from the final years of Esarhaddon's father Sennacherib (704–681),[19] and none of these discusses arrangements for the succession explicitly; we are left to reconstruct the early stages of Esarhaddon's rise to power from a series of indirect references in texts concerned with other matters.

A passage from one of Sennacherib's annals,[20] for example, implies that the first heir to the throne named by Sennacherib was not Esarhaddon, but an older brother named Aššur-nādin-šumi. The text reports that Aššur-nādin-šumi was appointed king of Babylonia by Sennacherib, and it gives Aššur-nādin-šumi the title *māru rēštû*, "pre-eminent, or first-born, son." Both the title and his appointment to the prominent position of king of Babylonia imply that he held a special position among the king's sons and suggest that he was being groomed to follow Sennacherib as king of Assyria.

Whether the title *māru rēštû* should be taken as conclusive evidence of his appointment as crown prince is not entirely clear, however, since the term is not reserved for sons of kings alone and its precise meaning in this passage remains somewhat ambiguous; in Akkadian, as in English, the word "first" (*rēštû*) can mean either "first" chronologically, or "first" in quality. Taken in either sense, however, the use of this term creates a strong presumption that Aššur-nādin-šumi was Assyria's crown prince. If *māru rēštû* is taken here in the sense of "first in quality, pre-eminent," Aššur-nādin-šumi's role as heir seems likely, since a title meaning "first, or pre-eminent, son," would seem appropriate for the crown prince alone; if the title is understood in the chronological sense, as meaning "first-born,"[21] the implication that Aššur-nādin-

---

[19] The latest well-preserved royal inscription of Sennacherib to give a year by year account of political and military events in his reign is the Taylor Prism, which ends with an account of the battle of Ḫalulē, around 691; although that text was recopied in later years, and some of those copies survive, the text was not updated to include later events, nor has any later edition of Sennacherib's annals been discovered. We thus have no year by year account between 691 and Sennacherib's death in 681.

A few less comprehensive accounts do survive from the final decade of Sennacherib's reign, providing reports on isolated events, most notably Sennacherib's attack on Babylon, his raid against the Arabs, and his last building projects, such as the *bīt akīti* at Aššur. Only two of these late inscriptions mention Esarhaddon: the so-called "Will of Sennacherib" (ABL 1452) and a barrel cylinder (Nin. J) commemorating Sennacherib's construction of a palace at Aššur for Esarhaddon. A fragmentary text recording an oath to support arrangements for the succession imposed during the reign of Sennacherib (Parpola and Watanabe, *Treaties*, text 3) may well come from the time of Esarhaddon's appointment as crown prince. Aside from this, however, there is no reference in any of Sennacherib's extant inscriptions to Esarhaddon's appointment as crown prince nor to his subsequent difficulties; for knowledge of these events, we are largely dependent on Esarhaddon's own accounts.

[20] Daniel David Luckenbill, *The Annals of Sennacherib*, Oriental Institute Publications, II, Col. III, p. 35, ll. 71–74.

[21] Von Soden (*AHw* "rēštû," 2b) takes the passage in this sense, as one instance of a larger pattern: that occurrences of the word *rēštû* as a modifier of the words *māru* (when used to mean "son") or *aplu* ("heir") should be understood in the chronological sense, as "erstgeboren." See also *AHw* "aplu."

šumi was the presumptive heir to the throne is even stronger, since circumstantial evidence seems to indicate that the Assyrians in this period normally
followed the principle of succession to the throne by the eldest son of the
reigning king.[22]

The hypothesis that Aššur-nādin-šumi was at this point next in line for
the throne is supported by the few surviving pieces of evidence for his career.
We know, for example, that Sennacherib built a palace for him at Aššur;[23]

[22] The principle that was followed in determining the selection of a successor to the Assyrian
throne is never explicitly stated in Assyrian sources and is not easy to deduce from practice. Paul
Garelli comments (in "L'État et la légitimité royale sous l'empire assyrien," *Power and Propaganda*,
ed. Mogens Trolle Larsen, 321), "Les Assyriens ne réussirent pas plus à résoudre le problème de la
succession légitime que les empereurs romains, et ils procédèrent de la même manière, par coopta-
tion." He concludes, however, "Le droit d'aînesse restait néanmoins une norme de référence . . .,"
using the situation of Esarhaddon (discussed below) as a case in point. Garelli notes elsewhere ("The
Achievement of Tiglath-Pileser III: Novelty or Continuity?" in *Ah, Assyria . . .: Studies in Assyrian
History and Ancient Near Eastern Historiography Presented to Hayim Tadmor*, Scripta Hierosolymitana,
33, ed. Mordechai Cogan and Israel Eph'al, 46) that Assyrian king lists show the Assyrian preference
for inheritance of the throne by sons by tending to describe all kings as their predecessors' sons—
even in cases where it is almost certain that the successor was instead his predecessor's brother. The
evidence of Neo-Assyrian royal inscriptions also supports the conclusion that when succession occurred without resort to arms, the usual pattern was inheritance of the throne by a son of the previous king.

It is more difficult to establish whether the son selected was normally the eldest. So little evidence survives about the birth order of children in royal families in Assyria that it is not possible
to derive the principle from actual practice. (The relatively ample evidence about Esarhaddon's children found in letters to the king is a rare exception, and even in this case the birth order of most
of the children is uncertain.)

There is circumstantial evidence, however, implying that succession by the eldest son was in
fact the expected pattern, as Garelli suggests. The evidence comes from the reign of Esarhaddon
himself and from the reign of his son Assurbanipal. The principle of succession by the eldest is implied by Esarhaddon's comments on his own accession (see below), which lay emphasis on the fact
that he was a younger brother, an emphasis that seems puzzling in context unless it responds to
an assumption that the eldest would ordinarily have been chosen instead. The same principle is
also implied in Assurbanipal's similar comments on his succession (Maximilian Streck, *Assurbanipal
und die letzen assyrischen Könige bis zum untergange Nineveh's*, 258, col. i, ll. 30 ff., quoted in English
translation in Parpola's commentary to LAS 129, *Letters* IIb, p. 116): "By order of the great gods,
my father and begetter loved me more than the assembly of my older brothers; in the month Ajâru
. . . I entered the Succession Palace . . . and . . . he elevated me above (all) princes and called my
name to the kingship." The principle of succession by the eldest is also implied in a letter to Esarhaddon (LAS 129) from one of his advisers, who comments on the appointment of the younger
son Assurbanipal to the Assyrian throne while the elder son was named to the Babylonian throne
by remarking, "What has not been done in heaven, the king, my lord, has done upon earth and
shown us: you have girded a son of yours with headband and entrusted him the kingship of Assyria;
your eldest son you have put (up) to the kingship in Babylon." As Parpola remarks, the king here
has "decidedly violated the accepted order of succession, as plainly stated at the outset of the letter"
by naming the younger son as king of Assyria (*Letters* IIb, p. 117). These texts, taken together, offer
what seems to me convincing evidence that the throne of Assyria would normally pass to the eldest
son.

[23] Leopold Messerschmidt, *Keilschrifttexte aus Assur historischen Inhalts*, WVDOG, 16, vol. I,
no. 49. This is a brick inscription commemorating the construction of a palace at Aššur by Sennacherib for Aššur-nādin-šumi.

this was an honor also accorded later to Esarhaddon, while he was crown prince, and was probably a necessary courtesy, providing each crown prince with needed office space and audience rooms for his duties as the king's second-in-command, as well as space for the officials in his personal retinue. It is not possible to establish an exact date for the construction of Aššur-nādin-šumi's palace, nor for the appointment as heir apparent that probably occasioned it, but the palace's northern location suggests a date sometime before the year 700, when Aššur-nādin-šumi was appointed ruler of Babylonia, an appointment that would have meant a move to southern quarters.

This appointment, as I have suggested, is a further indication of Aššur-nādin-šumi's special status. As the Assyrian ruler in Babylonia, he would hold a delicate and politically important office, a position that could provide valuable practical experience to a future ruler of Assyria. As it happened, however, the problems of governing Babylonia proved to be more than Aššur-nādin-šumi, or perhaps anyone, could handle. The Babylonians continued to plot against Assyria, and in 694, six years after Aššur-nādin-šumi's appointment, they succeeded in having him kidnapped and put to death by their allies, the Elamites, ending his short rule over Babylonia and his role as heir to the Assyrian throne as well.[24]

This brings us to Esarhaddon. With Aššur-nādin-šumi dead, it was necessary that a new heir to the throne be named. To the best of our knowledge, Sennacherib was left at this point with four sons among whom to choose: Arda-Mulišši, Aššur-šuma-ušabši, Aššur-ilu-muballitsu, and Esarhaddon.[25] The choice fell in the end upon Esarhaddon.

It was a surprising decision, since Esarhaddon was one of the younger surviving brothers[26] and would not ordinarily have been next in line for the succession. The texts offer no reason why elder sons were passed over in favor of Esarhaddon. It seems likely that his mother Naqi'a, a powerful figure in the kingdom, had intervened on Esarhaddon's behalf,[27] but there is too little

---

[24] Chr. 1, ii, ll. 42–43. A letter published by Simo Parpola ("A Letter from Šamaš-šumu-ukīn to Esarhaddon," *Iraq*, 34 [1972]: 21–34) confirms the kidnapping of Aššur-nādin-šumi and the Babylonians' role in it.

[25] Maximilian Streck, *Assurbanipal und die letzen assyrischen Könige bis zum untergange Nineveh's*, I, pp. CCXXXVIII–CCXXXIX. The name cited as "Ardi-Ninlil" by Streck is here corrected to "Arda-Mulišši," following Simo Parpola, "The Murderer of Sennacherib," in *Death in Mesopotamia*, Mesopotamia, 8, ed. Bendt Alster, 174.

[26] The account at this point makes a special point of Esarhaddon's age, commenting, "Among my big brothers, I was their little brother" (Nin. A, Ep. 2, l. 8). For a discussion of the principle of succession by the eldest son in Assyria, see above, n. 22.

[27] This possibility is supported by the comment of Berossus that Sennacherib's successor on the throne had a different mother than that of the murderer: "He [Sennacherib] was assassinated by his son Adremelos. But Axerdis, his brother by the same father but not by the same mother, killed him" (Stanley M. Burstein, *The Babyloniaca of Berossus*, 25, 5b). The name of the avenger, "Axerdis," seems to be a slightly garbled rendering of the name "Esarhaddon." Further confirmation

evidence to permit any firm conclusion. (See plate I, page 9, for an unusual bronze plaque depicting Naqi'a together with an Assyrian king, who is probably Esarhaddon, to judge from the accompanying inscription.) Perhaps it was to pave the way for the unorthodox naming of a younger son as heir that Sennacherib changed Esarhaddon's name from Esarhaddon (in Akkadian, Aššur-aḫa-iddina, meaning "Aššur has given a brother," a younger brother's name), to the more impressive name Aššur-etel-ilāni-mukīn-apli ("Aššur, prince of the gods, is establishing an heir"), a name that suggests its owner's status as heir to the throne. By happy chance, a text commemorating this change of name has survived. It is an odd document, sometimes referred to as the "Will of Sennacherib" but clearly not a will, in which Sennacherib records the gift of various jewelry and a tiara to ". . . Esarhaddon, my son, who hereafter shall be named Aššur-etel-mukīn-apli . . .," a slightly shortened form of the unwieldy new name.[28] The gifts, the text says, are booty from Bīt-Amuk. This comment, unfortunately, does not provide a clue to the date of the document, nor to the date of Esarhaddon's renaming, since the Bīt-Amukāni tribe was defeated by Sennacherib several times during his reign. Whatever its date, the "Will" seems to mark Esarhaddon's change in status from younger son to probable heir to the throne.

Esarhaddon's own inscriptions offer the only surviving record of the next step, his formal selection as heir and his public installation in that position. The account comes down to us in the set of dedicatory inscriptions for a palace and arsenal complex built by Esarhaddon at Nineveh in the latter part of his reign. We will see later that there are significant differences among these inscriptions, but for our purposes here it is sufficient to extract Esarhaddon's account of his accession and treat it as a single text, since it is identical in each

---

is provided by the text of an oracle concerning Esarhaddon cited by Parpola in this connection in "The Murderer of Sennacherib," 178, n. 40.

[28] ABL 1452. The new name is usually referred to as Esarhaddon's throne name, but the term is misleading, since the name was seldom used after he became king—at least not in written contexts, which are all that survive for us. The new name appears in one other text from his days as crown prince, inscribed on a barrel cylinder commemorating the construction of a palace for him at Nineveh (Nin. J). In inscriptions from the reign itself, the name appears only on three small objects: a small stone tablet, a piece of lapis lazuli, and an onyx amulet. The three inscriptions are identical and are published together as Assur F. In each, the new name is followed by Esarhaddon's titles as king. The new name appears a fourth time in a letter (ABL 308) written by Esarhaddon's daughter, who is writing to her sister-in-law to remind her that the latter's social position is inferior to that of a daughter of the reigning king. To underline her point, she refers to her father Esarhaddon with full royal titles as well as with the long formal name. Her use of the name in a letter, a genre that seems to reflect spoken usage, suggests that the king's new name was used in spoken contexts as well as in the few written examples known to us. Its use here also confirms that the new name was the more impressive of Esarhaddon's names—the one most likely to put a sister-in-law in her place.

of the texts in which it appears.[29] Despite some obvious omissions which underline the selective nature of the account they present, the Nineveh inscriptions provide at least an outline of the events which brought Esarhaddon to the throne.

The account begins by emphasizing the legitimacy of Esarhaddon's selection as heir to the throne, despite the problems which later resulted. It concedes at the outset that Esarhaddon was younger than his brothers, but asserts that Sennacherib nevertheless chose him and announced him as heir apparent, a choice (so the account asserts) resoundingly confirmed by the gods:

> Among my big brothers, I was their little brother. At the command of (the gods) Aššur, Sîn, Šamaš, Bēl, and Nabû, Ištar of Nineveh, (and) Ištar of Arbela, my father and begetter in the assembly of my brothers truly raised my head, saying, "This is my son (and) successor." He consulted (the gods) Šamaš and Adad through liver omens, and they replied with a true affirmative, "He is your replacement!" (Nin. A and F, Ep. 2, ll. 8–14).

Although direct quotation is rare in Assyrian inscriptions, usually reserved for emphasis, it occurs here twice in the space of three lines ("This is my son (and) successor," and "He is your replacement"), as if to impress upon the reader the unanimous approval of Sennacherib and all the major gods, a point that the texts further emphasize by adding, "He (Sennacherib) honored their solemn command." This insistence on the general approval of Esarhaddon's appointment seems to anticipate resistance on the part of the reader and suggests that there was in fact opposition to Esarhaddon's unconventional appointment from the outset.

This was probably unavoidable. Aššur-nādin-šumi, in his days as crown prince, would have acquired as a matter of course a circle of supporters among the members of the power elite of Assyria—people such as officials, army officers, temple administrators, and major land owners for whom it was expedient to cultivate a close relationship with the future king and his personal staff. Because Esarhaddon was one of the younger princes, not immediately in line for the throne, the circle of his supporters and dependents would in all likelihood have been much smaller. When Sennacherib broke with normal

---

[29] The account of Esarhaddon's accession appears as a long passage of eighty-nine lines in the set of thirty-five duplicate inscriptions Borger refers to as "Nineveh A." Lines 9–22 of this passage also survive in the middle of a long broken section in the single inscription Borger publishes as "Nineveh F," and ll. 56–68 of the Nineveh A account also survive in a broken section of the text Borger publishes as "Nineveh D," a text represented by two inscriptions. Nineveh F is undated, but was probably written in 676 or later, in the same period as the other texts commemorating the construction of the Nineveh palace and arsenal complex. Six copies of Nineveh A are dated, five to the years after 673 and one to 672. The dates on the Nineveh D inscriptions have not survived. Although the text of the Nineveh A inscription published by Borger in *Asarh.* has now been supplemented by additional material (see Appendices III and IV under "Nineveh A"), the passage describing Esarhaddon's rise to power is not affected.

precedent and named Esarhaddon as heir, he risked antagonizing not only the princes he had passed over, but their supporters as well, a substantial and influential group of people.

It was probably to counter their expected opposition and to force support for Esarhaddon that Sennacherib conceived the idea of a national oath-taking ceremony and formal induction into the *bīt redûti* for the new heir.[30] This is the significance of the new title now given the crown prince, *mār šarri (rabî) ša bīt redûti*, "(great, or pre-eminent) king's son, of the Succession House," a title coined for this occasion.[31] The *bīt redûti*, or House of Succession, was already an established center of Assyrian royal activity; Sennacherib had lived there as crown prince and king, and Esarhaddon himself had been born and raised there.[32] Sennacherib's innovation was to add a solemn ceremonial entry into the *bīt redûti* that would publicly confirm Esarhaddon's still shaky status as heir to the throne.

As the final touch, Esarhaddon's entry into the *bīt redûti* was preceded by a national oath-taking ceremony:

> (My father) assembled the people of Assyria, young and old, together with my brothers, the seed of my father's house, and before (the gods) Aššur, Sîn, Šamaš, Nabû, and Marduk, the gods of Assyria, the gods who dwell in heaven and earth, he made them swear a solemn oath to guard my claim to succession (Nin. A and F, Ep. 2, ll. 15–19).

A small tablet, now badly fragmented, may be a record of the oath itself; it binds the oath-taker to protect someone, apparently the crown prince, "and the other princes" at Sennacherib's command, and imposes "an indissoluble, grievous curse" on anyone who fails to do so.[33] In a world in which magic, curses, and the ill will of the gods were understood to be the source of most illness and misfortune, such an oath would have carried considerable weight. Esarhaddon's account continues, "In a propitious month, on a favorable day, in accordance with the lofty command (of the gods), in joy I entered the *bīt redûti*, that awesome place in whose midst kingship is bestowed" (Nin. A and

---

[30] The discovery at Calaḫ of the texts recording oaths administered in a similar ceremony which took place during Esarhaddon's reign have focused interest on Esarhaddon's use of the ceremony for his own sons. It is not generally recognized that the ceremony and title were first introduced a generation earlier by Sennacherib to bolster the precarious position of Esarhaddon himself.

[31] See "ridûtu" and "bîtu" in *AHw*.

[32] See Assurbanipal's Rassam Cylinder Inscription (Streck, *Assurbanipal*, II, p. 4, ll. 23 ff.). The *bīt redûti* as an institution to which the intended successor of a high official was assigned in order to gain practical experience in administration may date back to the days of the Ur III dynasty (2112–2004) in Mesopotamia. See note 18, p. 424, in Thorkild Jacobsen, *Toward the Image of Tammuz*, ed. William L. Moran.

[33] "Sennacherib's Succession Treaty," text 3, p. 18, with description on p. xxviii, in Simo Parpola and Kazuko Watanabe, *Neo-Assyrian Treaties and Loyalty Oaths*, State Archives of Assyria, II.

F, Ep. 2, ll. 20–22). In entering the *bīt redûti* Esarhaddon had formally assumed the role of crown prince of Assyria.

Two further texts seem to confirm that Esarhaddon was actually appointed as crown prince. The first, engraved on a stone lion's head, records
the gift of that lion's head to Esarhaddon and refers to him as the *māru rabû*
("eldest, or pre-eminent son"),[34] a term which recalls the similar title *māru
rēštû* ("first, or pre-eminent son") assigned earlier to his brother Aššur-nādin-
šumi, and was probably also a title of the crown prince. The second text, inscribed on a barrel cylinder found at Nineveh (Nin. J), records the dedication
of a small palace for Esarhaddon and accords him the full formal title of the
crown prince, *mār šarri rabû ša bīt redûti* ("eldest, or pre-eminent, king's son
of the Succession House"). Since there are only two texts that refer to Esarhaddon as crown prince,[35] it seems likely that Esarhaddon's tenure as crown

[34] Borger, section 108 (=B.M. 91678). The title used for Esarhaddon is not entirely clear. It
reads *māri-šú ÁŠ*. Borger suggests, correctly I think, that the ÁŠ sign was a scribal error for the
GAL sign, making its intended reading *rabû*. The term *māru rabû*, "eldest, or pre-eminent, son,"
seems to have been a title reserved for the crown prince to designate him as *primus inter pares*. In
the case of Esarhaddon, *rabû* clearly means "pre-eminent" rather than "eldest," since he was by his
own admission not the eldest surviving son during his time as crown prince. (That *rabû* could, however, mean "eldest [surviving] son" in Assyrian usage is suggested by a passage in the Assyrian Law
Code [section 43=*KAV* 1 vi 25, cited in *CAD* "ṣiḫru" 1c] that discusses the marriage of a betrothed
girl whose fiancé has died and refers to the father's "remaining sons" [*mārēšu rīḫāte*] "from the oldest to the youngest son," using *māre rabê* as the term for the oldest [surviving] son.)

A third Esarhaddon text, the treaty with Ba'al, king of Tyre (Borger's section 69), was thought
by Borger to include the term *māru rabû* in its opening lines. A new edition of the text, however,
published by S. Parpola and K. Watanabe, *Neo-Assyrian Treaties*, 24–27, indicates that this reading
of the signs, which are badly preserved and difficult to read, was in error.

The occasional ambiguity of the adjective *rabû* in references to people—that it may mean
either "elder" or "pre-eminent, first in rank," much like the term *rēštû* discussed above—arises
from its range of meanings in Akkadian, which is similar to that of the word "big" in English, by
which it is often translated. For the wide range of meanings of *rabû* in Akkadian usage, see von
Soden, *Ahw* "rabû," which cites examples of *rabû* as an adjective referring, for example, to the size
of buildings, plants and weights, the heaviness of punishments, the importance of kings or gods,
the greater age of brothers and sons and the high rank of various officials. Since the position of
an elder brother in Assyria was often one of higher status than his younger brothers (see n. 22 above
for a brief discussion), it is not always clear in a given situation whether *māru rabû* was intended
to mean "elder son," "son highest in status," or both, since the first often implied the second. It
is perhaps worth remarking that the antonym of *rabû*, the word *ṣiḫru* (defined in the *CAD* as
"small, young, second in rank" etc.) had a similarly wide range of meanings, and a similar ambiguity.

[35] Sami Ahmed argues (*Southern Mesopotamia in the Time of Ashurbanipal*, Studies in Ancient
History, 2, 56, n. 45) that ABL 152 provides evidence of Esarhaddon's participation in affairs of
state during his term as crown prince. The "king's mother" mentioned in the letter, however, is
almost certainly Naqi'a, Esarhaddon's mother, making the crown prince addressed in the letter not
Esarhaddon, but his son Assurbanipal. Of all the Neo-Assyrian letters from Nineveh which are addressed to a *mār šarri* (literally, "king's son," a term reserved in the letters for the crown prince
alone), none can be assigned unequivocally to the period in which Esarhaddon served as crown
prince. Even those which might tentatively be assigned to the period describe no significant
political or military developments.

Nor was Esarhaddon governor of Babylonia in this period, despite the long popularity of that

prince was brief and probably should be placed near the end of Sennacherib's reign.[36]

Esarhaddon's brothers, Esarhaddon's account continues, responded to his appointment as crown prince by launching a campaign to discredit him:[37]

> Proper behavior[?] was lavished upon my brothers, but abandoning the gods, they trusted in their own monstrous acts and plotted evil. And they caused evil talk against me, slander, misleading statements which were contrary to the will of the gods—lies and wickedness! They spoke maliciously behind my back (Nin. A, Ep. 2, ll. 23–28).

Whether there was any basis in fact for the accusations Esarhaddon's brothers leveled against him is impossible to decide, since the texts avoid telling us what they were; they were, however, evidently convincing to Sennacherib. The account reports, "They alienated from me, against the will of the gods, the heart of my father, which had been well-disposed (toward me). Secretly his heart was merciful to me; his eyes remained fixed on my exercising the kingship" (Nin. A, Ep. 2, ll. 29–31).[38]

Hidden in these lines is a significant admission. If it was only "secretly" (*šaplānu*) that Sennacherib remained committed to Esarhaddon's future rule,

---

idea. (See Friedrich Schmidtke, *Asarhaddons Statthalterschaft in Babylonien und seine Thronbesteigung in Assyrien 681 v. Chr.* [Leiden: 1916] for an early statement of the theory.) This idea rested on the statement of the first century BC Greco-Roman historian Cornelius Alexander Polyhistor, quoted by the fourth century AD chronicler Eusebius (Stanley Mayer Burstein, *The Babyloniaca of Berossus*, Sources from the Ancient Near East, 1/5, p. 23), that Sennacherib had placed a son named "Asordanios" on the throne of Babylonia after capturing Babylon, who had then reigned in Babylonia for him. This comment Schmidtke and others took as a reference to Esarhaddon. In the face of a complete lack of supporting evidence for the contention that Esarhaddon was ever governor of Babylon, it seems preferable to equate "Asordanios" instead with Aššur-nādin-šumi, whose name fits the garbled Greek version equally well and whose rule of Babylon in this period is attested both by Assyrian annals and by Babylonian contracts dated to his reign.

[36] Benno Landsberger and Theo Bauer originally argued in "Zu neuveröffentlichten Geschichtsquellen der Zeit von Asarhaddon bis Nabonid," *ZA*, 37 (1926–27): 71 ff., that Esarhaddon was named heir apparent as early as 687, basing their claim on the appearance of his name in eponym list Ca5 as eponym official for that year, a position which they argued was given the new crown prince as a special honor. Arthur Ungnad, however, in "Eponymen," *RLA*, II, 412–457, had already suggested that the appearance of Esarhaddon's name was a copying error by the scribe, a position which Landsberger later accepted (*Brief des Bischofs von Esagila an König Asarhaddon*, 18, n. 14). This conclusion effectively erases Esarhaddon's career as an eponym official and leaves us with no benchmark by which to measure his term as crown prince. Ernst Weidner, in his article "Die assyrischen Eponymen," in *AfO*, 13 (1941), 311, had already argued that the *KAR* 14 reference to Esarhaddon as eponym was in fact a reference to an eponym of the time of Tiglath-Pileser I, long before the seventh century king.

[37] On the interpretation of the difficult phrase *riddu kēnu*, translated here, following Borger, as "proper behavior [?]," see Borger's comments, *Asarh.*, 41, n. 23.

[38] The passage as it stands reads ". . . merciful to him/it," which is almost certainly a scribal error for "merciful to me," since there is no antecedent for the pronouns "him" or "it" (see *CAD* "šaplānu" 2).

it follows that publicly Sennacherib had withdrawn his support from Esarhaddon as heir to the throne.

The situation became so difficult, in fact, that Esarhaddon apparently went into hiding. His account first describes Esarhaddon's consternation at his brothers' actions: "I communed with my heart and thought in my mind, 'Their acts are monstrous, and they have relied on their own ideas; what ungodly thing will they do?'" (ll. 32–34). The account then describes at some length Esarhaddon's prayers for guidance to the gods Aššur and Marduk, "to whom treacherous words are an abomination," and asserts that the gods remained firmly on Esarhaddon's side. This passage, with its further emphasis on his brothers' unholy activities in contrast to his own pious and upright behavior, suggests by its defensive tone that Esarhaddon had indeed been seriously discredited in Assyria by his brothers' accusations, a conclusion further supported by the concluding lines of the passage, which contain the veiled admission that Esarhaddon had now gone into hiding: "They (the gods) made me dwell in a hidden (or "secluded") place and stretched their good shadow over me; they guarded me for the kingship" (Nin. A, Ep. 2, ll. 39–40). He was, as we will see, certainly in the north. In view of his statement that he was in a secluded place and his admission that Sennacherib was only secretly well disposed toward him, it is unlikely that he had been assigned there to command border troops, something that might be part of the normal duties of a crown prince.

The location of the place to which Esarhaddon withdrew is not recorded,[39] but a later passage (Ep. 2., ll. 63ff.), describing Esarhaddon's return after his father's death, offers clues to where he had been in this period. The passage reports first that the road to Nineveh which he took on his return was difficult and was often snowbound in the month Šabāṭu (January–February). The second clue it offers is that his path was blocked by an opposing army as he tried to cross through Ḫanigalbat,[40] a region in the plains to

[39] Schmidtke suggested (*Statthalterschaft*, 82) that Esarhaddon had spent this period, or else the time of his reign as crown prince, in the otherwise unknown town of Zaqqap, mentioned in a broken line in ABL 1216 as the dwelling place of a crown prince, which from the context he concluded might well be Esarhaddon. René Labat, however, working from a corrected reading of the line by D.J. Wiseman, has since demonstrated ("Asarhaddon et la ville de Zaqqap," *RA*, 53 [1959]: 113–118) that the reference to the town came into existence only through a misreading in the modern edition of the text. The original line reads not "URU ZAG.GAP" but instead "URU ZAG.MU," or "town on my frontier"; the entire phrase, as Labat notes, is then recognizable as a quotation from tablet 56 of the omen series "Enūma Anu Enlil." Since the king's son in the "town on my frontier" in that omen "did not take the throne," the passage is unlikely to be a reference to Esarhaddon, who did.

[40] The writing of the place-name in Nin. A1 as "Ḫal-NI-gal-bat" surely reflects a Neo-Assyrian pronunciation of the area referred to earlier in Assyrian annals as "Ḫanigalbat." The same spelling appears also in Nineveh H, which lists an eponym official as governor (*šaknu*) of Ḫal-NI-gal-bat. Whether the NI sign should be pronounced "li" or "ni" here is unclear.

The location of Ḫanigalbat at this period is hard to pin down, since the term was by Esarhaddon's time archaic and rarely used. For the period of Shalmaneser I (1274–1245), when docu-

the west of Assyria, around Nisibis on the tributaries that feed into the Habur River from the north. His hiding place, then, was beyond Ḫanigalbat and in mountainous regions where snow might be expected. An arc of mountains lies to the north of Ḫanigalbat—the Malatya Mountains to the northwest, and the southern extensions of the Armenian highlands to the northeast; most of this region would fit Esarhaddon's description. It is an area of high, wooded valleys, thickly covered with snow in winter, an area which would have been hard for an army to traverse in winter, as the text describes, and which would have offered ideal hiding places for an Assyrian political fugitive. Any of the local authorities in the region, whether in Kummuḫu, Meliddu, or Šubria, would have been potentially sympathetic to an enemy of those in power in Assyria; all three areas, in fact, were to rebel against Assyria in the ensuing ten years, and Šubria in particular was to be accused by the Assyrians of having sheltered fugitives from Assyria. Esarhaddon's withdrawal was to a place somewhere in this arc of mountains north of Ḫanigalbat, where he would be beyond the reach of his enemies at the Assyrian court and could prepare the military force he would need to claim the throne later.

In the meantime, events in Assyria precipitated his rapid return home. Contemporary Assyrian sources are silent about the death of Sennacherib, but one of the Babylonian Chronicles preserves an account of the murder and of the events that followed it:

> On the twentieth day of the month Ṭebētu Sennacherib, king of Assyria, was killed by his son in a rebellion. For [twenty-four] years Sennacherib ruled Assyria. The rebellion continued in Assyria from the twentieth day of the month Ṭebētu until the second day of the month Addāru. On the twenty-eighth [or, eighteenth] day of the month Addāru Esarhaddon, his son, ascended the throne in Assyria (Chr. 1, iii, ll. 34–38).

The Chronicle's report is laconic but seems to be essentially accurate in reporting the death of Sennacherib at the hand of a son or sons. Both Greek and Hebrew sources confirm Sennacherib's murder.[41] Although it was Esar-

---

mentation for Ḫanigalbat is much more complete than in the Neo-Assyrian period, the area referred to as Ḫanigalbat stretched approximately to Ḫarrān in the west and to modern Diarbekir in the east (see Elena Cassin in the *Fischer Weltgeschichte*, ed. Elena Cassin, Jean Bottéro and Jean Vercoutter, II, p. 81). E. von Weiher ("Ḫanigalbat," *RLA*, vol. H, p. 105) ascribes an even larger area to Ḫanigalbat in its fifteenth century heyday, but concludes that it had shrunk to encompass only a small area northwest of Assyria by the Neo-Assyrian period.

[41] The Biblical account of Sennacherib's death is given in II Kings 19:37. The two Greek accounts are from the first century BC Greco-Roman writer Cornelius Alexander Polyhistor (Burstein, *Berossus*, p. 24, #3) and from the second century AD writer Abydenus (Burstein, #5b, p. 25), both quoted in Eusebius and both based on an account of Mesopotamian history and culture written in Greek by Berossus, a Chaldean priest of Bēl who wrote ca. 281 BC for the Seleucid ruler Antiochus I.

haddon who ultimately benefitted most from his father's death, it is now fairly well established that he was not responsible for the plot, which seems to have been engineered by another son, Arda-Mulissi.[42]

It was late in the winter of 681 that the plan to murder Sennacherib was successfully carried out;[43] the immediate result was a full-scale uprising. Esarhaddon's account passes over the murder in silence, but offers some account of the subsequent fighting, supplementing the report of the Babylonian Chronicle: "Afterwards, my brothers fell into a mad rage and did what was not good in the sight of gods and man: they plotted evil. And they drew swords in Nineveh, without the gods' blessing. They butted each other like goats over the exercise of kingship" (Nin. A, Ep. 2, ll. 41–44).

This account suggests that the uprising that followed the attack on the king had degenerated quickly into a war between factions supporting the various brothers as contenders for the throne. It adds, "The people of Assyria who had pronounced, with oil and water, the oath of the treaty to support my kingship before the great gods, did not go to their support" (Nin. A, Ep. 2, ll. 50–52).

The passage implies that Esarhaddon, although out of favor, had not yet been officially deposed as crown prince; if we accept the evidence of the text, the oath to support Esarhaddon was still nominally in force and weakened support for his brothers.

According to Esarhaddon's account, word of the uprising was quickly carried by his supporters in Assyria to the place where he was encamped with his troops in the mountains. There are several ways in which he could have gathered such troops despite his relative isolation. It seems likely that his own personal troops came with him when he left Assyria, and he might also have brought with him (with or without his father's approval) any units from the main army that had been under his direct command. Once he had left Assyrian territory, Esarhaddon might also have been joined by fugitives from Assyrian justice and people who had otherwise fallen out of favor with the current Assyrian government. In addition, the authorities in the area where Esarhaddon had gone into hiding might well have thought it worthwhile to offer him support, as well. It is thus plausible that he had a body of troops at his disposal, as the account asserts, but these forces must have been small in comparison to the massed army of Assyria that they would have to fight if any of the brothers succeeded in defeating his rivals and consolidating the armed forces. The momentary fragmentation of political and military force in Assyria offered Esarhaddon his best chance.

---

[42] The evidence for this is convincingly presented by Simo Parpola, "The Murderer of Sennacherib," in *Death in Mesopotamia*, ed. Bendt Alster, 171–182.

[43] By modern reckoning, the murder took place late in January of the year 680.

His troops were in winter quarters, almost certainly dispersed among the mountain villages. Esarhaddon's account reports that he left quickly, not waiting to check over the equipment or collect provisions for an extended campaign:

> I did not delay for (even) one or two days; I did not wait for my infantry; I did not inspect the rear guard; I did not supervise a review of the chariot horses and battle equipment; I did not lay in a stock of provisions for my campaign. The snow and cold of the month Šabāṭu, the severity of the winter, I did not fear; like a winged eagle, I spread my wings to thrust aside my enemies. Despite the difficulties, swiftly I took the road to Nineveh. . . (Nin. A and D, Ep. 2, ll. 63–69).

It was by then the month of Šabāṭu (January/February); the rebellion had been underway for at least ten days since Sennacherib's murder. Normally, Assyrian troops would have waited until spring and melting snow before moving in the mountains. Esarhaddon was counting on the element of surprise.

The inscription reports that as he reached the plains of Ḫanigalbat, northwest of Nineveh, he found the way blocked by his brothers' troops, "sharpening their swords" in preparation for him (ll. 70–71). The account of the battle that follows is somewhat confusing, but the outcome is clear:

> The fear of the great gods, my lords, threw them down, and when they saw the rush of my mighty attack, they became like ecstatics. The goddess Ištar, lady of war and battle, who loves my priesthood, stood at my side and shattered their bows. She broke their ranks. They gathered together, saying, "This is our king!" At her lofty command they kept coming over to my side. Standing behind me like lambs, they tumbled about and implored me to be their ruler (Nin. A, Ep. 2, ll. 72–79).

If we discount the effects of Ištar's intervention, how had Esarhaddon, whose troops were outnumbered, managed to win? First of all, Esarhaddon's sudden appearance had probably caught his brothers' armies before full preparations for confronting him could be completed. In addition, Esarhaddon's troops had a special incentive. They had not, he tells us, taken time to gather provisions; they had no chance of winning a sustained war. Their success, and their lives, depended on winning in this single thrust. Some were, moreover, Esarhaddon's personal troops, bound to him and his fortunes. They had every reason to attack with a fervor that unmanned their opponents. Faced with this determination and perhaps touched by the charisma of Esarhaddon himself, his brothers' troops surrendered to Esarhaddon in groups, pledging to support him. Perhaps, as the text claims, the oath of fealty to Esarhaddon imposed earlier on the Assyrians among them had also added to their misgivings and made them fight less well. However we explain it, the gamble had paid off.

The text reports that when word of the defeat reached Nineveh, the bodyguards of the brothers fled. The brothers themselves then fled the country, to Urartu, according to the Bible.[44] Esarhaddon marched toward the city with his enlarged army, crossed the Tigris "as if it were the side-branch of a canal" (l. 86), and entered Nineveh on the eighth of the month Addāru (February–March) in the year 681/80.[45] Ten days later he was crowned king.[46]

The picture of Esarhaddon that most modern historians have drawn is that of a weak and vacillating king; René Labat, for example, has described Esarhaddon as "by nature a delayer," a king who was "indecisive, superstitious, anxious, and often a toy in the hands of his advisers."[47] The picture of the king that emerges from a close examination of his rise to power, however, is strikingly different; he appears in these events as a decisive leader who took advantage of a moment of crisis to seize the throne his brothers had tried to deny him.

The other important point to emerge from this reconstruction of Esarhaddon's rise to power is the precariousness of Esarhaddon's position at the time of his accession. His brothers were in hiding somewhere in the north; so long as they remained alive, there was a constant danger of assassination attempts or new rebellions. On the field in Ḫanigalbat Esarhaddon had won the support of much of the Assyrian army. To keep his throne he would need to gain the support of the political and administrative leaders of Assyria as well, reassuring those who had not expected him to rule and those who still harbored misgivings. Military daring had won him the throne; it remained to be seen if Esarhaddon would now show the political astuteness to consolidate his precarious position and hold the restless Assyrian empire together.

---

[44] II Kings 19:37. Esarhaddon's Nineveh A inscription says only that the rebels fled "to an unknown land" (l. 84). Erle Leichty, "Esarhaddon's 'Letter to the Gods,'" in *Ah, Assyria . . .*, 52–57, argues plausibly that the brothers and their supporters eventually took refuge in Šubria.

[45] Nin. A, I, ll. 82–87, and II, l. 1.

[46] This date, cited in Chr. 1, iii, l. 38, follows a break in the tablet large enough to permit the addition of one more wedge in the writing of the number, so that the day of the enthronement could be either the 18th or the 28th.

[47] "Das Assyrische Reich unter den Sargoniden," in the *Fischer Weltgeschichte*, Bd. 4, p. 81 (translated by me from the German). Similar evaluations of Esarhaddon are offered by Wolfram von Soden in his portrait of Esarhaddon, *Herrscher im alten Orient* (Berlin: 1954), 118–126, and by Albert T.E. Olmstead, *History of Assyria*, 347.

CHAPTER THREE

Babylonia at the Beginning of Esarhaddon's Reign

ESTABLISHING CONTROL OVER BABYLONIA WAS one of the most daunting problems Esarhaddon faced in the empire at large; the Babylonians' entrenched resistance to Assyrian rule represented a formidable problem, further complicated by the shifting coalitions that had come to characterize Babylonia's political life.[48] To understand the complexities of Babylonia's relationship to Assyria at the time of Esarhaddon's accession, it is necessary to trace the history of Babylonia's conflict with Assyria in some detail. Serious warfare between the two countries had first emerged in the thirteenth century, with the Assyrian king Tukulti-Ninurta I's conquest of the city of Babylon (ca. 1230), followed by his seven-year rule over Babylonia through client kings. After his death, however, Babylonia quickly reestablished independence, and in the three centuries that followed, neither state dominated the other for any extended period, despite periodic conflicts.[49] The twelfth century raids of the Assyrian king Aššur-dan I (1179–1134) into Babylonian territory, for example, were balanced by later raids into Assyrian territory by the Babylonian king Ninurta-nādin-šumi (ca. 1132–1127); the Babylonian king Marduk-nādin-aḫḫē's theft of gods' statues from the Assyrian city of Ekallāte was repaid almost immediately by an Assyrian raid on Babylon itself led by Tiglath-Pileser I (1115–1077).

This period of mutual testing was followed by a long and rather sparsely documented period that seems to have been marked by relatively peaceful relations between the two states, encouraged by their mutual preoccupation with invading Arameans.[50] The accession of Šamaš-mudammiq to the throne

---

[48] The summary of Babylonian political and military history below, except where otherwise noted, follows the reconstructions proposed by John A. Brinkman in his detailed study of the early period, *A Political History of Post-Kassite Babylonia, 1158–722 BC*, Analecta Orientalia, 43 (hereafter *Post-Kassite Babylonia*); his articles, "Babylonia under the Assyrian Empire, 745–627 BC," in *Power and Propaganda*, 223–250 and "Babylonia c. 1000–748 BC," in *The Cambridge Ancient History*, 2nd ed., Vol. 3, pt. 1, 282–313; and his excellent extended survey of Babylonia in this period, *Prelude to Empire: Babylonian Society and Politics, 747–626 BC*.

[49] For a detailed account of the events of these years, see Brinkman, *Post-Kassite Babylonia*, 86–226. The dates of Babylonian kings used here are those he proposes in Pl. II, between pages 76 and 77.

[50] The period from the late tenth century to the middle of the eighth century is discussed by Brinkman in "Babylonia c. 1000–748 BC," and in *Post-Kassite Babylonia*, 168–170 and 177–226.

of Babylonia late in the tenth century began a period of more active contact between the two states that Brinkman has characterized as a time of "battles, alliances, shifting of borders, and diplomatic marriages, most of which seem to have bound the two countries closer together."[51] By the mid-ninth century, friendship between the two states had become close enough that the Assyrian king Shalmaneser III (858–824) conducted two extensive campaigns in Babylonia in support of the legitimate Babylonian claimant to the throne, who in turn later supported Shalmaneser's son, Shamshi-Adad V (823–811), against a widespread revolt in Assyria. This incident, however, provoked the beginning of a change in the once cordial relationship between the two states; the Babylonian king, in exchange for his support, imposed a demeaning treaty on Shamshi-Adad, who later took his revenge by conducting four successive campaigns in Babylonia, taking the next two Babylonian kings in turn captive to Assyria. These abductions produced a period of near anarchy in Babylonia and a claim by Shamshi-Adad to Assyrian suzerainty there, a claim never acknowledged in Babylonia itself. Assyria, however, was now increasingly aggressive in her relations with Babylonia. Both Adad-nīrārī III (810–783) and Aššur-dan III (772–755) conducted further campaigns in Babylonian territory; while these campaigns were a mark of growing Assyrian power and influence in Babylonia, neither king pursued his advantage to the point of imposing direct Assyrian rule.

This changed with Tiglath-Pileser III (744–727). In the final years of his reign he defeated the Chaldean tribal leader and king of Babylonia, Nabû-mukīn-zēri, and became the first Assyrian king in almost five centuries to rule as king of Babylonia and be acknowledged as king in later Babylonian traditions.[52] Like earlier Assyrian kings, he made active efforts to win the friendship of the Babylonians by sacrificing to Babylonian gods in eight Babylonian cities. There is some doubt about the extent of his control of Babylonia, however, since the former king, Nabû-mukīn-zēri, remained free and apparently still in control of his capital city in Chaldea. That Tiglath-Pileser played the role of the Babylonian king in the *akītu* festival at Babylon in the two years in which he reigned over Babylonia is perhaps an indication of at least partial acceptance of his reign in northern Babylonia; a stronger indication of Tiglath-Pileser's acceptance in Babylonia is the fact that the dating formulae of Babylonian economic texts acknowledged him as king of Babylonia during the two years of his reign there, and later Babylonian king-lists also recognize him as Babylon's king in this period.[53] Tiglath-Pileser's reign marks the beginning of a series of Assyrian attempts to impose direct rule on

---

[51] *Post-Kassite Babylonia*, 169.

[52] For the events of Tiglath-Pileser's reign, see Brinkman, *Post-Kassite Babylonia*, 228–243 and *Prelude*, 40–43.

[53] *Post-Kassite Babylonia*, n. 1545 and p. 242.

Babylonia, as well as the emergence of the Chaldeans as leaders in resisting those attempts.

Within six years of Tiglath-Pileser's death, the Babylonians were again independent, led by another Chaldean, Merodach-Baladan II, who emerged as the new leader of the Babylonian resistance.[54] Supported by a coalition of various groups in Babylonia, and with military aid from neighboring Elam, Merodach-Baladan managed to hold the throne of Babylon for nearly twelve years. It was not until 710 that the new Assyrian king, Sargon II (721–705), attacked the Babylonian coalition, finally defeating it a year later and formally reclaiming the throne of Babylon for Assyria. Merodach-Baladan's final stand against Sargon at his capital city of Dūr-Jakīn in 709 was a failure; he fled to Elam, leaving Sargon in control of Babylonia.

Babylonia's resistance to Assyrian rule persisted, however, reaching a climax in the reign of Sargon's successor, Sennacherib (704–681).[55] Early in the reign, Merodach-Baladan again assembled a coalition and revolted against Assyria, successfully repelling the first attack by the Assyrian army, only to suffer crushing defeat in a second engagement. Sennacherib then installed a native Babylonian named Bēl-ibni as puppet king in Babylonia in an effort to end the revolts, only to see the arrangement collapse within three years, requiring another Assyrian campaign in Babylonia and the removal of Bēl-ibni and his officers. Sennacherib's next arrangement for rule of Babylonia, the appointment of his own son, Aššur-nādin-šumi, as king of Babylonia, lasted for only six years before Aššur-nādin-šumi was kidnapped and killed, a development which incidentally opened the way for Esarhaddon's appointment as heir to the throne of Assyria, as we saw earlier. In Babylonia, Sennacherib succeeded in quickly deposing the next king, a protégé of the neighboring Elamites, but was almost at once faced with yet another Chaldean king, who succeeded in forging another powerful Elamite-Babylonian coalition. Sennacherib's response was a long and bloody period of campaigning in Babylonia[56] in which he finally succeeded in reimposing Assyrian rule, taking the city of Babylon itself in 689 after a prolonged siege. According to his own inscriptions, Sennacherib was merciless in his punishment of the city, burning and plundering, destroying walls and temples, and finally flooding the ruins. For eight years until Sennacherib's death Babylonia was quiet, and it appeared

---

[54] For the conflicts between Merodach-Baladan II and Sargon II in these years, see Chr. 1, i, ll. 31-ii, l. 6'; A. G. Lie, *The Inscriptions of Sargon II, King of Assyria*, 40–67; and Brinkman's discussion in "Babylonia under the Assyrian Empire," 229–230.

[55] For the documentary evidence for Sennacherib's southern campaigns, see Sidney Smith, *The First Campaign of Sennacherib, King of Assyria, BC 705–681*; Chr. 1, ii, l. 19-iii, l. 36; and Daniel David Luckenbill, *The Annals of Sennacherib*, OIP, 2. For further discussion, see Brinkman, "Babylonia under the Assyrian Empire," 223–250, and *Prelude*, 54–70; and Louis D. Levine, "Sennacherib's Southern Front: 704–689 BC," 28–58.

[56] Beginning probably in 691. See Brinkman, *Prelude*, 63 and n. 306.

that his relentless use of force might at last have ended the long series of Babylonian revolts against Assyrian rule.

When Esarhaddon came to the throne after Sennacherib's death, however, it was already apparent that Babylonian resistance had only been lying dormant, recovering strength. With the Assyrian army preoccupied by the civil war that had broken out in the north at Sennacherib's death, one of Merodach-Baladan's sons, Nabû-zēr-kitti-līšir, now leader of the Chaldean tribe of Bīt-Jakīn and governor of the Sealand area in southern Babylonia,[57] had seized the opportunity to revolt, laying siege to the Babylonian city of Ur, an important administrative center and garrison city under Assyrian control. In Assyria, Esarhaddon had managed to suppress the civil war by the beginning of 680 and was engaged in setting up a new administration, but in the south the rebellious Nabû-zēr-kitti-līšir continued his siege.

Recognizing the importance of suppressing this revolt before it could engulf all of Babylonia, Esarhaddon promptly dispatched Assyrian troops to attack the rebels at Ur. Fortunately for Assyria, the governor of Ur remained loyal, refusing to open the city gates to the rebels, and Nabû-zēr-kitti-līšir, unable to confront an Assyrian army without local support, abandoned his siege and fled to Elam, where his father Merodach-Baladan had in the past found military aid and asylum. This time, however, the Elamites, whose king had recently died of a sudden illness, were apparently unwilling to risk direct confrontation with the Assyrians; they seized Nabû-zēr-kitti-līšir and put him to death, effectively ending the revolt.[58] With this unexpected help, Esarhaddon had resolved the immediate crisis. Given the long history of Babylonian revolts, however, it promised to be at most a temporary reprieve.

The Assyrians urgently needed to establish a lasting peace with Babylonia. The warfare that repeatedly swept Babylonia had disrupted the southern trading network of which she was a part, depriving Assyria of a profitable source of tax revenue and trade goods.[59] The cost of keeping troops available to deal with Babylonian revolts, and the loss of Assyrian lives when such revolts broke out, were also taking their toll. Assyria's military situation in the empire at large put additional pressure on the king to resolve the problem of Babylonia. Sennacherib's campaigns had led him nearly to the borders of Egypt; Esarhaddon needed to pursue this advantage and attack Egypt itself in order to

[57] Whether Nabû-zēr-kitti-līšir had been appointed by the Assyrians as governor there or was merely recognized by them as the current ruler of the Sealand is unclear. Esarhaddon's Nineveh A inscription (II, l. 41) claims that Nabû-zēr-kitti-līšir had a formal agreement (adû) with the Assyrians, which he broke, but the terms of that agreement are never specified. For these events, see Nin. A, B, C, and D, Ep. 4, and Chr. 1, iii, ll. 39–42.

[58] On the political history of Elam in this period, see Matthew W. Stolper, "Political History," in *Elam: Surveys of Political History and Archaeology*, ed. Elizabeth Carter and Matthew W. Stolper (Berkeley: 1984), 3–100, and Pamela D. Gerardi, "Assurbanipal's Elamite Campaigns: A Literary and Political Study."

[59] For Babylonia as a source of revenue and trade products, see Brinkman, "Babylonia under the Assyrian Empire, 745–627 BC," in *Power and Propaganda*, 228–229.

end Egypt's repeated support of rebellions by Assyrian vassals on the Mediterranean coast.[60] Esarhaddon was probably aware in addition that trouble was already brewing among these western vassals; it was to erupt in open war against Assyria within the next three years, in the revolt of Sidon on the coast and of her allies Kundu and Sisû in Asia Minor. There were also problems in the eastern mountain regions, where the Assyrians were finding it increasingly difficult to collect the tax in horses essential for their army.[61] Given the limited manpower resources of Assyria, Esarhaddon needed to free troops from Babylonia in order to deal with these and other problems. The pacification of Babylonia had become important for Assyria's prosperity, perhaps even for her survival.

After all these years of warfare, however, Babylonian resistance to Assyrian rule was deeply entrenched, and the complexities of the political situation in Babylonia compounded the problem of dealing with that resistance. Opposition to Assyria was being mounted not by a single group, "the Babylonians," but by shifting coalitions of the various ethnic and political groups settled in Babylonia. Successful revolts against Assyria had usually involved alliances among three groups that together dominated Babylonian politics: the Elamites, Babylonia's neighbors to the east, who provided military know-how and troops; the Chaldean and Aramean tribes of Babylonia, who provided both soldiers and political leadership; and the "native Babylonians"—whom the Assyrians describe as the citizens of the ancient cities (the *mārē āli*) and distinguish as a separate and clearly recognizable social and political group—who provided money, additional troops, administrative experience, and at times the protection of their cities' massive walls. Together, these three groups made a formidable force, and Esarhaddon would have to deal with each of them in turn to create a lasting peace with Babylonia.

The first of the three, the Elamites, occupied an area that lay immediately to the east of Babylonia in the lowlands of what is now the Iranian province of Khuzistan and in the valley systems and highlands to their east and north.[62] For years the Elamites had made efforts to expand their sphere

---

[60] Sennacherib's confrontation with Egyptian troops at Eltekeh in Palestine, echoing Sargon's earlier confrontation with Egyptian troops at Râpi'u, made it almost inevitable that the Assyrians would in time try to cross the desert and defeat the Egyptian armies at their source in order to end Egyptian interference with Assyria's vassals in Palestine and also to gain control over Egypt's lucrative trade.

[61] The Assyrians' increasing difficulties in the Zagros Mountain regions are reflected in the king's requests for omens to predict the outcome of proposed Assyrian actions in those areas (published in Jörgen A. Knudtzon, *Assyrische Gebete an den Sonnengott für Staat und königliches Haus aus der zeit Asarhaddons und Asurbanipals* and Ernst G. Klauber, *Politisch-Religiöse Texte aus der Sargonidenzeit*). The Assyrians' fear that their horse-tax collectors might be kidnapped by Medes, Manneans, Scyths, or others in the Zagros is reflected in Klauber, nos. 20, 21, and 22, and Knudtzon, nos. 30, 31, and 33.

[62] Stolper in Carter and Stolper, *Elam*, 4. The precise boundaries of Elam in this period remain uncertain.

of influence into Babylonia at Assyrian expense, providing military support
for Babylonian rebellions against Assyria and occasionally placing their own
candidates on the Babylonian throne. Sennacherib's annals report, for example,
that the Elamites had sent horsemen, officers, and 80,000 bowmen to join the
coalition army that unsuccessfully fought Sennacherib ca. 703.[63] Later in
Sennacherib's reign, the Elamites had also aided in the kidnapping and death
of Sennacherib's son Aššur-nādin-šumi,[64] had raided the Babylonian cities of
Sippar and Uruk,[65] had briefly installed their own candidate as king of Babylonia,[66] and had even led the coalition army which defeated Sennacherib's
army in battle at Ḫalulē.[67] Elam, in short, had proven to be a formidable and
active opponent of Assyrian rule in Babylonia.

There was little Esarhaddon could do, however, to influence Elam's activities directly, aside from posting garrisons on Babylonia's borders to discourage Elamite invasion. Ultimately, his best approach to the problem of Elamite
interference in Babylonian affairs was to try to win over the Chaldean tribes-
men and the native Babylonians, who were accessible to Esarhaddon because
they lived in areas directly under Assyrian rule and whom the Elamites would
need as allies in any attempt to take control of Babylonia. If Esarhaddon could
succeed in winning the support of these two groups, Elam would be isolated
and unable to undermine Assyrian control of the south.[68]

This, however, was easier said than done. The Chaldeans, and the Arameans with whom they were frequently allied, represented a large and varied
group of tribes, each under its own leaders and only loosely linked to one
another by shifting military alliances.[69] Assyrian inscriptions, our main source

---

[63] Sidney Smith, *First Campaign*, 31 and 58, l. 9. The exact date of this battle is uncertain.

[64] Chr. 1, ii, l. 42. See also Simo Parpola, "A Letter from Šamaš-šumu-ukīn to Esarhaddon,"
21–34.

[65] Chr. 1, ii, ll. 39–41 and iii, ll. 2–3.

[66] Chr. 1, ii, l. 44–iii, l. 6.

[67] Chr. 1, iii, ll. 16–18. Sennacherib's inscriptions, probably less reliable on this point than the
Babylonian Chronicles, claim an Assyrian victory; see Brinkman, *Prelude*, 63–64.

[68] Gerardi, "Assurbanipal's Elamite Campaigns," 12, plausibly suggests that the Elamite attack
on Sippar and the deportation of the Chaldean leader Kudurru along with the governor of the
Nippur province, described in the Babylonian Chronicle entries for 675, may reflect a final attempt
at a Babylonian-Elamite alliance gone awry. The treaty made by Esarhaddon with the Elamite king
Urtak, mentioned by Assurbanipal (*AS* 5, 17 ff.), should probably be connected, Gerardi suggests,
with the friendly overtures by "the Elamite" that are mentioned in Esarhaddon's Nin. A inscription,
Ep. 19. Gerardi dates this treaty to ca. 674, after the death of the previous Elamite king in 675 and
before the composition of Nin. A, dated to 673. If this is correct—and it seems plausible—the sign-
ing of the treaty shortly after the Assyrians had thwarted an attempted Elamite-Chaldean alliance
against them and deported its Chaldean leader, Kudurru, would seem to imply that the Elamites
themselves recognized the futility of efforts to oppose the Assyrians in the absence of such an alliance.

[69] See the sections on Arameans and Chaldeans in Brinkman, *Post-Kassite Babylonia*, 246–247
and 260–285, as well as his discussions there of the reigns of individual Chaldean kings. For a more
conjectural analysis of the role of the Arameans and Chaldeans in Babylonian politics in the seventh
century, see Manfried Dietrich, *Die Aramäer Südbabyloniens in der Sargonidenzeit (700–648)*, AOAT, 7

of information about these groups, identify five distinct Chaldean tribes and some forty Aramean ones. Whether the two large groups of tribes were related to each other by kinship or language, as has sometimes been asserted, is unclear;[70] it is clear, however, that tribes from both groups, whatever their differences, frequently united in political and military relationships that were the basis of most anti-Assyrian coalitions in Babylonia.

The Aramean tribes were the first to appear in Babylonia, coming as border raiders in the closing centuries of the second millennium and settling in southern Babylonia by the late eighth century. Their language was West Semitic in pattern, but evidence about their precise place of origin is still lacking. Although many Aramean tribes joined in the anti-Assyrian rebellions of the eighth and early seventh centuries, providing troops to the coalition armies on several occasions,[71] they did not themselves organize or lead the revolts. The Aramean tribes, on the whole pawns in the Babylonian politics of Esarhaddon's day, were seldom the direct focus of Esarhaddon's Babylonian policy.[72]

Unlike the Arameans, the Chaldeans had quickly become leaders in Babylonian politics. Appearing in Babylonia in the early ninth century, again from a location that is still unknown, the Chaldeans provided a total of six kings to govern Babylonia in the century before Esarhaddon's reign.[73] Beginning

---

(reviewed by Brinkman, "Notes on Arameans and Chaldeans in Southern Babylonia in the Early Seventh Century BC," 304–325, who takes exception to many of Dietrich's conclusions). In most cases discussed here, I have found Brinkman's reconstruction to be the more convincing; I am also indebted to Dietrich, however, for arguments on specific points, as noted.

[70] Although Dietrich treats the Chaldeans as a sub-group of the Arameans, Brinkman ("Notes on Arameans," 306–307) notes that the Chaldeans can be distinguished from the Arameans by distinctive tribal name-forms and settlement patterns, as well as by their extensive involvement in national politics in Babylonia. Assyrian inscriptions consistently treat Arameans and Chaldeans as two distinct groups of tribes.

[71] In the time of Sargon, for example, the reign of the Chaldean Merodach-Baladan II in Babylonia was supported by the Ru'a, the Ḫindaru, the Iadburu, the Puqūdu, and the Gambūlu, all Aramean tribes. During Sennacherib's reign, seventeen Aramean tribes sent troops to join the army which fought Assyria in the battles at Kutha and Kish ca. 703, and Sennacherib reports that the coalition army which the Elamites led against him at the battle of Ḫalulē included ". . . all the Arameans" (OIP, 2, p. 88, l. 45).

[72] A minor exception is the role played in Esarhaddon's reign by Bēl-iqīša, leader of the Gambūlu, an Aramean tribe settled in a swampy area on the edge of the mountains east of Babylonia. Esarhaddon's annals record (Nin. A and B, Ep. 13) that Bēl-iqīša came of his own free will to do obeisance to Esarhaddon, apparently reacting to the Assyrian raid on the Chaldeans described just before this incident, and that he was installed by Esarhaddon in the Gambūlaian fortress of Šapî-Bēl with a garrison, to serve the Assyrians "like a door" to shut out Elam. Later, in Assurbanipal's reign, the Gambūlu were to become an aggressive anti-Assyrian force (see Brinkman, "Notes on Arameans," 308), but in the time of Esarhaddon they had not yet emerged as an initiating force in Babylonian politics.

[73] The Babylonian kings Marduk-apla-uṣur (ca. late 770s), Erība-Marduk (ca. 770–761), Nabû-šuma-iškun (ca. 761–748), [Nabû]-mukīn-zēri (731–729), Merodach-Baladan II (721–710 and 703),

with the reports of Shalmaneser III's campaign of 850 against the three major Chaldean tribes, Bīt-Jakīn, Bīt-Amukāni, and Bīt-Dakkūri, the Chaldean tribes began to appear frequently in Assyrian annals, usually as Assyria's opponents.

By the time of Sargon II (721–705), the tribe of Bīt-Jakīn, settled in the swampy Sealand area deep in southern Babylonia, had emerged as the leader of the Chaldeans, quickly becoming the dominant force in Babylonia as a whole. Its chief, Merodach-Baladan II, ruled all Babylonia as king from 721 to 710 and again briefly in 703, organizing the large coalitions of Elamites, Arameans, Chaldeans and urban Babylonians that were necessary to hold the Assyrian military machine at bay. We have already seen that Merodach-Baladan was Sennacherib's principal opponent in Babylonia, and that when he withdrew from active political life after his defeat in 700, his son Nabû-zēr-kitti-līšir continued Bīt-Jakīn's leadership of the anti-Assyrian coalitions. Of all the tribal groups, it was the Chaldeans, and in particular Bīt-Jakīn, with whom Esarhaddon needed to come to terms if he was to establish a lasting peace in Babylonia.

The Elamites' refusal to grant Nabû-zēr-kitti-līšir asylum unexpectedly provided Esarhaddon with the opening he needed for dealing with Bīt-Jakīn.[74] At the same time Nabû-zēr-kitti-līšir's brother, Na'id-Marduk (who had also fled to Elam for asylum) managed to slip through the Elamites' hands and flee to Assyria, where he now threw himself on the mercy of Esarhaddon. Esarhaddon, recognizing an opportunity to make common cause with Bīt-Jakīn at last, pardoned Na'id-Marduk and appointed him Assyrian governor of the Sealand, the area of Babylonia in which Bīt-Jakīn had its hereditary seat.

The Elamites had thus unintentionally provided Esarhaddon with the lever he needed to make Bīt-Jakīn a loyal ally. Although the Elamites quickly tried to rectify their mistake by making alliance with yet another son of Merodach-Baladan and proposing him to the elders of Bīt-Jakīn as the new leader of that tribe, it was too late to make amends. The elders of Bīt-Jakīn, perhaps suspecting that Assyria now had the upper hand in Babylonia, rejected the proposed alliance with Elam and instead avowed their support

---

and Mušēzib-Marduk (692–689) were each members of Chaldean tribes (see Brinkman, *Post-Kassite Babylonia*, 221, and 262–263, "Babylonia under the Assyrian Empire . . .," 231, and his detailed study, "Merodach-Baladan II," in R.D. Biggs and J.A. Brinkman, ed., *Studies Presented to A. Leo Oppenheim*, 6–53). Note that in some of Sennacherib's annals Mušēzib-Marduk is referred to by the shorter name "Šūzubu" (OIP, 2, p. 83, l. 46 and p. 87, l. 28), while elsewhere in Sennacherib inscriptions the same shortened name is used to refer to the Babylonian leader Nergal-ušēzib. Cf. Grayson, *Chronicles*, 227.

[74] In a similar move, the Elamites also refused the invitation of Nabû-aḫḫē-iddina to join in a Babylonian revolt against the Assyrians, an incident which should probably also be dated to this period. See Ernst Weidner, "Hochverrat gegen Asarhaddon," 5–9.

for Na'id-Marduk and thus for alliance with Assyria.[75] Na'id-Marduk now had strong incentives to remain faithful to his pact with Esarhaddon. With the memory of his brother's death and of his own flight from Elam still fresh in his mind, he would have been reluctant to depend on the Elamites again in the future, and the Elamites' unsuccessful attempt to sponsor his surviving brother instead of himself as head of Bīt-Jakīn would surely have driven the wedge between Elam and Na'id-Marduk even deeper. No record survives of the agreement Esarhaddon made with Na'id-Marduk, but it evidently granted Na'id-Marduk sufficient power and prestige in the Sealand not only to make him accept the post—of course he had little choice at this point—but also to win his continued loyalty.[76] The specter of Merodach-Baladan was thus laid to rest, and Bīt-Jakīn led no further revolts against Assyria in Esarhaddon's reign.

This agreement with Bīt-Jakīn was a turning point for Assyria. The Elamites were now isolated from Babylonian affairs by their estrangement from Na'id-Marduk, while Na'id-Marduk's role as Assyrian governor of the Sealand meant that the opposition of his tribe to Assyrian rule was silenced as well. Without Bīt-Jakīn's leadership, attempts by other Chaldean tribes, such as Bīt-Dakkūri, to form a coalition against Assyria proved, as we have seen, ineffectual.[77] Within a year of his accession, Esarhaddon thus found

---

[75] These events emerge from a series of letters written to Esarhaddon almost immediately after Nabû-zēr-kitti-līšir's death, discussed by Dietrich in *Die Aramäer*, 24–25. In ABL 1114, the authors of the letter, probably the elders of the Sealand, report to the Assyrian king the arrival of an Elamite messenger announcing Na'id-Marduk's alleged death (1. 23) and urging acceptance of his brother Nabû-ušallim as their new leader (ll. 15–18). In ABL 576, again from the elders of Sealand, this report is repeated, along with protestations of loyalty to Assyria by the Sealand elders, who add that they believe Na'id-Marduk to be still alive (obv., ll. 15–16), a correct supposition. Finally, in ABL 1131 we hear of Nabû-ušallim's invasion of the Sealand with Elamite troops. Both Esarhaddon's annals (Nin. A, Ep. 4) and the later letter ABL 917 suggest that this invasion failed.

[76] In a letter evidently written later in the reign, ABL 917, Na'id-Marduk appears as a loyal Assyrian subject, asking the queen-mother for troops to help him deal with Elamite incursions in the area under his supervision, asserting his loyalty to Assyria, and reporting suspicious behavior by a son of the former Assyrian governor of Ur. The picture which emerges—and we have no particular reason to doubt it—is that of a faithful vassal of Assyria. Dietrich, however, in *Die Aramäer*, 34 ff., argues that Na'id-Marduk was replaced by Esarhaddon as governor of the Sealand about 678, presumably for disloyalty; his evidence for this seems to me unconvincing. Parpola (*Letters*, IIb, p. 37), pointing to the evidence of LAS 30, supports Dietrich's conclusion. LAS 30, however, reports only that the alleged rebel Ṣallāju had "inquired about" Na'id-Marduk in the same context in which he had inquired about Šamaš-ibni, a Bīt-Dakkūri leader who was later deported (cf. *Letters* IIb, p. 516 for the date); there is, however, no evidence that Na'id-Marduk himself was ever deported or that he was in any way involved in the anti-Assyrian activities of either Ṣallāju or Šamaš-ibni.

[77] The deportations of leaders of Bīt-Dakkūri on two occasions in Esarhaddon's reign may have been in response to anti-Assyrian plots involving that tribe, although the Assyrians' actions are the only evidence of such a plot (Chr. 1, iv, ll. 1–2 and iv, ll. 14–15, and Chr. 14, ll. 10–11 and 19). Dietrich suggests (*Die Aramäer*, 39 ff.) that Bīt-Amukāni also attempted a revolt during Esarhaddon's reign, led by Ṣallāju, but there is no evidence that this rebellion ever progressed beyond the planning stage.

himself in a situation in which both the Elamites and the Chaldeans were effectively neutralized as anti-Assyrian forces in Babylonian politics.

It was to the third powerful group in Babylonian politics, the citizens of the ancient city-centers, that Esarhaddon now turned his attentions, and it was this group which was to become the focus of his public relations program throughout the reign. The citizens of the long-established cities, who constituted the older Babylonian native stock—if one can use the term "native" for any people in such a melting pot—were a complex ethnic mixture, blended by centuries of intermarriage within the cities; in the Assyrians' eyes, however, they were a distinctive sociopolitical group, distinct from other groups more recently settled in the cities. Sennacherib, for example, reporting on his first Babylonian campaign, lists as his captives, "Arabs, Arameans, and Chaldeans, who were in Uruk, Nippur, Kish, Ḫursagkalamma, Kutha and Sippar, together with the citizens of (each) city (mārē āli)."[78]

Although the Chaldeans had become increasingly influential in Babylonian political life, this native Babylonian population remained an active force, important to anyone seeking control of Babylonia. In the seventy-five years preceding Esarhaddon's reign, several kings of Babylonia had come from native Babylonian stock,[79] perhaps not as many kings as the Chaldeans had provided, but enough to establish that the native Babylonian population remained a force to be reckoned with in Babylonian national politics. In local politics as well, certain powerful families from the old Babylonian population seem to have provided key civil and religious administrators for their cities for generations,[80] a situation which, if it was in fact the case in Esarhaddon's

[78] a-di DUMU.MEŠ āli (Sidney Smith, First Campaign, pp. 42 and 68, l. 52).

[79] Some of the kings who are either identified as Babylonian by the ancient sources or can be conjectured to be Babylonian were Assyrian-sponsored. These include Nabû-nāṣir (747–734) and Bēl-ibni (702–700). Independent kings of Babylonian stock who ruled in the period after the mid-eighth century include Nabû-nādin-zēri (733–732) Nabû-šuma-ukīn II (732), Marduk-zākir-šumi II (703), and Nergal-ušēzib (693). See Brinkman, "Babylonia under the Assyrian Empire," 231.

[80] The evidence for control of certain key positions by particular families in certain periods and cities in the south is suggestive but will require further research, period by period and city by city, before any clear pattern emerges. The evidence which raises the question is briefly summarized below.

In Borsippa, members of the Arkât-ilī-damqā, Iliya, and Nūr-Papsukkal families dominated top-level administration throughout much of the seventh century; see Grant Frame, "The 'First Families' of Borsippa during the Early Neo-Babylonian Period," 67–80.

In the case of Uruk, a letter (K. 4670+ B.M. 99229, published in CT 54, no. 60, and discussed by Manfried Dietrich, "Neue Quellen zur Geschichte Babyloniens (II)," 227–230, seems to involve a claim by a certain Aḫḫēša of Uruk for the reinstatement of his family as priests in the Eanna temple of Uruk on the grounds that they had held that position under an earlier Assyrian king. While K. 4670 refers only to a temple post, the recent study by Hans Martin Kümmel, Familie, Beruf und Amt im spätbabylonischen Uruk, suggests hereditary continuity in Uruk in secular posts also. While Kümmel's evidence is drawn from the period about a century after Esarhaddon, it seems likely that such practices were longstanding.

Brinkman notes evidence of high offices being handed down in certain families considerably

time, would have made such leading families a powerful political network. While it is not yet established that major posts were the property of particular families in Esarhaddon's day, it is in any case likely that families whose members had professional training and had held professional or administrative posts provided the pool from which leaders for each city were largely drawn, generation after generation.

The native Babylonians who largely controlled the life of the cities were important from a military point of view as well. Although the major Babylonian cities sometimes supported the Assyrians in time of war, most of them had at one time or another been important factors in revolts against Assyria as well, refusing to open city gates to the Assyrian armies and supplying troops and assembly points for the rebel effort despite the severe punishment such cities routinely received from Assyria when rebellions failed.[81] As strongholds from which to fight or refuges into which threatened armies could retreat, the cities were a valuable military resource. Merodach-Baladan II's effective use of cities during Sennacherib's first campaign against him is an example of their tactical importance. When Sennacherib advanced into Babylonia, Merodach-Baladan assembled his coalition army, "brought them together into Kutha, and from there observed the advance of Sennacherib's army."[82] As the Assyrians approached, Merodach-Baladan led half of his army into the city of Kish, trying to entice the Assyrian army to divide and assault both strongholds to prevent being attacked from the rear, a strategy that nearly won the day for the Chaldeans.[83] If Esarhaddon could win the support of the cities, it would clearly be much more difficult for rebels to sustain a revolt against him.

In times of peace, the cities were equally important because they were the natural and traditional administrative centers for their districts. Esarhaddon, like previous Assyrian kings of Babylonia, chose to adopt the traditional city-based pattern of administration, a decision that made the cities of central importance to him. Babylon, for example, ruled by an Assyrian-appointed governor, became the hub of an administrative district that included the cities of Kish, Sippar, and (until late in the reign) Borsippa,[84] with their surrounding

---

earlier in Babylonia, in the late ninth century (*Post-Kassite Babylonia*, 206–207). William W. Hallo, ("The House of Ur-Meme," 87–95) cites evidence suggesting that members of a single family dominated certain secular and religious posts in Nippur during the Ur III period, the earliest evidence of the practice known to me.

[81] See Brinkman, "Notes on Arameans," 315; *contra*, see Dietrich, *Die Aramäer*, 5.

[82] Smith, *First Campaign*, 33, l. 18.

[83] OIP, 2, p. 50, ll. 20–26.

[84] Benno Landsberger, *Brief des Bischofs von Esagila an König Asarhaddon* (Amsterdam: 1965), 30. By year five of Esarhaddon (676), Borsippa had its own *šakin ṭēmi*, a local man named Šamaš-zēra-iqīša (see Grant Frame, "Babylonia 689–627 BC: A Political History," 251).

territories. Other cities, including Nippur, Ur, Uruk, and (toward the end of the reign) Borsippa, also served as administrative centers for provinces in Esarhaddon's reign, under the supervision of Assyrian-appointed administrators.[85]

Many of these Assyrian-appointed administrators were themselves native Babylonians resident in the cities. Esarhaddon's governor of Ur, for example, a man named Ningal-iddina, was a member of an upper-class Babylonian family from the Sealand area.[86] The *šakin ṭēmi*, or local governor, of Borsippa during Esarhaddon's reign was Šamaš-zēra-iqīša, a member of the Arkât-ilī-damqā family, which had already provided one governor for Borsippa and was to dominate government there for generations. The chief administrator of the Borsippa temple under Esarhaddon, Nabû-nādin-šumi, was likewise a member of an important family, who identified themselves as the descendants of a certain Nūr-Papsukkal.[87] Ubāru, Esarhaddon's appointee as governor of Babylon, was probably also Babylonian; although nothing is explicitly stated about his lineage, the name "Ubāru" is rare in Assyrian settings in this period, but common as a Babylonian name.[88] The appointment of such people suggests that Esarhaddon was sensitive to the advantages of using as administrators people who were already accepted as leaders in the community.

Many middle- and lower-level officials under Esarhaddon must also have been Babylonian, as a matter of practical necessity. Various activities in which the Assyrian government played a role, such as the administration of Babylonian temples, required people with specialized local knowledge.[89] In particular, the storage and distribution of water for irrigation, a major activity of government in Babylonia, demanded the use of local people experienced in the workings of an intricate irrigation system. Officials such as lockkeepers and irrigation supervisors would be much more effective if they already knew the farmers and landowners they were working with; their jobs moreover required experience in technical matters, such as how to minimize damage from silting.[90] The resulting involvement of Babylonians in Esarhaddon's Baby-

[85] On the administration of Babylonia under Esarhaddon, see Landsberger, *Brief*, section G, pp. 28–37; Brinkman, "Babylonia under the Assyrian Empire," 227–228 and 232–233; and Frame, "Babylonia," esp. 251, App. A, Table 7, which lists Babylonian officials of Esarhaddon mentioned in economic texts. H. Lewy, in "Nitokris-Naqi'a*," 264–286, argues that Naqi'a was regent of Babylonia in the early years of Esarhaddon's reign. Although there is evidence that she was head of an administrative structure of some size based in the eastern Babylonian city of Laḫīru, there is no indication that she exercised control over Babylonia as a whole. It seems more likely that she was acting as a provincial governor in the Diyala area.

[86] ABL 920 reports that a group of people from the Sealand being held by the Assyrians were long-term members of Ningal-iddina's household.

[87] For both these men, see Frame, "Babylonia," 251 ff., and "First Families," 67–80.

[88] *Ahw*, "ubāru."

[89] For Esarhaddon's supervision of the activities of certain Babylonian temples, see for example LAS 281 and in particular the letters of Mār-Ištar (LAS 275–297), Esarhaddon's personal representative in Babylonia, who was active in supervising temple affairs on Esarhaddon's behalf.

[90] For an example of the complexities of administering water distribution in Babylonia, see

lonian administration on all levels, as well as the strategic importance of the cities and their pivotal role in Babylonian politics, made it crucial that Esarhaddon win the cooperation of the Babylonian cities and their leaders, rather than attempting to rule by force alone.

Although it may seem at first glance unlikely, Esarhaddon in fact had a reasonable chance of eventually winning such support. In the first place, the inhabitants of the cities had suffered greatly in the Assyrian campaigns of recent years. Sennacherib, for example, boasts that in a single campaign in Babylonia he had taken prisoners from the city of Kutha, looted the palace of Babylon, captured and burnt 88 walled cities and 820 hamlets in Chaldean Babylonia, returned to despoil the cities of Uruk, Nippur, Kish and Ḫursagkalamma, and had eventually departed with a booty of 208,000 men, 7,200 horses and mules, 11,073 donkeys, 5,230 camels, 80,050 cattle and 800,100 sheep and goats, as well as the booty that his soldiers carried off for their personal use.[91] Even if these figures are inflated, the basic message such accounts convey is probably reliable: that Babylonia had paid an enormous price in the last twenty-five years both economically and in human terms for its continued resistance to Assyrian rule. There can be little doubt that the Babylonians would have welcomed an end to the wars and plundering. In addition, Esarhaddon had the advantage that he himself had never engaged the Babylonians in warfare, since the rebellion at the beginning of his reign had collapsed before any major military engagement occurred. He could present himself with more credibility than his predecessors as a friend of the Babylonians. Moreover, the political situation in Babylonia was for the moment favorable; the neutralization of the Elamites and the defection of the Chaldeans to Assyria left the native Babylonians with no allies. To win their positive support, Esarhaddon began a program of actions and statements designed to present himself to the Babylonians as an acceptably Babylonian king and to demonstrate to them the benefits that could come with Assyrian rule. The keystone of this effort was an extensive program of gifts and public works, beginning with the rebuilding of the city of Babylon itself.

Stanley D. Walters' description of the water distribution system of the Babylonian city of Larsa in an earlier period, *Water for Larsa: An Old Babylonian Archive Dealing with Irrigation.* On the need for technical and local knowledge in this kind of operation, see Robert C. Hunt, "The Role of Bureaucracy in the Provisioning of Cities: A Framework for Analysis of the Ancient Near East," 172–173 in McGuire Gibson and Robert D. Biggs, ed., *The Organization of Power: Aspects of Bureaucracy in the Ancient Near East.*

[91] Smith, *First Campaign*, pp. 35 ff., ll. 24–61; the number of donkeys has been corrected following Luckenbill, OIP, 2, p. 55, l. 60.

CHAPTER FOUR

Gifts and Public Works Projects in Babylonia and Assyria

AS PART OF HIS EFFORT TO WIN THE SUPPORT of the traditional city-centers, Esarhaddon became a major patron of building projects in Babylonia, sponsoring the construction or restoration of some eight Babylonian temples, far more than any Assyrian king before him. The effect of this building program, and of the gifts and royal favors that accompanied it, was to provide tangible evidence of the benefits of Assyrian rule, evidence that would be widely visible to urban dwellers throughout Babylonia. In rebuilding and redecorating temples in Babylonia's major cities, Esarhaddon was suggesting in a concrete and visible way that he would rule Babylonia as generously as if he were indeed a native king, rather than a foreign overlord.

The centerpiece of Esarhaddon's building program in Babylonia was the rebuilding of the city of Babylon and of its main religious centers, the temple of the god Marduk, known as Esagila, and the adjoining temple-tower, or "ziggurat," complex, known as Etemenanki, both of which had been heavily damaged in Sennacherib's attack nine years before. The city of Babylon had a special importance; it had been the religious and political center of Babylonia for many generations. In the previous reign, Sennacherib had attempted to undermine the political independence of Babylonia as a whole by attacking and partly destroying the city. In proposing now to rebuild it, Esarhaddon was proposing to recreate the ancient focus of Babylonia's vision of itself as a nation, becoming himself the city's new patron, so that Babylon's magnetic force might draw the south together again, this time in support of Assyria.[92]

Plans for the project are described in the group of building inscriptions

---

[92] Simo Parpola, "The Murderer of Sennacherib," in *Death in Mesopotamia*, Mesopotamia, 8, ed. Bendt Alster, 179, n. 41, suggests a possible additional motive impelling Esarhaddon to restore the south's great temples. The letter ABL 1216 recalls an astronomical omen that had been applied to Esarhaddon, predicting that he, although not the chosen heir, would seize the throne from a prince who would rebel against his father, and that Esarhaddon would then restore the temples of the great gods. Parpola notes that the astronomical events cited in the oracle, although quite rare, had actually been observed in the area on 18 May 681, and had been reported. Since the first part of the resulting prophecy had seemingly been fulfilled by Esarhaddon's defeat of his brothers in Ḫanigalbat, there was strong incentive for him to confirm his legitimacy further by fulfilling the second part of the prophecy as well.

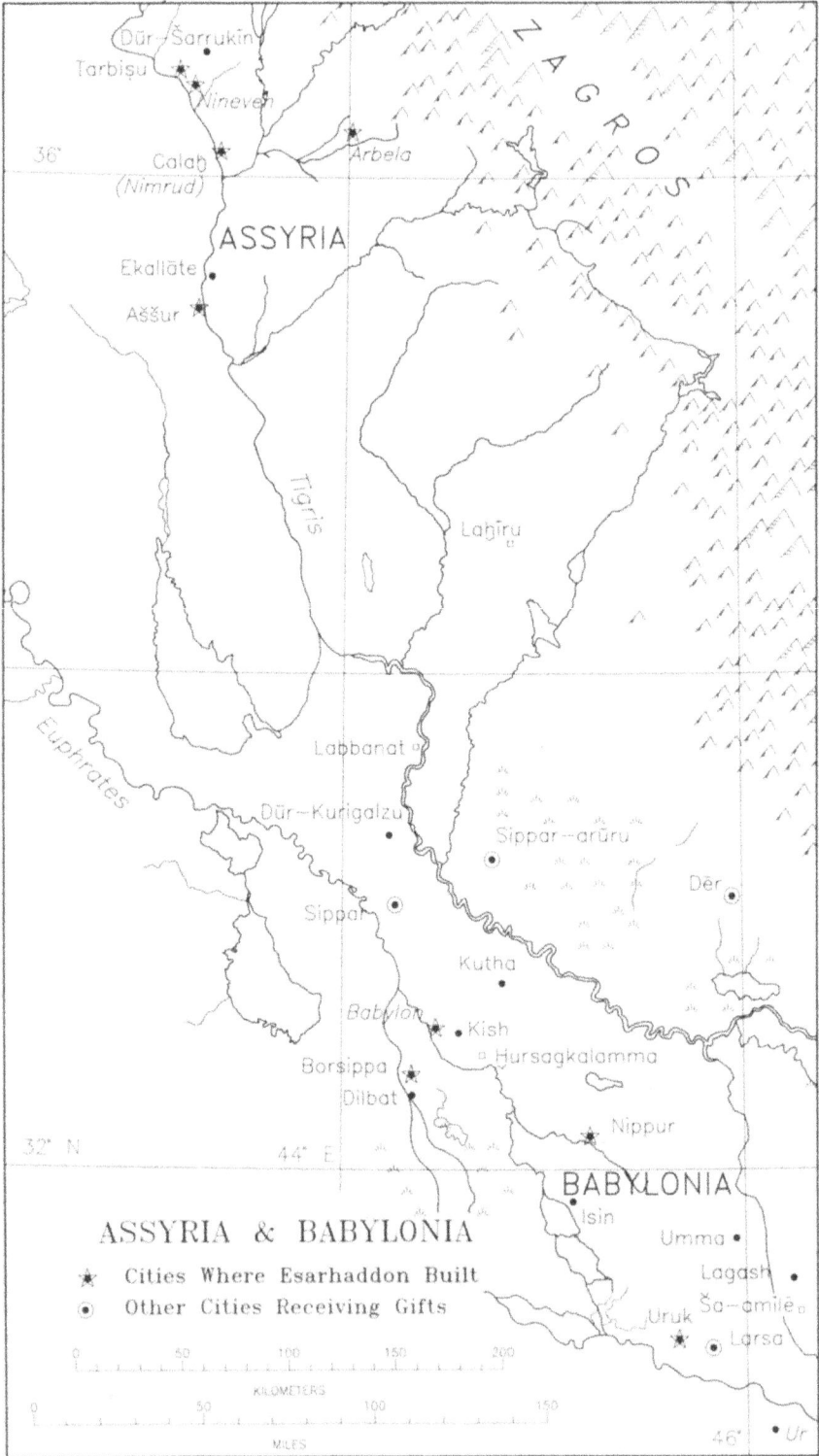

Assyria and Babylonia

that Borger labels "Babylon A–G." Like most Assyrian building inscriptions, these texts are proleptic, set in the past tense as a matter of convention, but actually describing work that was only beginning at the time when the first of these texts were composed, probably in the year 680; while the texts describe how the repair of Babylon and its temples had already been completed, as we will see, most of these texts, like other building inscriptions, were probably buried as foundation deposits in walls or under floors during the initial stages of reconstructing the various parts of the buildings—a point whose significance will be discussed at greater length below. To complicate matters further, assigning dates to each copy of the various building inscriptions for Babylon is a complex problem (my reasons for concluding that most of them should be assigned to the first few years of the reign are discussed in detail in Appendix II). Because of their early dates and because of their proleptic nature, it seems clear that most of the Babylon building inscriptions, although they celebrate the completed restoration of the city, were actually written when the project was just beginning and much of the work was only in the planning stages.[93] Rebuilding the city of Babylon, as these texts describe it, was a formidable project: it was to include the clearing away of debris from the damaged city; the rebuilding of its main temple, Esagila; the resettlement and reconstruction of the city itself; and the remaking of the city's two inner walls. The Babylon D text outlines the project: "Esagila, the palace of the gods, and its cultrooms; Babylon, the *kidinnu* city; Imgur-Enlil, its wall; (and) Nēmet-Enlil, its outer wall—from their foundations to their battlements I caused to be built anew. I had them made great, and high, and lordly" (Bab. D, Ep. 23). Other inscriptions fill out Esarhaddon's proposal in more detail. In them the king declares his intention to dig down to the original foundations of the Esagila temple and lay new foundations following the ancient pattern (Bab. A, B and C, Ep. 26), and to add rich ornamentation to the buildings after basic construction was completed (Ep. 26, 27, 28, 29, and 31). The damaged statues of the gods of Babylon were to be replaced or repaired (Ep. 32), the huge ziggurat complex Etemenanki was to be rebuilt (Ep. 34), and, to crown it all, the people of Babylon, now scattered and enslaved, were to be returned to the city, their ancient freedoms restored, and their lands and goods returned (Ep. 37). It was an ambitious program.

The proposed rebuilding of the city was significant both practically and figuratively. As a statement of political policy, it proposed a reversal of

---

[93] The first announcement of the project was in the Babylon G inscription, dated to April/May of Esarhaddon's first year of kingship, here probably a reference to the year 680 (for a discussion of the complexities of dating the inscriptions describing Babylon's reconstruction, see Appendix II). It seems probable that preliminary work on the project was actually undertaken soon after this announcement, since any significant delay could have cast doubt on Esarhaddon's intentions and undermined the effect of his conciliatory gestures toward Babylonia.

Sennacherib's punitive treatment of the city, item by item. In figural terms, it permitted Esarhaddon to assume the role of a traditional Babylonian king. While Assyrian royal inscriptions of this period typically present Assyrian kings as both military leaders and builders, Babylonian inscriptions had long presented their kings almost exclusively as builders, as if building was in Babylonian eyes the quintessential royal activity. As Sylvie Lackenbacher demonstrates in her study of the *topos* of the builder king in Assyria, the image of the king as builder was one of great antiquity in southern Mesopotamia.[94] It had been the focus of Sumerian royal inscriptions since earliest times and had continued to be important in southern Mesopotamian royal inscriptions even after the ancient Sumerian cities had passed under Babylonian rule early in the second millennium.

Because the building and repair of temples was seen in Babylonia as one of the essential functions of a ruler and the mark of a proper king, it became particularly the focus of attention in times of difficult transitions. Over the centuries, it had become a pattern in the political life of southern Mesopotamia that the founder of a new dynasty would restore or embellish the ancient temples of Babylonia's major cities with assiduous attention in order to demonstrate that he was indeed a proper king and a legitimate successor to the southern traditions of kingship. Even as early as Sumerian times, for example, Ur-Nammu, founder of the Sumerian Third Dynasty of Ur after the collapse of the Sargonic empire around 2100, began his reign with a massive building program in honor of the chief gods of the city of Ur. He continued by reconstructing the temples of the national Sumerian deities Enlil and Ninlil in Nippur, and later by working on ancient sanctuaries in the cities of Eridu, Uruk, Larsa, Kish, and (probably) Umma. This program of building was instrumental in winning Ur-Nammu support from the politically powerful priesthood in Nippur, and eventually acceptance in southern Mesopotamia as a whole.[95] In similar fashion, Išme-Dagan, a member of the Isin Dynasty that took control of southern Mesopotamia after the collapse of the Third Dynasty of Ur, restored the damaged sanctuaries at Ur and also those of Nippur, an action that William W. Hallo has characterized as "a politically astute move designed to ingratiate the new dynasty with its Sumerian

---

[94] Silvie Lackenbacher, *Le roi bâtisseur: les récits de construction assyriens des origines à Teglatphalasar III*. Commenting in her introductory essay on this difference in the royal ideology of the two nations, Lackenbacher notes that the titles used to characterize Assyrian kings in Assyrian royal inscriptions traditionally included references to both building and fighting, but put greater emphasis on the "heroic virtues" of warrior-kings than on the role of the kings as builders, a situation that began to change (under Babylonian influence, she suggests) in the time of Esarhaddon's immediate predecessors and culminated in a new emphasis on the role of the king as builder in the titulary of Esarhaddon's inscriptions. It is the reasons for this growing Assyrian emphasis on the more traditionally Babylonian image of the king as builder that will concern us particularly here.

[95] William W. Hallo in William W. Hallo and William Kelly Simpson, *The Ancient Near East: A History*, 78.

subjects."[96] Hammurapi, founder of the First Dynasty of Babylon, continued the tradition with meticulous care; the Prologue to his law code records his gifts and restoration of the temples and divine statues of a long list of cities in southern Mesopotamia.[97] Three hundred years later the restoration of major temples remained an important gesture for new rulers in the Babylonian south. One of the first acts of Agum-kakrime, a founder of the new Kassite dynasty in Babylonia (ca. 1600), was to sponsor lavish embellishments of the Babylonian god Marduk's temple and to arrange to bring the statues of Marduk and his consort back from foreign captivity, gestures that helped the kings of the new Kassite dynasty to win favor and to present themselves as legitimate successors to the native dynasty they were replacing.[98] Esarhaddon, like these rulers before him, followed a traditional Babylonian pattern of royal behavior by using royally sponsored building projects to lay the foundation for his rule of Babylonia.

There was a direct Assyrian precedent for his actions, as well. Esarhaddon's immediate predecessors, Sargon II and Sennacherib, had already played to some extent upon this Babylonian tradition to encourage acceptance of their rule in Babylonia. Sargon, the first Assyrian king to sponsor building in Babylonia, had built a quay in Babylon along the Euphrates and constructed on it the city walls Nēmet-Enlil and Imgur-Enlil; he had also sponsored construction in the city of Kish, had restored the temple Eanna in the city of Uruk, and had sponsored work on a canal connecting the cities of Borsippa and Babylon. Sennacherib, although his efforts were considerably more limited, had sponsored construction of a processional walkway in Babylon. The magnitude of Esarhaddon's proposed public works projects in Babylonia, however, far outstripped these earlier undertakings. By beginning with Babylon, and by proposing such major building projects there, Esarhaddon was presenting himself as the embodiment of Babylonia's royal traditions on a grand scale.

The extent of the project Esarhaddon was undertaking in proposing to restore Babylon was in part determined by the amount of damage Sennacherib had inflicted on the city in his last campaign. Unfortunately, the extent of this damage is difficult to establish, and there is still some debate about how much of the city of Babylon had actually been destroyed.[99] Sennacherib's own accounts report that the damage was extensive. One inscription reports, for example:

---

[96] *Ibid.*, 89.

[97] For a translation of the Prologue by Theophile J. Meek, see *Ancient Near Eastern Texts Relating to the Old Testament*, 2nd ed., James B. Pritchard, ed., 164–165.

[98] Georges Roux, *Ancient Iraq*, 222.

[99] Benno Landsberger, in *Brief des Bischofs*, 18–20, argues, following Albert T.E. Olmstead, that the destruction of Babylon was less complete than Sennacherib and Esarhaddon's descriptions suggest and that Esarhaddon built only minimally in Babylon, despite the claims of his inscriptions.

The city and (its) houses, foundation and walls (*lit.*, from its foundation to its walls), I destroyed, I devastated, I burned with fire. The wall and outer wall, temples and gods, temple-tower of brick and earth, as many as there were, I razed and dumped them into the Araḫtu-canal. Through the midst of that city I dug canals, I flooded its site (*lit.*, ground) with water, and the very foundations thereof (*lit.*, the structure of its foundation) I destroyed. I made its destruction more complete than that by a flood. That in days to come, the site of that city, and (its) temples and gods, might not be remembered, I completely blotted it out with (floods) of water and made it like a meadow (OIP, 2, pp. 83–84, ll. 50b–54a).

A later document from Sennacherib's reign offers further detail:

After I had destroyed Babylon, had smashed the gods thereof, and had struck down its people with the sword,—that the ground of that city might be carried off, I removed its ground and had it carried to the Euphrates (and on) to the sea. Its dirt (*lit.*, dust) reached (was carried) unto Dilmun, the Dilmunites saw it, and the terror of the fear of Aššur fell upon them and they brought their treasures (OIP, 2, p. 137, ll. 36b–41).

It is clear that Sennacherib's accounts of the city's devastation are deliberately somewhat exaggerated, since they report, for example, that his soldiers dumped earth from the city into the river in such quantities that the resulting silting was seen at the island of Dilmun (modern Bahrain) in the Persian Gulf, some six hundred miles away.

While such claims make it clear that Sennacherib's purpose in these texts was something other than presenting a precise factual assessment of the extent of the destruction the city had suffered at his hands, other sources do confirm the basic accuracy of his description, if not its details. A contemporary account of Sennacherib's siege of Babylon, written in Babylon itself, confirms beyond doubt that the siege of Babylon did occur and that the city suffered extensively from it. The text, a legal document dated at Babylon fifteen months before the fall of the city to Sennacherib, describes the city's plight in vivid terms:

In the time of Mušēzib-Marduk, king of Babylonia, the land was gripped by siege, famine, hunger, want, and hard times. Everything was changed and reduced to nothing. Two *qa* of barley (sold for) one shekel of silver. The city gates were barred, and a person could not go out in any of the four directions. The corpses of men, with no one to bury them, filled the squares of Babylon.[100]

A later letter, written to Esarhaddon by his newly-appointed governor of Babylon, confirms that Sennacherib's armies had plundered the city after its fall and deported some of the city's citizens:

[100] Y.B.C. 11377, quoted by John A. Brinkman, "Sennacherib's Babylonian Problem," 93. The text is dated to month V, day 28, year 3 of Mušēzib-Marduk, that is, to August of the year 690.

I have entered Babylon. The Babylonians have received me kindly, and daily they bless the king, saying, "What was taken and plundered from Babylon, he returned," and from Sippar to Bāb-marrat the chiefs of the Chaldeans bless the king, saying, "(It is he) who resettled (the people) of Babylon" (ABL 418, obv., l. 10-rs., l. 9).

Esarhaddon and Assurbanipal's inscriptions also corroborate Sennacherib's descriptions of the damage to some extent. Esarhaddon's Babylon building inscriptions, for example, echo Sennacherib's accounts of flooding and report that its effects were still evident almost ten years later: "Swamp reeds and willows grew thick in the midst of her and sent up shoots; birds of the heavens and fish of the sea beyond counting were there" (Bab. G, Ep. 7). Both Esarhaddon and Assurbanipal's inscriptions offer indirect confirmation of the accuracy of Sennacherib's accounts by reporting that both kings undertook restoration projects in precisely those parts of the city in which Sennacherib claims to have inflicted the most damage: the walls, the temple, and the temple-tower or ziggurat.

None of these later documents, however, directly confirms that Sennacherib completely destroyed the walls and temple, as he claimed, and the archeological evidence that would allow us to evaluate these claims is unfortunately equally inconclusive. There is archeological evidence of extensive building on the city wall in the time of Esarhaddon's son Assurbanipal, as we will see,[101] but it is unclear whether this construction work was a response to earlier damage to the wall or was simply routine maintenance. The temples similarly show no clear signs of destruction;[102] this is not necessarily significant, however, since we would expect that most of the debris resulting from any destruction would have been cleared away as part of normal preparations for repairing the damage, and that signs of destruction would have been further obscured by later restorations, which were extensive in the case of Esagila and Etemenanki.[103]

---

[101] See pp. 50 ff., below, for a discussion of Assurbanipal's work on the city walls.

[102] See the site report on the section of Babylon in which Esagila and Etemenanki were located: Friedrich Wetzel and F.H. Weissbach, *Das Hauptheiligtum des Marduk in Babylon, Esagila und Etemenanki.*

[103] Neo-Babylonian rebuilding in Babylon continued for several generations and was concentrated in the very areas in which Sennacherib's attack and Esarhaddon's rebuilding are said to have occurred, i.e., Etemenanki, Esagila, and the city walls. F.H. Weissbach published (in *Hauptheiligtum,* Section II, 42 ff.) sixteen exemplars of building inscriptions of Neo-Babylonian kings, and these represent only a small sample of the total. For a more complete collection, see Stephen Langdon, *Die neubabylonische Königsinschriften,* which includes numerous examples of building inscriptions for Babylon—some 75 documents—representing most of the Neo-Babylonian kings. These inscriptions report extensive building activity in Babylon throughout the period. Nabopolassar, for example, claims to have rebuilt Etemenanki from the ground up, a project continued after his death by Nebuchadnezzar; considering the amount of later building activity, it is surprising that so much remains as witness to Esarhaddon's efforts.

For archeological evidence of the disturbance of the Assyrian levels by Neo-Babylonian con-

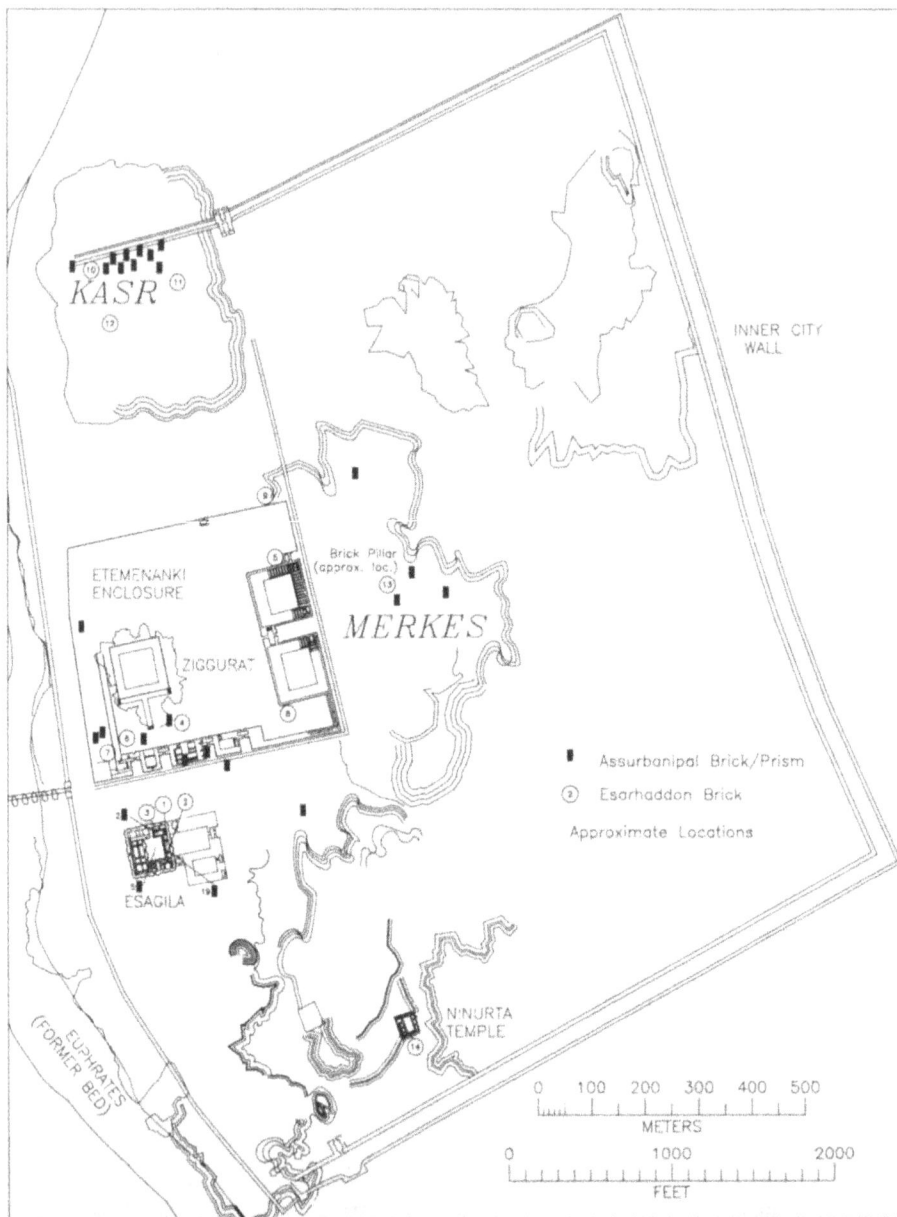

Central Babylon
Numbers refer to texts listed on p. 54.

Although the archeological evidence in the area of these public buildings is inconclusive, the one residential area of Babylon that was excavated, the section of the ruins now known as Merkes, does offer evidence that confirms Sennacherib's accounts to some extent, suggesting that houses were abandoned and the population of the city markedly diminished at roughly this time.[104] Merkes, one of the several mounds comprising the site of ancient Babylon, included numerous private houses as well as an Ištar temple and some administrative offices. In the materials dating from the Assyrian period, a level of substantial houses in this area is followed by a layer of debris, that is, sand and clay mixed with shards of pottery, fragments of bricks, and occasional hearths and ashes. In the excavation report, Oscar Reuther suggested that this layer of debris might represent the period immediately after Sennacherib's destruction of the city in 689.[105] The houses, except in two cases, do not seem to have been burned, as one would think likely from Sennacherib's accounts, but do show signs of abandonment;[106] after this abandonment, it appears that people returned to a few areas in this section of the city, living in rude huts that have left no traces except a few hearths. The archeological evidence from Merkes thus presents a picture that fits Sennacherib's account of his attack and the city's abandonment fairly well.[107]

---

struction, see, for example, Koldewey's comment that the gate complexes of the south wall of the Etemenanki enclosure rest on a rubbish fill which consists in part of stamped building bricks of earlier Assyrian kings (*Hauptheiligtum*, 25); Assyrian and Babylonian building inscriptions routinely describe the leveling of old walls to make way for new building, which was almost certainly the fate of many of the Neo-Assyrian walls.

[104] See Grant Frame, "Babylonia," 65–66, for a brief summary of the evidence. The site report for Merkes [Oscar Reuther, *Die Innenstadt von Babylon (Merkes)*], discusses this material in Bd. 1 on 21–25 and 60–64; the plans of Merkes for this period appear in Bd. 2 as Tafeln 15 and 16.

[105] This date depends on Reuther's dating of this entire sequence of levels in Merkes. He suggests that the widely scattered and poorly built houses that appear next in this area represent the beginnings of resettlement in Sennacherib's reign. In the level above these, Reuther unearthed evidence of a more prosperous period of settlement with fairly substantial houses, which he links to the era of Esarhaddon's reconstruction and resettlement of the city. The presence of tablets associated with the foundations of some of the more prosperous of these homes, bearing dates from the reigns of Esarhaddon's son Šamaš-šumu-ukīn and his successor Kandalānu, suggests, however, that at least some of the rebuilding in this section of the city occurred after Esarhaddon's death. There is not conclusive evidence to link any of the undated foundations to the earlier period associated with Esarhaddon himself, but in Reuther's opinion such a date is possible for at least some of the houses. If his proposed dating is correct, the level of debris with rude hearths and ashes probably reflects the plight of the city in the period immediately after Sennacherib's attack and offers some supporting evidence for Sennacherib's description of his treatment of the city.

[106] Such as the house partially uncovered at #22/23q2 on the plan, described by Reuther, *Innenstadt*, 63.

[107] There is only one reference in the excavation reports to possible evidence of flooding, a reference to river mud found in the temple area. An Esarhaddon-inscribed brick listed in the inventory list as 41230 (Wetzel and Weissbach, *Hauptheiligtum*, 86) is shown (plate 6) as lying beside a little column of tiles, in a deposit of river mud. The location is Trench 15, which parallels the

Beyond this general confirmation of Sennacherib's attack, however, neither the archeological nor the documentary evidence allows us to measure the extent of the damage he inflicted with any degree of certainty. It is, however, clear that the attack occurred, and the details of Sennacherib's account, although they cannot be independently confirmed, have a certain credibility, since they describe Sennacherib as doing what one would logically expect— destroying the walls to make self-defense impossible and discourage rebellion, and destroying temples and statues of the city's gods to demoralize the city and undercut its attraction as a religious and political center. It seems reasonable to conclude that Esarhaddon's relatively moderate accounts of the city's plight at the beginning of his reign can be accepted as by and large accurate. This gives us a rough idea of Esarhaddon's starting point in his program to rebuild Babylon; he needed to clear away debris, perhaps drain water from the low-lying areas where Esagila and Etemenanki are located, and then fulfill his promise to resettle the city, reconstruct its two fortification walls, and restore the religious centers Esagila and Etemenanki.

To what extent did Esarhaddon in fact undertake and complete these projects? The question is not easily resolved because Assurbanipal, Esarhaddon's son, also claims credit for major rebuilding projects in Babylon, in many cases the same projects that Esarhaddon claims as his own, i.e., Esagila, Etemenanki, and the city walls. Because of these apparently conflicting claims, it has sometimes been argued that Esarhaddon did relatively little work in Babylon, despite his proposals, and that it was instead his son Assurbanipal who was responsible for most of the reconstruction.[108] To resolve this question, we need to survey the documentary and archeological evidence for Assurbanipal's building projects in Babylon in order to establish what projects Assurbanipal actually worked on in the city. We can then compare that to the evidence for Esarhaddon's efforts, in order to assess the actual role of each king in the rebuilding.

Assurbanipal's inscriptions state clearly that he himself was responsible for the final steps in the city's reconstruction. His Cylinder C inscription, for example, reports, "The chapels of Assyria and Akkad [i.e., Babylonia], of which Esarhaddon, king of Assyria, my father who created me, had laid the foundations, but not completed, I at the command of the great gods, my lords, completed their work" (Streck, *Assurbanipal*, p. 146, X, ll. 4–9). More specifically, Assurbanipal claims to have laid new brickwork for Etemenanki and to have rebuilt the inner and outer city walls of Babylon. Other inscriptions

---

east wall of Etemenanki and lies within the Etemenanki enclosure, just south of the main gate (see the Babylon plan, page 48). It is tempting to associate this mud with the alleged flooding by Sennacherib, but it seems unwise to draw any conclusion from such scant evidence.

[108] Primarily by Benno Landsberger, *Brief des Bischofs*, 18–20.

repeat these claims and add detailed accounts of his work on the temple of Esagila and its chapels.[109]

Archeological evidence from the city supports these claims. A total of twenty-six copies of Assurbanipal inscriptions were found still in place in the Esagila temple complex, confirming Assurbanipal's claims that he sponsored work on the temple.[110] Building activity by Assurbanipal is also evident in the area of the ziggurat Etemenanki; a total of eight bricks bearing inscriptions of Assurbanipal were found at various points in this area, one of them in the main gateway into the Etemenanki enclosure.[111] In addition, a series of bricks bearing Assurbanipal inscriptions commemorating his work on these two religious centers were found in other areas of the site as well, bringing the total of Assurbanipal-inscribed bricks found in the city to thirty-nine.[112] If one adds to these the ten Assurbanipal clay prisms discussed below which commemorate his work on the city walls, it brings the grand total of Assurbanipal-inscribed objects found in Babylon to forty-nine, substantial evidence that the king sponsored construction in Babylon, particularly on Esagila and Etemenanki, the projects commemorated in his brick inscriptions.

The walls of the city are more difficult to assess, but here again the evidence suggests that Assurbanipal's claims are essentially correct. The walls of Babylon as they now stand date from the later Neo-Babylonian period.[113]

---

[109] Assurbanipal inscriptions C, L1, L2, L6, P1, S2, S3, and the text known as the E-Maḫ cylinder all provide some account of his work on Esagila and its chapels; these are published by Maximilian Streck, *Assurbanipal und die letzen assyrischen Könige bis zum untergange Nineveh's*. His work on Etemenanki is described more briefly, in a series of brick inscriptions, e.g., Streck, *Assurbanipal*, II, p. 350, texts a and b. For an account of Assurbanipal's work on the city's walls see, for example, Cyl. L6, ll. 16b–21 (Streck, 236–238).

[110] Nineteen copies of an Assurbanipal inscription for Esagila were found in the paving of the entryway ("Durchgang") to the Esagila temple, four more copies in the central court, or "Binnen-hof" (labeled on Tf. 3 as the "Haupthof") and yet another in the paving of the courtyard (i.e., "Hof," evidently also referring to the central courtyard); for the locations of these pieces, see Wetzel and Weissbach, *Hauptheiligtum*, "Inventarnummern der Deutschen Babylon-Expedition," 86 and Tf. 3. In room 12 of Esagila, identified by Koldewey as the Ea chapel, the third and fourth layers of paving each included bricks stamped with Assurbanipal inscriptions (Wetzel and Weissbach, 9–10, citing Koldewey's excavation report for this section, *MDOG*, 7 [1900–1901], pp. 18 ff.). The number of Assurbanipal bricks recovered from this paving is not recorded; the total of twenty-six Assurbanipal-inscribed bricks found *in situ* in Esagila is a minimum number based on the conservative assumption that there was only one inscribed brick in each layer of pavement in room 12.

[111] Wetzel and Weissbach, 86. The brick in the gateway was found at "Süd am 37," shown in plan 8, Friedrich Wetzel, *Die Stadtmauern von Babylon*.

[112] These are included in the "Inventarnummern" list in *Hauptheiligtum*, 86 and in Weissbach's publication of the Assurbanipal texts from Babylon on 39–40; these texts (where provenance is noted) were found on Merkes, or in one case, in the "*Stadt-gebiet*," the excavators' term for the area surrounded by the inner city wall. The total number of inscribed bricks given here reflects in addition two bricks representing the two layers of Assurbanipal-inscribed brick paving in the "Ea chapel," or room 12, of Esagila, texts which were not included in the list on p. 86, *Hauptheiligtum*.

[113] Friedrich Wetzel, *Die Stadtmauern von Babylon*; Tafel 6 shows the location of the walls identified by Wetzel as Neo-Babylonian.

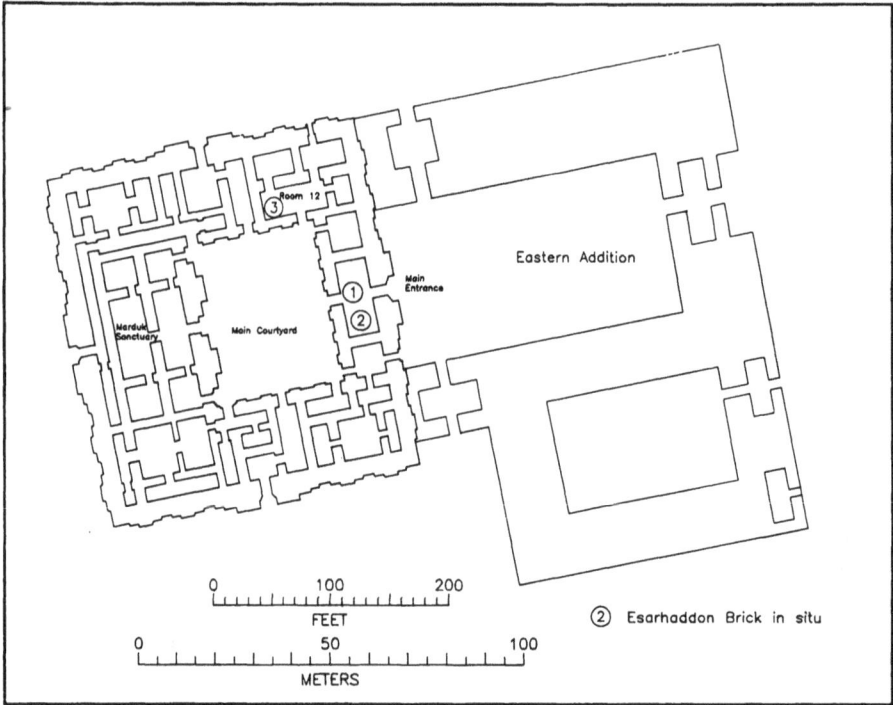

Esagila

Numbers refer to texts listed on p. 54.

Although no building inscriptions, either of Esarhaddon and Assurbanipal, or of later kings, were found anywhere in the excavated parts of the walls,[114] ten baked clay prisms with inscriptions describing Assurbanipal's building of the walls Imgur-Enlil and Nēmet-Enlil were found elsewhere in the city.[115] None of these were actually discovered encased in the wall as foundation deposits; most were found in refuse at various points on the mound Kasr. Several, however, were found lying near the inner city wall, and Friedrich Wetzel suggests in his excavation report that these prisms might have fallen here from the fore-wall or the nearby main wall when those walls collapsed in later times.[116] While the discovery of the prisms in these locations is not conclusive evidence that Assurbanipal worked on the walls, it does offer support for his claims. Overall, the archeological evidence corroborates Assurbanipal's assertions that he sponsored considerable construction work in Babylon, particularly on Esagila and Etemenanki, and probably on the city walls, as well.

[114] Wetzel, *Stadtmauern*, 7 and 66–67.
[115] The text of a duplicate of these is published by Streck, *Assurbanipal*, II, 234 ff., as cylinder L6. See Wetzel, *Stadtmauern*, 80, for the locations in which the various prisms were found.
[116] *Stadtmauern*, 67.

When we compare this picture of Assurbanipal's efforts in Babylon to the one that emerges from the documentary and archeological evidence for Esarhaddon's building activity in Babylon, a surprisingly similar pattern emerges—once again supported by archeological evidence, as we will see. Like Assurbanipal, Esarhaddon claims to have built extensively in the temple of Esagila, rebuilding it, he says, "from its foundations to its battlements" (Bab. E, Ep. 26). He also claims to have rebuilt the ziggurat complex Etemenanki (Bab. C, Ep. 34) and to have reconstructed the city's inner and outer walls (Bab. A, C, E, and F, Ep. 35).

In Esagila, Esarhaddon's claims are corroborated by the discovery *in situ* in the temple of three objects bearing Esarhaddon dedicatory inscriptions (see the plan of Esagila, facing page), two found beside Assurbanipal inscriptions in the entryway to the temple complex, and a third in the paving of the Ea chapel beneath two layers of inscribed brick paving of Assurbanipal.[117] (For the inscriptions and precise locations of the objects discussed here, see the table on the next page.) An unusual addition to the evidence for Esarhaddon's attentions to Esagila is a lapis lazuli cylinder seal found in a collection of precious objects buried under the floor of a house from the later Parthian period, located near the temple; its inscription identifies the seal as a gift from Esarhaddon to the treasury of Esagila, evidence of the royal gifts that supplemented the temple's restoration.[118]

The reports of Esarhaddon's building activity in the temple-tower Etemenanki and its precincts are also corroborated by archeological evidence. In the Etemenanki complex itself, four bricks with Esarhaddon inscriptions were found *in situ*: at gate IV, a side gate leading from the east into the huge courtyard in which the temple-tower was located; in the area of gate IX, a gate leading from the south into the section of the courtyard facing the foot of the ziggurat; and at a nearby point within the courtyard, just south of the ziggurat itself.[119] (See the plan of Etemenanki, page 55.)

---

[117] The entryway text inv. 8084 commemorates Esarhaddon's work on a brick walkway or processional street (*tallaktu*) for Esagila. The verb describing Esarhaddon's activity in the inscription was reconstructed by Borger, following a Nippur text, to read "he made shine" (*unammir*); Weissbach had reconstructed instead "he repaired" (*ikšir*). Either reading is feasible, leaving the precise nature of Esarhaddon's work on the walkway—repair or adornment—still a matter of conjecture.

[118] R. Koldewey, *Die Tempeln von Babylon und Borsippa*, WVDOG, 15 (Leipzig: 1911), 45–46 and 48. For the text of the seal, see Borger's Babylon H.

[119] Inventory #39840, found at Gate IV of Etemenanki, inscribed with Borger's Babylon J text; #41099, found at Sahn south at ad38, in the area of gateway IX and its complex of rooms, and stamped with the Babylon J inscription; #41054, found beside it at ad38 of Sahn, and inscribed with the Babylon K inscription; and #41183, found at Sahn south at ai34, at the foot of the ziggurat within the Etemenanki enclosure, and stamped with the Babylon I inscription commemorating Esarhaddon's construction of the procession street for Esagila. For all of these, see *Hauptheiligtum*, inventory list, 86.

Esarhaddon Texts Found at Babylon

Inventory Number	Text Describes . . .	Inscription (Borger Number)	Location*
Texts Found *in situ* in Esagila			
8084	*tallaktu* of Esagila	Babylon I	(1) Entryway
8050	unknown	?	(2) Entryway
?	*tallaktu* of Esagila	?	(3) Room 12, Pavement
Texts Found *in situ* in Etemenanki			
41183	*tallaktu* of Esagila	Babylon I	(4) Sahn Süd, ai34
39840	Esagila and Babylon	Babylon J	(5) Sahn Ost, Tor IV, as20
41054	Esagila and Etemenanki	Babylon K	(6) Sahn Süd, ad38
41099	Esagila and Babylon	Babylon J	(7) Sahn Süd, ad38
Texts Reused or otherwise not *in situ*			
41230	Esagila and Etemenanki	Babylon K	(8) Sahn Süd, at33
41419	Etemenanki	Babylon N	(9) Sahn Nord, aq15
32167	Esagila and Etemenanki	Babylon K	(10) Kasr, k21
41472	*tallaktu* of Esagila or Esagila and Etemenanki	Babylon I or K	(11) Kasr
44638	Esagila and Etemenanki	Babylon K	(12) Kasr, surface
46374	Etemenanki	Babylon M	(13) later Brick Pillar, Merkes
46402	Esagila and Etemenanki	Babylon K	(13) later Brick Pillar, Merkes
46403	Esagila and Etemenanki	Babylon K	(13) later Brick Pillar, Merkes
46404	Esagila and Etemenanki	Babylon K	(13) later Brick Pillar, Merkes
46405	Esagila and Etemenanki	Babylon K	(13) later Brick Pillar, Merkes
46406	Esagila and Etemenanki	Babylon K	(13) later Brick Pillar, Merkes
46407	Etemenanki	Babylon L	(13) later Brick Pillar, Merkes
46408	Esagila and Babylon	Babylon J	(13) later Brick Pillar, Merkes
46410	Etemenanki	Babylon N	(13) later Brick Pillar, Merkes
46435	Etemenanki	Babylon N	(13) later Brick Pillar, Merkes
46436	Etemenanki	Babylon N	(13) later Brick Pillar, Merkes
15316	Etemenanki	Babylon N	(14) Ninurta Temple, Südtor, Hoftür

* Number in parentheses refers to plans; ai34, etc., refers to *Stadtmauern*, Tafeln 5 & 8.

In addition to these seven bricks with Esarhaddon inscriptions discovered *in situ* in Esagila and Etemenanki, seventeen other bricks bearing inscriptions commemorating Esarhaddon's work on Esagila and Etemenanki were found scattered in other sections of the site, most of them probably reused at a later period and displaced from their original locations. The substantial number of Esarhaddon building inscriptions for Esagila and Etemenanki found in the city, a total of twenty-four inscribed bricks and one seal, many found still *in situ*, supports Esarhaddon's assertions that he sponsored restoration of both buildings.

The large number of surviving Esarhaddon texts found at Babylon is par-

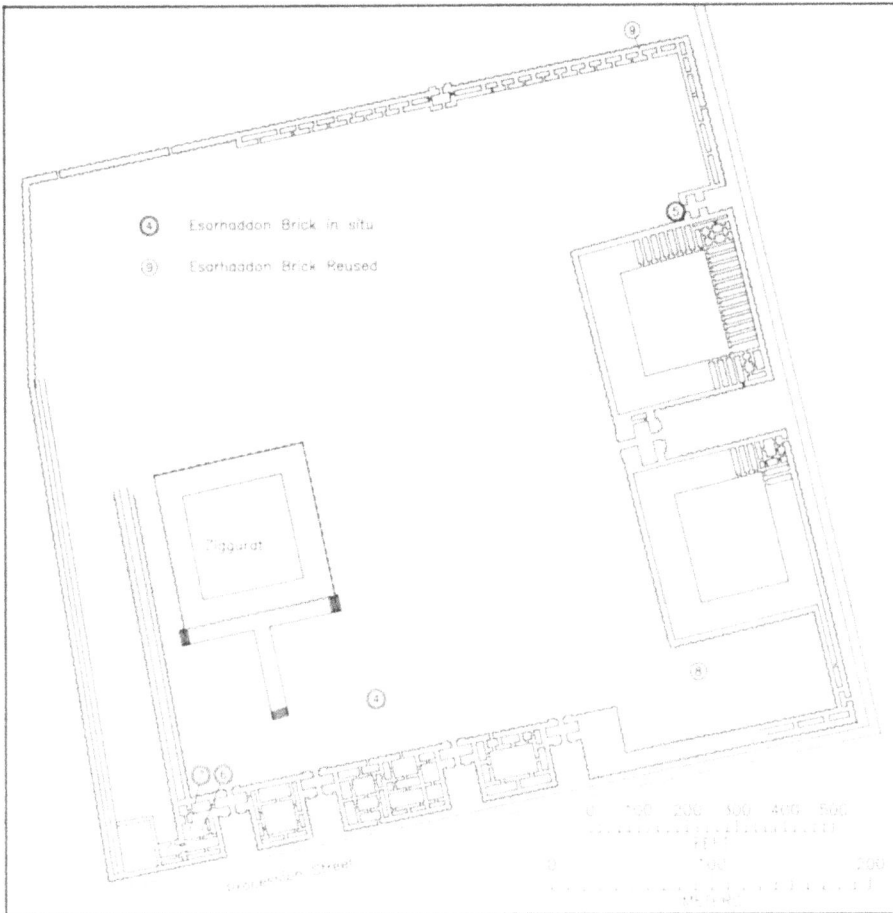

The Etemenanki Enclosure
Numbers refer to texts listed on p. 54.

ticularly striking in view of the extensive disturbance of the site in modern times. In his book, *By Nile and Tigris: A Narrative of Journeys in Egypt and Mesopotamia on Behalf of the British Museum between the Years 1886 and 1913* (London: 1920), I, pp. 268–273, E.A. Wallis Budge describes his mission to Mesopotamia for the British Museum to see why antiquities from supposedly closed and guarded excavation sites in Mesopotamia were appearing for sale in large numbers on the European antiquities market. He discovered that for centuries local people had mined the ancient sites for bricks and stone to use as building materials, and that the new European interest in Mesopotamian antiquities had recently led them to search for ancient objects to sell, as well. Babylon was among the sites being mined, even though formal excavation of the site had not yet begun. Budge, finding the practice widespread and impossible to stop, gave in and simply bought what he could. Significantly, his purchases included "several large pieces of cylinders of Esarhaddon" (I, p. 273). These were bought from local people who brought them to Budge as he traveled from Hillah (the city nearest to the ruins of Babylon) toward the ruins themselves. It seems likely that these texts were found on the mounds of Babylon and that at least some of them should be identified with the prism fragments on which Babylon A, C, E, and F are inscribed. J.E. Reade of the British Museum kindly informs me that the texts Bu. 88-5-12, 75–80, -101 and -103 (inscribed with the Bab. A, C, E, and F texts) are registered in the British Museum basic inventory in Budge's handwriting, with the provenance "Hillah," and that Bu. 88-5-12, 74 (inscribed with part of the Babylon C text) and Bu. 88-5-12, 102 (Babylon F) are also registered as coming from Hillah, although the entry for these latter texts is not in Budge's handwriting. All six of these texts, although bought rather than found *in situ*, thus probably came from the ruins of Babylon and should be added to the total of Esarhaddon inscriptions from that site. If the prisms purchased by Budge in fact represent foundation documents deposited by Esarhaddon in Etemenanki and Esagila, as seems likely, this would indicate that the unofficial digging had penetrated to the areas in which some of the most important Esarhaddon building documents on the site were located. The prisms bought by Budge are thus additional proof of Esarhaddon's building activity at Babylon, and suggest that further remains of Esarhaddon's work in the city have probably been lost or destroyed in unrecorded digging.

The surviving archeological evidence offers strong corroboration for Esarhaddon's claim that he carried out substantial restoration work on the temple of Esagila and its adjoining ziggurat complex, Etemenanki. Only in the case of the city walls does the archeological evidence suggest that Esarhaddon may not have fulfilled his promises to the city. While we have seen that Assurbanipal's work on the walls seems confirmed by inscriptions found in the city, some discovered in positions where they might have fallen from the walls themselves, no archeological evidence has emerged to support Esarhaddon's claims of work on the walls. In the excavation report, Wetzel notes that foundation texts of either Esarhaddon or Assurbanipal might still lie hidden at the base of the walls, which were never excavated (*Stadtmauern*, p. 67), but it is clear that Esarhaddon's work did not advance beyond the laying of foundations for the walls, if, indeed, it advanced that far. In sum, the archeological evidence from Babylon confirms that both Esarhaddon and Assurbanipal sponsored work on the temple Esagila and the ziggurat Etemenanki, but suggests that Assurbanipal was largely responsible for the reconstruction of the city walls.

If both kings restored the same buildings, however, is it possible to assess the extent of Esarhaddon's contributions to the projects more precisely? The answer, I suggest, lies in the way the projects are described in the two kings' building inscriptions. Like most building inscriptions, these texts are proleptic, as I have already noted; often buried in the foundations or walls of the buildings whose construction they describe, Assyrian building inscriptions typically outlined a plan of construction still being carried out when the texts were put in place. In any particular text, certain parts of the construction plan are described in detail, suggesting that these sections of the project were already fully planned and perhaps even under construction when the text was composed, while other parts of the project are described briefly and in general terms, suggesting that this part of the work was to be undertaken at a later time.[120] If we look at the two kings' building inscriptions for Babylon in this light, the problem of their apparently overlapping efforts is largely resolved. In his Babylon inscriptions, Esarhaddon's claims to have worked on Esagila and Etemenanki are explicit and detailed, and the preparation and clearing of the site are described in convincing detail. Babylon G, for example, gives a careful account of the initial stages of clearing away debris to prepare Babylon for rebuilding: "I called up all my workmen (and) all the land of Karduniaš (Babylonia). They felled trees and swamp reeds with axes; they uprooted them. The waters of the Euphrates . . . I removed from its midst. . ." (Bab. G, Ep. 18).

Esarhaddon's Babylon texts continue with descriptions of ritual preparations for construction: the anointing of the slope of the excavation, ". . . with fine oil, honey, ghee, *kurunnu*-beer, and *mutinnu*-wine, pure drink of the mountains . . ." (Bab. A, B, C, D, and E, Ep. 20); the king's bearing of a basket as a sign of his involvement in the project (Bab. A, C, D, and E, Ep. 21); and the presentation of offerings to the great gods and the brick god, followed by the anointing of the foundations (Bab. B, Ep. 27). Esarhaddon's inscriptions also describe efforts to recover the original plans of the building and follow them in the reconstruction, reporting, ". . . the site of Esagila before . . ., I caused to be opened up [and] I saw its lay-out" (Bab. A and C, Ep. 25).[121] The texts go on to describe deepening the excavation to build a massive new foundation platform (Bab. C, Ep. 30), and making bricks, ". . . in brick forms of ivory, willow, boxwood, and mulberry" (Bab. A, B, C, D, and E, Ep. 22). And they conclude this report of preliminaries with a description of laying the foundations: "In a favorable month, on a propitious day, I laid its founda-

---

[120] Mordechai Cogan has used this same principle in his efforts to establish relative dates for the Babylon inscriptions in "Omens and Ideology in the Babylon Inscriptions of Esarhaddon," in *History, Historiography and Interpretation*, 85–87. Note, however, that while we agree in principle, we differ on the resulting dates we propose for some of the Babylon texts. For further discussion, see Appendix II.

[121] Borger's text in *Asarh.* has been supplemented here with new material; see his revised edition in "Zu den Asarhaddon-Texten aus Babel," 143–148.

tion upon the former foundations, not leaving out a (single) yard, not adding (even) half a yard, following its original plans" (Bab. A and C, Ep. 26, ll. 41b–46).

With descriptions of these preliminaries out of the way, the inscriptions provide equally detailed accounts of the various steps in the actual building, reflecting a project in the final planning stages or already under way. They describe placing roof beams for ceilings: "With beams of lofty cedar, a product of the pure Amanus Mountains, I made its roof stretch (across)" (Bab. A and C, Ep. 28). They list the types of wood used in construction, "mulberry, cedar, pistachio, pure woods" (Bab. C, Ep. 29), and they describe the installation of ornate doors: "Door leaves of cypress whose scent is sweet I fastened with a covering of gold and silver, and I hung them in their gateways" (Bab. A and C, Ep. 31).

Esarhaddon's texts conclude by describing the final steps in restoring the temple to working order: the repair and replacement of the damaged gods' statues (Bab. A, Ep. 32); the equipping of the temple with cultic vessels "of whatever kind, things desirable for Esagila, made of gold and silver, whose (weight) was 50 minas, cleverly made with artful skill" (Bab. C, D, and F, Ep. 33); and finally the reinstitution of regular offerings and the appointment of temple personnel, including "*ramku*- and *pašīšu*-priests and ecstatics," and "purification-priests, exorcists, lamentation-priests, and musicians" (Ep. 33). The rich detail with which even these final steps of the project are described suggests that work on Esagila and Etemenanki was nearing completion by the end of Esarhaddon's reign.

The discussion of the building of walls in Esarhaddon's Babylon inscriptions is by comparison brief and perfunctory,[122] suggesting in contrast that rebuilding the city walls was delayed until late in the reign or not ever begun—a delay that makes sense if we understand it as a security measure intended to keep the city relatively defenseless until Assyrian-Babylonian relations improved. With the exception of the walls, however, the detail in Esarhaddon's descriptions of building suggests that he actually undertook extensive construction work in the city, which is also the conclusion to which the archeological evidence points.

Assurbanipal's inscriptions, in their turn, also support the conclusion that Esarhaddon, rather than Assurbanipal, was responsible for the bulk of the construction work in Babylon. In describing his own achievements, Assurbanipal freely gives his father credit for the main part of the work on Esagila, calling

---

[122] Ep. 35 (in Babylon A, C, and F, and more briefly in Babylon E, whose texts are completed by new material listed by Borger in *BiOr*, 21 [1964]: 143–148) describes the reconstruction of the two city walls in a general statement whose only touch of detail is the measurements of the wall, taken before work began. No more detailed account of work on the walls survives, probably because Esarhaddon did not reach the point of rebuilding the walls until shortly before his death, if at all.

Esarhaddon "builder of Esagila" (*ēpiš Esagila*) (Cyl. L2, l. 5)[123] and saying of himself only, "the work on Esagila that the father who engendered me had not finished, I myself completed" (Cyl. L1, ll. 8–9). Assurbanipal reports that he completed Esagila, but the work he describes is limited to the final steps of placing roof beams and doors and supplying equipment (Stele S3, ll. 58–65), and to decorative work ("With silver, gold, (and) precious stones, I provided for Esagila" [Cyl. L2, l. 13]; "he who provides for Esagila, palace of the gods, who makes its lock (*šigaru*) shine like the stars of the firmament" [Stele S2, ll. 8–10]). He also claims credit for the building or adornment of two chapels in Esagila, Ekarzagina, the chapel of the god Ea ("At that time I caused to be made anew Ekarzagina, the house of Ea which is in the midst of Esagila" [Stele S3, ll. 65–67]), and the Marduk chapel in Esagila called Ekua, whose adornment by Assurbanipal is mentioned in Cyl. L2, l. 14 and in Cyl. L6, l. 16 ("like the stars of the firmament I made Ekua shine"). In a more detailed account, he adds,

> Their pasturelands, cellas (*di'āni*), and the remaining cultic platforms (*parakkē*)
> of Esagila according to their ancient custom I surely put into their places for
> all time (Cyl. P1, ll. 18–20).

The work is more limited than that described by Esarhaddon, and it is said explicitly to be the completion of work already begun; the inscriptions of Esarhaddon, in contrast, describe the advancing construction work in full detail. Assurbanipal's inscriptions claim that he sponsored the completion of two chapels in Esagila and the final outfitting and adornment of Esagila as a whole, but they give credit for most of the basic restoration work on the temples to Esarhaddon.

The passages discussing the construction of the walls, as we have seen, show a different picture, also confirmed by the archeological evidence. In contrast to Esarhaddon's brief lines about work on the walls, Assurbanipal describes at some length their need for repair and his work on the inner walls in particular, including the final step of hanging door-leaves in the massive gateways in the walls, but his texts significantly make no mention in all this of any work by his father on the project (Cyl. L6, ll. 16–22). In the case of the walls, it was evidently Assurbanipal who was responsible for most of the work completed.

With this one exception, Assurbanipal's inscriptions confirm the image Esarhaddon himself presents of his work in Babylon. The two kings' claims are not contradictory, but complementary, and are well supported by archeo-

---

[123] Streck, *Assurbanipal*, 228. The Assurbanipal texts in the following pages are cited according to the identifying labels Streck assigns them.

logical evidence. Just as Esarhaddon was to complete work on the Ešarra temple in Aššur which his father Sennacherib had left unfinished, so Assurbanipal completed Esarhaddon's work on Esagila and Etemenanki, acknowledging his father's major contribution to the project as he did so.[124]

With the apparent contradictions between Esarhaddon and Assurbanipal's reports resolved, we have no reason to doubt that Esarhaddon's reconstruction work in Babylon was, as he claimed, a major public works project. The archeological evidence confirms that Esarhaddon honored his promises to rebuild Babylon and made substantial progress in its resettlement and restoration before his death in 669, particularly in the reconstruction of Esagila and Etemenanki.[125]

Since the city of Babylon served as the capital for all Babylonia, its revitalization was in a sense a gift to the south as a whole. Esarhaddon nevertheless took pains to extend the tangible benefits of Assyrian rule to other Babylonian cities, as well. (For the location of these cities, see map, p. 42.) His first gesture in this direction was the return of statues of Babylonian gods that had been captured in wars and were being kept in Assyria:[126] in the first year of Esarhaddon's reign, the god Anu and several other gods were returned to the city of Dēr, and Ḫumḫumia and other gods were returned to Sippar-arūru.[127]

---

[124] Simo Parpola argues (in *Letters*, IIb, 235 and 238) that Assurbanipal was co-regent with Esarhaddon in the final days of Esarhaddon's reign. If this is so—and it seems likely—both kings could legitimately have claimed credit for sponsoring the same construction work in Babylon in that period, which may be an additional reason for their apparently overlapping claims.

[125] Esarhaddon also claims to have restored a temple called Esabad (AsBbB, IV, l. 10), which may also have been located in Babylon. The line is broken, but seems to be part of a list of restorations and gifts. William W. Hallo, "The Royal Correspondence of Larsa: I. A Sumerian Prototype for the Prayer of Hezekiah?" 214–215, l. 7, cites a letter of Sîn-iddinam of Larsa which refers to a temple called Esabad in Larak ("who has founded [in] Larak the Eniggar [as] a throne, the Esabad as their lofty dais"). Stephen Langdon, *Die neubabylonischen Königsinschriften*, 302, identifies Esabad as a temple of Gula in Babylon on the basis of references in two Nebuchadnezzar inscriptions. Erich Ebeling ("Esabad," 474) lists three known temples of this name: an early temple from the time of Naram-Sîn, probably located in Kish; a second in Babylon, renewed by Assurbanipal and later by Nebuchadnezzar; and a third in Aššur, mentioned by Assurbanipal. Esarhaddon's temple, because of its date, is probably to be identified with one of the latter two. The Esabad project might thus be another example of Esarhaddon's building activity in Babylon.

[126] See AsBbA, rs., ll. 42–44 for the most complete account; the event is also reported in both the Babylonian Chronicle and the Esarhaddon Chronicle for the year 680 (Chr. 1, iii, ll. 44–46; Chr. 14, ll. 3–4).

[127] The return of Ištarān and other gods to Dēr is recorded in Chr. 1, iii, ll. 44–45. Anu's statue had been carried off from Dēr by Sennacherib, so that this return of gods in the first year of Esarhaddon's reign marked a clear reversal of Sennacherib's policy toward Dēr. Line 46 of Chronicle 1, now broken, probably reported the return of other gods and gives Dūr-Šarrukīn as their destination. Borger (*Asarh.*, p. 122) argues this should be recognized as a name for Sippar-arūru, an identification I have tentatively accepted here. Chr. 14, ll. 3–4, reports the return of Anu and other gods to Dēr in the first year and also a return of the gods Ḫumḫumia and Šimalya. AsBbA, rs., l. 44, also reports Esarhaddon's return of these latter two gods and names their destination as Sippar-arūru, which lends further support to Borger's identification.

Later other Babylonian gods were also repatriated: Šamaš to Larsa, Il-Amurrû to Babylon, and Uṣur-amatsa to Uruk (AsBbA, rs., ll. 40–44).[128]

In addition to the repatriation of gods, the program of temple building and adornment, begun in the first year with Babylon, was extended to other southern cities in a program of Assyrian building in Babylonia that was to continue until the end of the reign.[129] In the city of Uruk, Esarhaddon sponsored construction work on the Eanna temple of the goddess Ištar. According to his inscriptions, he uncovered the original foundations of the temple, cleared away debris from the collapse of walls and rebuilt the structure in its entirety (Uruk A, ll. 30–33). Within Eanna, the chapels Enirgalanna, dedicated to Ištar, and Eḫilianna, dedicated to the goddess Nanâ, were largely rebuilt. Seven exemplars of the three foundation inscriptions (Uruk B, C, and D) for these chapels still survive, but there is to my knowledge no archeological evidence yet available to corroborate Esarhaddon's work on Eanna. Not confining himself to the reconstruction of the Eanna temple alone, Esarhaddon also built a new ziggurat at Uruk dedicated to the god Anu; although no foundation documents from the project have survived, an inscribed Esarhaddon brick found *in situ* in the ziggurat confirms his role in its construction.[130]

In addition to building at Uruk, Esarhaddon acted as patron of the Uruk temples in other ways, as well. A broken text[131] describes his gathering of scattered herds belonging to the temple of Ištar of Uruk. A letter from Mār-Ištar, Esarhaddon's personal envoy to Babylonia, reports that people were working on the statue of Uruk's goddess Nanâ under his supervision in Uruk, and that the work was nearly completed (LAS 277). Mār-Ištar's supervision

---

[128] The most significant of all these projects was the proposed return to Babylon of the statues of Marduk and Ṣarpanītum along with several minor Babylonian gods, a project discussed at length in the final chapter. This project, however, was not actually completed in Esarhaddon's reign.

[129] The dating of the building projects in Borsippa, Nippur, and Uruk is uncertain, but they seem to have begun later than the building in Babylon, at least in the case of the two latter cities. The building inscription for Borsippa, Brs. A, is undated and gives no internal evidence for dating. The Nippur building inscriptions are also undated. However, one of them, Nippur A, was probably written near the end of the reign, since it refers to the return of Marduk to Babylon, a late *topos* (l. 9 of 6N-T 1046; copy in Albrecht Goetze, "Esarhaddon's Inscriptions from the Inanna Temple in Nippur," 120). The same is true of Uruk A (l. 18). Parpola's suggested dates for certain letters suggest a late date for construction work in Uruk and in Borsippa. He argues a date of October, 671 for LAS 277, which discusses work on the goddess Uṣur-amatsa of Uruk (*Letters*, IIa, p. *16), and a date in 670 for LAS 284, which discusses a silver coating being applied to the *parakku* of the Ezida temple, probably the temple in Borsippa mentioned elsewhere in Esarhaddon inscriptions, rather than the chapel of the same name in Babylon (*Letters*, IIa, p. *17). LAS 291 describes proposed building operations in Borsippa and is dated by Parpola to the year 669 (*Letters*, IIa, p. *17). These dates suggest that Esarhaddon's patronage of projects in Babylonia continued to the end of his reign. For further discussion, see Appendix II, p. 175.

[130] See Grant Frame, "Babylon," 75, n. 4, and p. 16.

[131] Adam Falkenstein, *Literarische Keilschrifttexte aus Uruk*, no. 46. See Riekele Borger, "Die Inschriften Asarhaddons (AfO Beiheft 9)," 116–117 for the argument that this is an Esarhaddon text, not that of a grandson of the earlier Sargon, as Falkenstein had thought.

of the work is an indication that the statue was being refurbished under the sponsorship of the Assyrian king. The same letter also reports that a statue of the goddess Uṣur-amatsa had arrived elegantly costumed in Uruk after refurbishing in Assyria, and that it needed only to have gold leaf applied to its hands and feet; evidently Esarhaddon's contributions to the gods of Uruk were fairly lavish. Mār-Ištar remarks that his letter had been written in response to a direct inquiry by the king about progress on the projects, an indication that Esarhaddon was taking an active interest in the work being done at Uruk in his name.

Esarhaddon also sponsored building projects in the city of Nippur. The Ekur temple of Enlil in Nippur was restored, and a processional street for it was "made to shine like the day."[132] Ebaradurgarra, the temple of Inanna in Nippur, was also restored.[133] Esarhaddon's work on this building was for the most part destroyed in the course of later restorations of the temple, but in the surviving northern front section and gate, the excavators found one undisturbed inscribed brick of Esarhaddon, confirming his claims.[134] In addition, fragments of some fourteen clay cylinders bearing Esarhaddon dedicatory inscriptions for Ebaradurgarra have been found widely distributed on the site, particularly in the area of the Inanna temple itself.[135] These texts and their provenance provide ample evidence of Esarhaddon's attentions to the religious centers of Nippur.

A fourth southern city on which Esarhaddon's attentions were concentrated was Borsippa. Here he rebuilt and strengthened the temple of Gula, weakened by flood.[136] He claims also to have made generous donations to the Ezida temple in that city:

> [For?] Ezida, the temple of Nabû in the midst of Borsippa, . . . [2 bulls?] of gold, 2 bulls of silver, 2 bulls of bronze, 2 *suḫurmašu* fish of bronze, . . . through the art of (the gods) Guškin-banda and Ninagal, I had cleverly made and . . . [a *parakku* of fates], the place where Nabû gives advice—he who is entrusted with all the heavens and the earth—of pure [sil]ver (?) . . . artfully I formed, and a chariot of bright bronze, . . . bulls of pure bronze artfully I formed. . . (Smlt., rs., ll. 10–15).

[132] Nippur C, ll. 14–15. The inscriptions for the Ekur temple of Nippur are published as Nippur B, C, and D. Miguel Civil, "Note sur les inscriptions d'Asarhaddon à Nippur," 94, cites a new fragment confirming that Nippur B is indeed an independent text, a point that had not been certain previously.

[133] See Albrecht Goetze, "Esarhaddon's Inscription from the Inanna Temple in Nippur," 119–131, for his edition of the Esarhaddon Inanna temple dedicatory text.

[134] Goetze, 119. The text is that of Borger's Nippur C.

[135] See Goetze, *op. cit.*, 119; James E. Knudstad, "Excavations at Nippur," 111–114; Giorgio Buccellati and Robert Biggs, *Cuneiform Texts from Nippur: The Eighth and Ninth Seasons*, AS 17, pp. 4 and 13; Francis Rue Steele, "Esarhaddon Building Inscription from Nippur," 69; and Civil, *op. cit.*, 94.

[136] See Borsippa A. The attribution of the text to Esarhaddon, although not certain, is likely because of parallels between the titulary used here and in Uruk A, in particular the use of the title *šakkanak Bābili*, used in Assyria only by Sargon II and Esarhaddon.

Esarhaddon also commissioned the construction of a tiara for Nabû of Borsippa.[137] A letter of Mār-Ištar to Esarhaddon (LAS 284) refers to still another project in Borsippa, the adorning of the *parakku*'s of Ezida with silver.[138] It is possible that Esarhaddon sponsored at least one more building project in Borsippa, as well; rising water prompted Mār-Ištar to recommend to the king the construction of a quay for Borsippa's Ezida temple and the strengthening of its embankment to protect it from flooding (LAS 291). However, Esarhaddon may not have begun work on the project, since the letter was written in late June of 669,[139] only four months before the king's death. In any case, Mār-Ištar's suggestion implies Esarhaddon's continued interest in Borsippa to the end of his reign.[140]

The city of Akkad (a Babylonian city whose identity and location are still debated) also benefitted from a building program.[141] According to an inscription of the Neo-Babylonian king Nabonidus, Esarhaddon was known in later times as a king who had restored Eulmaš, the ancient temple of Ištar in Akkad.[142] A letter reports that Esarhaddon also intervened to restore compulsory contributions to this temple, which had been discontinued after Ištar's statue was carried off to Elam in Sennacherib's reign.[143]

What has been emerging in these pages is the outlines of a large public

---

[137] LAS 57, 276, and 281 ("LAS" refers to letters published in Simo Parpola, *Letters from Assyrian Scholars to the Kings Esarhaddon and Assurbanipal, Part I: Texts*, AOAT, 5/1 [Neukirchen-Vluyn: 1970].) Parpola suggests a date for LAS 281 in the spring of the year 670 and places LAS 276 in the summer of 671 (*Letters*, IIb, p. 264). The letters LAS 281 and 292, which Parpola cites in reference to construction projects in Borsippa (p. 429), seem to me to make no clear reference to building projects.

[138] The passage could refer to the Ezida chapel in Etemenanki in Babylon, but it seems more likely that it refers instead to the Ezida temple in Borsippa, which is mentioned in another Esarhaddon inscription (Smlt., rs., ll. 10–15).

[139] Parpola (*Letters*, IIa, p. *17) dates this letter to Du'ūzu 10, 669.

[140] There is no archeological evidence from Esarhaddon's reign available from Borsippa. Its site, now called Birs Nimrud, received only brief attention from the German expedition to Babylon and has not since been re-opened. See Robert Koldewey, *Die Tempel von Babylon und Borsippa*, 72–73.

[141] It is not clear whether Akkad should be identified with Babylon (as Landsberger, *Brief des Bischofs*, 38, n. 56, and 39, n. 57, argues is the case in the letters of Akkullânu and Mār-Ištar, as a learned usage); with Sippar (as is suggested by Eckhard Unger in "Akkad," *RLA*); or should simply be considered a still unidentified city in northern Babylonia (A. Leo Oppenheim, *Ancient Mesopotamia*, 388). Landsberger's position, however, has much to recommend it. Mār-Ištar refers, for example, to the resettling of the city of Akkad by the king (LAS 275); the only city attested as being resettled in Esarhaddon's reign is Babylon. Parpola has recently readdressed the question (*Letters*, IIb, pp. 263–264 and 515–516), initially concluding that Akkad should be identified with the mound Ishan Mizyad, following Harvey Weiss, but later suggesting a site near Sippar as more likely. Because the question remains unresolved, I have presented the evidence for Akkad separately from that for Babylon.

[142] Stephen Langdon, *Die neubabylonischen Königsinschriften*, VAB, 4, p. 246, Col. II, ll. 36b–38. The inscription is written on a large clay cylinder found at Ur recording temple restorations by Nabonidus (p. 48).

[143] LAS 275.

works program that Esarhaddon developed throughout Babylonia. The work on the temples of Babylon was its centerpiece, but it was only one facet of a construction program that was extended also to the cities of Uruk, Nippur, Borsippa and Akkad.[144]

Esarhaddon conferred other benefits on the Babylonian cities, as well. Fields taken by the tribe of Bīt-Dakkūri were retaken by the Assyrians and returned to their original owners in the cities of Babylon and Borsippa (Nin. A, Ep. 12; Nin. B, Ep. 10), a forceful demonstration of the king's intention to protect the interests of the southern cities. To the citizens of Babylon, he restored ancient freedoms from obligations to the king, the freedoms variously referred to as *andurāru, kidinnūtu* and *zakûtu*;[145] he also restored to Babylon the right to trade freely with all nations, a right that had evidently been curtailed (Bab. A, C, and F, Ep. 37, ll. 38–42). To the cities of Nippur, Borsippa and Sippar, he granted the similar freedoms of *šubarû* status.[146] The king also intervened to solve problems in the operation of southern temples, in one case sending an official to assure the delivery of regular ram offerings for the god Nabû in Borsippa (LAS 281). Twice, southern cities were permitted to share in booty brought home by the Assyrian army from conquest abroad; after the campaign against Šubria in 673, a portion of the booty was sent as a gift to Uruk,[147] and later, after the conquest of Egypt, booty was shared with

---

[144] On the basis of the letter LAS 291, Parpola believes that Esarhaddon also sponsored construction work in the city of Kutha, under way in summer of 669. The letter does not offer conclusive evidence of building, however, since the passage in question only refers to a wall and then breaks before it becomes clear if rebuilding is actually occurring or is only being proposed.

[145] Bab. A, C, D, and F, Ep. 37. The terms are roughly synonymous and refer to privileges of one kind or another; *kidinnūtu* is a protected status, apparently granted within certain physical limits, such as within a given city. See *CAD* and *AHw* "kidinnu." The exact nature of the protection granted is not completely clear, but it seems to include protection from physical harm, since the shedding of blood of people who hold this status is treated as a transgression (see the references to the shedding of blood in the Era Epic, IV, l. 33, and in "The Poor Man of Nippur," *STT*, 38, l. 106, both cited in *CAD* "kidinnu," b1' and b4'). The status is sometimes associated with a particular god, so that Esarhaddon here may be not so much conferring *kidinnu* status, as acknowledging that he will respect it. *Zakûtu* is more specifically a grant of exemption from certain taxes or corvée duties (see *CAD* and *AHw* "zakûtu"). The status of *andurāru* confers either remission of commercial debts (*CAD*) or perhaps a more general freedom from either debts or taxes (*AHw*). Esarhaddon's use of the term in another passage referring to the city of Aššur (Assur A, III, ll. 8–13), implies the latter meaning, if the phrase *andurāršunu aškun* is understood as a summary of the lines before it.

[146] AsBbA, obv., l. 41. The exact meaning of *šubarû* is unclear. In general terms, it seems best defined as "freedom from burdens or charges" (cf. *Ahw*). In Babylon A, C, and F, Ep. 37, the *ṣābē kidinni*, i.e., the people protected by *kidinnu* status, are also referred to as *šubarê Anim u Enlil* (ll. 14–15), suggesting a near equivalence of the two terms.

[147] Chr. 1, iv, ll. 19 ff., for the year 673. There is some confusion over the date of this delivery of booty. The Babylonian Chronicle dates the fall of Šubria to the tenth month of the eighth year, i.e., 673, and then surprisingly reports the delivery of booty from it as occurring in the ninth month of that year. The Esarhaddon Chronicle, which does not mention booty, places the fall of Šubria in the twelfth month of 673 (Chr. 14, ll. 24–25). Esarhaddon's only description of the fall of Šubria places it in the ninth month of an unnamed year (GBr. II, col. ii, l. 3). Possibly the city fell in 673, as reported, but the booty was not sent to Uruk until well into the next year.

a number of southern cities: "I covered [the holy places?] of Sumer and Akkad [with the lus]ter(?) of gold, silver, precious stones . . . and booty from Egypt and Ethiopia, [which through tr]ust in Aššur, my lord, [my hands had t]aken, and I made (them) shine like the day . . ." (Smlt., obv., ll. 28–29).

Such distribution of booty was an unusual favor, ordinarily reserved for the homeland cities of Assyria alone. Like the building projects and other favors, it was both a tangible gift and a sign of the change in Assyrian relations with Babylonia; although Babylonia remained a subject state, Esarhaddon was conferring benefits upon its cities that they would normally have received only from their own Babylonian king.

The cities that received favors from Esarhaddon included by the end of the reign Nippur, Uruk, Borsippa, Dēr, Sippar, Sippar-arūru, Larsa, Akkad, and above all, Babylon itself. It is possible that Esarhaddon sponsored building projects in some of the other cities of Babylonia as well, such as Dilbat and Kish, but of this we have no record—perhaps because these, like so many of Babylonia's ancient cities, have not been extensively excavated, so that both archeological evidence and building inscriptions may still lie hidden. Even with these gaps in our evidence, however, the list of Esarhaddon's building projects in Babylonia and of his gifts and favors to southern cities is impressive, comprising by far the most extensive southern building program conducted by an Assyrian king.[148]

While the king's personal pieties and the state of dilapidation of the temples in question may both have been factors in Esarhaddon's decision to build so extensively in the south, the political impact of such a program of gifts and building was certainly a major element in the decision as well. In the first millennium in Mesopotamia, as Thorkild Jacobsen has pointed out, gods came "to embody more and more the political interests of their cities and countries."[149] As a consequence, a king's treatment of the temple or statue of a god had political as well as religious ramifications; as Jacobsen puts it, "Since the gods were in large measure identified with their main places of worship as local and national gods, they became, of course, unavoidably drawn into political conflicts as partisans; and they, their statues and their temples were felt to be at the mercy of the conqueror."[150] The reverse, of course, was

---

[148] This may have been partly the result of opportunity, but was also a matter of deliberate policy. His nearly twelve years of relatively peaceful relations with Babylonia offered Esarhaddon more extensive opportunities for building in the south than had been available to any of his Assyrian predecessors, but it is surely significant that he took advantage of the opportunity to build extensively in Babylonia. His father Sennacherib, in control of Babylonia from 689 until his death late in 681, sponsored in contrast only a single construction project in Babylon, suggesting that such decisions to build were indeed matters of deliberate choice.

[149] Thorkild Jacobsen, *The Treasures of Darkness*, 231.

[150] *Ibid.*, 232.

also true: benefits conferred upon the gods of a city or upon their statues and temples were understood as fundamental favors to the city as a whole. Esarhaddon's rebuilding of the temples of Babylonia was thus a strong demonstration of his concern for the welfare of his southern subjects. By repairing and adorning southern temples and acting as the patron of the Babylonian cults, Esarhaddon was assuming in Babylonia an important aspect of the persona of a Babylonian king, echoing the gesture of southern rulers over the ages such as Ur-Nammu, Išme-Dagan, Hammurapi, and Agum-kakrime, who had also consolidated their position as ruler over the ancient southern cities by sponsoring building projects and donations to the cities' temples, as we have seen. His gifts and temple building projects in the south, both as contributions to the cities' welfare and as statements of the king's respect for Babylonia and her traditions, provided tangible evidence of the benefits of Assyrian rule and formed the core of the public relations program Esarhaddon developed to win Babylonian acceptance of his rule.

Although Esarhaddon's building projects in the Babylonian cities provided visible confirmation of his intentions to provide liberally for Babylonia and also presented him to his southern subjects as a ruler who would to some extent carry on the traditions of their own Babylonian monarchy, it is important that Esarhaddon's attentions to Babylonia should not be interpreted as diminishing his role as king of Assyria. Esarhaddon has sometimes been referred to by scholars as the "Babylonian" king of Assyria,[151] but this usage reveals a fundamental misunderstanding of Esarhaddon's relationship to the Babylonians and of the thrust of his Babylonian policy.

Esarhaddon's public image as king, his role as ruler of both Assyria and Babylonia, was reflected in the projects he undertook in Assyria as much as in those he sponsored in Babylonia. His building program in Assyria was different in character from his southern building program, and its nature makes it abundantly clear that whatever Esarhaddon's attentions to the south, his real political and military base remained unequivocally in Assyria. This is the message of the Assyrian public works program, and it supplies an important qualification to our understanding of Esarhaddon's Babylonian policy. Esarhaddon's building program in Babylonia, as we have seen, was largely confined to work on temples; his building program in Assyria, in contrast, included not only temple construction, but also extensive work on palace and arsenal complexes, as well. We will begin by reviewing Esarhaddon's program

---

[151] Theo Bauer, "Review of R.C. Thompson, *The Prisms of Esarhaddon and of Ashurbanipal*; Bruno Meissner, *Neue Nachrichten über die Ermordung Sanheribs und die Nachfolge Asarhaddons*, and Hans Hirshberg, *Studien zur Geschichte Esarhaddons*," 179. See also Alfred Boissier, "Notes Assyriologiques II: A) Asarhaddon," 77: "Asarhaddon parait par moments se désintéresser des états du Nord, tant il témoigne de piété à Marduk et d'amour à Babylone." For a rather different opinion, see Landsberger, *Brief des Bischofs*, 14–16.

of temple construction in Assyria and will then turn to consider the significance of his equally extensive program of secular construction in the north.

In the spring of 679, a year after announcing the beginning of work in
Babylon, Esarhaddon inaugurated his northern temple building program with
ceremonies in the city of Aššur that marked the beginning of restoration
work on the national temple Ešarra.[152] This project closely paralleled the project he had just begun in Babylon; just as Esagila in Babylon was the national
religious center of the south, Ešarra served the same function in the north.

The Esagila project, announced early in 680 and probably begun shortly
thereafter, was the first public works project of Esarhaddon's reign; the reconstruction of Ešarra, begun in 679, was the second. This latter project seems
to have been intended in part to demonstrate to the Assyrians from the outset
that Esarhaddon's favors to Babylonia would be matched by equivalent attentions to Assyria. To underline this point, Esarhaddon's inscriptions shortly
began to include references to both projects in the formal listing of his
achievements in the royal epithets, calling Esarhaddon "builder of the house
of Aššur, maker of Esagila and Babylon"; the two phrases are invariably
linked in these texts, as if to emphasize the king's evenhanded treatment of
the two groups.[153] The "Aššur-Babylon" inscriptions, written toward the end
of the reign, would later claim that the two projects were so closely related
that they should be understood as a single undertaking, but in these early
stages, the two projects were presented as equivalent but clearly separate
undertakings.

This equivalence was underlined by repeating as part of the foundation
ceremonies at Aššur the basket-bearing ceremony which had been introduced as part of the foundation ceremonies for Esagila in the previous year.[154]
We will talk further about the significance of the basket-bearing ceremony
below, but at this point its importance for us lies in the fact that these were
the only two occasions on which Esarhaddon performed the basket-bearing
ceremony, a further indication that the building of Ešarra was meant to be
understood as the northern counterpart of the reconstruction of Esagila in
Babylonia. To emphasize his evenhanded treatment of the two peoples even
further, Esarhaddon accompanied the beginning of work on Ešarra with a

---

[152] The construction of Ešarra was announced in the Assur A texts, which describe the project
in some detail and indicate that it was expected to take several years to complete (Assur A, v, ll.
1 and 27). One copy of this text, Assur A4, is dated to the month Simānu (May–June) of 679. A
slightly later copy, Assur A1c, is dated to the following month. The Assur B inscription, which is
undated, offers a second, much shorter, account of the building of the temple. The reconstruction
of Ešarra by Esarhaddon is also described in two texts from the latter years of the reign, AsBbA
(rs., ll. 46 ff.) and AsBbE (obv., ll. 17b ff.).

[153] *bānû bīt ᵈAššur ēpiš Esagil u Bābili^{ki}*: see, for example, the royal epithet lists in Assur F
(undated), Kalach A (676) (l. 5), Nineveh A (673) (Ep. 3, ll. 21–22), and Uruk A (undated), l. 16.

[154] Assur A, iv, ll. 36–40. Cf. Babylon A, C, D, and E, Ep. 21.

grant of freedoms and tax exemptions to the city of Aššur similar to the grant made to Babylon a year earlier.[155] Although the archeological evidence from the Ešarra temple is meager, some confirmation of Esarhaddon's claim that he restored Ešarra is provided by a series of limestone foundation blocks found *in situ* in the cultroom of the temple, blocks which the excavator, Walter Andrae, identified as typical of Esarhaddon's architectural style.[156] In addition to his work on Ešarra, Esarhaddon also sponsored construction of a massive wall of limestone blocks running along the river at Aššur; the blocks, found *in situ*, carry a series of inscriptions that identify the work as his.[157]

The beginning of construction on Ešarra in 679 was the first step in the delicate balancing act the new king needed to maintain if his program to win the favor of the Babylonians was not to produce active resentment in the north, his real power base. As he moved to include more cities in his program of southern public works, he also expanded his program of northern building projects. After beginning work on Ešarra, Esarhaddon turned his attention to Nineveh, the political capital of Assyria. Here he sponsored construction work on the temple Emašmaš of the goddess Ištar in 677, supplementing the building project with a donation of precious objects to the shrine.[158]

Also in Nineveh, Esarhaddon rebuilt a temple of the gods Sîn and Šamaš and their consorts. The mention of a "temple of Šamaš" (l. 7) in the building inscription for the Emašmaš temple of Nineveh discussed above suggests that the two projects were closely connected; other inscriptions make it clear, however, that this building was not just a chapel in Emašmaš, but an independent construction project of some size.[159] The Nineveh I inscription, for example, describes the Sîn and Šamaš temple as a substantial building:

> [In a] favorable [month] (and) propitious day, [I built a terrace] of limestone, stone of the mountains . . . Upon that terrace I laid its foundation . . . That house in its totality I built, . . . beams of lofty cedar I caused to stretc[h out over

[155] Assur A, ii, ll. 27–iii, l. 15. Cf. Babylon A–G, Ep. 37.

[156] Walter Andrae, *Das Wiedererstandene Assur*, Sendschrift der Deutschen Orient-Gesellschaft, 9 (Leipzig: 1938), 230.

[157] See Walter Andrae, *Die Festungswerke von Assur*, 228, for the archeological evidence, and 177–78 for the inscriptions. Borger published these as Assur E (a palace inscription) and Assur G (a *mušlālu* inscription). On the basis of the latter inscription, Andrae identified the entire structure as the much-debated *mušlālu* structure. On this point, see *AHw* "mušlālu"; Eckhard Unger in *RLA*, "Aššur," sections 11 and 37; and G. van Driel, *The Cult of Aššur*, 29.

[158] Nineveh G, which contains the description of this project, is dated to Ulūlu 20, 677. The surviving text is badly broken, but it is clear from what remains that this is a building text. The references to the court of Emašmaš in line 6 suggest that the building whose construction is commemorated here is Emašmaš itself. The precious object donated to Emašmaš—something of silver—is mentioned in a broken passage in a later text, Smlt., rs., l. 5, written in mid-671 or later.

[159] Nineveh H and Nineveh I. The title of the eponym official (*šakin māt Ḫanigalbat*) survives in the date section of the Nineveh H document, but no eponym official with that title is known from Esarhaddon's reign. Borger (p. 67, n.13+x) suggests the eponym may be Abi-rāmu, the eponym official for 677, but the minimal traces of the name that survive permit no firm conclusion.

it . . .] Door-leaves of cypress whose scent is good. . . . whatever equipment was desirable for the temple, of silver and gol[d . . .] (Nin. I, ll. 6–11).

The date is broken in each of the building inscriptions that describe the project, but the reference to it in the Emašmaš inscription of 677 suggests a date early in the reign.

Two documents from later in the reign attest to Esarhaddon's continuing favors to the gods of Nineveh. As part of the project of renewing statues of gods (most of them Babylonian), Esarhaddon also refurbished the statues of two Ninevite gods, Abšušu and Abtagigi, minor gods whose chapel was in one of the temples of Ištar in Nineveh (AsBbA, rs., ll. 40–41). Esarhaddon seems to have restored a third temple or chapel in Nineveh, as well; the "Sammeltext," a late inscription describing an assortment of building projects in Assyria and Babylonia, briefly reports, "[the temple?] of Nabû and Tašmētum, (which had grown) old, I renewed, (and) that which had fallen I repaired . . ." (Smlt., rs., l. 6). Although the location of this temple is not mentioned, it should probably be placed in Nineveh, since the passage describing its construction is sandwiched between descriptions of two other construction projects in that city. It is difficult to pinpoint the extent of the project, since the description is brief and somewhat broken. The verb (*maqātu*, "to fall") used in the passage, however, ordinarily refers in building inscriptions to the collapse of walls, suggesting that the passage describes fairly substantial repairs, not just decorative additions.

Esarhaddon's northern temple building program extended beyond the Assyrian national centers of Aššur and Nineveh to include other northern cities. At Calaḫ (a site better known today as Nimrud, from the modern town located beside the ruins), a city Esarhaddon was redeveloping as a military center for Assyria, Esarhaddon was probably responsible for extensive repairs made to the Ezida temple of the god Nabû in this period; the excavator, M.E.L. Mallowan, although he attributes much of the reconstruction of Ezida in this period to Sargon II, notes the resemblance of the masonry in the great hall of the Ezida temple (NTI) to that of Esarhaddon's great defensive wall at Fort Shalmaneser, elsewhere on the site, and suggests that Esarhaddon instead may have been responsible for much of the work in this area.[160] The attribution of the work to Esarhaddon is strengthened by the discovery in the temple of three inscribed prism fragments which describe the restoration work; although the name of the builder king is broken away in all three inscriptions, the excavation epigraphist, Barbara Parker, notes that stock phrases used in the texts suggest them to be the work of Esarhaddon's scribes.[161] The

---

[160] M.E.L. Mallowan, *Nimrud and its Remains*, v. I, p. 348, n. 12. See also v. I, pp. 239 and 286, and v. II, p. 601.

[161] ND 4313–5 (=Klch. E1–3). The largest fragment was found on the pavement of the entry

archeological evidence indicates that the repair of this temple was a substantial project, involving a nearly complete rebuilding of the sanctuary.

Esarhaddon also sponsored work on the temple of Ištar in the Assyrian city of Arbela. This temple, Egašankalamma, he sheathed with *zaḫalû*, a silver alloy, and ". . . made it shine like the day."[162] In addition to this expensive piece of decoration, he also commissioned the construction of statues of lions, *anzû*-birds, *laḫmu* monsters, storm demons, and cherubim in silver and bronze, and had these set up in the gateways of the temple.

Another temple construction project of Esarhaddon that was probably also located in Assyria is the *bīt akīt ṣēri*, or New Year's Festival House of the Fields, whose construction is described along with other Esarhaddon building projects in a text dating from late in the reign (Smlt., rs., ll. 19–33). The location of this temple is uncertain, since no site is mentioned in the text and *akītu* temples are known to have existed in at least seven and perhaps eight different cities in Assyria and Babylonia.[163] The text seems, however, to link this temple to the goddess Ištar, which would suggest an Assyrian location, since *akītu* festivals in Babylonia at this period centered on the god Marduk alone.[164] There are two Assyrian *akītu* temples known to be associated with Ištar in this period, one in the city of Milkia (somewhere near Arbela) and a second in Nineveh. Esarhaddon's work may have involved the restoration of one of these, or the construction of an entirely new *akītu* temple in a different place. In either case, the references to brickwork (l. 22), cedar beams (l. 23), and sacrifices accompanying the gods' entry into the completed temple

---

to the Tašmētum shrine in the temple. The texts were published by D.J. Wiseman, "Fragments of Historical Texts from Nimrud," 122–3, and pl. XXVII. For their attribution to Esarhaddon, see the comments of Barbara Parker, cited by M.E.L. Mallowan, "The Excavations at Nimrud (Kalḫu), 1955," 11.

[162] His work on Egašankalamma is briefly described in Kalach A and Tarbisu A, ll. 8–11. There is not sufficient evidence to permit a date to be assigned to these projects. The earliest Kalach A text, however, is dated to Abu 21, 676, suggesting that work on Egašankalamma had by then begun.

[163] Nineveh, Milkia (somewhere near Arbela), Ḥarrān, Aššur, Babylon, Uruk, Dilbat, and perhaps Sippar. See *CAD* "akītu" for references. There is no evidence to link Esarhaddon's *akītu* temple with that rebuilt by Assurbanipal in Milkia, despite the *CAD*'s conclusion that the two are identical. While the description of the *akītu* temple of Esarhaddon does appear in the Smlt. text immediately following a description of a temple in Arbela, the appearance earlier in that text (Rs., l. 10) of a passage about Nabû of Borsippa sandwiched between a discussion of Nineveh and one of Arbela makes it clear that the Smlt. text can shift geographical context without notice.

[164] See Svend Aage Pallis, *The Babylonian Akîtu Festival*. The passage dealing with the *akītu* temple in the Smlt. text begins, ". . . after Ištar my lady had made my kingship greater than that of the kings, my forefathers. . . . I had (them) make her appearance surpassing great(?). A New Year's temple of the fields, a temple of joyful song [I] . . ., and I performed in full her religious rites. . . . That [temple?] . . . in brick, hematite, (and) lapis lazuli . . ., [beams of] lofty cedar I made, and. . . ." (Smlt., rs., ll. 19–23). The references to "*her* appearance" and "*her* religious rites" indicate that the passage continues to refer to the goddess Ištar.

(l. 27) make it clear, despite the fragmentary nature of the passage, that this was a substantial project.[165]

This brings the total of Esarhaddon's temple construction projects in Assyria to seven, providing a rough balance to his eight temple building projects in Babylonia. The program of northern temple building projects seems to have been intended to demonstrate to the Assyrians their king's continued interest in his own Assyrian religious institutions, whatever his attentions to the cults of the southern cities.

While the construction work on northern temples paralleled the work Esarhaddon was sponsoring in Babylonia, the rest of his northern building program was quite different in nature from the work he was doing in Babylonia. There, as we have seen, Esarhaddon limited his construction projects almost entirely to work on temples.[166] While he worked on almost as many temples in Assyria, he also built in Assyria major military and administrative complexes that were also designed to serve as royal residences.

This point is crucial for understanding Esarhaddon's policy toward both Babylonia and Assyria. Esarhaddon's construction of massive military and administrative centers in the north—and the complete absence of such secular construction in the south—makes it clear where the king's priorities lay. Temple building in the south helped Esarhaddon present himself to the Babylonians as the representative of their traditions of kingship, but represented no real shift of power. Simultaneous temple construction in Assyria established Esarhaddon's equal support for his own northern religious traditions, while at the same time, his secular constructions in Assyria made it abundantly clear that the north was, and was intended to remain, his real base of operations, the unchallenged military and administrative center of the empire.

A closer look at the pattern of Esarhaddon's secular construction in the north makes it clear that preferential treatment for Assyria was part of his policy from the beginning. As early as 678, Esarhaddon was actively engaged in the expansion of the already large fort and palace complex, or *ekal māšarti*, in the Assyrian city of Calaḫ (Nimrud), not far from Nineveh.[167] This build-

---

[165] Following shortly after this are passages that seem to refer to construction on Ešeriga (l. 41), probably to be identified with the temple of that name in Dūr-Šarrukīn, near Nineveh; see Bruno Meissner and P. Rost, "Die Bauinschriften Asarhaddons," *BA* III, p. 362, n. 41. If this identification is correct, the Ešeriga project would be another instance of Esarhaddon's temple building in the north. The same passage in Smlt. also refers to objects of ". . . silver, gold, and iron . . ." given to the god Nergal (ll. 42–43). Since Nergal is associated with temples in both Babylonia (at Kutha) and Assyria (at Tarbiṣu), it remains unclear whether this passage records further grants by Esarhaddon to a northern religious site.

[166] The one possible exception was the reconstruction of the city walls of Babylon, a project promised but perhaps not undertaken before Esarhaddon's death, as we have seen.

[167] D.J. Wiseman reports (*The Vassal-Treaties of Esarhaddon*, 5, n. 37) that 678 is the date given in Esarhaddon's still unpublished inscriptions for the new monumental entryway he constructed

ing was the centerpiece of Esarhaddon's extensive program to redevelop Calaḫ as a military and administrative center for Assyria, a program that continued to the end of his reign.[168] When Esarhaddon's project expanding the *ekal māšarti* at Calaḫ was completed, the building covered some 18 acres of ground and included military barracks, quarters for administrators, workshops, storage rooms, a royal residential wing and throne room, and five large courtyards, three of them big enough to permit reviews of mounted troops—a palace of some 200 rooms in all.[169] Esarhaddon's inscriptions report that his work on the building included enlarging the area of the palace, raising its terrace by roughly 18 meters,[170] sheathing its foundation platform (*tamlû*) in stone, adding a residential suite for his own use, and making a new monumental entryway on the palace's southeast corner.[171]

Archeological evidence from Calaḫ supports these claims. The monumental entryway that Esarhaddon built still stands, a series of ascending corridors leading to a gateway on the southeast corner of the palace, with inscriptions of Esarhaddon framing the doorway at the bottom (Mallowan, II, pp. 466–7). Esarhaddon's sheathing of the massive south wall of the mound (Klch. A, 11. 40–50) also survives, as a great revetment of limestone ashlar masonry covering the earlier mud-brick (Mallowan, II, pp. 374 and 467). Within the palace itself, an inscribed brick bearing Esarhaddon's name, discovered *in situ* in courtyard S31–45, confirms his work in that area (II, p. 389). Mallowan also attributes to Esarhaddon a variety of other seventh-century renovations to the *ekal māšarti* on the basis of architectural style, including the new brick wall of the northeastern courtyard (II, pp. 394–5) and new walls for terrace T6 (II, p. 455).

In addition, Esarhaddon sponsored repairs to a mile-long rock-cut tunnel and canal designed to carry water from the Great Zab River to irrigate the

---

in the southern corner of the *ekal māšarti* at Calaḫ. Since these inscriptions were not buried under the walls, but inscribed on blocks of masonry framing the gateway itself, their date marks not the beginning, but a fairly advanced stage in work on the gateway. It thus offers a fixed point for dating his work on the *ekal māšarti* as a whole.

[168] Copies of Esarhaddon's building inscriptions from the *ekal māšarti* at Calaḫ are dated to 676 (the three Kalach A inscriptions published by A.R. Millard, "Esarhaddon Cylinder Fragments from Ft. Shalmaneser, Nimrud," 176–8) and to 672 (later copies of the Kalach A inscription, published by Borger, 32–35, and by P. Hulin, "Another Esarhaddon Cylinder from Nimrud," 116–118). The unfinished condition of the Southwest Palace of Esarhaddon at Calaḫ suggests that work on the city continued until the very end of his reign.

[169] Mallowan, *Nimrud and its Remains*, II, pp. 371–377.

[170] Mallowan, II, p. 467, estimates that the 120 *tibku's*, or courses, of brickwork by which Esarhaddon claims to have raised the terrace should equal about 18 meters in height, judging from the average height of a course of brickwork in surviving walls from his time.

[171] The construction of the residential suite is described in Kalach A, 11. 40–55, and work on the entryway, in the still unpublished inscriptions carved into the ashlar masonry framing the gate itself, described by Mallowan, II, pp. 466–67.

fields around Calaḫ; Austin Henry Layard in his early excavations at Calaḫ found a stone tablet bearing an Esarhaddon inscription in the remains of the tunnel itself. The tablet is badly worn, but the surviving sections of the inscription suggest that it was originally an account of Esarhaddon's rebuilding of the aqueduct.[172] Esarhaddon also began work, probably late in his reign, on a second palace located on the acropolis itself, the so-called Southwest Palace, his second palace in Calaḫ. Winged lions and bulls, the latter bearing Esarhaddon inscriptions, line the monumental entrance-way, but the palace itself was never finished.[173]

Esarhaddon's program of building at Calaḫ was one of the major architectural projects of his reign. Begun soon after Esarhaddon's accession, work on Calaḫ was still underway at the time of the king's death some nine years later, a highly visible reminder to the Assyrians, if any was needed, of Esarhaddon's intention that his administrative and military base would remain in the Assyrian north.

This message was repeated in the construction of a second arsenal and palace complex (*ekal māšarti*) in the city of Nineveh, similar to the great *ekal māšarti* being built at Calaḫ. At Nineveh, the inscriptions claim, the *ekal māšarti* project involved completely replacing a small palace with a complex large enough for gathering and provisioning a large body of soldiers (Nin. A and B, Ep. 21–22). As at Calaḫ, Esarhaddon included a royal residential suite within the building to serve as his residence in the city.[174]

This palace, the *ekal māšarti* of Nineveh, has never been fully excavated because it lies beneath the modern village of Nebi Yunus, whose mosque, the reputed burial-place of the prophet Jonah, makes the mound a sacred site. Several discoveries at Nebi Yunus, however, confirm that this is where Esarhaddon's Nineveh palace was located. In 1851, Sir Austen Henry Layard, the early excavator of Nineveh, obtained permission to dig a cellar for a house on Nebi Yunus and by this expedient unearthed a chamber whose walls were

[172] Sir Austen Henry Layard, *Nineveh and its Remains*, v. 1, 80–81. See David Oates, *Studies in the Ancient History of Northern Iraq*, 46–47 for a description of the surviving remains of the canal and tunnel. The remains of the inscription are published by Borger as Kalach C.

[173] After digging a series of fruitless exploratory trenches to the east of the palace (in his opinion the only direction in which the palace could have continued), Mallowan concluded that the building had never been completed. See R.D. Barnett and Margarete Falkner, *The Sculptures of Aššurnaṣir-apli II (883–859 BC), Tiglath-Pileser III (745–727 BC), and Esarhaddon (681–669 BC) from the Central and South-west Palaces at Nimrud*, 20 and 24. Mallowan's conclusion is supported by the fact that the walls of the surviving rooms of the palace are partly lined with stone slabs taken from Tiglath-Pileser III's Central Palace and placed here with their reliefs facing the wall or chiseled away. The exposed faces are still undecorated, and some slabs lie in piles on the floor, suggesting work in progress. See Layard, *Nineveh and its Remains*, plan 2, for a plan of Layard's discoveries here, and his *Discoveries*, 160 and 598, for a description of the bulls and sphinxes and their inscription. For a description of the rooms as they appeared in the nineteenth century, see E.A. Wallis Budge, *By Nile and Tigris*, 80 and 87. The inscription is published by Borger as Klch. D.

[174] Nin. A, Ep. 22, l. 3: a-na mu-šab be-lu-ti-ia ("for my royal dwelling-place").

lined with alabaster slabs bearing Esarhaddon's name, titles, and genealogy.[175]
Layard's foray established the presence of Esarhaddon's palace on the Nebi
Yunus mound, but was halted by local officials before further exploration of
the building could take place. In 1954 city officials of Nebi Yunus granted
permission to the Directorate-General of Antiquities of Iraq to do a limited
excavation in the southeast corner of the mound so that a road might be put
through. These brief excavations, led by Sayid Mohammed Ali Mustafa, succeeded in the first season in uncovering the entryway and several chambers
of a large palace.[176] In the following year, the Iraqi team unearthed in the platform underlying the palace a nearly perfect clay prism inscribed with the full
text of Esarhaddon's foundation inscription for the Nineveh *ekal mašarti*,
confirming the identity of the palace.[177] It is clear that Nineveh, as well as
Calaḫ, was being equipped to continue to serve as a base for Esarhaddon's
government and armies, and as a royal residence.

The building inscriptions for Nineveh are dated variously to the years 676
and 673, an indication of the period when active building was taking place.[178]
The inscriptions for Calaḫ range, as we have seen, from 678, in the early years
of Esarhaddon's reign, to 671 or later, near the end, while the Southwest Palace
at Calaḫ was evidently still under construction at Esarhaddon's death in 669.
These dates indicate that soon after work began on Esagila and Ešarra, the
two showpieces of Esarhaddon's temple construction program, the king also
began work on a series of major secular projects in the north, at both Calaḫ
and Nineveh, and continued work on these projects until his death.

In addition to these, Esarhaddon sponsored a series of other secular building projects in Assyria, as well. In Aššur, he built yet another palace, to serve
as a royal residence in that city (Ass. E). In Tarbiṣu, Esarhaddon enlarged an
existing palace to serve as a *bīt redûti*, or princely residence, for the crown-
prince Assurbanipal (Trb. A–D). In addition to this already formidable number of Assyrian palaces built by Esarhaddon himself, his mother Naqi'a built
a palace in Nineveh for him, "behind the Sîn and Šamaš temple."[179] No date
for this latter project survives, but it must have been begun fairly well into
the reign, since the inscription reports that the labor was done by captives
from Esarhaddon's campaigns whom Naqi'a had received as gifts.

These northern palaces, six in all, represent a major commitment by the

---

[175] Austin Henry Layard, *Discoveries in the Ruins of Nineveh and Babylon . . .*, 598. He also reports
finding here bricks and fragments of stone bearing the same inscription.

[176] Naji al Asil, "Editorial Notes: The Assyrian Palace at Nebi Yunus," 110–111.

[177] Alexander Heidel and A. Leo Oppenheim, "A New Hexagonal Prism of Esarhaddon (676
BC)," 9–37 and pls. 1–12; also published in outline by Borger as Nin. B7, in an afterword, p. 125.

[178] Nineveh B7 is dated to 676, and five exemplars of Nineveh A are dated to the year 673.
These are all *ekal mašarti* inscriptions.

[179] K. 2745 + Rm. 494; with its duplicate, published by Borger on pp. 115–116. The location
is mentioned in column II, l. 16. This palace has not been identified in excavation.

king to Assyria. They make it clear, if indeed there was ever any doubt, that Esarhaddon had intended from the outset to keep Assyria as the base of operations for his government and as his place of residence. In Babylonia, his building was extensive, but it was limited almost entirely to work on temples; while this activity produced tangible improvements in temple buildings and in the local economy of the cities, the impact of Esarhaddon's Babylonian building program was as much ideological as practical, linking Esarhaddon to the practices of earlier southern kings and casting him as the protector of southern sanctuaries. Esarhaddon's northern building program, in contrast, not only confirmed his links to his own native cults, but also underlined his primary political and military commitment to the north. However effectively he may have managed to convince the Babylonians—and at times his modern readers—that he wished to be seen as a truly Babylonian king, Esarhaddon's two massive arsenals in Nineveh and Calaḫ stand as monuments to his unwavering intention to remain fundamentally a northern and Assyrian king.

Seen in this light, Esarhaddon's Babylonian building program falls into proper perspective. Even as he continued to demonstrate that his primary commitment was to Assyria and her welfare, Esarhaddon was able to suggest to the Babylonians through his program of temple building in the south his willingness to rule Babylonia benevolently, fulfilling the traditional responsibilities of a Babylonian king in ways that even Babylonians might find acceptable. This, finally, was the message his building program in Babylonia was designed to convey.

CHAPTER FIVE

Images of the King
The Royal *Persona* as an Instrument of Public Policy

THE IDEOLOGICAL MESSAGE UNDERLYING ESARhaddon's program of building and gifts was arguably as important to the success of his Babylonian policy as the tangible benefits his building projects and gifts conferred on the two states. That the king and his advisers were aware, at least on an intuitive level, of this importance is suggested by the elaborate public relations program that they developed to reiterate and make more explicit the ideological messages that the building program and gifts had only implied. This public relations program took a variety of forms; in Babylonia it included, for example, the king's adoption of certain Babylonian royal titles, his personal enactment of an ancient Babylonian royal ceremony, and his use in Babylonian settings of statements carefully shaped to appeal to Babylonian audiences. At the same time that messages of reconciliation were being presented in Babylonia, a different message was being presented to Assyrian audiences to reassure them of their king's continuing commitment to their needs and traditions, despite his attentions to Babylonia; this message was presented through a different building program for Assyria, as we have seen, and also through different, Assyrianized versions of the royal inscriptions commemorating Esarhaddon's restoration work in Babylon. Esarhaddon's attention to the ideological impact of his statements and activities suggests an astute political leader's awareness of the figurative impact of his actions, as well as of their concrete results.

In the early years of his reign, Esarhaddon's program for dealing with the Babylonians showed a remarkable political sophistication by not only dealing with the Babylonians' practical needs for resettlement, economic revival and temple repair, but also by directly addressing the Babylonians' perception of their situation and the Assyrians' role in it. Kingship in Babylonia and Assyria, as in many states, had a figurative as well as a practical aspect. Attired in his traditional royal garments, performing the required royal ritual, addressed by the traditional titles and epithets of an Assyrian or Babylonian ruler, the king, in both states, served not only as an individual ruler, but also as a personification of that state's ideal of kingship and as a living emblem of the state he ruled. It was therefore the image of the king that was chosen in the early years as the focus of Esarhaddon's efforts to draw the Babylonians into a closer union with Assyria, appealing to them both through practical benefits and through the royal *persona* presented to them. By assuming the key figurative elements of Babylonian kingship in his own person without in any way renouncing his role—figurative and practical—as king of Assyria, Esarhaddon was suggesting to the Babylonians that their own sense of nation could find a valid life within the Assyrian empire. By assuming some of the trappings of Babylonian royal ritual and titulary, in addition to the Babylonian king's traditional responsibility to care for Babylonian temples, Esarhaddon offered the Babylonians the possibility of absorption into the Assyrian empire without a complete loss of national identity. He offered them, as well, a special status within the empire, reflected in the adoption of their national traditions of kingship by a ruler of the Assyrian empire—an honor not accorded to any other conquered state.

Like the building program, this intangible side of Esarhaddon's Babylonian policy was not a radical departure from earlier practice, but was rather an extension of the policies of some of his predecessors. Both Tiglath-Pileser III (744–727) and Sargon II (721–705) had combined their claims to direct Assyrian rule over Babylonia with conciliatory gestures toward the Babylonians similar to those Esarhaddon was to make, both assuming the Babylonian king's traditional role in the ritual of the *akītu* festivals at Babylon and both adopting certain Babylonian royal titles.[180] Sargon had in addition become the first Assyrian king to commission a building inscription for Babylonia, a text commemorating his restoration of the temple Eanna in the Babylonian city of Uruk.[181] Even Sennacherib, despite his aggressive approach to Babylonia in the later years of his reign, had earlier assumed the traditional role of a Babylonian builder-king in a limited way by sponsoring the construction of a cere-

---

[180] Tiglath-Pileser III was the first Assyrian king in almost five centuries to assume the crown of Babylon, and the first to participate in the Babylonian *akītu* festival. According to the eponym chronicles, he did so twice, in both 729 and 728 (see J. A. Brinkman, *A Political History of Post-Kassite Babylonia 1158–722 BC*, 241 and note 1547). Shalmaneser V, his successor in Assyria, was acknowledged as king in Babylonian records, but it is not recorded that he participated in the *akītu* festival. Sargon II, his successor, participated in the *akītu* festival in Babylon in his thirteenth year, the year following his reconquest of Babylon (Chr. 1, ii, l. 1') and is acknowledged as king of Babylon in Babylonian records. Both Tiglath-Pileser III and Sargon II sent gifts to Babylonian sanctuaries as well and made sacrifices in the major southern temples (see Brinkman, *Post-Kassite Babylonia*, 230 and 240–43; Paul Rost, *Die Keilschrifttexte Tiglat-Pilesers III*, I, 56–57, ll. 11–13; and A.G. Lie, *The Inscriptions of Sargon II, King of Assyria, Part I: The Annals*, 51, ll. 331–332; 57, ll. 374–375; and 59, ll. 386–389).

Tiglath-Pileser III adopted the title *šar māt Šumeri u Akkadi* (Rost, 42, l. 1) and also *šar Bābili* (Rost, 48, l. 2) to assert his claims to Babylonia. Sargon II used the titles *šakkanak Bābili* and *šar māt Šumeri u Akkadi*; see, for example, his gateway paving inscriptions (Hugo Winckler, *Die Keilschrifttexte Sargons nach den papierabklatschen und originalen neu herausgegeben*, I, ll. 136 f., and II, pl. 37), and the bull inscription (David G. Lyon, *Keilschrifttexte Sargon's Königs von Assyrien (722–705 v. Chr.) nach den Originalen neu herausgegeben, umschrieben, übersetzt und erklärt*, 13).

[181] Albert T. Clay, *Miscellaneous Inscriptions in the Yale Babylonian Collection*, no. 38.

monial walkway in Babylon.[182] Esarhaddon, however, expanded on the conciliatory practices of these earlier kings, creating a complex ideological framework for his building program which, as we will see, repeatedly presented him to the Babylonians as a genuinely Babylonian ruler.

One important step in this effort was his revival of royal titles asserting his claim to rule Babylonia. From the earliest days of the reign, the formal lists of royal titles in Esarhaddon's inscriptions refer to him as *šar māt Šumeri u Akkadi*, or "king of Sumer and Akkad," an ancient term for Babylonia, and as *šakkanak Bābili*, "governor, or viceroy, for Babylon."[183] These two titles chosen by Esarhaddon in his first years to assert his claims to Babylonia had been originally the titles of southern rulers, but by the seventh century were frequently included in the royal titulary of Assyria, as well. The choice of these titles permitted Esarhaddon to present himself as the legitimate heir of the royal traditions of both nations, in terminology that already had an accepted role in Assyria. In the south, *šar māt Šumeri u Akkadi* had first been commonly used late in the second millennium by the Sumerian kings of the Ur III dynasty (ca. 2112–2004), and had then been adopted by the kings of the First Dynasty of Isin (ca. 2000–1800).[184] The title was taken up by Hammurapi of Babylon (1792–1750) and thereafter continued to appear occasionally as a title of the kings of Babylon into the eighth century.[185]

In Assyria, *šar māt Šumeri u Akkadi* was first adopted as a royal title by Tukulti-Ninurta I (1244–1208), who added it to his official titles after his conquest of Babylon. After his time, however, Babylon quickly regained independence, and the title was not used again in Assyria until the eighth century, when Tiglath-Pileser III reintroduced it to mark his own Babylonian conquests. Sargon II (721–705), who regained control of Babylonia in the last years of his reign, continued its use.[186] Under his successor Sennacherib, however, the title *šar māt Šumeri u Akkadi* was again discarded, as we have seen. Paul Garelli argues that the adoption of this and other southern royal titles by Assyria represented not only a formal assertion of sovereignty over Babylonian territory, but also implied the Assyrians' intention to lay claim to "the prestige of the first empires of Akkad and of Ur, and of the great Babylonian kings";[187]

---

[182] Walter Andrae, *Das Wiedererstandene Assur* [Leipzig: 1938], 218.

[183] Beginning with Babylon G, dated to Ajāru (April–May) of 680, and Babylon A, probably written in the first few years of the reign (for a discussion of these dates, see Appendix II).

[184] For earlier occurrences of the title, see M.-J. Seux, *Épithètes royales akkadienes et sumériennes*, 302–303; and William W. Hallo, *Early Mesopotamian Royal Titles*, 77–88.

[185] It appears in the titles of the Babylonian kings Ammiditana (1683–1647), Merodach-Baladan I (1173–1161), Marduk-nādin-aḫḫē (1098–1081), and Merodach-Baladan II (721–710 and 703) (see Seux, 302–303).

[186] The title is not attested in the reign of Tiglath-Pileser III's immediate successor, Shalmaneser V, but documentation for that reign is so sparse that the omission is not necessarily significant.

[187] "L'État et la légitimité royale sous l'empire assyrien," in *Power and Propaganda: A Symposium on Ancient Empires*, Mogens Trolle Larsen, ed., 320.

his point is supported in that conquest over other states is only rarely reflected in Assyrian titulary at all, and never, to my knowledge, by the adoption of the titles of a conquered ruler except in the case of Babylonia. In reinstating a title such as *šar māt Šumeri u Akkadi*, Esarhaddon was both styling himself as successor to the ancient kings of Babylonia and signaling a return to the beneficent Babylonian policy of his grandfather Sargon, the last Assyrian king to use these titles.

Šakkanak Bābili, "governor, or viceroy, of Babylon," the second southern Mesopotamian title reintroduced by Esarhaddon at the beginning of his reign, had a history nearly as long.[188] Used without modifiers, the term *šakkanakku* had been a title of provincial governors since ancient times in both the north and the south. In the south, however, it had also been incorporated in the titles of kings, beginning with the reign of Lugal-zagesi, ruler of the Sumerian city-state of Umma ca. 2300. In the Old Babylonian period (ca. 1900–1600), it emerged as a common element in the royal titles of Babylonia, and after about 1300, the title *šakkanakku* appeared occasionally in the royal titles of both nations.[189]

The coupling of the title with the name of Babylon in the phrase *šakkanak Bābili*, however, was a special case, occurring once in Babylonia, in the reign of Itti-Marduk-balāṭu in the twelfth century, and then disappearing for centuries until it was adopted as an Assyrian title by Sargon II (721–705). Like *šar māt Šumeri u Akkadi*, the title *šakkanak Bābili* was discarded by Sennacherib, but revived by Esarhaddon. Esarhaddon's use of these titles was particularly significant because his father Sennacherib, despite his control over Babylonia during much of his reign, had dropped all references to Babylonia in his official titles, an act that implied the reduction of Babylonia to the status of other provinces, which were only rarely mentioned in Assyrian royal titles.[190]

---

[188] For occurrences of *šakkanakku* as a royal title, see Seux, 276–280; Hallo, *Titles*, 100–107; and *AHw*, "šakkanakku."

[189] Before Sargon, it had last been used in Babylonia by Merodach-Baladan II, who called himself *šakkanakki māt Šumeri u Akkadi* (Seux, p. 278). Sargon's adoption of the term *šakkanakku* may have been intended to echo Merodach-Baladan, just as Sargon's building inscription for the Eanna temple of Uruk replaced Merodach-Baladan's Eanna inscription and was modeled after it. For this text, see C.J. Gadd, "Inscribed Barrel Cylinder of Marduk-apla-iddina II," 123–134.

[190] On this point, see the comments of Brinkman ("Through a Glass Darkly: Esarhaddon's Retrospects on the Downfall of Babylon," *JAOS*, 103 [1983], 35): "Though *de facto* monarch of Babylonia for ten of his twenty-four years on the Assyrian throne, he [Sennacherib] seems never to have acknowledged formally this role: in contrast to his predecessor and his two successors he did not authorize the use of Babylonian royal titles in his titulary," by which, Brinkman suggests, Sennacherib "distanced himself ideologically from the southern kingdom." It is not certain that this distancing was part of Sennacherib's policy in the early days of his reign; when his son Aššur-nādin-šumi ruled as king of Babylonia, it seems likely that he assumed the normal Babylonian royal titulary, although no royal inscriptions from his brief reign survive to confirm this. After Aššur-nādin-šumi's assassination, Sennacherib besieged and conquered Babylon and could himself have claimed those titles had he wished. However, the *bīt akīti* foundation inscription from Aššur (OIP, 2, pp.

In addition, Esarhaddon's use of the title implies his intention to suggest a connection between himself and the ancient kings of the south, where *šakkanakku* had been a common element in early royal title lists.

Since the term *šakkanakku*, used without modifiers, was a title of governors as well as of kings, Sargon and Esarhaddon's choice of this particular title was a way of stating their claims to control of the city of Babylon and its lands in the least strident terms possible.[191] On the other hand, a king could appropriately be called "governor," only in the sense that he was understood to be the subordinate and regent of the gods themselves; the term *šakkanakku* when used of a king thus had religious overtones as well, an implication sometimes made explicit by expanding the title to *šakkanak ilāni*, or "governor of the gods."[192] It may be this aspect of the term that Sargon, and later Esarhaddon, intended to emphasize, the idea that each ruled Babylonia by the choice of Babylonia's own gods, a point Esarhaddon made explicit in one of his first inscriptions, where he claims he was appointed to kingship by the Babylonian god Marduk.[193] The introduction of these two titles into Esarhaddon's official title lists was an important early step in presenting himself as a legitimate Babylonian king, a claim expressed in terms of Babylonia's own royal traditions.

135–139) and the Bavian Inscription (OIP, 2, pp. 78–85), both of which can be dated to the period after Babylon's destruction (which they describe), assign Sennacherib traditional Assyrian royal titles and epithets, and in the latter text even list the chief Babylonian gods Marduk and Nabû among Sennacherib's divine patrons, but rather pointedly do not include royal titles referring to Babylonia in the list.

[191] Except for short brick inscriptions, which were probably not read publicly, Esarhaddon avoided styling himself explicitly "king of Babylonia," preferring the more euphemistic *šar māt Šumeri u Akkadi* and *šakkanak Bābili* until relatively late in the reign. Only one extant full-length inscription, written for use in Babylonia, calls him *šar Bābili* ("king of Babylonia"); this is a temple inscription, Uruk D, which is undated but describes a building project probably undertaken in the latter years of the reign (a date suggested by the reference to the late theme of Marduk's return in the closely related Uruk A text, ll. 18–20). The other title directly claiming kingship of Babylonia, the more archaic term *šar māt Karduniaš*, was used in two monument inscriptions, Mnm. A and Mnm. C, both datable to 671 or later and both erected outside the homeland and thus directed to a foreign audience. Aside from these two texts, the latter title occurs only in a short inscription on an alabaster vase from Nineveh (Nin. N), which is undated and, like the brick inscriptions, was probably not a text with high public visibility. Esarhaddon publicly asserted his rule of Babylonia from the first, but tactfully refrained from asserting that he was king of Babylonia until well into the reign.

[192] For Assyrian kings, variously as "governor of the god Aššur" (Shalmaneser III and Assurnasirpal II), "governor of the gods Bēl and Marduk" and "governor of Nabû and Marduk" (Sargon II), "governor of the gods" (Adad-nīrāri I, Shalmaneser I, and Tukulti-Ninurta I), and "governor of the great gods" (Aššur-dan II, Adad-nīrāri II, Shalmaneser III, and perhaps Aššur-bēl-kala). For Babylonian kings, as "governor of Enlil" (Naram-Sîn of Akkad and Simbar-šipak). See Seux, 279–80.

[193] "(With the) shepherdship of the land of Aššur you(s.) filled my hands" (Babylon A, Ep. 11, ll. 22–23). Although the god is not addressed by name here, it is clearly Marduk, whose appeased anger is discussed in Episode 10, immediately before this passage.

Another aspect of Esarhaddon's effort to present himself in Babylonia as an essentially Babylonian king was his enactment of an ancient southern royal ritual, the bearing of a laborer's basket by the king as part of ceremonial preparations for the building of a temple.[194] The enactment of this royal ritual, which Esarhaddon introduced into his foundation-laying ceremonies for Esagila in Babylon, publicly presented Esarhaddon in Babylonia in a role formerly reserved for southern kings alone.

Esarhaddon's accounts of his own "bearing of the basket" as part of the inaugural ceremonies for construction work at Esagila (and later at Ešarra in Aššur also, as we will see) make no explicit mention, however, of royal basket-bearing as an ancient southern activity—in fact, these passages make no reference to the history of the ceremony at all. If Esarhaddon is to be understood as deliberately performing a southern ceremony, in these two settings a dramatically public bow to southern royal tradition by an Assyrian king, then we must establish the links between the ceremony as Esarhaddon performed it and the ceremony as it was performed by earlier kings of the south, and we must further establish that Esarhaddon and his contemporaries were aware of the ceremony's historical significance.

The evidence for the early practice of basket-bearing in the south, however, is somewhat problematic. Only one text, a set of building inscriptions from the time of the ancient Sumerian ruler Gudea of Lagash (ca. 2130), offers a verbal description of the early practice of basket-bearing by a ruler. The remaining early evidence for the ceremony is not verbal but iconographic, consisting of basket-bearing figures depicted on plaques, and of small statues. The earliest piece of evidence goes back to the time of the Sumerian ruler Ur-Nanše, who governed the city-state of Lagash in southern Babylonia around 2500. It consists of a carved limestone plaque showing a ruler who carries a steep-sided basket on his head while his family and courtiers look on;[195] a label

---

[194] On rites associated with preparations for building in Mesopotamia, including offerings, sacrifices, prayers, and activities of ášipu and kalú priests, see Richard Ellis, *Foundation Deposits in Ancient Mesopotamia* (New Haven and London: 1968), 5–34. I am using the term "ritual" here in the sense of a religiously charged ceremony or ceremonial action evidently intended to invoke or propitiate a god or gods.

[195] Family Relief A, described by Richard Ellis in *Foundation Deposits in Ancient Mesopotamia*, 20, and illustrated in Morris Jastrow, *Bildermappe zur Religion Babyloniens und Assyriens* (Giessen: 1912), Fig. 74, and in Samuel N. Kramer, *The Sumerians* (Chicago: 1963), following p. 64. The inscription on the plaque is published in translation by Edmond Sollberger and Jean Kupper, *Inscriptions royales sumériennes et akkadiennes* (Paris: 1971), 46.

Jacobsen argues that another inscription of Ur-Nanše describes that king's enactment of a royal basket-bearing ceremony; if Jacobsen's contention is correct, the text would represent a second, very brief verbal description of royal basket-bearing and one even earlier than that of Gudea, discussed below (Thorkild Jacobsen, "Ur-Nanshe's Diorite Plaque," *Or.* [n.s.], 54 [1985]: 65–72). In the inscription, the god Šul-utul, who Jacobsen suggests was represented in the ceremony by Ur-Nanše, carries a DUSU.KÙ ("a pure DUSU-basket") in a ceremonial setting. Ur-Nanše's impersonation of Šul-utul in the ceremony, however, remains conjectural.

a label carved on the plaque confirms that the basket-bearing figure is Ur-Nanše, and a brief inscription near the figure lists temples built by him, implying a context of temple-building for the scene that the plaque depicts.

The next piece of evidence for basket-bearing by a ruler, in roughly chronological order, is the set of building inscriptions mentioned above. Written in the reign of Gudea, temple-builder and ruler of Lagash around 2130, the inscriptions include an account of how the ruler carried a basket as part of ceremonial preparations for building the temple Eninnu. In these texts, Gudea, after a night of vigil and prayer, begins the building rituals for Eninnu by entering the temple area carrying a "holy basket" on his head, accompanied by various gods. He proceeds to perform a variety of ritual actions, involving the beating of drums and the making and anointing of a special brick:

> The holy basket and the effective brick-mold of destiny in the temple . . . he carried; with head high he went. (The god) Lugalkurdub went in front of him, (the god) Igalim went with him, (the god) Ningišzida, his god, took him by the hand. He put propitious(?) water on the case(?) of the brick-mold. Copper kettle drums and *ala*-drums were played for the *ensi* (Gudea). . . .; the stamp(?) and the brick he prepared(?). He put together honey, ghee, and precious oil(?); (with) KUŠU-plants, PI-plants, and (different kinds of) wood he made it into a paste. He carried the holy basket, he put together(?) the brick-mold. Gudea put clay into the brick-mold; he carried out the operation perfectly. He made the brick for the temple splendid[196] (Cyl. A, XVIII, ll. 10–27).

[196] The translation is that of Richard Ellis, prepared in collaboration with Miguel Civil and published in Ellis, *Foundation Deposits*, 22 and Appendix A, 170–172.

The object carried by Gudea in these passages is somewhat problematic. It is called in Sumerian a DUSU, translated by Ellis (*Foundation Deposits*, App. A, ll. 10 and 24) as "basket," but sometimes argued to have been the head pad worn by those carrying a basket, which would make this a *pars pro toto* reference to basket-bearing; see, for example, the translation by François Thureau-Dangin, *Les Cylindres de Goudea*, V, l. 5. Other translators take DUSU as meaning "hod," that is, a device for carrying bricks (e.g., Thorkild Jacobsen, "Ur-Nanshe's Diorite Plaque," col. iv, ll. 1–2).

The preponderance of the evidence, however, suggests that the DUSU was in fact a basket. While DUSU is sometimes introduced by a GI sign (mark of a reed object) and sometimes by a GIŠ sign (denoting an object made of wood), there is no evidence that even the wooden DUSU object, despite its use as a brick carrier, in any way resembled the European hod, a triangular wooden trough mounted on a pole used to hand bricks upward. Although the DUSU may have been like the European hod in function, there is no indication that it was like a hod in form. Lexical texts indicate that the word DUSU was in later times considered to be the equivalent of the Akkadian *tupšikku*, which has been defined as a type of basket (CAD) or as both a basket and a "Ziegel-Tragrahmen," or "brick-carrying frame" (*AHw*), the latter again a definition in terms of function that does not specify the physical form, whether basket or other object. In the occurrences cited in *AHw*, the *tupšikku* is used for carrying bricks (in mathematical texts), clay tablets, barley, and earth. The carrying of loose materials in the latter examples supports the definition of *tupšikku* as some sort of basket; the other references offer no indication of the shape of the carrying container. Unless clearer evidence emerges for the existence in Mesopotamia of a wooden-frame-and-pole brick carrier, it seems best to conclude that both the DUSU and its Akkadian equivalent, the *tupšikku*, were some sort of basket, even when used as a hod. The occasional use of GIŠ with DUSU may indicate that the DUSU-basket was in some cases woven of sticks or of wooden splits to give it greater rigidity for brick carrying, although this remains conjectural.

Although the precise meaning of each step in the ritual is not made explicit, it is evident that the ceremonies were intended to solemnize the beginning of the temple's construction. Gudea's carrying of the basket is presented as a central part of the elaborate series of rituals; it introduces the ceremonies ("the holy basket and the effective brick-mold of destiny in the temple . . . he carried; with head high he went"), and it reappears to introduce the brick-making that is the climax of this section of the text ("He carried the holy basket, he put together(?) the brick-mold; he carried out the operation perfectly"). In the summary statement that concludes the account of the ceremonies, carrying the basket appears as the central element, emblematic of the dedicatory ceremonies as a whole: "Gudea, the builder of the temple, in the temple put the basket on his head like a holy crown; he laid the foundation, erecting the walls on the ground" (Cyl. A, XX, ll. 24–26).

Gudea's account is important for our purposes because it establishes the characteristic elements of the basket-bearing ceremony in this early period, that it was a ritual act, that it was performed by the ruler himself, and that it was part of ceremonies marking the beginning of temple construction; these elements, as we shall see, are all characteristics of Esarhaddon's basket-bearing ceremony as well.

Gudea's reign also marks the first appearance of a series of small figurines, ca. 10–12" in height, each representing a male figure with shaven head, dressed in a simple kilt and raising both hands to support a shallow basket that he carries on his head.[197] (For a picture of a typical basket-bearing figurine, see plate II.) These figures were usually deposited in brick boxes set into the floors or walls of temples, often accompanied by deposits of herbs and precious materials.[198] The appearance of these basket-bearing statues in the time of Gudea, whose inscriptions stress that he personally performed the basket-bearing ritual, makes it likely that they were intended (despite the simple dress of the figures) as representations of the ruler; this conclusion is supported by the appearance of a brief, label-like inscription on most such figures, naming a ruler and a building project he sponsored.[199] These figurines, and the con-

[197] See Ellis, 61–62, for a description of the basket-bearing figurines from the reign of Gudea and the single figurine that survives from the reign of his son, Ur-Ningirsu. For sketches of typical examples of basket-bearing figurines, see Ellis, figs. 22–25. Ellis argues persuasively that in almost all cases the figures are clearly intended to represent men, despite the rounded breasts of a few of the statues (73–74).

[198] For a discussion of the archeological contexts in which basket-bearing figurines (both from Gudea's reign and from the subsequent Ur III and Isin-Larsa periods) were found, see Ellis, 61–71, and William W. Hallo, "The Royal Inscriptions of Ur: A Typology," 11 and notes 78 and 79.

[199] See Ellis, 23. That the Assyrians themselves understood the figures to represent kings is suggested by the depictions on stelae of Šamaš-šuma-ukīn and Assurbanipal bearing a basket in the traditional pose and wearing the characteristic hat and dress of an Assyrian king. For the texts of inscriptions on basket-bearing figurines, see E. Sollberger and J. Kupper, *Inscriptions royales sumériennes et akkadiennes*, 46 (Ur-Nanše); 118 (Ur-Ningirsu); 141 (Šulgi); and 202–203 (Rīm-Sîn).

PLATE TWO
Inscribed copper figurine showing Ur-Nammu of Ur (2112–2095)
as a basket-bearer (The Pierpont Morgan Library, New York)

texts in which they are found, offer further evidence for an early basket-bearing ceremony performed by rulers and associated with building.

Basket-bearing figurines continued to be used as a standard element in foundation deposits by the kings of the Third Dynasty of Ur (Ur III), who led the cities of the Mesopotamian south in the period that followed (ca. 2100–2000). Richard Ellis's study of Mesopotamian foundation deposits lists twenty-two extant basket-bearing figurines from this period, unearthed in the cities of Ur, Nippur, Uruk, and Lagash, and even in the distant Elamite city of Susa, and representing the kings Ur-Nammu, Šulgi, Amar-Sîn and Šu-Sîn; additional examples of the figurines have since come to light in further excavations at Nippur.[200] These basket-bearing figurines are a characteristic element of Ur III foundation deposits and suggest widespread use of the royal basket-bearing ceremony in that period. In addition, a stele showing the Third Dynasty ruler Ur-Nammu carrying a basket as part of ritual activities associated with building[201] adds further evidence that the ritual was associated with the ruler and with temple-building activities. Figurines of basket-bearing kings continue to appear through the reigns of Warad-Sîn (1834–1823) and Rim-Sîn (1822–1763) of the Dynasty of Larsa, which eventually succeeded Ur as the strongest power in southern Mesopotamia. These Larsa figures attest to a continued interest in royal basket-bearing in southern Mesopotamia into the eighteenth century.[202]

The basket-bearing figurines of Rim-Sîn, however, are the last evidence of any kind, documentary or iconographic, for the basket-bearing ceremony until Esarhaddon's inscriptions describe his performance of a basket-bearing ceremony some eleven hundred years later, a lacuna which suggests that the ceremony may have fallen into disuse at some time in this long period.[203]

---

[200] See Ellis, 63–69, and Hallo, "Typology," 24–26 and 29–31. For the more recent Nippur material, see Naji al-Asil, "Recent Archaeological Activity in Iraq," 4, which reports the discovery of two more canephoric figurines of Ur-Nammu, found at the entrance to the temple of Enlil; V.E. Crawford, "Nippur, the Holy City," 74–83, which includes photos and a summary of material from foundation boxes; Richard C. Haines, "A Report of the Excavations at Nippur during 1960–61," 67, which reports the discovery of seven more bronze figurines of the Ur III ruler Šulgi in the Inanna temple area.

[201] See Henri Frankfort, *The Art and Architecture of the Ancient Orient*, 2nd ed., 50–51 and pl. LIII; also James B. Pritchard, ed., *The Ancient Near East: An Anthology*, fig. 85.

[202] Ellis, 70–71.

[203] There are large gaps in both the archeological and documentary evidence for Babylonia for much of this period, however, so the absence of basket-bearing figurines may be less significant than it appears. Figurines do continue to appear in foundation deposits, however, but none of the figurines after Rim-Sîn's time depicts a basket-bearer. (For a survey of the evidence, see Elizabeth Douglas van Buren, *Foundation Figurines and Offerings*. Van Buren's examples include both Babylonian foundation deposits from the years of the Kassite kings, ca. 1600–1150 [34–38], and Assyrian deposits, from the early periods, ca. 1300–900 [39–48], and from Neo-Assyrian times, ca. 900–600 [48–56].)

Ellis, using documentary evidence, argues that basket-bearing probably continued uninter-

Despite the possible discontinuity, there is considerable evidence that Esar-haddon and his contemporaries knew of the ancient ceremony, at least in out-line, and were aware of its antiquity. Their knowledge of the ancient cere-mony is suggested in part by the marked similarities between the ceremony in its early form and Esarhaddon's performance of it, as we will see shortly. The Assyrians' familiarity with the ceremony is further suggested by three un-usual stelae from Babylonia, two showing Esarhaddon's son Assurbanipal and one showing his older son Šamaš-šumu-ukīn as basket-bearing kings. Each of these stelae depicts the king in question and carries a text describing one of his building projects in Babylonia (see plates III and IV). In each case the figure is clearly identified as a king by his characteristic Assyrian royal hat and clothing. The king is represented, however, in the stereotyped pose charac-teristic of the ancient basket-bearing figurines, facing forward with both arms raised to support a basket balanced on his head. The stelae are particularly strik-ing because the two Assyrian kings are depicted with their faces turned toward the viewer, although in Assyrian iconographic tradition, kings represented in bas-relief were always presented with the face in profile, even when the body faced forward.[204] The baskets on the heads of the kings and the unmistakable familiarity of the pose are indications that the figures of the Assyrian kings on the three stelae were intended as allusions to the basket-bearing figurines of the ancient rulers of the south.

The familiarity with the ancient figurines which these stelae reveal sug-gests that the figurines themselves were the medium through which the Assyrians learned of the ancient Babylonian ceremony, if it had indeed fallen into disuse centuries earlier. The figurines, as we have noted, were customar-ily buried in the walls or floors of temples; the restoration of such temples

---

rupted between the time of Rim-Sîn and Esarhaddon (26). His evidence, however, consists of a single reference to royal brick-making (in a text known as Astrolabe B, from ca. 1000), an activity which, he argues, always followed royal basket-bearing, since the purpose of the basket-bearing, he suggests, was to bring clay for making the ceremonial brick (23). It is not certain, however, that royal brick-making and basket-bearing were always performed together. (One of the three descrip-tions of basket-bearing in Gudea's inscription [XX, l. 24] makes no reference to brick-making. In Assur A, iv, l. 16-v, l. 2, Esarhaddon makes a brick and only then bears the basket; in this case, at least, royal basket-bearing was not a preliminary step in brick-making.) Since it seems possible that ritual basket-bearing was an independent activity in its own right, the reference to royal brick-making in Astrolabe B is not convincing evidence that basket-bearing was being practiced ca. 1000. This leaves us with no evidence, documentary or archeological, for royal basket-bearing during the more than one thousand years between the reigns of Rim-Sîn and Esarhaddon.

[204] See, for example, the Calaḫ relief of Assurnasirpal II enthroned, shown in Frankfort, *Art and Architecture*, pl. 89, where the torso faces us, but the head is turned sharply to give a profile view. For representative examples of first millennium Assyrian kings depicted in bas-reliefs, see Frankfort, pls. 84, 87, 88, 89, 91, 92, 93, and 109. For the somewhat rarer first millennium Babylonian reliefs depicting kings, see Frankfort, pls. 120 and 121. In both Assyria and Babylonia, kings were depicted in frontal view only when sculpted in the round or on seals.

PLATE THREE

Red sandstone stele found in the Nabû temple at Borsippa showing Assurbanipal
as a basket-bearer; an inscription on the back and side of the stele names
the king and describes his reconstruction of the Nabû temple
(BM 90865; photo courtesy of the Trustees of the British Museum)

PLATE FOUR

Red sandstone stele found in the Nabû temple at Borsippa showing Šamaš-šumu-ukīn as a basket-bearer; here again the inscription on the back names the king and describes his reconstruction of the Nabû temple (BM 90866; photo courtesy of the Trustees of the British Museum)

usually involved leveling dilapidated walls and searching for original foundations, in the course of which builders could hardly have avoided finding foundation boxes containing the basket-bearing figurines. By this means, Babylonians would have remained familiar with the figurines even if the ceremony
itself had been long discontinued.[205] When Esarhaddon's grandfather Sargon
began sponsoring temple repairs in Babylonia, Assyrians, as well as Babylonians, were brought into direct contact with southern sites containing such
deposits. These deposits survived not only to Sargon II's day, but even into
our own time. Modern excavations of the Eanna temple at Uruk, which
Sargon repaired, uncovered six foundation boxes, four with contents intact,
and each including a basket-bearing figurine depicting an Ur III ruler.[206]
There is ample evidence, moreover, that Mesopotamian kings were interested
in such foundation deposits and aware of the information contained in
them.[207] It is not surprising, then, that Assyrians in Esarhaddon's time knew
about the Babylonian basket-bearing ceremony and were aware of its great
antiquity. In choosing to perform the royal ceremony that the ancient
figurines depicted, Esarhaddon was assuming a public role once played by
Babylonia's ancient kings, implying to the Babylonians that he himself was the
king in whom Babylonia's ancient traditions might find new life.[208] The great

[205] One possible source of this information for Assyrians would have been Babylonian priests
resident at Esarhaddon's court, such as Urad-Ea, the descendant of a *galmāḫu* priest of Esagila who
was himself priest and appeaser for Esarhaddon (Parpola, *Letters*, IIa, p. 43).

[206] Ellis, 64.

[207] The request that future kings should find, anoint, and rebury the foundation inscriptions
of earlier kings was a commonplace in Assyrian inscriptions and a tradition still very much alive
in Esarhaddon's time. This passage from an inscription of Sargon II is typical: "On tablets of gold,
silver, bronze, tin, lead, lapis lazuli and alabaster I inscribed my name, and I placed these in their
foundation walls. Let (some) future prince restore its ruins, let him inscribe his memorial stele and
set it up alongside of mine. (Then) Aššur will hear his prayers" (Lyon, *Sargon*, 23–34 and 52).
Ellis cites evidence that such reburial actually occurred: the curious mixture of contents in
Gudea's deposit boxes, which suggests ancient reburial (Ellis, 62); the reburial of Adad-nīrārī I's
tablets for the Ištar temple in Aššur in the time of Tukulti-Ninurta (Ellis, 97 and 99); and the discovery of a gold foundation tablet of Shalmaneser I in a context that again suggests reburial (Ellis,
97–98). Assyrian and Babylonian inscriptions often describe the construction history of a building
in such detail as to suggest that foundation boxes were not only opened in the course of preparing
for reconstruction, but their contents routinely read, as well. Esarhaddon's Assur A inscription (III,
16–40) is a typical example, listing the precise number of years between each rebuilding, the reason
for each rebuilding, such as fire, old age, etc., and the name of each builder king. This familiarity
with the history of each building, not unique to Esarhaddon texts, is an indication that the Assyrians
were not only reburying foundation inscriptions, but were also reading them.

[208] Ancient Greek canephoric (that is, basket-bearing) figurines are often mentioned in connection with Mesopotamian basket-bearing, with the implication that Greek ceremonies, rather
than Mesopotamian ones, might have been the forerunners of the ceremony used by Esarhaddon.
Ellis concludes (23–24), I think correctly, that this scenario is unlikely. The earliest Greek references
date from well after the time of Esarhaddon (see Pauly-Wissowa, *Real-Encyclopädie der classischen
Altertumswissenschaft*, V, pp. 1862–66, for the Greek canephoroi). Moreover, the differences between
the basket-bearing ceremonies of Mesopotamia and Greece—that the Greek baskets were borne
by young women chosen for their beauty, rather than by kings, and that the Greek ceremonies

antiquity of the basket-bearing ceremony gave Esarhaddon's performance of it special significance, recalling a time when the cities of Babylonia had been independent and powerful, and implying that under Esarhaddon's patronage the ancient cities of the south might in time regain something of their former stature.

Esarhaddon's own performance of the basket-bearing ritual is described in a series of inscriptions, most of which can be dated to the beginning years of his reign.[209] His first performance of the ceremony occurred in Babylon and is described in slightly varying accounts in Babylon A, C, D, and E (Ep. 21). An account of the second performance of the ritual, which took place in Aššur a year later, is preserved in Assur A (iv, ll. 36–40).

According to the Babylon inscriptions, the first performance of the ritual was part of ceremonies marking the beginning of reconstruction work on the temple Esagila, the national religious center of Babylonia. These ceremonies were of great importance to the Babylonians, marking what they must have hoped would be a turning point in their relationship with the Assyrians. Their last Assyrian ruler, Sennacherib, had attacked Babylon; his son Esarhaddon was now about to restore the city's main temple, the center of Babylonia's national life. By personally performing an ancient Babylonian royal ritual in this prominent setting and at the very beginning of his reign, Esarhaddon was making a dramatic public statement, presenting to the Babylonians an image of himself as king that offered the possibility of a new relationship between his country and Babylonia.

In Esarhaddon's accounts of the foundation ceremonies for Esagila, the basket-bearing ceremony plays a central role. The texts begin with an account of the city's earlier destruction (Eps. 2–10) and assert that Esarhaddon has now been made king of Assyria by Babylon's own patron gods in order that he might repair the city of Babylon (Bab. A and D, Ep. 11). The king decides to undertake the repairs, omens confirm the correctness of his decision, and

---

were part of annual religious festivals with no connection to building—suggests that there was no connection between the two customs, beyond a superficial resemblance in the objects carried. What we are really seeing here, I think, is a world in which specialized baskets of various types were used as containers in the performance of carefully distinguished carrying and storage jobs. For a sampling of the multiplicity of baskets used for distinct tasks in Mesopotamia alone, see the list of baskets discussed in early volumes of the *CAD*, compiled by Jack Sasson, *English-Akkadian Analytical Index to the Chicago Assyrian Dictionary: Part 1*. If something solid were to be carried in an ancient Near Eastern context, the chances were good that it would be carried in a basket adapted for the purpose. We should be cautious, therefore, in assuming any connection between instances of basket-bearing in the ancient Near East, particularly if those instances occurred in different societies, in different periods, and in different contexts. There is ample evidence within Mesopotamia alone to account for Esarhaddon's use of a basket-bearing ceremony as the revival of a purely Mesopotamian tradition.

[209] Some of the Babylon texts, although dated to 680, may have been written later, but retain the pattern of the earlier texts in that group. For discussion and dates, see Appendix II.

the great day approaches when work can start. Workmen are assembled, and the foundation ceremonies are performed:

> With good oil, honey, ghee, *kurunnu*-beer (and) *mutinnu*-wine, pure drink of the mountains, I (the king) sprinkled the scarp of the excavation. In order to show the people his (the god Marduk's) great godhead and to cause them to fear his lordship, I lifted the *kudurru* basket onto my head, and I myself carried it (Babylon A, C, D, and E, Ep. 20 and 21).

The king's bearing of the basket appears here as the final step in the building ceremonies and as the climax of this section of the text, underscoring the importance of the ceremony in the king's account of his work on the temple.

The significance of the king's enactment of the ceremony in this setting was complex. On the one hand, the ceremony presented Esarhaddon as the living continuation of an ancient and exclusively Babylonian tradition of kingship. At the same time, bearing the basket symbolized the king's personal involvement in the labor of building the temple ("I myself carried it"), just as modern public officials ceremonially dig the first spadeful of earth in the construction of a new building as a visible sign of their involvement in the project. That Esarhaddon carried a *kudurru* basket, however, gave his involvement a special meaning. The *kudurru* was an ordinary laborer's basket, not reserved for ceremonial or religious use.[210] By Neo-Assyrian times, it had become a metaphor for corvée labor performed for the state; the phrase *kudurra emēdu*, for example, meaning "to place the *kudurru* (upon someone)," had become by extension the standard expression meaning, "to impose forced labor," just as *kudurra epēšu*, literally "to do the *kudurru*," had come to mean "to perform corvée work," and *zābil kudurri*, or "*kudurru* carrier," had become the term for a "basket carrier (to do corvée work)."[211] In carrying the *kudurru*, an emblem of menial physical labor, Esarhaddon was both demonstrating his solidarity with the people of Babylon assigned as laborers on the project, and also, as he tells us, "showing the people" proper respect for their god Marduk by

---

[210] The *CAD* defines *kudurru* primarily as "a basket to carry earth, bricks," but notes that at Nuzi the word was written with a GIŠ determinative, denoting a wooden object, and therefore offers a secondary meaning, "wooden container," the latter usage attested only at Nuzi. The *AHw* offers the more generalized definition "Tragestell," that is, "carrying arrangement, pack frame." Lexical list entries cite *kudurru* as a synonym for *tupšikku*, a basket whose usual ideogrammatic writing as GI.ÍL ("reed" + "to lift") indicates that it was ordinarily a carrying container made of reed, i.e., a basket (for further discussion of the function of *tupšikku*'s, see note 196, above). Except for the Nuzi references and an anomalous Neo-Babylonian passage where *kudurru* seems to be a term for a canal revetment of some sort, it seems clear that the term *kudurru* ordinarily referred to a type of basket. This definition accords well with the range of uses attested for the *kudurru*: as an object for carrying earth, or mushrooms, or bricks, and as a tool commonly used in compulsory labor. The representations of Assurbanipal and Šamaš-šumu-ukīn carrying baskets, described above, support the conclusion that the *kudurru* carried by Esarhaddon was a basket.

[211] For these expressions, see the *CAD*, "emēdu," 3j; "epēšu," 2c; and "zābilu," 3.

personally laboring for him (Bab. A, C, and E, Ep. 21), thus publicly assuming a Babylonian king's traditional role as religious leader of his people.

Esarhaddon performed the basket-bearing ceremony again a year later, this time as part of ceremonies inaugurating the reconstruction of the temple Ešarra in Aššur. Ešarra, as the national religious center of the north, was the Assyrian counterpart of Esagila. The foundation ceremonies performed for Ešarra included some additional rituals, but were on the whole similar to the ceremonies for Esagila a year earlier. As before, the king anointed the scarp of the excavation with a mixture of pleasant liquids. He made bricks ceremoniously in brickmolds of precious woods and ivory. Then, the king says,

> I, prayerful slave who fears him (the god Aššur), I smote my *ḫulduppu* garment;[212] with my pure hands I made a brick. I caused the people to see the might of the god Aššur, my lord. I lifted the *kudurru* basket onto my head, and I myself carried it. In order to make the lands fear (their god), I showed the people (Assur A, iv, ll. 27–40).

In this account, after a single sentence describing the year-long manufacture of bricks which was to follow, the text returns to further descriptions of ceremonies, so that the basket-bearing ritual is here made less central than in the Babylonian version, overshadowed by further descriptions of anointing the foundations and of the king's carrying and placement of a "first brick" (v, ll. 1–26).

It is somewhat surprising that the Babylonian ritual of basket-bearing appears at all in this quintessentially Assyrian setting. It may have been included mainly for the benefit of Babylonian emissaries present at the ceremonies, to confirm that Esarhaddon's performance of the ceremony at Esagila had not been an isolated gesture for Babylonian consumption alone, but had signaled a lasting change in royal policy. For the Assyrians, however, the possibly jarring effect of seeing the Babylonian ceremony performed in an Assyrian setting was cushioned by surrounding it with impeccably Assyrian foundation rituals, such as the king's mixing of special mortar with which to anoint the scarp of the excavation, and his anointing of the *šallaru* with a similar mixture.[213] Its impact was perhaps also muted because the basket-bearing ritual itself was so ancient that Assyrians could easily have seen it as no more than

---

[212] The *ḫulduppu* garment mentioned here (^{TÚG}ḫul-dúp?]-*pi*(*sic?*)-*ia*) is otherwise unattested. There is a GIŠ *ḫultuppû* attested as a wooden object used in expiatory rites, perhaps a whip or rod (see *CAD* "ḫultuppû"), but the TÚG determinative used here indicates that this *ḫulduppu* was a type of garment.

[213] Col. iv, ll. 19–22, and v, ll. 17–20. The Assyrian practice of mixing ceremonial mortars and sprinkling, or smearing on, precious liquids in building ceremonies is attested for the reigns of the kings Erišum I, Shamshi-Adad I, Shalmaneser I, and Esarhaddon (see Ellis, 29–31). See also *CAD* "balālu" ("to mix") for references to mixing or anointing with ceremonial mortars as an element in Assyrian building ritual.

a reference to the antiquity of kingship in Mesopotamia and to Esarhaddon as successor to that tradition.

By repeating the basket-bearing ritual in the foundation ceremonies inaugurating work on Ešarra, Esarhaddon also underlined the parallel nature of the two building projects, a point made explicit in the later AsBbA text, where the reconstruction of the two temples is presented as part of a single project.[214] By the end of the reign, this parallelism was to become part of a larger pattern linking the national self-images of the two nations. In this earlier period, however, the function of the parallelism in the foundation ceremonies was probably to suggest to the Assyrians that every gift to Babylonia would be balanced by an equal or greater gift to Assyria, and in this case, that work on Ešarra would balance similar attentions to Esagila. By performing the basket-bearing ceremony in Assyria, Esarhaddon at once reassured the Babylonians of the seriousness of his commitment to their traditions, and at the same time demonstrated to the Assyrians through his personal participation in the building of Ešarra that he remained the faithful servant of Assyria and her gods.

The basket-bearing ceremony is thus presented slightly differently in Babylonia and Assyria, but in each case it presents Esarhaddon in an important public event as a legitimate successor of ancient kings, as a benevolent ruler personally active in the care of his people, and as the religious leader of each nation. In Babylonia, the basket-bearing ceremony also presents him as the preserver of a uniquely Babylonian tradition; in performing the basket-bearing ritual, an act simultaneously religious and political, Esarhaddon presents himself as the embodiment of Babylonian kingship in its most traditional form.

So far we have examined Esarhaddon's use of royal titles and of ritual in the early days of his reign to present differing images of himself in Babylonia and Assyria, presenting in Babylonia the image of a genuinely Babylonian king, and in Assyria a subtly different and more Assyrian royal *persona* designed to reassure his own people of his continued loyalty to them, despite his attentions to Babylonia. We turn now to consider a third tool Esarhaddon used to present different royal *personae* to the two groups: the royal building inscriptions themselves.

We have already seen how certain individual elements of royal building inscriptions, such as the titles assigned to the king, are used to project a particular image of the ruler. The image of the king a particular inscription presents, however, is not only suggested by isolated elements in the text, but is shaped by the whole series of events the text describes; the text as a whole

---

[214] "In a favorable month, on a propitious day, of Eḫursaggalkurkurra, bond of heaven and earth . . . (and) of Esagila, palace of the gods . . . I laid their foundations together; I made firm their br[ickwork]" (AsBbA, rs., ll. 46–48).

becomes a tool for creating an image of Esarhaddon as the appropriate ruler of the nation for which that text is composed.

To identify the techniques by which this is achieved, we will begin by focusing on two building inscriptions from the same time period, one written for a building project in Assyria and the other, for a project in Babylonia, which present quite different images of Esarhaddon as king. We will then go on to consider a set of inscriptions which appear on the surface to be a single inscription commemorating work in Babylon, but which prove, on closer examination, to present similarly differentiated images of the king to different audiences.

The texts we will begin with are the Babylon A inscription, which commemorates building in the city of Babylon and is dated to the year 680, and the Assur A inscription, which commemorates building in the city of Aššur and is dated to the following year.[215] In the Babylon A text, Esarhaddon appears as a remarkably Babylonian royal figure, who is only incidentally king of Assyria as well. The topic of the text, which we have already encountered in our discussion of Esarhaddon's building activities above, is the destruction of the city of Babylon and its eventual reconstruction by Esarhaddon. It begins by introducing the king, describing the city's earlier sins and its abandonment by the gods, and finally describing its destruction by a flood—a flood actually produced by Sennacherib's army, a detail that is tactfully not mentioned here. The inscription then describes how the gods relented and called Esarhaddon to rebuild Babylon, how the king called up workmen and began reconstruction with all necessary ritual, and how he restored the city's temple and walls and resettled its scattered inhabitants. The text concludes with the king's request for blessing from the gods of Babylon and his hope that his inscription will be treated respectfully by future kings. In presenting each of these events, the Babylon A inscription focuses on the figure of the king, emphasizing his active role in the projects and presenting him consistently as ruler of Babylonia and servant of Babylonia's gods. The Babylonian character of the king is suggested from the very outset:

> Esarhaddon, great king, mighty king, king of all, king of Assyria, governor of Babylon, king of Sumer and Akkad; true shepherd, favorite of the lord of lords, pious prince, beloved of (the goddess) Ṣarpanītu the queen, goddess of all that is; humble king who from the days of his youth was mindful of their lordship

---

[215] For the provenance and description of the various exemplars of these two inscriptions, see Appendix IV. For Assur A6 (VAT 9642), not identified as a copy of the Assur A text until after Borger's edition, see Borger, "Die Inschriften Asarhaddons (AfO Beiheft 9)," 113. Exemplars of Babylon A published after Borger's edition include Babylon A4 and A5, published by A.R. Millard, "Some Esarhaddon Fragments relating to the Restoration of Babylon," 117–118, and Babylon A6, discussed by Mordechai Cogan, "New Additions to the Corpus of Esarhaddon Historical Inscriptions," 75.

and praised their strength; prayerful slave, humble, submissive, fearing their great godhead (Babylon A, Ep. 1).

This text exemplifies Esarhaddon's use of Babylonian titles and makes little reference to his Assyrian antecedents, omitting his genealogy, usually included after the titles. Instead, the passage emphasizes his role as a Babylonian ruler by using epithets claiming the gods of Babylonia as his patrons; Esarhaddon is called "favorite of the lord of lords . . . and beloved of (the goddess) Ṣarpanītu," "humble king who from . . . his youth was mindful of their lordship." The reference to Ṣarpanītu, consort of the Babylonian chief god Marduk, makes it clear that it is Marduk himself who is evoked in the phrase "lord of lords," and that it is Marduk and Ṣarpanītu to whom Esarhaddon is "prayerful slave." The effect of the titles and epithets is to present Esarhaddon as a ruler whose patrons are the chief gods of Babylon.

The text then turns to an account of how the city of Babylon fell from favor and was destroyed at its own gods' command (Ep. 2–9); since this was a sore subject in Babylonia, the king is not mentioned in this section, which focuses attention instead on the gods of Babylon as the instigators of the unpleasant action. With this topic out of the way, however, the scribe turns to the main subject of the text, the rebuilding of Babylon, and here the text returns to its earlier focus on the figure of the king, a focus underlined by having the king speak in the first person as he addresses Marduk, the patron deity of Babylon:

> Me, Esarhaddon, you truly chose from among my assembled older brothers in order to restore these things to their places, and your good shadow you placed over me. All my enemies you destroyed like a flood and all my opponents you killed, and you caused me to achieve my desires. In order to quiet the heart of your great godhead and to soothe your feelings, you filled my hands with the shepherdship of Assyria (Babylon A, Ep. 11).

The passage asserts unequivocally that Esarhaddon's selection for kingship of Assyria itself came from the gods, not of Assyria, but of Babylonia, whom he addresses here, and that the purpose of his rule is to restore the shattered city of Babylon. This is the call to rule that one might expect for a Babylonian ruler, not for an Assyrian king such as Esarhaddon.

As the text moves on to describe the actual rebuilding of the city, it continues to focus on the figure of the king, setting the account in the first person so that the steps of rebuilding are presented as the king's personal actions: "I summoned all my workers . . ." (Ep. 19); "I myself bore the basket . . ." (Ep. 21); "I laid its foundation . . ." (Ep. 26); "The gods and goddesses who dwell in the midst of it, whom the flood waters . . . had carried away . . ., I made them dwell in their holy places for all time. . . ." (Ep. 32).

As the text draws to its conclusion, it maintains its focus on the king, underlining his role as a Babylonian ruler. Speaking still in the first person, the king asks, "May Marduk and Ṣarpanītu, the gods who are my helpers, look joyfully upon my good deeds . . .; the seed of my priesthood [i.e., my descendants], together with the foundation of Esagila and Babylon, may they make firm. . . ." (Ep. 39). In conclusion, the king requests that any future king among his heirs, "whose name the king of the gods, Marduk, calls to rule of the land and peoples" (Ep. 41, ll. 21–23), will respect the object on which the account of his rebuilding has been inscribed. Throughout these final passages the chief gods of Babylon, Marduk and his consort, are the only gods invoked, and Esarhaddon and his heirs are again said to receive the right to rule from them alone.

From beginning to end, the image of the king presented by the Babylon A text is that of a Babylonian ruler. After an initial acknowledgment of Esarhaddon's role as king of Assyria, there is no further mention of the king's Assyrian connections; the text instead devotes its attentions to the king's actions on behalf of the city of Babylon and his acceptance by Babylonia's gods as rightful king of that land. The Babylon A inscription as a whole effectively presents an image of Esarhaddon as an essentially Babylonian king.

In the Assur A text, written a year later, in 679, to commemorate construction on Ešarra in the city of Aššur, we see in contrast Esarhaddon's Assyrian royal *persona*. Like Babylon A, the Assur A inscription begins its account with a list of the king's titles and epithets; in this case, however, they are almost without exception the traditional titles and epithets of an Assyrian ruler. Esarhaddon is called,

> . . . great king, mighty king, king of all, king of the land of Aššur, governor for the god Enlil, priest of the god Aššur; son of Sennacherib, great king, mighty king, king of all, king of the land of Aššur, governor for the god Enlil, priest of the god Aššur; king who from his youth had feared the word of Aššur, Šamaš, Bēl, and Nabû . . . (Assur A, ll. 1–12).

The first five lines—"great king, mighty king, king of all, king of the land of Aššur"—include the most traditional of the royal titles used by the kings of Assyria. These are followed by the title *šaknu Enlil* ("prefect, or governor, for the god Enlil"), somewhat less common in Assyrian titulary, but of great antiquity.[216] It had been first introduced by Shamshi-Adad I (1813–1781) and had become a frequent element in the official titles of Assyrian kings from the time of Aššur-uballiṭ I (1365–1330) on; it was, moreover, a title that had never been used in association with Babylonian kings. It is followed by *šangû Aššur*, or "priest of the god Aššur,"[217] a standard royal Assyrian title used here

---

[216] See *AHw* "šaknu" for a summary of occurrences of the title. See also M.-J. Seux, *Épithètes royales*, 280 ff.

[217] Written with the ideogram SANGA. Seux notes (110, note 21) that the sign can be read

to emphasize the king's connection to the national god Aššur, to whom the temple under repair belonged. The titles assigned to Esarhaddon's father Sennacherib, which follow, repeat exactly the titles assigned to Esarhaddon himself, underlining his role as successor and heir to the Assyrian royal line, whose work on Ešarra he was now about to continue. The epithets conclude with a reference to Esarhaddon's piety toward Aššur and the other great gods worshipped in Assyria,[218] part of the traditional image of Assyrian rulers. Together, the titles and epithets set the tone for the document that follows.

After a passage describing the appearance of omens favorable to Esarhaddon's reign comes an account of the actual restoration of the temple, which expands the characterization of Esarhaddon as a traditional Assyrian king. The history of the Ešarra temple is used to link Esarhaddon to the earlier Assyrian kings who worked on the temple, with Esarhaddon calling each of them in turn, "my forefather, priest of Aššur" (iii, ll. 17 ff.). This passage concludes with the statement that Esarhaddon is now following in their footsteps by restoring Ešarra. As in Babylon A, the description of the actual restoration work that follows emphasizes the king's personal role in the work by having him speak in the first person: "I, Esarhaddon, king of Assyria . . . assembled the peoples of the lands . . ." (iv, ll. 7–13); "I anointed the scarp of the excavation . . ." (l. 22); "I myself carried the basket . . ." (l. 38); "its foundations . . . I laid" (v, ll. 8–11); and "that temple from its foundations to its parapets I erected, I completed . . ." (vi, ll. 1–3).

As its climax, the Assur A text describes how the gods were returned to their places in the refurbished temple: "Aššur, king of the gods, I made dwell in the lofty cella of his lordship . . .; Ninurta and Nusku, (and other) gods and goddesses, I made firm in their positions, right and left. . . ." (vi, ll. 28–36). It is noteworthy that the Assyrian god Aššur, rather than Marduk, is here named as "king of the gods." The contrast between Babylon A and Assur A is equally clear in the king's requests for blessing, which follow; the prayer is here addressed to Aššur, again styled "king of the gods" (vii, l. 17), and the request that future rulers care for the building, phrased just as it is in the Baby-

---

either as *iššakku*, "regent, vicar, feudatory, etc.," or as *šangû*, "priest," and that it is often difficult to be certain which reading was intended by the ancient author. Seux's decision to read "*iššakku*" in all cases in which the SANGA sign is followed by the name of the god Aššur alone seems to me somewhat arbitrary in view of the few occurrences in which such a reading can be confirmed; I have tentatively retained here the more traditional reading of the sign as *šangû*, "priest."

[218] Alongside the traditional Assyrian gods Aššur and Šamaš, Nabû and Bēl (another name for Marduk), originally Babylonian gods with strong nationalist associations, are also included. The reference to these two gods is the only Babylonian note in an otherwise thoroughly Assyrian text, and its impact is muted by the almost complete assimilation of the god Nabû into the Assyrian pantheon by this period, despite his still lively Babylonian connections, and by the partial assimilation of even the Babylonian national deity Marduk into Assyrian worship, a point that we will discuss at greater length in the chapter that follows.

lon A text, is now addressed not to Marduk, but to Aššur, and it is he who
will "name their names for the rule of the land and peoples" (viii, ll. 4–8).

The similarities between the two building inscriptions, Babylon A and
Assur A, are evident, but the images of the king that the texts present to their
respective audiences are markedly different. In Babylon A, Esarhaddon's role
as king of Assyria is passed over almost in silence; if that text were by some
accident our only source for Esarhaddon, we might almost think him a Babylonian ruler. In Assur A, in contrast, Esarhaddon is presented as the embodiment of Assyrian kingship and the heir to Assyria's ancient royal traditions.
In each of these texts, the king speaks in the voice of his Assyrian or Babylonian *persona*. In each case, the entire inscription is used to shape and refine
the image of the king which that text presents to its intended audience in
Assyria or Babylonia.[219]

The idea that different texts, projecting two different images of the king
and his activities, were being prepared by Esarhaddon's scribes for audiences
in Assyria and Babylonia is further confirmed when we examine the larger
group of texts to which Babylon A belongs, Borger's Babylon A–G inscriptions, the building inscriptions written to commemorate Esarhaddon's public
works projects in Babylon. It is surprising to discover that even here, in a
group of texts describing a single set of building projects in a single city, two
different images of the king emerge; in some of the texts, Esarhaddon is
presented as essentially Babylonian in his sympathies, responsive to Babylon's
plight and tactful in describing her difficulties, while in other texts, he appears
in contrast as a ruler who is bluntly critical of the Babylonians' behavior and
evidently well satisfied with their subsequent downfall. The two groups of
texts, as we will see, were in fact found in different locations, some in Babylonia, the others in Assyria, and the differences in outlook that they reflect
again seem intended to appeal to the different national audiences in those two
areas. This difference in outlook between the two groups of texts makes the
Babylon inscriptions unique among Assyrian building inscriptions for a single
project, which ordinarily reflect a single uniform point of view; the unusual
step of preparing two sets of building inscriptions for this project underlines

---

[219] That the text was intended in one case for use in Assyria and in the other, for use in Babylonia, is suggested not only by internal evidence, but also by the discovery of copies of those texts
in the areas in question. Five of the six surviving copies of Assur A were excavated in Aššur, three
of them within the Aššur temple precincts. One of the copies of Babylon A (Bab. A1) was bought
near the ruins of Babylon and was almost certainly unearthed in the city in unofficial digging. Another copy, Babylon A4, was found in the Babylonian city of Sippar; whether it was actually
presented to a Babylonian audience in that city, or was placed there for safe-keeping while the rebuilding of Babylon was under way, or for some other purpose, however, remains unclear. (Of the
three remaining copies of Babylon A, two have no recorded place of discovery, and one was discovered in Aššur, suggesting that it represents an Assyrian record of the text, or possibly a presentation copy placed in the Aššur temple.)

the importance to Esarhaddon's administration of presenting different images of the king and his activities to audiences in the two nations.

The differences between the two sets of texts are relatively subtle, and their effect is somewhat muted by the many similarities, perhaps reflecting an intentional effort to minimize any offense to Esarhaddon's Babylonian advisers who might be present at the public presentation of the Assyrian versions of the text; the texts are, in fact, so similar in broad outline that they were published by Borger as a single composite text, "Babylon A–G," with variant accounts of each incident printed side by side. Two of the texts Borger included in the group, Babylon AC and F, I will not discuss here because they are too fragmentary to permit an over-all analysis, and a third, Babylon D, must also be set aside from the rest of the group since it represents a different genre of text, not a building inscription but more probably the formal legal record of the king's grant of special privileges to Babylon.[220] The five remaining texts, Babylon A, B, C, E, and G, appear on first examination to be a typical set of building inscriptions for a single project, offering parallel, at times identical, accounts of the various stages of Esarhaddon's rebuilding of Babylon. When we examine the texts more closely, however, a pattern of differences emerges that separates the texts into two distinct groups and offers an important clue to their intended use.

These differences occur in one particular section of the text, the historical summary, a section that explains why the reconstruction project at hand had become necessary. Ordinarily, such historical summaries in Assyrian building inscriptions explain that the building in question had grown old, had burned down, or had become too small for current needs. In this case, however, Babylon needed restoration because Esarhaddon's father had sacked it in the course of a campaign against Babylonia. Faced with the awkward problem of having to describe this Assyrian attack on the city before they could celebrate Esarhaddon's restoration of it, Esarhaddon's scribes fell back upon the notion that the Babylonians themselves had caused their city's destruction, having behaved so badly that their gods had punished them by ordering the city's downfall. It is noteworthy that this explanation, usually used by a defeated

---

[220] Babylon D is not inscribed on a clay prism, but on a rectangle of black stone with an unusual pattern of images—a plow, a palm-tree, a more stylized tree, an altar, etc.—carved into the top, a form more reminiscent of contemporary Babylonian *kudurru* documents, which record grants of land, tax exemptions, or privileges, than of Assyrian building inscriptions. The contents of the text also suggest something other than a building inscription; although the text describes the decision to rebuild the city and the preliminary building rituals, it deals with the actual restoration of Esagila and the city walls in the briefest of summaries, suggesting the main interest of the author was elsewhere. The text concludes with a description of the return of the Babylonians and the restoration of *kidinnu* status to the city (Ep. 37); it seems probable that this concession to the Babylonians was the real focus of the text. The stone on which the text is inscribed was found in Nineveh; it may represent the formal record of the grant of *kidinnūtu*, perhaps used initially in ceremonies in Babylon and then removed to Nineveh as a permanent record of the grant.

city to explain the failure of its gods to protect itself, is here used by the conqueror instead. This approach conveniently reduces Sennacherib to the role
of an insignificant agent of the gods, of so little importance that he is not even
mentioned in the texts.

All five texts begin by describing the situation in Babylon which led, they
suggest, to the city's downfall.[221] In Babylon A, C, and E, the accounts of this
are brief. Babylon E, the most laconic, avoids any reference to wrongdoing
and simply states, "Before my time, the great lord Marduk was angry; he felt
stormy toward Esagila and Babylon" (Ep. 5). Babylon A and C offer more
explanation: "At that time, in the reign of a former king, there were evil signs
in the land of Sumer and Akkad.[222] The people who lived in (the city) an-
swered 'yes' and 'no' to one another. They spoke lies. They pushed away and
neglected their gods. Their goddesses forsook their ordained practices and
rode (away). . . . On the possessions of (the temple) Esagila—a place where
entry is forbidden—they laid their hands, and gold and silver and precious
stones they gave to the land of Elam as a purchase price" (Eps. 2, 3, and 4).

While this account is scarcely complimentary to the Babylonians, it seems
mild when it is compared to the version offered by Babylon B and G, where
the events leading to the downfall of the city are described with a certain
relish:[223] "[When] in the reign of a form[er king, there were] evil [omens,
all the shr]ines. . . . Violence (and) murder was inflicted upon their bodies,
and they oppressed the weak—they give them to the strong.[224] Within the
city there was oppression (and) accepting of bribes, and daily without ceasing

---

[221] Both Babylon B and G are broken at the beginning in the copies available to Borger when
he prepared his edition. A.R. Millard (*AfO*, 24, 118–119 and plate XIV) has now published newly
identified pieces of Babylon G, as well as a fragment he identifies as part of either B or G (called
Babylon "H" by Brinkman; see App. IV under "Babylon B2"). Both texts begin, after a broken
section, with line 9 of the Babylon A text in each case and roughly paraphrase the remainder of
the Babylon A introductory epithets section (Borger's Episode 1). Babylon C was also missing these
beginning passages in the version available to Borger. A new copy of Babylon C (BM 78221), sub-
sequently published in *CT* 44 (London: 1963), plates V, VI, and VII, includes the material of Episode 1 and continues through four columns of text. Borger added this material to the revised edition of Babylon C published in "Zu den Asarhaddon-Texten aus Babel," 143–148.

[222] Written Á.MEŠ. Borger reads the sign Á as *idu* ("arm, side, strength") so that Á.MEŠ
ḪUL.MEŠ becomes "siding with evil" (cf. *CAD*, "idu A," 2b6), or, in Borger's translation, "evil
forces." A possible alternative, which seems to offer a better reading here, is to take Á as *ittu*, "mark,
omen" (see *CAD* "ittu A"), giving the reading "evil signs."

[223] The two extant exemplars of Babylon B are badly broken here, but the surviving traces
("in the reign of a former king" and then "all cult cities"), which also occur in Babylon G, suggest
that the two texts were roughly identical here, a supposition strengthened by the fact that the Babylon B text becomes available again at just the point where the text of the Babylon G inscription
itself breaks, in the midst of a description of the Babylonians' sins, and Babylon B completes the
phrase and the thought as if the texts had indeed been identical throughout the now broken passage.
The initial lines come from the additional pieces of Babylon B and G texts published by Millard.

[224] Note Borger's changed emendation, *[ḫa(b)]-ba-lu* ("brutality, violence") rather than *[naḫ]-
ba-lu* ("snare"), in line 4 (*BiOr*, 21 [1964], p. 144).

they stole one another's goods. The son in the marketplace has cursed his father, the slave [has disobeyed?] his master, [the female slave] does not listen to her mistress" (Ep. 3). As if this weren't bad enough, the Babylon B text adds, in a now fragmented line, "having infringed the taboo of the sacred meal . . .," and concludes ". . . the [regular offer]ing they discontinued, and they plotted a conspiracy" (Ep. 3, c3). Although all five texts are critical of the Babylonians, only Babylon B and G are truly scathing. Where Babylon A, C, and E accuse the Babylonians of deviousness in their dealings with one another and neglect of their cultic duties, Babylon B and G talk about murder and oppression of the weak and accuse the Babylonians of disregarding the fundamental relationships of parent and child, master and slave on which the order of society depended. Babylon B further expands the list to include neglect of the gods and conspiracy.

In the next section, the texts deal with the god Marduk's reaction to this wrongdoing. Here the differences in tone are subtler, but still clearly evident. Babylon E, which had already mentioned Marduk's anger, now adds, "His heart was angry; he felt wrath" (Ep. 5). Babylon A and C report, "The Enlil of the gods, Marduk, flared up in anger. He considered bad things for the leveling of the country (and) the destruction of its people" (Ep. 5). Babylon B and G, however, combine the elements of both and add further detail: "The Enlil saw (this) and his heart grew angry, his bowels burned. The Enlil of the gods, the lord of the lands, considered bad things for breaking up the land and the people. His heart was angry (enough) to level the land and cause its people to disappear, and in his mouth was placed a curse of hardship" (Ep. 5). Babylon B and G append to this passage a description of unfavorable astral omens (Ep. 6), extending the image of a world out of joint.

The texts conclude their historical summaries with an account of the city's destruction. Babylon E describes the painful event in a single sentence: "Through the anger of his heart and the burning of his bowels, Esagil and Babylon became wasteland and turned into empty fields" (Ep. 5 and 7, ll. 7–11). Babylon A and C, this time joined by Babylon B, are also relatively brief: "The Araḫtu Canal, river of abundance, was brought to (the stage of) angry flood, violent onrush of water, mighty inundation, an image of the deluge, and the water swept over the city (and) its dwellings and made (them) a ruin" (Ep. 7). Babylon G, however, once again offers further detail: "Swamp reed and willows grew thick in the midst of her and sent up shoots. Birds of the heavens and fish of the watery deep beyond counting were there in the midst of her" (Ep. 7). In this version, downtown Babylon has become a lake, an unfortunate end for a beautiful city.

It is clear that the Babylon inscriptions, superficially so similar, fall into two distinct groups with significant differences in tone and outlook. Babylon A, C, and E, on the one hand, are relatively sympathetic to the Babylonians' situation, outline the Babylonians' shortcomings only to the extent necessary to justify the Assyrian destruction of the city, and describe that destruction as laconically as possible.[225] Babylon B and G, in contrast, sharply criticize the Babylonians' behavior and describe the city's destruction and subsequent plight with a wealth of detail that suggests a certain satisfaction in the city's misfortunes. Esarhaddon, as the protagonist in the texts and the king responsible for their composition, emerges as a markedly different figure in the two accounts. In Babylon A, C, and E, he appears as a king fully sympathetic to Babylonian concerns, while in Babylon B and G, he appears as a ruler who is sharply critical of the Babylonians and well satisfied with the city's punishment.

It seems clear that this set of building inscriptions, in a departure from normal Mesopotamian practice, was prepared not only for the people of Babylon—the city that the inscriptions discuss—but also for an audience in Assyria. Indeed, the biting tone of Babylon B and G would seem to make them appropriate for use only in an Assyrian setting, since the presentation of such texts in Babylonia would have appeared as a deliberately offensive gesture. Esarhaddon, as we have seen, was in the midst of an extensive and expensive southern building campaign designed to demonstrate to the Babylonians the benefits of being loyal subjects. His performance of the basket-bearing ceremony and his use of Babylonian titles seem calculated to encourage further Babylonian acceptance of his rule. It is hardly likely that Esarhaddon would have undermined these efforts by gratuitously offending the Babylonians in these documents announcing his benevolent attentions to their capital city and holy places.

It is significant that although most of the Babylon building inscriptions were bought or found in Babylonia, the prism inscribed with the Babylon G text—and probably the pieces of tablet inscribed with the Babylon B text,

[225] Mordechai Cogan (in "Omens and Ideology in the Babylon Inscription of Esarhaddon," *History, Historiography and Interpretation: Studies in Biblical and Cuneiform Literatures*, 76–87) argues, in contrast, that Babylon E would have been offensive to a Babylonian audience and was designed instead for presentation to Assyrians. He points first to the text's failure to refer to celestial omens (mentioned at this point in other texts), an omission that Cogan suggests reflects a typically Assyrian lack of interest in celestial divination in this period, and second, to its failure to mention that the Babylonians were eventually released from corvée duty in Babylon, an omission that Cogan suggests reflects an insensitivity to a matter of great importance to the Babylonians.

Neither of these arguments seems to me convincing. In the first place, celestial divination *was* being practiced in Assyria in Esarhaddon's time (see A. Leo Oppenheim, "Divination and Celestial Observation in the Last Assyrian Empire," 97–135, as well as the detailed account of celestial omens that introduces Esarhaddon's Assur A inscription [i, l. 31-ii, l. 11]). As to the text's silence about the Babylonians' release from doing demeaning corvée work, the text could hardly mention that the Babylonians had been freed from that work without indicating that they had been obliged to do it in the first place, if only to insure their own survival until the city's economy began to revive. The text's silence on this point may well reflect a tactful sensitivity to Babylonian feelings, rather than the other way around.

as well—were found in the Assyrian city of Nineveh and are written in Assyrian script, lending further support to the suggestion that these more critical texts were intended for use in Assyria. Even within the set of inscriptions written to describe Esarhaddon's work in the single city of Babylon, Esarhaddon's scribes found it necessary to compose two quite distinct accounts presenting different images of the king and his activities to the two nations.

In the context of Esarhaddon's reign, it is not difficult to see why it was felt necessary to create two separate sets of building inscriptions for this particular project. The various texts prepared for Babylonia served the normal function of building inscriptions, announcing the project publicly at its beginning and reporting on progress as construction advanced. At the same time, they offered Esarhaddon an opportunity to justify to the Babylonians the earlier Assyrian destruction of the city. While the justification offered was probably not particularly appealing to the Babylonians, it nevertheless was couched in terms of their own traditions, offering them a way to save face if they should prove willing to forget the past and accept Esarhaddon's offer of peace and prosperity in exchange for an end to Babylonian resistance. The set of building inscriptions prepared for use in Babylon thus had an important function in laying the groundwork for reconciliation with Babylonia.

It is perhaps not so obvious that it was equally important to explain the reconstruction of Babylon to the Assyrians as well. In order not to offend his own countrymen, Esarhaddon had to find an adequate justification for rebuilding a city that they had only recently gone to considerable effort and expense to destroy. The Babylon inscriptions offered such a justification (in Ep. 10) by asserting that the god Marduk, relenting of his anger against Babylonia, had decided to reduce the number of years he had ordained as the time of Babylon's abandonment, changing it from seventy to eleven, thus permitting immediate reconstruction of the city and, in addition, shifting all responsibility for the decision to rebuild from Esarhaddon to the god.[226]

Although this argument needed to reach the Assyrians, it would not in itself have been offensive to the Babylonians and would not have required the creation of special Assyrian versions of the texts.[227] There was a second message, however, that Esarhaddon needed to present to the Assyrians, and it was this message that required the more critical tone, appropriate for Assyrian audiences alone. The rebuilding of Babylon was the first public works

---

[226] This explanation is offered in Babylon A, B, and D. The text of Babylon G is difficult to reconstruct, because much is still missing and because the extant text suggests that events were presented in a somewhat different order than in the other texts in the group. Although there is no trace of this passage in the extant portions of Babylon G, it could have appeared in the broken sections, possibly in the missing first section of column iv.

[227] Accounts of Marduk's change of heart do in fact appear in two Babylonian versions, Babylon A and C, where they serve as announcements of Marduk's reconciliation with the city, providing a logical completion for the theological sequence of sin, punishment, and forgiveness.

project of Esarhaddon's reign, announced early in his first year; the equivalent Assyrian project, the rebuilding of Ešarra in Aššur, would not be organized and announced until the following year. In the meantime, Esarhaddon needed to reassure the Assyrians of his unwavering commitment to them, despite his conspicuous activities in Babylon. The Assyrian versions of the Babylon building inscriptions performed this function, allowing the king to speak of the rebuilding of Babylon in terms that showed him to be unequivocally Assyrian in his attitude toward the project, critical of the Babylonians and well satisfied with their punishment. The preparation of two contrasting sets of inscriptions for this single building project is an unusual and striking example of Esarhaddon's use of building inscriptions as tools of propaganda, vehicles for presenting differing images of the king and his activities to Babylonian and Assyrian audiences.

In order to be used for such a purpose, however, the inscriptions had to be accessible to a contemporary audience, and there is a substantial body of opinion among contemporary scholars that this was not the case. A. Leo Oppenheim, for example, argues in *Ancient Mesopotamia* that Assyrian and Babylonian building inscriptions were typically buried in the buildings whose construction they described, making them apparently inaccessible to contemporaries. Other building inscriptions, although displayed in palaces or temples, were erected in rooms that must have been dark enough to make reading such texts exceedingly difficult, even for people skilled in reading cuneiform.[228] Oppenheim argues that building inscriptions were thus not intended for contemporary audiences, but only for the gods or for future kings who might unearth the texts in the process of rebuilding, an argument that has gained wide acceptance.[229]

---

[228] No display inscriptions of Esarhaddon were discovered in the arsenal and palace complex at Calaḫ. If such inscriptions were displayed in his Nineveh palace, they remain buried beneath the mound of Nebi Yunus. This means that in Esarhaddon's case we are concerned only with building inscriptions on clay prisms or cylinders, or with copies or drafts of such texts on clay tablets, rather than with publicly displayed building inscriptions.

[229] A. Leo Oppenheim, *Ancient Mesopotamia: Portrait of a Dead Civilization*, 146–148. A similar argument had been made a short time before in reference to Sumerian building inscriptions by William W. Hallo, "The Royal Inscriptions of Ur: A Typology," 1–43. The idea that such texts were not intended for contemporary audiences has been accepted, for example, by Ellis, 166–167 and by Edmond Sollberger and Jean Kupper, *Inscriptions royales sumériennes et akkadiennes*, 28–29. A. Kirk Grayson, in "Assyria and Babylonia," 140–194, concludes that royal inscriptions placed in prominent places in temples and palaces "could be seen and read" (151), but reaches essentially the same conclusion about buried texts as does Oppenheim. He does note, however, that at least in Babylonia, some copies of foundation documents are also found unburied in archives where they may have served as records or as models for scribal training (n. 116, 164).

Recent discussion of the function of Assyrian royal inscriptions as propaganda has to some extent reopened the question of the intended audience for texts inscribed on clay prisms or cylinders, the usual physical vehicles for building inscriptions buried in buildings. See, for example, Mario Liverani, "The Ideology of the Assyrian Empire," 297–317, in *Power and Propaganda*, Mogens T.

There are, however, several mechanisms by which even buried building inscriptions might well have reached contemporary audiences despite the eventual burial of the texts, and there is considerable evidence from Esarhaddon's own reign that seems to require the conclusion that such transmission to contemporary audiences in fact occurred. Two aspects of the Nineveh A text (one of Esarhaddon's later building inscriptions) seem puzzling, for example, if the text was intended only for gods and future kings, but are easily accounted for if it was intended as well for an audience of Esarhaddon's contemporaries. The Nineveh A text is one of the longest and most important of Esarhaddon's building inscriptions, written relatively late in the reign to commemorate Esarhaddon's construction of a large palace and arsenal complex at Nineveh. The first element suggesting that the text was prepared with a contemporary audience in mind is the long introductory passage (Ep. 2) describing the struggles that accompanied Esarhaddon's rise to power, a subject that earlier texts had passed over in silence. Hayim Tadmor has made a study of ancient Near Eastern accounts of this type describing how a particular king rose to power, accounts that he terms "autobiographical apologies." He begins by noting that while such royal apologies had a wide distribution in both space and time in the ancient Near East, they nevertheless shared a common pattern: royal apologies were typically included in documents composed on behalf of rulers who had experienced difficulties in reaching the throne.[230] In addition, Tadmor points out, the royal apology did not, in the case of Assyrian kings, appear in inscriptions until well into the king's reign, at the point when he was preparing to name a successor to the throne. At that juncture, Tadmor suggests, the royal apology was introduced to establish the legitimacy of the ruler despite his early difficulties in becoming king. The apology offered a format in which the king could present his own version of his rise to power, minimizing its difficulties and asserting his gods' early, unwavering commitment to his rule despite human opposition, an approach evidently intended to prevent later challenges to the legitimacy of his chosen successor. Since it was contemporaries whose support the king was trying to enlist to insure a peaceful transfer of power to his chosen successor at the time of his death, Tadmor's model implies a contemporary audience for any text in which a royal apology occurs.[231]

Larsen, ed., esp. 302, who acknowledges the difficulties in concluding that foundation deposit inscriptions reached a broad contemporary public and yet is loath to dismiss the possibility entirely. I suggest that the idea of multiple intended uses for such texts—such as ceremonial presentation to a contemporary audience followed by burial for a future audience—would resolve the difficulties Oppenheim and others have perceived.

[230] "Autobiographical Apology in the Royal Assyrian Literature," in *History, Historiography and Interpretation,* Hayim Tadmor and M. Weinfeld, ed., 36–57.

[231] Tadmor himself stops short of making this conclusion explicit, but notes, "It is our con-

It is thus significant that Esarhaddon's Nineveh A inscription, as Tadmor notes, fits the classic pattern of royal apology texts precisely. The story of Esarhaddon's accession (a stormy one, as we have seen) was completely omitted from texts composed in the early years of Esarhaddon's reign;[232] the account we have followed above comes primarily from the Nineveh A inscription, dated in four copies to 673, one year before Esarhaddon appointed two of his sons to succeed him on the thrones of Assyria and Babylonia, respectively.[233] If gods and future kings had been the only intended audience for his inscriptions, there would have been little point in omitting the account of Esarhaddon's difficulties from earlier building inscriptions, since the Nineveh A text, which does tell the story, would have been equally available to a future audience.

It seems likely that the reason for Esarhaddon's silence in the early texts about his problems in reaching the throne, and for his discussion of those problems in the later Nineveh A text, is the one Tadmor suggests, that he wished to avoid raising the dangerous question of his right to rule at the beginning of the reign, when that right had just been hotly contested, but needed to raise the question and deal with it directly as soon as his position on the throne was relatively secure. By then, the likelihood of an immediate rebellion based on that issue was small, and it had become necessary to break the silence and lay to rest any doubts about the legitimacy of Esarhaddon's claims to the throne, lest those doubts later make problems for the sons he was about to appoint to succeed him. The absence of the apology passage in texts dating from early in the reign, and its inclusion in the later Nineveh A text, written one year before the appointment of his successors, makes sense only if Esarhaddon expected those inscriptions to reach an audience of his contemporaries.

The presence of a royal apology in Nineveh A is not the only indication that Esarhaddon expected that text (and by implication, other building inscriptions as well) to reach contemporary audiences. Additional evidence is pro-

---

tention that they [Assyrian apologetic documents] were composed not so much in order to reflect apologetically upon the past but rather to serve certain imminent political aims in the present or some particular design for the future" (37).

[232] For a list of these early texts, see Appendix II, 173 ff. The brief account of Esarhaddon's rise to power in Babylon A and D omits any mention of his early difficulties, saying only: "Me, Esarhaddon, you truly chose from among my assembled elder brothers to set these matters (i.e., Babylonia's problems) right again, and you placed your good shadow over me . . . " (Ep. 11, 9–16).

[233] Nin. F includes thirteen lines which were also included in the Apology, the passage reporting Esarhaddon's selection in the assembly of his brothers (=ll. 9–22 of Nin. A); Nin. D includes twelve lines of it, the passage in which Esarhaddon exclaims in woe at hearing of trouble in Nineveh, consults with the gods, and starts off posthaste for Nineveh to claim the throne (=ll. 56–68 of Nin. A). Both passages are brief excerpts from the account of the rise to power in the Nineveh A text (Ep. 2, which is ninety lines long) and neither discusses Esarhaddon's fall from favor and subsequent difficulties.

vided by a second element in the Nineveh A text, in this case a significant omission. The passage in question is again the long historical introduction (Ep. 2) describing Esarhaddon's selection as heir and his rise to power. As we saw earlier in the discussion of Esarhaddon's rise to power, this historical introduction begins with an account of Esarhaddon's selection as heir apparent, his brothers' critical attacks on him, and his eventual decision to withdraw to safety outside Assyria. The next section, which follows immediately, briefly describes the fighting which, it says, broke out in Nineveh among Esarhaddon's brothers after his departure. The passage is as important for what it fails to mention as for its actual description of events:

> After this, my brothers went mad and did what was not good in the sight of the gods and of mankind. They plotted evil and drew swords in the midst of Nineveh, contrary to the will of the gods. Like goats they butted against each other over the exercise of the kingship (Nin. A, Ep. 2, ll. 41–44).

The section concludes, as we saw earlier, with an account of how Esarhaddon learned that his brothers were fighting among themselves, returned to Assyria with an army, defeated the warring factions, and took the throne. What is missing from the entire account is any mention that his brothers were fighting together about who would be king because the reigning king, their father, had just been killed—murdered, in fact, by one of his sons. We know this from the Babylonian Chronicles, from the Bible, and even from later Assyrian texts, but not from Nineveh A. Why was all reference to Sennacherib's death—such a crucial part of the story—omitted?

The first explanation is that Esarhaddon himself was the son who had arranged the murder, and that the reference to his father's death was omitted out of guilt. As noted earlier, however, Simo Parpola has argued that the letter ABL 1091, when correctly translated, provides convincing evidence that it was not Esarhaddon, but his brother Arda-Mulissi, who had arranged the assassination of Sennacherib.[234] Since there is no evidence that Esarhaddon was involved in the murder in any way, we must find another explanation for the Nineveh A text's silence about it.

A second possibility is that the subject of assassinating Assyrian kings might itself have been considered inappropriate in Assyrian royal inscriptions. But Esarhaddon's son Assurbanipal later mentions the murder of Sennacherib, without any apparent reservations, in the text in which he describes himself as killing Babylonians by the statues where they had killed Sennacherib,[235] an indication that the subject of the murder of Assyrian kings was not forbidden *per se*.

The most plausible explanation is that Esarhaddon did not mention the

---

[234] Simo Parpola, "The Murderer of Sennacherib," in *Death in Mesopotamia*, 171–182.
[235] Rassam Cylinder, iv, 70–76 = Streck, *Assurbanipal*, 38–39.

murder of his father because of an understandable reluctance to raise the subject of the successful murder of a recent king, a topic that might set people's minds going in an undesirable direction. The story of the Biblical King David offers a possible analogy. According to the account in II Samuel 1:1–16, shortly after David's predecessor and enemy, King Saul, died in battle, a man came to David proudly asserting that he himself had killed Saul during the fighting. David reacted, according to this account, by tearing his clothes in mourning, exclaiming, "How wast thou not afraid to stretch forth thine hand to destroy the Lord's anointed?" and commanding that the man be put to death. Although Saul had been his deadly enemy, David's first reaction was to reject forcibly the idea that it was acceptable to kill an anointed king, however helpful that death might prove to David himself. Esarhaddon may have been motivated by similar considerations. Later, after Esarhaddon's death and the peaceful installation of his successors, the subject of Sennacherib's murder was less charged, so that Assurbanipal could raise it freely, particularly in the context of announcing that he had now avenged that murder. Esarhaddon, however, evidently felt constrained to omit any reference to his father's murder in the Nineveh A inscription, an omission that makes good sense politically if we understand that the text was expected to reach not only gods and future kings, but also an audience of his own contemporaries.

These two aspects of the Nineveh A inscription—its inclusion for the first time of an account of Esarhaddon's early difficulties and its omission of any reference to Sennacherib's murder—suggest that this text, and probably other foundation documents as well, were intended for dual use: first, for presentation to a living audience of the king's contemporaries; and second, for burial in the walls or floors of the building whose construction the text described, so that the texts would be preserved for an audience of gods and future kings.

But how could the texts of such building inscriptions have reached the contemporary audiences for which they seem to have been at least in part designed, if such inscriptions were ordinarily interred in the foundations of buildings? In the first place, the inaccessibility of the texts after they had been placed in foundation boxes would not in any way have precluded their reaching a variety of contemporary audiences before their burial. One contemporary audience that building inscriptions certainly reached, for example, was that of the scribes who composed the texts, and their associates at court. These scribes drafted the formal documents presenting royal public policy and no doubt discussed their work with their colleagues in the palace. As they did so, the king's messages about himself, his intentions and his achievements reached these scribes and a wider contemporary audience in the king's court.[236] In reaching these members of the Assyrian ruling elite and reinforc-

---

[236] In some cases, the composing scribes may also have served as royal counselors and have

ing their conviction of the king's power and right to rule, the messages presented in the royal inscriptions filled an important first function by contributing to the self-confidence and effectiveness of the Assyrian administration.[237]

Later, after the composition of the texts, at least one group of building inscriptions of Esarhaddon was made available to a second selected audience of contemporaries. The discovery in the city of Aššur of several copies of Esarhaddon building inscriptions describing construction projects that took

---

been involved in formulating the policies presented by the texts. The extent to which royal inscriptions in a given reign reflected the opinions of the king himself, his counsellors, or the joint decisions of both reached after consultation, is a vexing question and one that can.be addressed only briefly here. At this point there appears to be little explicit evidence to shed light on the relative importance of individual kings or their counsellors in developing public statements of policy or shaping the king's public image. (Parpola's suggestion in *Letters*, IIa, 20 that the letter fragment LAS 305 records a request to a king to review a document and suggest deletions or additions was not repeated in Parpola's revised commentary on the letter in *Letters*, IIb, probably because the fragment does not identify the object the king is to review, which could be anything from a document to a statue. The letter thus cannot serve as evidence of the king's editing of inscriptions, as Parpola had originally proposed.)

It is interesting to note in this connection, however, that there was considerable continuity in the king's professional staff in the reigns of Esarhaddon and Assurbanipal. Parpola's list of twenty-five scribes and royal advisers identified by profession and office or specialty in letters to Esarhaddon or Assurbanipal shows that at least nine of these men served both kings in important advisory positions, and an additional three may have done so. At least one, possibly two, of these men had moreover served under Sennacherib as well. Although the profession of many of them was listed in texts as scribe, their professional specialties differ, and we have no way of knowing whether the professional responsibilities of some of them included composing drafts of royal inscriptions. Both inscriptions and letters are silent on this point. If in fact there was considerable continuity in royal advisers from reign to reign, as Parpola's list on a brief inspection seems to suggest, then the sometimes marked differences in the inscriptions of two successive kings—in matters such as the royal *personae* the texts present or the tone the texts take toward a particular event, such as the destruction of Babylon—may reflect to some extent the input of the king himself into the messages the texts present, either because his own ideas on those points differed from those of his predecessor, or because he was relying more heavily on different advisers from those his predecessor had chosen to follow. For our purposes here, however, it is not significant whether the messages that were presented in the royal inscriptions had originated with the king himself, with his inner circle of advisers, or through some interaction of the two. In any of these cases (and the precise scenario probably varied from reign to reign) it seems probable that the official royal policy was formulated at a high level in the Assyrian court, was drafted into formal documents either by the king's counsellors themselves or by scribal specialists, and that these documents were then surely reviewed in some way by the king or his advisers before the texts were formally presented to their intended audience, human or divine. During this process, the official version of the king's achievements and his policies would have percolated through the king's court, reaching the bureaucrats, military officers, professional advisers, foreign dignitaries and messengers, royal relatives and others present at the court, but not necessarily participating in the discussions that led to the formulation of official public policy for the realm. Those present at court (on this point, see *Letters*, IIa, 8–9 and 21), I am suggesting, were, through oral transmission and informal discussion, the first audience for the official royal message encapsulated in the inscriptions.

[237] The importance of this group as an audience for royal pronouncements is discussed by Mario Liverani, "The Ideology of the Assyrian Empire," in *Power and Propaganda*, Mogens T. Larsen, ed., 298–299 and 302.

place in other cities suggests that at least in some cases, a duplicate of the building inscription, copied on a clay prism, was placed in a city other than the
one where the text was interred as a foundation deposit; this second copy of
the text presumably remained accessible to contemporaries even after the
main copy of the text was buried. This is at first glance a somewhat surprising
conclusion, since it has long been a working hypothesis among Assyriologists
that texts copied on clay prisms or cylinders were intended for use only as
deposits in foundation boxes in the buildings whose construction they describe; a number of clay prisms and cylinders have in fact been found in other
settings, however, suggesting that the hypothesis that prisms and cylinders
were invariably meant to be buried in the city and building they discuss needs
to be reexamined. A.K. Grayson, in his study of the various genres of Assyrian
and Babylonian royal inscriptions, comments at one point, "Copies of some
inscriptions were actually kept in a special kind of archive," citing here ancient
collections of texts from previous reigns found at Babylon and at Sippar.[238]
Although these collections were found in Babylonia (and Grayson does not
note whether they included prisms and cylinders), it begins to appear that
similar collections were made in Assyria, as well, and these did include texts
on prisms. In Esarhaddon's case, building inscriptions copied on prisms and
found at Aššur include records of construction projects in Nineveh (Nin.
A19), in Tarbiṣu (Trb. A), and in Babylon (Bab. A3), as well as a combined
account of construction in both Aššur and Babylon together (AsBbE).[239] Although the latter text might have been used as a foundation text in Aššur,
since it does include an account of work done there, it was discovered as part
of a group of texts from various reigns in a courtyard in the temple Ešarra (in
Aššur), not in a foundation box. The other Esarhaddon texts listed above as
found in Aššur are all building inscriptions describing work in other cities.[240]
The intended use for the texts in Aššur is unclear; that two of the three texts
for which we have a precise provenance were found in the Ešarra temple or
nearby (the third was almost certainly moved from its original site in antiquity)
raises the possibility that the texts were deposited by Esarhaddon in the Ešarra
temple, perhaps as formal records or as presentations to the god Aššur. Several
Esarhaddon inscriptions have been found in other temples, as well: a copy

---

[238] A. Kirk Grayson, "Assyria and Babylonia," 164.

[239] For the provenance of all four texts, see Appendix IV. The Nineveh A prism was found
at some distance from the remains of any sizable building, suggesting that it had been removed from
its original location and dropped here at some point.

[240] It has often been assumed in the past that building inscriptions inscribed on prisms or cylinders and not found in the city they discussed were either flawed copies, rejected texts, or texts
that for one reason or another had never been actually used and so remained in the city in which
they had been composed or copied. In the case of Esarhaddon's inscriptions in Aššur, however, we
know that some of the texts are not rejected versions because we have other copies of the same
text from the cities in which they were used, probably as building deposits.

of Nineveh D in the Ištar temple at Nineveh and a second copy of it in the
Nabû temple at Nineveh, and the vassal treaty texts recording oaths imposed
on certain vassals to insure their support of Esarhaddon's chosen successors,
in the Nabû temple at Calaḫ. In addition to these, a copy of one of
Sennacherib's annalistic inscriptions was found in the Nabû temple in Nineveh, as was a copy of one of Assurbanipal's building inscriptions.[241] The discovery of such texts in temples raises the possibility that several of the late
Assyrian kings may have routinely deposited formal duplicate copies of their
building inscriptions, along with other royal texts, in temples, as well as placing such building inscriptions in foundation deposits. Because the Esarhaddon
building inscriptions found at Aššur were not buried in foundation deposits,
these texts clearly remained accessible to contemporaries in Aššur, at least to
those who had access to the large collections of texts housed in the Aššur
temple. Such scribes and temple personnel represent a probable second contemporary audience for those building inscriptions.

Access to the inscriptions in these first two instances was limited to people
who were permitted entry to palaces or temples in Assyria, and who were
able to read or had scribes available to them. There were obvious advantages
to the Assyrians, however, in having the texts of building inscriptions also
reach a wider and more general contemporary audience in Assyria and Babylonia as well.

Although the presentation of building inscription texts to this wider audience remains conjectural, it is clear that mechanisms for presenting the texts
to a wider audience were readily available. The texts could easily have been
presented to contemporary audiences, for example, in the form of speeches
or proclamations read aloud at public gatherings. The ceremonies during
which building inscriptions were deposited in the foundations of buildings
are an example of one setting in which building inscriptions might appropriately have been read aloud to a large and varied contemporary audience. The
performance of rituals at various stages in the construction of public buildings
in Mesopotamia is well attested. The participation of the king in many of
these rituals is equally well attested, with examples ranging from the time of
Gudea in the third millennium to Esarhaddon's reign and long after him.[242]
These rituals were not performed by the king in private; in the accounts of
building ceremonies offered in royal inscriptions these ceremonies have all the
earmarks of major public events. Esarhaddon, in fact, makes this explicit; he
says of his enactment of the basket-bearing ceremony at the temple Ešarra,

---

[241] See Appendix IV for the locations of the Esarhaddon inscriptions. For the locations of the
Sennacherib and Assurbanipal inscriptions in the Ištar temple at Nineveh (at M15 and at W.6.91
on the site plan, respectively), see Wilfred G. Lambert and A.R. Millard, *Catalogue of the Cuneiform
Tablets in the Kouyunjik Collection of the British Museum: Second Supplement*, 35.
[242] See Ellis, *Foundation Deposits*, 5–34.

"In order to cause the lands to fear, I showed the people" (Assur A, iv, ll. 39–40). Building ceremonies, then, were specifically public gatherings, occasions for "showing the people."

Almost certainly, they were also occasions for "telling the people." We would expect foundation ceremonies to have had an accompanying script, a speech or public announcement in which the king or his representative described the construction project that was being inaugurated and presented—with the king as its sponsor. When we read Assyrian building inscriptions, it is hard to imagine texts better suited for such a purpose. Like the speeches made at modern ground-breaking ceremonies, Assyrian building inscriptions typically consist of pious references to divine help, glowing descriptions of the project at hand and of the king's role in making it possible, and a concluding wish that the gods might smile upon the project, upon the people who were to use it, and upon the sponsor who was having it built. Such inscriptions would have served admirably as speeches for the foundation ceremonies inaugurating building projects, a setting in which such inscriptions would have been effective vehicles for delivering the king's messages to his people in verbal form before the burial of the documents for audiences in the future.

The Assyrian versions of the building inscriptions describing projects in Babylon are a special case and suggest that at least in some instances, royal inscriptions were presented at other sorts of public gatherings as well, such as the city-wide assembly in Aššur that A. Leo Oppenheim posits as the setting for the presentation of Sargon II's eighth campaign report. The text explicitly addresses the people of the city of Aššur, and Oppenheim has argued that it represents the text of a speech made by the king to the citizens and gods of that city to report to them the results of the king's most recent campaign.[243] Esarhaddon's Babylon B and G texts, found at Nineveh and Assyrian in tone, may well have been publicly presented in similar fashion at such gatherings.

That Esarhaddon's building inscriptions reached contemporary audiences by being read aloud or presented as speeches at public gatherings seems likely in a society, such as that of Assyria and Babylonia, in which most people were unable to read. Mario Liverani, in an essay discussing Assyrian ideology and the mechanisms by which it was communicated, argues that reading aloud was a common method of presenting texts to the Mesopotamian public: "It is obvious . . . ," he says, "that the written message was complemented by other types of messages, in particular the visual one . . . and the oral one. The same written texts were to be orally divulged in ceremonial situations. . . ."[244]

---

[243] A. Leo Oppenheim, "The City of Assur in 714 BC," 133–47. Except for this instance, the vexed question of which other texts currently identified by scholars as "letters to gods" were actually read aloud is not relevant to the present discussion.

[244] Mario Liverani, "The Ideology of the Assyrian Empire," in *Power and Propaganda*, 302.

The idea that written texts were also presented orally is supported by numerous references indicating that reading documents aloud was a common mechanism for communicating information to the public throughout the ancient Near East over a long period of time. A second millennium Hittite treaty between the ruler Muwatalliš and Alaksandus of Wiluša is one example of reading aloud as a means of calling to mind information contained in an important public document; its instructions to the treaty signer include the stipulation, "Moreover, let someone read thee this tablet which I have made for thee three times every year."[245] A passage from the Biblical book of Esther suggests that reading public documents aloud was also the practice later in the Near East, under the Persian empire;[246] it reports that, "A copy of the document [ordering the extermination of the Jews] was to be issued as a decree in every province by proclamation to all peoples to be ready for that day" (Esther 3:14). One suspects that the practice of issuing public orders by oral proclamation, which this passage explicitly mentions, was assumed without comment in many other texts.

In both Israel and Mesopotamia, there are records of so-called "years of release" in which the king, by custom, granted the citizens of his nation exemptions, or release (in Akkadian, *mīšarum*), from certain obligations. In an article discussing such exemptions, Moshe Weinfeld argues that in both Israel and Mesopotamia such years of release were announced by the ruler through public proclamations,[247] citing in support, among other documents, the preamble to the edict of King Ammiṣadūqa of Babylon (1646–1626) which identifies that text as "the tablet (ordered) to hear at the time (the king) established the [*mīšarum*] for the land."[248] Weinfeld notes in addition that the release of property at Nuzi, performed by the king in a festival month in the god's city, was called a *šudûtum*, or "public proclamation" (p. 496).

Literary texts, as well, often mention reading aloud; the beginning of one Mesopotamian epic, for example, calls on its audience to listen: "A song of Bēlet-ili will I sing; oh friend, pay attention! oh warrior, listen!"[249] In similar fashion, a short hymn glorifying the early Assyrian king Tiglath-Pileser I closes with the instruction, "Let the present [generation] hear [this hymn] and

[245] F5, par. 19, III, ll. 73–74, cited in Dennis J. McCarthy, S.J., *Treaty and Covenant: A Study in Form in the Ancient Oriental Documents and in the Old Testament*, 3.

[246] The date of composition of the Book of Esther is debated; it has been argued to be either in the late Persian period, i.e., in the fourth century BC, or alternatively, in the Maccabean period, from the mid-second to mid-first centuries BC. The period in which the story is set is the reign of Xerxes I (485–465 BC), so there is some ambiguity about the period and culture whose social and legal practices are reflected in the story. For a discussion, see Bernhard W. Anderson, *Understanding the Old Testament*, 4th ed. (Englewood Cliffs, N.J.: Prentice-Hall, 1986), 607–610.

[247] Moshe Weinfeld, "Justice and Righteousness," in *Mesopotamien und seine Nachbarn*, 496.

[248] *tuppi [. . .] šami'am [qabi] inūma [šarrum mīšarum] ana mātim iškunu*, 496.

[249] Cited in Claus Wilke, "Die Anfänge der akkadischen Epen," *ZA*, 67 (1977): 154–55.

recite it to the later."[250] The extent to which such literary conventions reflect actual practice is not clear; the significant thing for our purposes is that these texts, too, contain references to reading aloud or reciting as common practice. The Enūma eliš myth is an interesting case in this regard. Not only do its concluding passages similarly exhort the father to "recite and impart to his son" the words of the epic, and urge that the "ears of shepherd and herdsman be opened" to it,[251] but also the instructions for carrying out the ritual of the annual *akītu* festival at Babylon indicate that the exhortation to recite and to hear was, in this case at least, taken literally and the Enūma eliš read aloud once a year during the festival.[252] The expectation that important texts would be read aloud appears from these examples to have been a commonplace throughout the ancient Near East, including Mesopotamia. It seems likely that building inscriptions, like many other types of texts, were presented orally to contemporary audiences.

We have at this point identified several mechanisms by which the texts of Esarhaddon's building inscriptions might have reached contemporary audiences in Assyria and Babylonia, despite their eventual burial as foundation documents. As we have seen, it is clear that they would have reached a contemporary audience of scribes and people at the royal court in the period when the texts were being composed; many of them probably reached an additional audience of temple officials and scribes in Aššur, as well, where copies of several Esarhaddon building inscriptions were deposited in the Ešarra temple and remained unburied. In addition, it seems likely that building inscriptions were also presented orally to a more general audience in the form of speeches or proclamations at public gatherings. The eventual burial of copies of building inscriptions in foundation deposits for future audiences would not in any way have prevented such texts from also reaching contemporary audiences.

That building inscriptions were written in Akkadian, rather than in Aramaic, which was increasingly becoming the vernacular of Mesopotamia, permits a more precise identification of their intended audience. Brinkman, discussing the use of Aramaic by Chaldeans, concludes that by "later Neo-Babylonian and Persian times . . . all the inhabitants of Babylonia used Aramaic as the vernacular"[253]—a change apparently already well under way in

---

[250] Cited by Jacob J. Finkelstein, *Propaganda and Communication in World History*, ed. H.D. Lasswell, et al., 72.

[251] The translation is that of E.A. Speiser in *Ancient Near Eastern Texts Relating to the Old Testament*, 2nd ed., James B. Pritchard, ed., 72.

[252] "Temple Program for the New Year's Festivals at Babylon," A. Sachs, transla., instructions for the fourth day, ll. 280–284 in *Ancient Near Eastern Texts Relating to the Old Testament*, James B. Pritchard, ed., 2nd ed., 332. The text is from the Seleucid period, but the practices it reflects may well be much older.

[253] J.A. Brinkman, *Post-Kassite Babylonia*, 267, n. 1716.

Babylonia by Esarhaddon's time. In an article on the use of Aramaic in Babylonia, Jonas Greenfield concurs, but suggests that Akkadian was probably still
at least comprehensible to certain groups in Babylonia in Esarhaddon's period:

> ... by the later seventh century the country [Babylonia] was highly aramicized—
> that is Aramaic was widespread in the vernacular, without forgetting for a
> moment the survival power of languages long after scholars have pronounced
> them dead. On the whole, the assertion that Babylonian was limited to the
> learned and priestly classes, a sort of clerks' Latin which continued to be used
> for another six hundred years and maintained its influence and position in certain
> areas, is correct.[254]

Tadmor argues that in Assyria also the use of Aramaic was widespread by
Esarhaddon's time.[255] Since Esarhaddon's building inscriptions are written in
Akkadian, not Aramaic, it seems likely that they were directed primarily at
an audience of the elite, who could still either read Akkadian themselves or
had scribes readily available to interpret for them.

This is a conclusion that makes sense politically. People such as scribes,
temple officials, powerful merchants, and administrators, the people in Assyria
who were either literate themselves or regularly employed scribes, were also
the most politically influential people in the kingdom. Their support was essential for controlling Babylonia, for administering the empire effectively, and
for preventing counter-revolution in Assyria. Greenfield's point about the
tenacious survival of languages adds an important qualification to this conclusion, however, because it suggests that to some extent the message of the building inscriptions would also have been comprehensible to the populace as a
whole, rather in the way that the archaic English of the King James Bible is
still relatively comprehensible to modern audiences because they are accus-
tomed to hearing it on ceremonial occasions. The nuances of the texts, however, would certainly have been most evident to the more limited group still
conversant in Akkadian. It was these members of the literate elite in both
states for whom the inscriptions were primarily intended.

We have been tracing in these pages the development of a large-scale, surprisingly modern public relations campaign that began in the first years of
Esarhaddon's rule and focused on presenting carefully differentiated images
of the king to audiences in Assyria and Babylonia, images designed to present
the king in each nation as the embodiment of that nation's own royal traditions. An important early step in this program was the dramatic gesture in
which the king himself appeared in the city of Babylon, and then in the city

---

[254] Jonas Greenfield, "Babylonian-Aramaic Relationship," in *Mesopotamien und seine Nachbarn*,
ed. Hans-Jörg Nissen and Johannes Renger, 471.

[255] Hayim Tadmor, "The Aramization of Assyria: Aspects of Western Impact," in *Mesopotamien
und seine Nachbarn*, 449–470.

of Aššur, symbolically beginning the restoration of the national temple by personally carrying a laborer's basket. The basket-bearing ceremony presented the king as the religious leader of each nation and at the same time linked the king to ancient Mesopotamian royal traditions.

In Babylonia, the ceremony in addition presented Esarhaddon in a role previously reserved for the kings of Babylonia alone, implying that in Esarhaddon's person and under his rule the traditions and national identity of Babylonia would be preserved and honored. At the same time, royal inscriptions presented in Babylonia further developed the image of Esarhaddon as a traditional and legitimate Babylonian ruler.

This image of the king, presented in the early texts written for the south, was hardly the message Esarhaddon wished to convey to the Assyrians, however, and Esarhaddon's early building inscriptions for Assyrian building projects present the king in a different light, as a traditional Assyrian ruler faithful to the needs of his people. Even the building inscriptions for Babylon were recast in special Assyrian versions to justify the rebuilding of Babylon to the Assyrians and to reassure them that despite his attentions to Babylon, Esarhaddon remained an unmistakably Assyrian king, properly critical of the Babylonians, but willing to be the agent of the gods' mercy toward them if the gods so required. Such texts represent the other side of the coin, the message Esarhaddon directed at the north in the early days of his reign.

The multifaceted public relations effort in both areas was essential to Esarhaddon's survival. In Assyria, it was a central element of the effort to stabilize his initially precarious position as a king who had come to power only by seizing the throne from his brothers. In Babylonia, it was designed to begin the slow process of diminishing the Babylonians' resistance to Assyrian rule, laying the foundations on which Esarhaddon could attempt to build a closer relationship between Babylonia and her northern conquerors.

CHAPTER SIX

Toward the Development of
a Single National Image

BY THE MIDDLE YEARS OF HIS REIGN, ESARHAD-
don had evidently begun to achieve a considerable degree of
acceptance in Babylonia as well as in Assyria. When he came to
the throne in 681, the prospects of any real acceptance of Assyrian rule by the
Babylonians must have seemed remote. Sennacherib's devastating attack on
Babylon had occurred only eight years earlier, and the Babylonians, led by
Bīt-Jakīn, were once again in active revolt. By some five years into Esarhaddon's reign, however, the situation had changed. Bīt-Jakīn, having made its
peace with Assyria at the very beginning of the reign, had apparently remained a faithful ally despite considerable temptations. Two attempted con-
spiracies against the Assyrians (organized by provincial governors in Nippur
in alliance with leaders of the Bīt-Dakkūri tribe in 678 and 675) had both
failed to produce an uprising.[256] Instead, Babylonia in the first half of
Esarhaddon's reign had remained essentially quiet under Assyrian rule, in
contrast to the turbulent resistance to Assyria that had marked much of the
reigns of Sargon and Sennacherib.[257] Even with the Assyrians distracted by an
attempted uprising in the west in 677, in the past often a signal for revolt, the
Babylonians had continued peacefully about their business.[258] The change
that was occurring in the relations between Babylonia and Assyria by the
middle of Esarhaddon's reign was a quiet one, but that a change was beginning
seems clear.

In the early years Esarhaddon seems, despite his turbulent accession to the

---

[256] See above, pp. 5–6. The incidents are reported in Chr. 1, iv, ll. 1–2 and 14–15; Chr. 14,
ll. 10–11 and 19; and Nin. A and B, Ep. 12.

[257] Six economic documents from Babylon dating from the years 678 to 675 use Esarhaddon's
name in their dating formulae, a mark of legal acceptance of his reign in that city at a fairly early
period. Eight texts from Dilbat, most dated between 675 and 672, and five from Uruk, most dated
between 675 and 673, indicate recognition of his rule in those cities in subsequent years. A total
of thirty Babylonian economic texts from Esarhaddon's reign use his name in dating formulae, a
mark of widespread formal acceptance of his rule in the ancient cities of Babylonia. These date
formulae refer to Esarhaddon as "king" ten times, "king of Assyria" eight times, "king of the uni-
verse" five times, "king of the lands" twice and "king of Babylonia" twice—both of these latter
dated at Babylon (Frame, "Babylonia," Table 1 and p. 70).

[258] This uprising, led by the king of Sidon, collapsed with the fall of Sidon in 677. It is described
in Nin. A–F, Ep. 5, Chr. 1, iv, ll. 3 and 6–7, and Chr. 14, ll. 12 and 14.

throne, to have achieved widespread acceptance as king in Assyria, as well. The documentary evidence from his reign shows no sign of problems in Assyria in the king's early years. Perhaps the momentum of Esarhaddon's rather spectacular success in defeating his brothers and winning the allegiance of their soldiers at Ḫanigalbat had captured the imagination of the Assyrians and made the majority of them willing, at least initially, to support the promising new king. His summary punishment of the few of his brothers' supporters who had not fled the country would have further discouraged any other response.[259] Esarhaddon's position in Assyria in the first few years had been further strengthened by early successes in military affairs: he defeated groups of Cimmerians and Manneans, invaded the exotic distant land of Bāzu, and conducted a very successful campaign in the west to defeat the Phoenician-led uprising.[260] In addition, the king's assiduous attentions to building projects in Assyria, supported by the image of the king presented in his royal inscriptions for Assyria, may also have contributed to what appears to have been a broad acceptance of his rule in Assyria in the early years of the reign.

The growing acceptance of his rule in both states made it feasible for the king and his advisers to begin to introduce further modifications in Esarhaddon's still-controversial Babylonian policy as time passed, subtly encouraging both groups to accept the concept of greater unity between them. The mechanisms chosen for encouraging this change in attitude were of two kinds: first, a gradual change in the language of the royal inscriptions so that they began increasingly to address the two groups in almost identical terms, as if to imply that Assyrians and Babylonians constituted in essence a single audience, united by common interests; and second, an effort to focus attention on the figure of the Babylonian god Marduk, already worshipped to some extent in Assyria, and to propose to the Assyrians a subtly changed image of the god that would permit him to become a major focus of worship in both states and an emblem of their divinely-approved unity. These two developments mark the final stages in Esarhaddon's program to draw Assyria and Babylonia into a lasting peaceful union under Assyrian rule. Since the changes introduced in the language of Esarhaddon's royal inscriptions for the two states were the first of these developments to appear, we will begin our examination of the later stages of Esarhaddon's public relations program with an analysis of these, turning later to examine the enhanced role of Marduk as the final step in Esarhaddon's efforts to develop support for his policy of reconciliation and unification.

One factor that may have influenced the decision to introduce this new theme in the second half of the reign was the growing pressure to name an

[259] Nin. A, Ep. 2, ii, ll. 8–11.
[260] The defeat of the Cimmerians is recorded in Chr. 14, l. 9, and placed there in 679; the defeat of the Manneans is mentioned in Nin. B7 and thus occurred before 676; the Bāzu campaign is placed in 676 by both Chr. 1 and Chr. 14; and the fall of Sidon is placed in 677 in both chronicles.

heir for Esarhaddon, who suffered from an increasingly troublesome chronic illness,[261] and the somewhat surprising choice of not one, but two sons as his future heirs, one to rule as king of Assyria, the other to rule in a subordinate role as king of Babylonia. This proposed arrangement for the succession, whose significance for Esarhaddon's policies we will later consider at greater length, meant that after Esarhaddon's death the figure of the Assyrian king would become a much less effective emblem of the union of the two states, since the role of king of Babylonia would be filled by a separate individual. These arrangements for the succession, announced in public ceremonies in both states in 672, required a change in the emphasis of Esarhaddon's public relations program, from its initial focus on the figure of the king himself to a greater emphasis instead on the unity of the Assyrian and Babylonian people.

This new emphasis first begins to be apparent in inscriptions composed in the middle years of Esarhaddon's reign. Its characteristics are most easily recognizable, however, in its final, fully developed form, in a series of inscriptions written almost at the end of the reign that address the Assyrians and Babylonians as a single audience, describing projects in both nations evenhandedly and in alternation, or even together in a single passage. In the interests of clarity, we will begin our analysis of the changing emphasis in the rhetoric of Esarhaddon's inscriptions with these later texts and will then look back to trace the gradual development of this theme in earlier texts.

As an example of a late inscription that emphasizes the unity of Assyrians and Babylonians, we start with the AsBbA inscription, one of the longest and best preserved of the texts Borger labels the "Assur/Babylon" group, so called because they take the unusual tack of dealing with projects in both cities in a single inscription.[262] The description of Esarhaddon in the introduction of the AsBbA inscription as king of the kings of Ethiopia (obv., ll. 28–29) places the composition of the text almost at the end of Esarhaddon's reign, after the successful Egyptian campaign of 671. There is no indication of the occasion for which AsBbA was written, but a subscript appended to it describes it as the "first excerpt" from a text that was inscribed "on the left stele,"[263] an indication that the text was intended for use on a monument and thus represents a formal, public document. Although both copies of the text were probably found in Nineveh[264] (which might suggest an Assyrian audience) there is, sig-

---

[261] See Parpola's extensive comments on the nature and course of this illness, tentatively diagnosed as lupus, in *Letters*, IIb, 229–238.

[262] See Borger's comments on these texts, 78–79. Although he includes the text AsBbG in this group, I will discuss it in a later context instead because it alone of Borger's AsBb group deals not with the reconstruction work on Ešarra and Esagila or the return of the gods, but rather with the king's dedication of his eldest son Šamaš-šuma-ukīn to the gods Marduk and Ṣarpanītum, a possibly related but nevertheless quite different topic.

[263] *ša eli a-su-mit-ti ša šumēli nis-ḫu maḫ(?)-ru(?)-u(?)*, (AsBbA, Unterschrift, following rs., l. 56).

[264] For the provenance of these texts, see Appendix IV.

nificantly, little or no indication in the tone or topics of the text of whether an Assyrian or Babylonian audience was intended; the AsBbA inscription addresses Assyrians and Babylonians throughout as one people, reflecting the interests of both.

This unifying approach makes itself felt from the outset, as the text begins with a list of gods who, it says, chose Esarhaddon for kingship (obv., ll. 1–21); the Babylonian gods Nabû and Marduk are included without comment among the more traditional gods of Assyria. While both Marduk and Nabû were by this time widely worshipped in Assyria, a point we will consider further below, both gods retained their strong Babylonian associations, with their main cult centers still located in cities in the Babylonian south. The brief list of royal titles that follows the god list (ll. 22 ff.) acknowledges Esarhaddon as king of both Assyria and Babylonia and is followed by references first to the goddess Tašmētum (wife of Nabû and a prominent figure in the Baby-lonian pantheon) and then to Ištar of Nineveh and Ištar of Arbela, important Assyrian goddesses.

The balance of northern and southern elements continues in the royal epithets. Esarhaddon is addressed, for example, as the king who "fears the word of Aššur, Nabû, (and) Marduk" (l. 30), and further on, the text asserts Esarhaddon's ties to the ancient origins of kingship in a phrase that again evokes the traditions of both states in a single line, calling him *zēr šarrūti dārû pir'i Baltil^ki*, that is, "lasting seed of kingship, scion of Baltil" (l. 35). The phrase "lasting seed of kingship" is a Babylonian royal epithet originating in the times of the ancient Sumerian kings,[265] while the phrase "scion of Baltil," links Esarhaddon to one of the most revered of Assyrian holy places, Baltil, the precincts of the god Aššur in the city of Aššur. The epithets continue the interweaving of Assyrian and Babylonian elements, first referring to Esarhad-don as "precious one, beloved of Ešarra" (l. 35b), the temple of Aššur in As-syria, and then immediately calling him, "he of the pure hands, *išippu* priest, who cleaned the statues of the great gods (of Babylon)" (ll. 35b–36a). In the same vein, the epithets characterize him first as "builder of the temple of Aššur" and then, in the same passage, as "the maker of Esagila and Babylon

---

[265] For a discussion of this title, see Wilfred G. Lambert, "The Seed of Kingship," in *Le Palais et la royauté*, 427–440. In the south, the phrase first appears in the time of the Sumerian kings of the Ur III dynasty (late third millennium), who used it, Lambert argues, as a claim to divine parent-age. Later, during the time of the First Dynasty of Babylon (1894–1595), it began to be used in claiming royal legitimacy by descent from earlier kings. The phrase was later adopted by several kings of the Kassite dynasty of Babylonia (1375–1157), was used in the post-Kassite Babylonian "Kedor-laomer" poems, disappeared for some time, and was then revived by Merodach-Baladan II (721–710 and 703), immediately before Esarhaddon's time.

Assyrian kings used the phrase "seed of kingship" from the thirteenth century on, in asserting their legitimacy as descendants of ancient kings of Assyria. The expanded phrase used by Esar-haddon, "lasting seed of kingship," first appears in the reign of Aššur-bēl-kala (1074–1057). The phrase was thus southern in origin, but had become accepted in Assyrian titulary, as well.

who returned the plundered gods of the lands to their places" (l. 36b–37). Esar-haddon is also called "the one who makes fast the exemptions of Baltil" (in Aššur) and then "the establisher of the freedoms of Nippur, Babylon, Bor-sippa and Sippar" (l. 41), all cities of Babylonia. He is called the king who reassembles the scattered Babylonians (l. 43), and also the king whom the god Aššur makes victor over the enemies of the land of Aššur (l. 44). Woven throughout the epithets is a consistent balance of elements designed to appeal alternately to Assyrians and Babylonians. The final passage of the introduction (ll. 47–51) epitomizes the entire section by characterizing Esarhaddon first as the descendant of a long line of Assyrian kings, and then remarking that it is the Babylonian god Marduk who has called him to rule! The figure of the king is central to the AsBbA text, as it was central to Esarhaddon's earlier in-scriptions, but here the king himself is an emblem of unity; the introduction presents the king not as the ruler of one or the other state, but as a ruler who combines Assyrian and Babylonian kingship in his own person.

In the body of the narrative, the balance of Assyrian and Babylonian ele-ments continues. The subject of the AsBbA text is the repair and adornment of the statues of various gods, principally Babylonian gods carried off after Sennacherib's attack on Babylon, a potentially divisive point which the text passes over in silence.[266] As the account begins (obv., ll. 52 ff.), Esarhaddon takes the throne, and "with the wisdom (given him) by Aššur and Marduk" (rs., l. 12) conceives the idea of renewing the statues of the great gods.

The text continues by indicating that the making of statues of gods, even at the command of the gods themselves, was considered an audacious under-taking for men (rs., ll. 14–17); an appropriate site for the work was therefore to be chosen by the gods themselves, who were to indicate their choice through liver omens. The choices offered the gods included two northern sites, the city of Nineveh and the Baltil section of the city of Aššur, and one southern site, Babylon (rs., ll. 20–21). Although Esarhaddon was loading the dice somewhat in favor of Assyrian sites, for reasons which will later become clear, it is important that Babylon was offered as a choice: Assyria and Baby-lonia were both represented. We are told that the gods' choice fell, not sur-

---

[266] There is some ambiguity about whether Marduk's statue had been destroyed or only carried off. Sennacherib's inscriptions report destruction of the statues (Bavian Inscription, OIP, 2, p. 83, l. 48: ". . . the gods dwelling therein [i.e., in Babylon]—the hands of the people took them, and they smashed them"; *bīt akīti* Inscription, OIP, 2, p. 137, ll. 36 f., "after I had destroyed Babylon, (and) had smashed the gods thereof . . ."), but Assurbanipal's inscriptions refer to "the great lord Marduk who, in the reign of an earlier king, had sat before the father his creator in the midst of Aššur . . ." (Streck, *Assurbanipal*, 242, ll. 24–26), suggesting the statue of Marduk had survived and was in Aššur in Esarhaddon's reign. Esarhaddon's inscriptions also assume the survival of the statue. For further discussion, see B. Landsberger, *Brief des Bischofs*, 20–27. For our purposes, whether the statues were being made from scratch or reconstructed from the remains of the original statues, the theological and political significance of Esarhaddon's actions remains the same.

prisingly, on the temple workshops in Aššur, where work began as soon as workmen and precious goods could be assembled.

In describing the work itself, the text continues the balance of Assyrian and Babylonian elements. Since most of the statues being restored were Babylonian, the scribe maintains the even-handedness of his account by inserting an unexpected excursus describing the making of a crown for the god Aššur:

> A cunningly made crown, symbol of the rule [of] Aššur, king of the gods, my lord, I caused to be made of red gold and precious stones, and I returned it to its place. That crown—dressed in light, adorned with dignity, possessed of glittering brightness, clothed with light—greatly pleased Aššur, the great lord; his heart was contented and his face glowed (rs., ll. 32b–34).

With this concession to Assyrian interests completed, the scribe at last describes the reconstruction of the statues, the event for which the twenty-three previous lines of text serve as an elaborate introduction. The adornment of the statues of the gods Bēl (an alternate name for Marduk), Bēltiya (his consort), Bēlet Bābili, Ea and Madānu is described in rich detail: ". . . with red *zāriru*, the product of Arallû, dust of its mountains, I made their forms lordly. With lofty ornament and precious jewels I adorned their necks" (ll. 36b–37a), and so forth. The elaborate language of the passage recalls the passage describing the making of Aššur's crown and provides a balance to it.

The passage describing the actual construction of the statues reveals a new aspect of the project: "(The gods) Bēl, Bēltiya, Bēlet Bābili, Ea (and) Madānu, great gods, were truly born in the midst of Ešarra, the house of their father, and (their) form was comely" (rs., ll. 35–36). The significant point is that Ešarra, the temple of Aššur, is here characterized as the "house of their father," and the reconstruction of the statues is represented as a kind of birth, a traditional usage in descriptions of the construction of statues. But in this case the metaphor was extended: by being "born" in Ešarra, the text asserts, the gods of Babylon would become in some sense Aššur's children. The political and theological implications of such a statement were considerable; the text was in effect proposing the adoption of major Babylonian gods, including Bēl/Marduk himself, into the Assyrian pantheon. This idea had been foreshadowed in the text's introduction, where Aššur was called "father of the gods" (*ab ilāni*, obv., l. 1), and Marduk "first heir" (*aplu rēštû*, obv., l. 8), an epithet usually accorded the eldest son and heir of a household. By extension, the text implies that the Assyrians and Babylonians were also being drawn into a new and closer relationship, through the now closer genealogical relationship of the patron gods who symbolized the two nations, and through their shared veneration of Marduk, who was now to be officially one of the most important figures in the pantheons of both nations. Implicit in the formulation, however, was not only the offer of an enhanced position in Assyrian eyes for Marduk (and by implication, for the Babylonians he represented), but also a clear statement of the limits of the enhanced status they were being offered. Marduk and his divine colleagues were being assigned permanent positions of great honor in the Assyrian pantheon as children of Aššur, but within that pantheon Aššur was to remain the father, while Marduk would take on a subordinate role as his son—a clear statement of the hierarchical relationship between Assyria and Babylonia envisioned in Esarhaddon's Babylonian policies, a relationship with Babylonia uniquely honored within the empire, but with Assyria firmly occupying the dominant position.

Since the crucial phrase identifying Ešarra as the "house of their father" appears only in this account of the statues' reconstruction and is missing in the only other surviving account of the reconstruction (the AsBbE text, discussed below), it seems probable that the AsBbA text was intended to present the story of the rebuilding, and the image of a unified Assyrian and Babylonian people that permeates the text as a whole, to an Assyrian audience. The AsBbE text, which omits the phrase, would seem more appropriate for a Babylonian audience, who would probably have found the proposed rearrangement of their chief gods' genealogy offensive.[267] This remains conjectural, however, since there is no clear indication in either text of its intended geographical setting and since the evenhanded tone of the texts offers no internal clue to their intended audience.

After describing the reconstruction of the statues, the AsBbA text reports that a throne and footstool for Nabû's consort were also constructed, and that in addition statues of several minor gods were repaired (ll. 39 ff.). These significantly included not only Il-Amurrû from Esagila of Babylon, but also Abšušu and Abtagigi from a temple in Nineveh, once again balancing. The text underlines the effect of balance by commenting that Esarhaddon restored these statues "and whatever gods and goddesses Aššur and Marduk commanded . . ." (l. 41b), reiterating the idea that his activities were being conducted at the command of the gods of both nations.

The rhetorical balance is made even clearer as the text goes on to describe preparations for the work of restoring the temples Eḫursaggalkurkurra (an alternate name for Ešarra) and Esagila. The events described in this passage and even the phrases used are already familiar to us from earlier inscriptions that described these same preparations for rebuilding Ešarra and Esagila in separate texts. What is different here is that the AsBbA inscription is now returning to those events in order to describe them as if they had been part of a single, unified project:

---

[267] In the past, I have argued that these two texts give no indication of their intended audience. For this modification in my position, I am indebted to the prodding of Prof. Robert C. Hunt of Brandeis University, who persistently observed from his vantage point as an anthropologist that the Babylonians would scarcely have found this rearrangement of their patron god's genealogy appealing.

> In a favorable month, on a propitious day, the foundations of Eḫursaggalkurkurra, bond (of) heaven and earth, dwelling of Aššur, king of the gods, my lord, and those of Esagila, palace of the gods, dwelling of the great lord Marduk (of) Babylon—city which is the seat of his godhead—upon gold, silver, abundant herbs, honey, fine oil, *karānu*-wine and *kurunnu*-beer . . ., together I laid their foundations (rs., ll. 46b–48).

Since the earliest building inscription for the Aššur temple is dated almost a full year after the earliest Esagila inscription, and since the two cities were located some 200 miles apart, the idea that the two projects began at the same time and that their foundations were laid "together" requires a strenuous act of the imagination. This passage is the climax of the text and suggests a strong desire on the part of the scribe to connect the projects in the minds of his readers, however separate the projects may have been in actuality.[268]

The concluding passage that follows, now partly broken, shifts attention briefly to Marduk ("Marduk, the great lord, noted the making of the sanctuary of his lofty godhead in all its aspects, and in order to show the people the mightiness of his acts and to teach [them] the glory of his godhead, . . . I made(?) a raging dragon. . . ." [ll. 49 ff.]), and then ends with a now fragmentary passage that once again balances Assyrian and Babylonian concerns: "Marduk, great lord . . . Aššur, my lord . . . his head" (ll. 55–56). Although its account of the rebuilding of Marduk's statue includes a subtle reminder of Assyria's dominant role in the relationship, the text consistently invokes both Assyrian and Babylonian gods, implying that they are part of the same pantheon, and through both subject matter and presentation suggests that Assyrians and Babylonians can be addressed together as a single audience.

By taking it as a given that Assyrians and Babylonians share an interest in each others' temples and gods and can be addressed as a single audience, the AsBbA text implies that the two are in essence one people, united not only by a common ruler, but also by a common outlook and interests, an assertion that had considerable basis in fact. The two nations spoke the same language, with only slightly different dialects, and to a great extent shared a common cultural and technological tradition as well. Modern political theorists emphasize the importance of such shared elements of culture and outlook in forging a sense of common nationality.[269] By projecting an image of Assyrians and Babylonians as one people, the AsBbA text reinforces in its audience a sense of community and encourages them to think of them-

---

[268] The earliest dated Ešarra inscription, Assur A4, is dated to Simānu (May/June) of 679; a second copy, Assur A1c, is dated to Du'ūzu (June/July), probably in the same year, since the inscriptions are identical and no separate year date was added. The first Esagila inscription, Babylon G, is dated to Ajāru (April/May) of the year 680, almost a year earlier than Assur A4.

[269] See, for example, the comments of Karl Deutsch, *Nationalism and Social Communication: An Inquiry into the Foundations of Nationality*, 1–14.

selves, and therefore to act, as distinct but interdependent parts of a single nation.

The presentation of a common national image to Assyrians and Babylonians in the AsBbA text was not an isolated occurrence; it is characteristic of several other inscriptions, as well, most of which can be dated to the late years of Esarhaddon's reign. The majority of the texts in Borger's "Assur/Babylon" group, for instance, seem to be characterized by this unified approach. Although several of them (AsBbB, AsBbC, AsBbD, and AsBbF) are fragmentary, making an analysis of their overall tone difficult,[270] the AsBbE inscription has fortunately survived nearly intact, permitting us to examine in detail a second major inscription that consistently interweaves Assyrian and Babylonian elements in a single text.

Like AsBbA, the AsBbE inscription can be dated to 671 or later by its reference to Esarhaddon's successful Egyptian campaign of that year, and like AsBbA, it deals mainly with the reconstruction of the temples Ešarra and Esagila, showing no trace of bias in favor of either Assyria or Babylonia in its account. The text consists of an introduction followed by two balanced main sections, the first describing Esarhaddon's restoration of Ešarra in Assyria, and the second describing Esarhaddon's restoration of Esagila in Babylon along with the restoration and return of its gods' statues. Here again, the two temple restoration projects are described as occurring at the same time, as if to emphasize the king's evenhandedness in dealing with the two nations. Even in descriptions of the two nations' gods, the AsBbE text maintains a neutral position, calling Aššur simply "Aššur, my lord," and Marduk and his consort, "the gods who love one another,"[271] epithets that avoid referring to either god as head of a national pantheon. The concluding passage describing the return of Babylon's gods, restored in Assyria and returned in honor to Babylonia, is used to lend theological support to the dominant theme of the AsBbE text, that under Esarhaddon's control, the temples and gods of both Assyria and Babylonia would be cared for and respected as if the religious welfare of both nations were of equal importance. Like AsBbA, the AsBbE inscription treats Assyrians and Babylonians as if they were one people, balancing the interests of both in an integrated account that is free of national bias—a striking departure from the pattern of separate and distinctive inscriptions composed for Babylonia and Assyria that characterized the beginning years of the reign.

Both the evidence of their colophons and the locations in which the

---

[270] AsBbG (as mentioned in n. 262 above) and AsBbH are also included by Borger among his "Assur/Babylon" texts, but I have not discussed them here because these two fragments as extant deal exclusively with Babylon, and it remains unclear whether they were originally part of texts that dealt with Aššur, as well. Although I have excluded them, their inclusion would not in any case alter my argument.

[271] *dBēl ù dBēlti-ia ilāni^meš mur-ta-a-me* (rs., l. 11).

various "Assur/Babylon" texts were discovered suggest that these texts do not represent a single set of inscriptions designed for some specific occasion, but are instead texts composed for use in a variety of different situations and probably in different locations, as well. AsBbA, for example, was found in Nineveh and, as we have seen, carries a subscript that identifies it as a text that was inscribed on a stele. AsBbE, found among a group of texts in the Ešarra temple at Aššur, is inscribed on an alabaster tablet, suggesting it was intended for use as a foundation deposit or as a formal record, while AsBbF, found at Nineveh, is identified in its colophon as a copy of the inscription on a pedestal supporting a statue of the god Bēl.[272]

Clearly the texts were intended for use in different settings. Whether they were intended for different audiences, as well, is more difficult to establish but seems to me probable, as I have already suggested in the case of the two longest texts, AsBbA and AsBbE. In addition, the AsBbF text, since it was intended to accompany a statue of Marduk, was very probably meant for display in Marduk's main temple (Esagila, in Babylon); its other possible site, Marduk's temple in Nineveh, seems to have been a much less important religious center, rarely mentioned even in Assyrian texts. AsBbF, then, seems to have been meant for a Babylonian audience.

The locations in which the texts were discovered are in this case not particularly helpful as indications of possible intended audience. While all of the "Assur-Babylon" texts were probably found in Assyria, one in Aššur and the rest probably in Nineveh, this is not necessarily an indication that they were meant for use there, since all but one of the texts are copied on clay tablets, suggesting that most of them represent archival records of texts, rather than the actual main copies of the documents, which could have been used anywhere. The one exception is the AsBbE inscription, which is inscribed on an alabaster tablet and thus is probably the formal document itself; it seems likely that this text, which omits the assertion that Marduk had now become Aššur's son, was intended for Babylon, rather than for Aššur, where it was found.

In addition to the "Assur/Babylon" texts, another late inscription,[273] which Borger calls the "Sammeltext," shows the same careful mix of Assyrian and Babylonian elements evident in the texts discussed above. The "Sammeltext" is almost unique among Assyrian royal inscriptions because it does not focus on a single building project, or even on two projects, like the AsBb inscriptions, but instead presents a panorama of royal temple building projects and donations in cities throughout Assyria and Babylonia, moving back and

---

[272] [i-n]a muḫḫi ki-gal-li ša ᵈBēl šà-tir (iv, l. 13). For the provenance of all these texts, see Appendix IV.

[273] Smlt. should be dated to 671 or later because of its reference to "booty from Egypt and Ethiopia" (obv., l. 28b).

forth freely without special attention to either area. After an introductory passage, now missing, the text begins its account on neutral ground, with a brief reference to the founding of a new city, Kār-Esarhaddon, on the site of a conquered city on the Mediterranean. It then describes the decoration of temples in Babylonia with booty from Egypt, moves to Assyria for the reconstruction of the Emašmaš temple of Nineveh, returns to Babylonia for a description of work on the Ezida temple of Borsippa, and then turns north again to describe work on the Assyrian temple of Ištar in Arbela, weaving in an assortment of other pious undertakings on the way. Throughout the text, the gods and building projects of both Assyria and Babylonia receive equal attention and respect as a matter of course, and national bias is consistently avoided.[274] Like the "Assur/Babylon" texts, the "Sammeltext" is a significant departure from the earlier building inscriptions we examined because it seems designed to appeal equally to Assyrians and Babylonians and to present to this audience a single, undifferentiated image of the king and his activities. The implication is once again that the two peoples represent in effect a single audience. Both surviving copies of the text are inscribed on clay tablets found at Nineveh, but the setting in which they were meant to be used, whether in Assyria or Babylonia, is unclear.

Most other Esarhaddon inscriptions adopt a position that lies part way between the position of these late documents and that of the early texts, suggesting that there was a gradual shift toward the integrated approach that characterizes the late inscriptions. Although a few texts from the intermediate years, such as Babylon C and E, retain the early pattern of a clear separation of audiences,[275] most texts that can be dated to the intermediate years show an increasingly even-handed treatment of Assyrian and Babylonian motifs and an increasingly integrated approach to the two audiences.

Nineveh B and Calah A, two long building inscriptions both probably used as foundation deposits in the Assyrian cities where they were found, and both dated to 676, are examples of such transitional texts from the middle years

---

[274] This is particularly evident in the epithets assigned the gods. Aššur, for instance, is called *bēlu rabû* (obv., l. 27), *bēli-ia* (obv., l. 29), and *šar ilāni*[meš] (obv., l. 31). Nabû is initially *bēli-ia* (rs., l. 1). Ninlil of Nineveh is called *bēlti-ia* (rs., l. 4). Nabû and Tašmētum, mentioned together, are not assigned epithets (rs., l. 6). Nabû of Borsippa is then called the god "to whom is entrusted the whole heavens and earth" (*pa-qid kiš-šat šamê erṣetim*[tim] [rs., l. 13]). Ištar of Arbela is simply *be-el-ti* ("my lady") (rs., l. 19), despite the claim that it was she who granted Esarhaddon kingship greater than that of his forebears (rs., l. 19). In short, no special emphasis is placed on any one god, Assyrian or Babylonian, although Aššur is once acknowledged as "king of the gods" (obv., l. 31). To counter even this epithet, however, the same passage (obv., ll. 28–34) deals with the adornment of Babylonian temples and the granting of privileges to people who had been scattered (l. 34), presumably the Babylonians.

[275] For the dating of Babylon C to 674 and Babylon E to about the same period, see Appendix II. The two texts are late versions of building inscriptions composed at the very beginning of the reign and retain the pattern established in those texts.

of the reign prepared for Assyrian audiences. Although each incorporates both Assyrian and Babylonian elements in its introduction, the body of each text emphasizes the national and local interests of the city where the construction work described was taking place.[276] The introduction to the Nineveh B text, for instance, calls Esarhaddon "great king, mighty king, king of all, king of the land of Assyria," all standard Assyrian titles, and follows these with titles and epithets which identify him as ruler of Babylonia, as well. The introduction to the Calah A text shows a similar balance of Assyrian and Babylonian elements.

In the narrative portions of both texts, however, this balance is rarely apparent. Instead, their summaries of the king's military achievements and their accounts of his construction of an arsenal and palace in Assyria show a consistently Assyrian outlook. In the account of the king's military undertakings presented in Nineveh B, for example, it is the god Aššur in whom Esarhaddon is said to "put his trust" in battling his enemy Sanduarri (i, l. 45), Aššur who overwhelms the Gambūlu lord Bēl-iqīša with fear (iii, l. 41), and Aššur whose might is praised in the inscription Esarhaddon sends to the land of Bāzu (iii, ll. 21–31). Although there are occasional references to favors granted to Babylonia (e.g., ii, l. 41 and iv, ll. 21–31), these references are the exception, and comments about the Babylonians and their gods are laid aside entirely in the account of the building of the Nineveh arsenal that forms the body of the text. Instead, it is the god Aššur whose mighty deeds are represented in the relief placed in the arsenal; Aššur, Ištar, and the great gods of Assyria who are invited into the palace for its dedication; and Aššur and "the gods of Assyria, all of them," who are appealed to for the final blessing that concludes the text.

The body of the Calah A text is equally Assyrian in tone, representing the king's military successes as contributions to Assyria's welfare and consistently attributing the king's success to the help given him by the Assyrian gods. The account of the construction of the arsenal at Calaḫ, which is the main focus of the text, presents Aššur as the king's patron god; prisoners working on the arsenal are said to have been captured "through the help of Aššur, my lord" (l. 41), and the text concludes by noting that texts deposited in the new palace were inscribed with "the might of Aššur, my lord" (ll. 56–57). Like Nineveh B, the Calah A text presents a balance of Assyrian and Babylonian elements only in its introductory titulary; in the body of the text its outlook is almost entirely Assyrian.

---

[276] The other dated building inscriptions for Assyrian sites (Nineveh A, dated to 673 and 672, and Tarbisu A, dated to 672) similarly show a balance of Assyrian and Babylonian elements in titulary and epithets and a contrasting regional outlook in their narratives. Nineveh G, dated to 677, shows a similar balance of elements in the introductory titles and epithets, but the body of the text is badly broken; it probably dealt (as Borger suggests, p. 66) with an Assyrian subject, the construction work on the Emašmaš temple in Nineveh, also described in Nineveh I.

This combination of Assyrian and Babylonian elements in introductory passages and a contrasting local outlook in the body of the text emerges as a characteristic pattern in several texts written for Babylonia, as well. The Uruk A and Nippur A texts, for example, two nearly identical inscriptions each commemorating the construction of a Babylonian temple, again balance Assyrian and Babylonian elements in their introductory titles and epithets, and follow this with a narrative which is by contrast consistently Babylonian in outlook and interests, in each case describing the construction of a temple on Babylonian soil and honoring the Babylonian patron deity of that temple. Although neither text can be precisely dated, both were probably composed in the middle years of the reign, since the two texts are closely related to the text of the Calah A inscription of 676 and since both contain references to the return of Marduk, a theme that appears most frequently in texts from the second half of the reign. Like their northern counterparts, Uruk A and Nippur A reflect a unified outlook in the introductory framework of the text, but still reflect a provincial point of view in their main narrative, suggesting that in Babylonia as well as in Assyria the emphasis in inscriptions was changing, but changing gradually.

This survey suggests that the changes in emphasis followed a roughly chronological pattern, although the problems in dating many of these inscriptions exactly make it difficult to date the stages of this development with any precision. Since the period of time we are considering here is relatively short, we would not in any case expect to find a fully developed and consistent pattern of changes in attitude, but at most some gradual shifts in emphasis, and this is in fact what the texts suggest. Inscriptions from the early years of the reign, such as Assur A and Babylon A, show a careful differentiation in their approach to Assyrian and Babylonian audiences and present a quite different message to the two groups. A few later texts, such as Babylon C and E, composed in 674 or later, still reflect this different approach to the two audiences despite their relatively late date, but most inscriptions from the middle years of the reign show the beginnings of a change, with introductory passages that now balance Assyrian and Babylonian concerns, but with a main narrative that retains the earlier provincial outlook. In the final years of the reign, a balanced and integrated approach to the two groups emerges more and more clearly. In late texts such as the AsBbA and AsBbE inscriptions and the "Sammeltext," the idea of a single king ruling both nations is no longer the sole element presented as unifying Assyria and Babylonia. Instead the entire narrative addresses Assyrians and Babylonians as a single community, weaving an integrated account that presents an image of the two nations as essentially one people.

One reason for introducing this new emphasis in the inscriptions may have been a desire to prod members of the power elite in both states toward acceptance of the closer cooperation between Assyria and Babylonia that was already beginning to be a political reality. Some scholars have gone so far as to argue that there was by this time a coherent pro-Babylonian faction at the Assyrian court, supporting the king's policy of greater unity with Babylonia, although opposed by a nationalist Assyrian party which continued to resist the idea of closer political and cultural relations. Although there were certainly conflicts in the cultural sphere about the appropriate relationship between the two states' traditions, I can see no clear evidence for the existence of coherent pro- and anti-Babylonian political factions at the court, whether related to these cultural opinions, or purely political in origin.[277] There is, rather, evidence of differences of opinion among individual advisers, some advocating a hard line toward Babylonia and others a more conciliatory stance, but I can see no evidence that people who shared such opinions were ever organized into coherent factions. Nor is it clear that either group should be thought of as less devoted to Assyria's national self-interests than the other; they seem simply to have been advocating different strategies for achieving Assyrian control over Babylonia. One adviser, for example, urges Esarhaddon to name a Babylonian as the next substitute king, commenting, "[the king my lord] knows the Babylonians . . .; [the]se plotters should be affli[cted]!" (LAS 185); his attitude is an example of the more obdurate approach to Babylonia. On the other hand, the adviser who tells the king about an alleged uprising in Babylon (whose occurrence he denies) in which people supposedly had thrown clods of dirt at the Assyrian commandant in protest against the imposition of more taxes, comments sympathetically that the citizens of Babylon are "poor wretches who have got nothing," and is clearly urging a lenient approach (LAS 276). Both writers, however, from all appearances, are equally committed to advancing Assyria's best interests; they simply differ in their opinions of how to go about it. Although there were clearly differences of opinion in Assyria both about Babylonian policy and about Babylonian culture, the growing acceptance of Esarhaddon as ruler in both Assyria and Babylonia by the middle years of the reign made it possible for him increasingly to urge both Assyrians and Babylonians to accept the idea of themselves as in essence a single people, despite some lingering resistance to closer relations within both groups.

[277] On the existence of such "parties," see Benno Landsberger and Theo Bauer, "Zu neu-veröffentlichten Geschichtsquellen der Zeit von Asarhaddon bis Nabonid," 65–72; Wolfram von Soden, *Herrscher im alten Orient*, 118f.; Hayim Tadmor, "The Sin of Sargon," *Eretz Israel*, 93*, English summary, and more cautiously, *SAAB*, 3 (1989), 32. See, however, the reservations of J.A. Brinkman, *Prelude to Empire*, 71. One of the more convincing formulations is that of Paul Garelli, "Les sujets du roi d'Assyrie," in *La Voix de l'opposition en Mésopotamie*, 197–199, who argues that while there was certainly opposition to the king at court, sometimes by groups of people sharing common interests or a common opinion, there is no evidence of real "parties" as such.

A second political development, however, made this change in the emphasis of Esarhaddon's public relations program not only possible, but imperative; this was the somewhat surprising appointment in 672 of two separate heirs to the thrones of Assyria and Babylonia.[278] The selection of separate future kings for the two states suggests, at first glance, that Esarhaddon might have decided to abandon his efforts to bind Babylonia more closely to Assyria, but a closer look at the political situation suggests that his decision was largely a response to internal political pressures in Assyria and that the change in the structure of Babylonia's government was not intended to alter her relationship to Assyria in any significant way.

The son whom Esarhaddon chose to name as future ruler of Assyria (and of the empire as a whole) was Assurbanipal, a choice that involved passing over the claims of an older son, Šamaš-šumu-ukīn.[279] Whether this choice had been forced upon Esarhaddon by pressure from powerful supporters of Assurbanipal, as has sometimes been suggested,[280] whether it was instead the result of Esarhaddon's conviction that Assurbanipal had greater abilities than his brother, as Parpola has suggested and as seems rather more likely,[281] or whether there were still other factors involved, remains unclear. Whatever the reasons may have been for choosing Assurbanipal as the future ruler of Assyria, Esarhaddon's choice of a younger son as principal heir will in turn have played a major role in other decisions. In Esarhaddon's own case, his father's decision to pass over older brothers in order to name Esarhaddon as heir had created problems which had almost prevented him from reaching the throne. His brothers' verbal attacks on him after his appointment had led

---

[278] There is evidence suggesting that Esarhaddon's original choice as heir was a single son named Sîn-iddin-apla. In an oracle inquiry (Knudtzon #107), the king asks if this son should enter the *bīt redûti*, that is, become the designated heir. There is no evidence of Sîn-iddin-apla's actual appointment, however, and his absence from two lists of Esarhaddon's children written during Esarhaddon's lifetime (ABL 113, and Assur 13956bq, the latter cited by Hildegard Lewy, "Nitokris-Naqî'a*," 281, n. 85 and published by Ernst Weidner, "Assurbânipal in Assur," pl. XIV and p. 214) suggests that Sîn-iddin-apla died before his appointment could take place.

[279] The letter LAS 129, addressed to Esarhaddon, refers to Šamaš-šumu-ukīn as "your elder son" (IBILA-*ka* GAL-ú, obv. l. 10). The vassal treaties, however, refer to Šamaš-šumu-ukīn as Assurbanipal's twin brother (*aḫu talīmešu*: Col. ii, l. 86); if this is to be understood literally, which is not certain, it would suggest that Šamaš-šumu-ukīn was the first twin to be born, making the two sons' claims to the throne on grounds of age almost, but not quite, equivalent.

[280] Wolfram von Soden (*Herrscher im alten Orient*, 124) suggests that Assurbanipal rejected his father's conciliatory policies toward Babylonia and that this had produced powerful support for Assurbanipal in Assyria which forced Esarhaddon to name him as heir apparent instead of Šamaš-šumu-ukīn. This seems unlikely, however, since Assurbanipal shows every sign of having continued his father's Babylonian policies unchanged when he himself took the throne. He completed the return of Marduk's statue initiated by his father, represented himself in his Babylon inscriptions as completing his father's public works projects there, and even had himself represented on stelae in Babylonia as a basket-bearing king.

[281] *Letters*, IIb, p. 116.

his father to repudiate Esarhaddon's claims, at least publicly, and had made it necessary for Esarhaddon to leave the country. In the end he had succeeded in taking the throne only by force and against considerable odds. Consequently, Esarhaddon was certainly aware of the threat the older brother Šamaš-šumu-ukīn might pose to Assurbanipal's succession, and Esarhaddon may have felt that he had no choice but to placate Šamaš-šumu-ukīn and his supporters by offering him a position of great importance. The kingship of Babylon may well have been the only appointment prestigious enough to serve the purpose.

The practical benefits of having an Assyrian ruler resident in Babylon may have made the perhaps unavoidable decision more palatable. A resident king in Babylonia would be spared the difficulties of long distance government which Esarhaddon had to contend with and could handle the day-to-day problems of government without delays. While this approach had failed in Sennacherib's time, with the assassination of Esarhaddon's brother Aššur-nādin-šumi, it now had a greater chance of success with Babylonia less belligerent.

Whatever the reasons for the decision to split the kingship and to appoint Assurbanipal as heir apparent to the throne of Assyria, there are signs that Esarhaddon anticipated resistance to the decision and that its announcement did in fact produce tensions in Assyria. One sign of these misgivings is that the arrangements for the succession were formally announced in a series of assemblies in Assyria and Babylonia in 672, during which Assyrian professional people and royal advisers, Babylonian elders, leaders of vassal states, ordinary Assyrians, and even members of Esarhaddon's own family were obliged to swear fealty to Assurbanipal and promise to support the arrangements for the succession. This extraordinary series of public meetings, involving even more people than the public assembly and oaths in Assyria by which Esarhaddon's own appointment as heir apparent had been made official, suggests that Esarhaddon and his advisers expected opposition to the arrangements for the succession and were attempting to encourage compliance with them by imposing formal oaths on a broad cross-section of people in Assyria, as well as on influential people in Babylonia and other conquered territories.[282] No explicit statement of opposition to the arrangement for the succession survives, which is not surprising, since open opposition to so public a royal policy might well have been interpreted as treason. There is, however, a curious comment made by one of Esarhaddon's closest advisers, the royal exorcist Adad-šumu-uṣur, in an ostensibly laudatory letter about the king's appointment of Assurbanipal over his elder brother. He remarks, "What has not been done in heaven, the

---

[282] See LAS 1, 2, and 3, ABL 202 and Streck, *Assurbanipal*, p. 2 (Rassam Cyl.), I, ll. 12–22. For comments, see Simo Parpola, *Letters*, IIb, pp. 3–6 and D.J. Wiseman, *The Vassal-Treaties of Esarhaddon*, 3–5.

king my lord has done upon earth and shown us: you have girded a son of yours with headband and entrusted him the kingship of Assyria; your eldest son you have put (up) to the kingship in Babylon" (LAS 129, ll. 5–11). In Akkadian usage, the comment that an action is something "not done in heaven" would ordinarily imply serious criticism;[283] in the context of the effusive praises in this letter, however, the comment appears intended instead as a compliment, but one wonders whether the ambiguity might be deliberate and whether this might not in fact be a carefully veiled expression of dismay at Esarhaddon's action. If this is the case, the comment is probably as explicit a statement of such misgivings as we will ever find in writing.

A more direct sign of serious problems in Assyria which may be a response to the appointment of the two heirs is the evidence suggesting the development of a plot to overthrow Esarhaddon, summarily suppressed early in the year 670. The clearest evidence for the plot is a series of letters to the king written at that time, which allege that a conspiracy against the king was underway, and suggest that the plot centered in the northwestern Assyrian city of Ḥarrān, and that it involved men very close to the king. A report in the Babylonian Chronicles that in 670 Esarhaddon executed many of his magnates lends support to these allegations. While no reason for the executions is given there, the severity of the punishment inflicted suggests that the king was indeed responding to suspected treason, as Parpola argues.[284] Whether the planned uprising was at least in part a response to the arrangements for the succession remains unclear, but its timing makes this a possibility. Esarhaddon's proposal to repair the captured statue of Marduk—a somewhat controversial figure in Assyria, as we will see—and return it with full honors to Babylonia was announced at about this time, as well, and may also have contributed to resentments against the king in some circles.

Whatever the reasons for the unrest in Assyria that culminated in the executions of 670, the unrest was clearly not a response to any enhancement of Babylonia's political power implied by the new arrangements. The documents recording oaths imposed on certain vassals to guarantee their support for the new arrangements for the succession make it clear despite the appointment of a separate ruler for Babylonia, that both her subordinate status vis-à-vis Assyria and her essential powerlessness in the empire were to remain unchanged. Several copies of these sets of oaths have come down to us, and their wording strongly implies that effective political power was to remain in the hands of the Assyrian king alone.[285] Throughout the oaths, Šamaš-šumu-

---

[283] See, for example, Esarhaddon's Apology, where he condemns his brothers' hostile actions toward him in precisely these terms, as *ša la ilāni*, "ungodly" (Nin. A, Ep. 2, l. 34 and, similarly, l. 46).

[284] For a discussion of the evidence, see Parpola's comments, *Letters*, IIb, pp. 238–243. The execution is reported in Chr. 1, iv, l. 29 and Chr. 14, l. 27.

[285] The first edition of these texts (here referred to as treaties) was that of D.J. Wiseman, *The*

ukīn, who is to rule Babylonia, is treated as a minor figure, consistently over-shadowed by his brother Assurbanipal, now heir to the Assyrian throne. The opening passages, for example, refer to the document as "the treaty . . . con-cerning Assurbanipal" (i, ll. 1 and 11–12), while Šamaš-šumu-ukīn is not even mentioned. Only at the very end, in the colophon to the text (ll. 666–670), is the document finally explicitly identified as one that concerns Šamaš-šumu-ukīn, as well. Of the thirty-one oaths required from the vassals to in-sure their support of the arrangements for the succession, only one (ll. 86–91) mentions Šamaš-šumu-ukīn; that oath requires the vassals to support Šamaš-šumu-ukīn's succession to the throne of Babylonia and his receipt of any gifts conferred on him by his father, a stipulation suggesting that Šamaš-šumu-ukīn was expected to have little real power. Assurbanipal, in contrast, domi-nates the text. Another document (published by Parpola and Watanabe as text 14, "Esarhaddon's Treaty Inscription," pp. 77–79 and XXXIV) describes a more balanced oath in which both brothers figure on a more equal footing, although Assurbanipal's name appears before that of Šamaš-šumu-ukīn. This latter text, which probably comes from Sippar in Babylonia, seems to reflect the Babylonian version of the oath imposed, and here the king intended for the south naturally plays a more prominent role.[286] The oaths imposed on the vassals in the longer text, however, make the future Babylonian king's sub-ordinate status in the larger political sphere quite obvious; despite the appoint-ment of an Assyrian of high status as king of Babylon, the division of political power between the two states was clearly to remain unchanged. Assyria and Babylonia would continue to be united under the rule of a single Assyrian high king, with Šamaš-šumu-ukīn ruling in Babylonia as his subordinate—a situation very little different in practical terms from Esarhaddon's administra-tion of Babylonia through governors. The only major difference would be the consolidation of Assyrian power in Babylonia in the hands of a single resi-dent administrator answering to the Assyrian king, with the provincial gov-ernors as his own subordinates.

Although in practical terms the changes in Babylonia's relationship to

---

Vassal-Treaties of Esarhaddon, reprinted from *Iraq*, 20 (1958), Part 1. The texts are now available in a revised edition prepared by Kazuko Watanabe, *Die adê-Vereidigung anlässlich der Thronfolgeregelung Asarhaddons*, and in a new transliteration and translation prepared by Simo Parpola and Kazuko Wata-nabe, ed., *Neo-Assyrian Treaties and Loyalty Oaths*, text 6, pp. 28 ff. and XLVIII. (Citations of passages here refer to this latter edition.)

[286] Also interesting in this context is the text (AsBbG) recording Esarhaddon's dedication of Šamaš-šumu-ukīn to the god Marduk, an unusual gesture probably intended to have a double effect, first, to make Šamaš-šumu-ukīn more appealing to the Babylonians, despite his Assyrian antecedents, by devoting him to a god who was first and foremost the Babylonians' patron deity, and second, to suggest subtly Šamaš-šumu-ukīn's subordinate position as ruler of Babylonia, the servant of a god who was himself relegated to a subordinate position in Esarhaddon's AsBbA inscription.

Assyria would be insignificant, the arrangements for the succession would nevertheless diminish the effectiveness of the Assyrian king as an emblem of the unity of Assyria and Babylonia once they were put into effect. Although the two nations would remain united under a single high king, the ruler of Babylonia would now represent a separate Babylonia under Assyrian control.

With this new arrangement for the future government of Assyria and Babylonia there was now a pressing need to provide a different figurative focus for the unity of the two states, and it is for this reason that the image of Babylonians and Assyrians as a single people, briefly alluded to in the introductions of texts from the middle years, becomes the dominant theme of Esarhaddon's late inscriptions. If the image of the Assyrian king would shortly become less powerful as an image of unity, a newly expanded concept of nation might effectively take its place.

This concept of a unified Assyrian and Babylonian people, developed abstractly in Esarhaddon's late inscriptions, finds a concrete and tangible emblem in the statue of the god Marduk. The statue (carried off from Babylon by Sennacherib, we recall) was still being held by the Assyrians in Aššur, and the project of restoring it and returning it to Babylon, already mentioned in early inscriptions, receives much greater emphasis in documents from Esarhaddon's final years.

Marduk held a unique position in both Babylonia and Assyria. Although the worship of Marduk in Assyria had for some time produced repercussions which we shall have to consider, he was an appealing god, central to the worship and identity of the Babylonians, worshipped to some extent in Assyria as well, and with the clear potential, if properly presented, of being a powerful rallying and unifying force. In Babylonia, Marduk, initially patron god of the then obscure city of Babylon, had risen early to importance in the area as a whole under the patronage of Hammurapi's dynasty, the First Dynasty of Babylon (1894–1595); later, in the reign of Nebuchadnezzar I (1124–1103), Marduk had been accorded an unprecedented position of supreme and absolute power in the Babylonian pantheon, a position he was to retain until long after the fall of the Assyrian empire.[287] Although Babylonian in origin, Marduk had begun to be worshipped in Assyria also by the fourteenth century, when an Assyrian building inscription mentions a temple of Marduk in the

---

[287] This summary of the rise of Marduk in Babylonia follows Walter Sommerfeld, *Der Aufstieg Marduks: Die Stellung Marduks in der babylonischen Religion des zweiten Jahrtausends v. Chr.*, AOAT, 213. Although it is sometimes argued that Marduk's name is Sumerian and that the god was Sumerian in origin, Sommerfeld (9–11) concludes that the first clear references to Marduk come from Babylon in the early Old Babylonian period. For Marduk's final ascendancy to absolute power in the reign of Nebuchadnezzar, see Wilfred G. Lambert, "The Reign of Nebuchadnezzar I: A Turning Point in the History of Ancient Mesopotamian Religion," 3–13.

city of Aššur.[288] The capture of Marduk's statue in Babylon by the Assyrian king Tukulti-Ninurta I in 1244 and its subsequent brief residence in Assyria encouraged the growth of the Marduk cult there. The greater importance of the cult in the following period is indicated both by references in ritual texts from the Middle Assyrian period (ca. 1500–1000) to the occasional inclusion of Marduk in Assyrian rituals,[289] and also by the increasing occurrence in Assyrian texts of personal names using Marduk as the divine element. By the beginning of the Neo-Assyrian period (ca. 950), Marduk was an established, if minor, figure in Assyrian religious life. He now began to play an increasingly important role in the official state religion, beginning with the reign of Assurnasirpal II (883–859), who includes Marduk's name in some lists of his patron gods.[290] The increasing importance of Marduk in Assyrian state religion culminated in the reign of Sargon II (721–705), who assigned Marduk a prominent role in his inscriptions, asserting for example, that it was Marduk who "truly called me from among all princes and lifted my head" (that is, made him king). Sargon's royal epithets routinely refer to him as "rightful ruler, to whom Aššur and Marduk have entrusted an unrivaled kingdom," or as the king who conquers "with the help of Aššur, Nabû, and Marduk."[291] Sargon's inscriptions also report that he sponsored construction of a temple in Nineveh itself for Marduk and Marduk's son Nabû,[292] a striking indication of the importance of Marduk in Assyria in Sargon's time.

Under Sargon's successor Sennacherib, however, Marduk's position in Assyria suffered a reverse, as Sennacherib rarely invoked his name in royal in-

---

[288] For the rise of Marduk's cult in Assyria, see Sommerfeld, pp. 193–195. The changes introduced by Tukulti-Ninurta are discussed by Peter Machinist, "Literature as Politics: The Tukulti-Ninurta Epic and the Bible," *Catholic Biblical Quarterly*, 38 (1976), pp. 455–482. See also the comments of Wilfred G. Lambert, "The Historical Development of the Mesopotamian Pantheon: A Study in Sophisticated Polytheism," in *Unity and Diversity: Essays in the History, Literature, and Religion of the Ancient Near East*, Hans Goedicke and J.J.M. Roberts, ed. (Baltimore and London: 1975), 197 ff.

[289] KAR #135, cited by G. van Driel in *The Cult of Aššur*, 54, and VAT 16435, cited on p. 54 and dated by Van Driel to the Middle Assyrian period (ca. 1500–1000) on the basis of script and dialect.

[290] For example, Marduk appears in the introduction to Assurnasirpal II's Monolith Inscription from Calaḫ (IR, pl. 27) just after the gods Aššur, Anu, Ea and Sîn as "the master, lord of oracles." He is also named in inscriptions of Shalmaneser III (858–824), Tiglath-Pileser III (744–727), and the latter king's official, Bēl-Ḫarrān-bēla-uṣur, who invokes Marduk as his principal god in an inscription commemorating construction of a city (Eckhard Unger, *Die Stele des Bel-harran-beli-usser: ein Denkmal der Zeit Salmanassars IV*). On the ascendancy of Marduk in the hierarchy of Assyrian gods in the ninth to eighth centuries, as evidenced in his position in god-lists in royal inscriptions, see now Hayim Tadmor, "The Sin of Sargon and Sennacherib's Last Will," 25–27.

[291] For these passages, see A.G. Lie, *The Inscriptions of Sargon II* (Paris: 1929), p. 42, l. 270, and Hugo Winckler, *Die Keilschrifttexte Sargons* (Leipzig: 1889), II, pp. 43 and 36.

[292] I R, 6, no. VII, a seven-line brick inscription of Sargon found on bricks from the edge of the Kuyunjik mound at Nineveh, reports that Sargon built a temple "for Nabû and Marduk, his lords."

scriptions and instead commissioned bas-reliefs for a temple in Aššur depicting the god Aššur as the hero of the Enūma eliš myth. This was a Babylonian
myth which in its traditional form exalted Marduk and was recited as part of
the main festival of the Marduk cult in Babylon.[293] In these reliefs, Sennacherib is both taking over for Aššur a heroic role previously reserved for
Marduk, and at the same time paying mute (if unintentional) tribute to
Marduk's increasing popularity.

In addition to this effort by Sennacherib to lessen the importance of
Marduk, there are indications of more widespread resistance to the role of
Marduk in Assyria. Besides the bas-relief commissioned by Sennacherib, there
was an Assyrianized version of the Enūma eliš in circulation as a text in
Assyria; several copies survive,[294] suggesting that the effort to undermine
Marduk's importance in Assyria by attributing his traditional exploits to Aššur
was fairly extensive.

An even more pointed attack on the image of Marduk appears in a set
of Assyrian documents known as the "Ordeal of Marduk" texts. These texts,
found in slightly differing versions at Nineveh and Assur, take the form of
commentaries on a ritual or series of rituals, which are said to represent
Marduk being seized and beaten, put on trial, and imprisoned.[295] Although

---

[293] The bas-reliefs were commissioned to decorate the *bīt akītu* at Aššur. A reference to the
fall of Babylon in one of the inscriptions commemorating that construction (OIP, 2, p. 137, l. 36)
suggests a date late in Sennacherib's reign. For a description of the relief, see OIP, 2, p. 140, obv.,
ll. 5–8 and pp. 141–142, ll. 10–15, and edge, ll. 1–2. It is clear from these passages that the reliefs
were to depict the adventures recounted in the Enūma eliš and that Aššur was to be shown in the
leading role.

It would be a mistake, however, to conclude from these reliefs that Sennacherib was a consistent foe of the Marduk cult throughout his reign, as is sometimes assumed. In his inscription
at Bavian (OIP, 2, p. 78, l. 1), for example, Sennacherib includes Marduk among his patron gods.
While this may be as much an expression of Sennacherib's new position as victor over Babylon
as of veneration for Marduk, it is at least a respectful acknowledgement. Van Driel cites a Sennacherib text which lists gods whose former cult places, apparently forgotten, were being relocated
by divination in order to make worship of those gods in the exact former location possible; Marduk
is included toward the end of the list (BM 121206, IX, ll. 24'–34', cited by van Driel, 99). Whether
this Marduk cult-place was in Babylonia or Assyria, Sennacherib's interest in it indicates that he
was not entirely inimical to the worship of Marduk.

[294] See Daniel David Luckenbill, "The Ashur Version of the Seven Tablets of Creation," 12–35
for these texts. Their script and language suggest that they were both composed and copied in
Assyria sometime in the first millennium. They cannot be more precisely dated, although it is tempting to place them in the context of Sennacherib's reign or perhaps in the time of Esarhaddon.

[295] For editions and discussion, see Wolfram von Soden, "Gibt es ein Zeugnis dafür, dass die
Babylonier an die Wiederauferstehung Marduks geglaubt haben?" and "Ein neues Bruchstück des
assyrischen Kommentars zum Marduk-Ordal," 224–234. A more recent edition, which argues that
the texts were meant to conclude with a vindication of Marduk (a position which I find unconvincing) is that of Tikva Frymer-Kensky, "The Tribulations of Marduk: The So-called 'Marduk
Ordeal Text,'" 131–141. A new translation has now been published, with commentary in the introduction, by Alasdair Livingstone, *Court Poetry and Literary Miscellanea*, SAA, III, 82–91. See also
his new edition and cogent comments on the texts in *Mystical and Mythological Explanatory Works*

the tablets are broken at several points and the details of the action they discuss are often unclear, the texts consistently present the image of Marduk as an ineffective and essentially powerless god. These "Ordeal of Marduk" texts, probably written in the final years of Sennacherib's reign or the beginning of Esarhaddon's, are further evidence of resistance to the worship of Marduk among certain literate and theologically sophisticated people in both Aššur and Nineveh.

These tensions in Assyria about whether Marduk could appropriately play any role in Assyrian religious life had potential political repercussions and made Esarhaddon's proposed restoration and return of Marduk's statue a controversial and somewhat risky undertaking. Because of his wide appeal to Babylonians and to many Assyrians as well, the figure of Marduk was potentially a powerful unifying force. To restore Marduk to the prominence he had enjoyed in Assyria before Sennacherib's reign, however, and to encourage his worship in Assyria without provoking open opposition from those who saw the worship of Marduk in Assyria as problematic would require considerable tact on Esarhaddon's part. Well aware of the tensions surrounding the figure of Marduk, Esarhaddon initially moved very slowly toward praising Marduk in Assyrian contexts or appearing to encourage his veneration in Assyria. Esarhaddon's extensive restorations of Assyrian temples, for example, begun early in the reign, were probably intended to reassure Assyrians of the king's loyalty to the traditional gods of the nation. Although praise of Marduk occurs in Esarhaddon's inscriptions from the beginning, such comments were initially confined to documents meant for use in Babylonia.[296] As the reign progressed, however, Marduk's name was invoked increasingly often in royal inscriptions intended for Assyria, as well. His name appears, for example, in the list of patron gods in the Nineveh B text, written in 676 to announce the beginning of work on a palace and military complex in Nineveh. Marduk's name also appears in Calah A, written in 672 to commemorate the construction of a similar building in the Assyrian city of Calaḫ, appearing there in

of Assyrian and Babylonian Scholars (Oxford: 1986), 205–253, which, to my regret, was not available to me until this study was essentially completed.

Von Soden argues a date of composition no earlier than the reign of Tiglath-Pileser III (744–727) (*ZA*, 51 [1955]: 163) and notes further that the script of one fragment from Aššur suggests it was copied in Nineveh in the seventh century (*ZA*, 52 [1956]: 225). He concludes that the texts were probably composed in the final years of Sennacherib's reign. Frymer-Kensky (132) proposes a later date.

[296] The Babylon inscriptions are the most obvious example; see the discussion in the previous chapter. In the two Babylon inscriptions designed for use in Assyria, Babylon B and G, Marduk is only mentioned once, obliquely, as "lord of lords," in introductory epithets (in the new fragment published by Millard in *AfO*, 24 [1973]: 117–119 and pls. 13 and 14), and again obliquely, as the "Enlil of the gods," in Ep. 5, where the texts written for Babylon (A and D) name him as Marduk in the parallel passage.

a list of gods to whose aid Esarhaddon attributes his widespread conquests (ll. 12–13). While the references to Marduk in these texts remain muted, it is nevertheless significant that the Babylonian national god should appear at all in texts dedicating military centers in Assyria.

In two other texts probably written for use in Assyria in the latter days of Esarhaddon's reign, however, Marduk is assigned a remarkably prominent position, suggesting increasingly open royal support for Marduk in Assyria that was to culminate in Esarhaddon's restoration of Marduk's statue and his attempt to return it to Babylonia. The first of these texts, fragmentary and still unpublished, is described in an article by René Labat.[297] Although badly broken, the text's extant lines suggest that it was an account of one of Esarhaddon's two Egyptian campaigns, which would place its composition in 674 or later. Since the text was found in Nineveh, a northern site, it seems likely that it was meant for an Assyrian audience, although the small size of the extant fragment limits the internal evidence that might confirm or refute this hypothesis. According to Labat's description, the text tells how Esarhaddon's soldiers, desperate for water during their desert crossing toward Egypt, were saved by a sudden rainstorm which, the text explains, was sent to them by Marduk. If the text was indeed intended for use in Assyria, this tribute to Marduk is unexpected and significant.

The second text attributing unexpected prominence to Marduk is the well-known "Letter to a God" inscription of Esarhaddon (Borger, Gbr., pp. 102 ff.), which describes the campaign of the year 673 against the land of Šubria and was probably written shortly after the conclusion of that campaign. Enough traces remain of the broken introduction to show that the text began by invoking "Aššur, king of the gods," in conventional Assyrian fashion (Gbr. I, 1). It also refers to Aššur as ". . . the hero . . . my lord," in a later passage (II, l. 7), a further indication that the text was probably intended for an Assyrian audience.[298] It is therefore striking that it is the god Marduk who is credited with giving Esarhaddon's troops victory in the battle that follows. The setting is an Assyrian siege against Uppume, a city in the land of Šubria, in the mountains northwest of Assyria. The text reports that the defenders

[297] René Labat, "Rapports sur les conférences: Assyrien," *Annuaire de l'École Pratique des Hautes Études, IVe section: Sciences Historiques et Philologiques, 1973–74,* 65–68.

[298] A. Leo Oppenheim, in "Neo-Assyrian and Neo-Babylonian Empires," *Propaganda and Communication in World History,* 111–144, esp. 124 ff., discusses this text as an example of the genre he refers to as "letters to a god" and argues that it was meant, like an earlier text of this genre from the time of Sargon II (cf. Oppenheim, "The City of Aššur in 714 BC," 133–47), to be read aloud in Assyria, in this case shortly after the Šubria campaign was completed, as a report to the god Aššur and to the city of Aššur on the events of that campaign. Although the identity of Esarhaddon's inscription as a text of the "letter to a god" type is somewhat conjectural, Oppenheim's willingness to entertain this theory underlines the strongly Assyrian character of the text.

of the city succeeded in pouring oil on a siege ramp the Assyrians had built, and in the dead of night set fire to the ramp, intending to destroy it. Their plan failed:

> At the command of Marduk, king of the gods, a north wind sprang up—pleasant breeze of the lord of the gods; it turned the flaring tongues of flame (back) against the city of Uppume, and it (i.e., the fire) did not seize the ramp. It burnt (the city's) wall and turned it to ashes (Gbr. II, col. II, ll. 5–7).

With one wall of the city in ruins, the Assyrians were able to penetrate the defenses and take the city. Although the text later gives credit for the victory to the god Aššur in the conventional Assyrian manner ("after I had conquered the land of Šubria with the help of Aššur my lord . . ."), it is actually Marduk, as we saw, who is credited with intervening at the crucial moment to assure the fall of the city.[299] The appearance of Marduk in such a decisive role in this text, and in an equally important role in the fragmentary account of the Egyptian campaign, is evidence of Esarhaddon's increasingly open espousal of Marduk in texts evidently intended for Assyrian audiences, a development that was now to culminate in Esarhaddon's project of restoring and returning the statue of Marduk to Babylon.

It is perhaps tempting to interpret this increasing prominence of Marduk in Esarhaddon's inscriptions as a reflection of Esarhaddon's own religious beliefs, and in emphasizing the political significance of such religious elements in Esarhaddon's inscriptions, it is not my intention to discount the role that the king's personal beliefs may have played in motivating his efforts in support of Marduk. The extent to which the king's personal religious convictions are reflected in his public actions, however, is exceedingly difficult to assess. In royal inscriptions and even in letters, it is the public faces of the king that are presented to us. We see Esarhaddon as a private person only obliquely, through the comments of his advisers; we have almost no evidence of his private beliefs. We do, however, have ample evidence of his public positions on certain religious questions, such as the veneration of Marduk, and there can be little doubt that his public support for the worship of Marduk would have had political repercussions in both Assyria and Babylonia that no intelligent political leader could have overlooked. It is these political aspects of Esarhaddon's theological positions that I am concerned with here. Whatever the king's personal beliefs, he evidently found it important to encourage greater acceptance of the Marduk cult in Assyria in order that religious life there should reflect and support the political changes Esarhaddon was attempting to introduce.

---

[299] The north wind is sometimes associated with the gods Sîn and Ninlil, but never, to my knowledge, with Marduk, except in this passage. (Cf. *CAD* "ištānu.") The appearance of Marduk here is therefore not occasioned by the north wind's role in the incident.

It is also important to realize that in a sense, the religious and political changes Esarhaddon advocated were essentially one and the same. Although politics and religion are for us to a large degree separable categories, for the ancient Mesopotamians they were inextricably interwoven. Marduk and Aššur were simultaneously both gods and emblems of their nations.[300] For Esarhaddon to assert in his inscriptions that Marduk had become the son of Aššur was at one and the same time an expression of Esarhaddon's unifying Babylonian policy and also an effort to encourage acceptance of that policy by bringing all the force of the community's shared religious beliefs to its support. It is not surprising, then, that the final step in Esarhaddon's effort to bring the two nations closer together was the simultaneously religious and political project of restoring the statue of Marduk and returning it to its home in Babylon under the patronage of the Assyrian king, a project through which Marduk would be transformed into an emblem of the unity of the two states, now in every sense a legitimately Assyrian god as well as god of Babylon.

Because Marduk was to some extent a controversial figure in Assyria, as we have seen, Esarhaddon approached this final project to elevate him to greater prominence gradually and with the same caution that had characterized the slowly increasing references to Marduk in his inscriptions. The project of restoring and returning the captive Babylonian statues was mentioned in inscriptions from very early in the reign, but was not made the focus of attention until its final years. Babylon A and Babylon D, for example, written within the first two or three years of Esarhaddon's reign, both contain brief accounts of repairing the damaged statues of the gods and goddesses of Esagila and also imply their eventual return to Babylon (Ep. 32). Inscriptions written during the next several years, however, such as Nineveh G (677) and Nineveh B (early 676), fail to mention either the repair or the return of the gods, sug-

---

[300] Thorkild Jacobsen, as we saw above (65), has pointed out the increasing identification of gods in first millenium Mesopotamia with their nations and places of worship and the consequent increasing role of gods, their statues, and their temples in political life. This politicizing of the gods, particularly marked in first millennium Mesopotamia, was part of a larger pattern of thought which saw what we call the political and religious aspects of public life as part of a single sphere of activity. The Assyrian king, for example, was by tradition both a secular and religious leader, ruling by the choice of the gods, waging war on their behalf and with their help, rebuilding and financing their temples, and acting as celebrant in a heavy schedule of state rituals honoring their divinity. Because of this interweaving of the religious and political life of the state, political theory itself often found expression in mythology, couched in terms of the gods' activities. See H. and H.A. Frankfort, John A. Wilson and Thorkild Jacobsen, *Before Philosophy: The Intellectual Adventure of Ancient Man*, 14–15 for the argument that in Mesopotamia, mythology served as a medium of expression for speculative thought in every sphere. For an example, see Jacobsen's analysis of the Enūma eliš myth as in part a political position paper supporting the idea of monarchical government, *op. cit.*, 167–191. It was natural enough in such a context that Esarhaddon should advocate theological change in support of his public policies for Babylonia, and that those policies should be given expression in terms of the relationship of the gods Aššur and Marduk.

gesting that the project had been temporarily shelved. The motif reappears with the Calah A inscription of mid-676, and after 674 it is mentioned regularly, in texts including Babylon C, Nineveh A, and Tarbisu A, but is still relegated there to brief references, usually in royal epithets.[301]

By this time, however, Esarhaddon's increasingly open praise of Marduk in royal inscriptions and in texts such as the ones cited above was already paving the way for finally beginning work on the project of restoring the god's statue. As a final step designed to reduce opposition to the project among those Assyrians who still harbored doubts about the appropriateness of Assyrian veneration of Marduk, a remarkable document was composed. This text, now known as "The Sin of Sargon," reports that Sennacherib himself, despite his final attack on Babylon, had revered Marduk, had himself intended to make a statue for the god, and had now returned from the dead to urge his son Esarhaddon to carry out the statue-making project which he himself had been prevented from completing.[302] These assertions, unconvincing as they may seem to modern readers, may well have seemed plausible to Assyrians, who believed their lives were affected by the activities of the dead and who were sometimes advised by them.[303] The "Sin of Sargon" text seems in-

[301] The earliest copy of Nineveh B is dated to the spring of 676 (Ajāru 22), and the motif is still not mentioned at that point. The motif reappears in the royal epithets of Calah A (earliest copies, mid-summer of 676, i.e., in late Abu and early Ulūlu), and then appears regularly, in Babylon C (674/3 or later), Ep. 32; Nineveh A (673), Ep. 3; Tarbisu A (672); Assur E (672 or later), and Calah D (671 or later). In most of these latter texts it appears in the royal epithets, typically as "rebuilder of Esagil and Babylon, renewer of the gods and goddesses that are in its midst," or more simply as, "renewer of the statues of the great gods." In addition, Nippur A, Nippur B, and Uruk A (all undated but probably composed in the middle years of the reign, or later) briefly mention both repair and return of the gods. The absence of references between approximately 679 and mid-676 may indicate that the project was tabled during that time.

[302] The 1958 revised edition of the text, prepared by Hayim Tadmor ("The Sin of Sargon," 150–162 and English summary, *98) has now been followed by a further revised edition with extensive commentary by Hayim Tadmor, Benno Landsberger, and Simo Parpola, "The Sin of Sargon and Sennacherib's Last Will," 3–52. (I am grateful to Simo Parpola, who generously made a synopsis of his preliminary work on this text available to me several years before its publication.) A new translation based on the revised Tadmor-Parpola edition was also published in 1989 by Alasdair Livingstone, Court Poetry, 77–79.

Tadmor suggests the text was probably written in the reign of Sennacherib, the style of whose inscriptions seems to mark the text, although he says it may also have been written at the very beginning of Esarhaddon's reign ("Last Will," 31–32). Landsberger, noting the same stylistic affinities, made the ingenious suggestion that the text was written in Esarhaddon's reign in deliberate imitation of the style of the dead Sennacherib, who, it asserts, is the ghostly author of the text (35). Parpola, seeing the text as fitting best in the political context of Esarhaddon's reign and noting marked affinities in its account to discussions of extispicy in Esarhaddon texts, argues for a date of composition in Esarhaddon's reign (45–47), a position which I find persuasive.

[303] See CAD "eṭemmu" ("spirit of the dead, ghost") and also LAS 132, a letter in which Esarhaddon's personal exorcist mentions advice received from the ghost of Esarhaddon's deceased queen.

tended to bring the authority of the venerable Sennacherib himself to counter any remaining objections on the part of conservative Assyrians to the project of restoring Marduk's statue, paving the way for the announcement that work on the project was at last beginning. Finally, in 671 or shortly thereafter, the AsBbA and AsBbE inscriptions were composed to present the restoration of the statue in full detail, as we saw earlier, and the project was at last accorded a prominent role in the royal inscriptions.

It is the AsBbE inscription which now gives a full account of the proposed climax of the project, the ceremonial return of the restored statue of Marduk, accompanied by the statues of lesser Babylonian gods, to the city of Babylon, an event here presented as an already accomplished fact:

> Out of the midst of Eḫursaggalkurkurra they have now taken the road for Šuanna, a festive way, just as Šamaš (i.e., the sun) goes out glowing to the land. From Baltil as far as the [quay] of Babylon, piles of brushwood were lit every 1/3 of a double-mile; every double-mile they slaughtered a fattened ox, and I, Esarhaddon, took the hand of his great godhead and [walked? . . .] before him. Into the midst of Babylon, the city of their honor, joyfully I had them enter. In the groves of fruit trees, orchards, canals, and gardens of Ekarzagina, a pure place, through the knowledge of the experts, (through the rituals of) Washing of the Mouth, Opening of the Mouth, washing and purifying before the sta[rs of the heavens]—(before) the gods [Ea], Šamaš, Asariluḫi, Maḫ, Kusu, Ninaḫaku[ddu, Ninkurra, Ninagal, Ǧuškin-banda, Niniginagargid, Ninzadim], they entered . . . (AsBbE, rs., ll. 17–24).

The tablet is broken at this point, so we do not know how the text concluded, but the eventual outcome—the gods' return to their temples in Babylon—has already been made clear. The rather flowery language ("as the sun goes out glowing to the lands"), the use of poetic names for Aššur and Babylon ("Baltil" and "Šuanna"), the elaborate ceremonies attending the procession as it moved toward Babylon, and the rituals of mouth-washing and mouth-opening used to endow the gods' statues with life when they arrived,[304] all seem intended to place the event on an elevated plane and to underline its solemn significance.

Although this account in AsBbE is the only completely preserved descrip-

---

[304] In a recent article ("Esarhaddon's Attempt to Return Marduk to Babylon," in *Ad bene et fideliter seminandum*, Gerlinde Mauer and Ursula Magen, ed., AOAT, Bd. 220, 157–174), Wilfred G. Lambert points out that Borger's Assur C text (here published in a revised and significantly expanded edition) includes a brief description of a mouth-washing (and probably mouth-opening) ritual performed on god's statues in the Ešarra temple in Aššur, almost certainly the statues of Marduk and Ṣarpanītu restored by Esarhaddon. Parpola (*Letters*, IIb, p. 429) suggests a date ca. Ajāru 8, 669 for this text. The text suggests that the revivifying ceremonies for the statues were performed in Assyria before the statues set off for Babylon, where the same ceremonies were to be repeated in a Babylonian setting; every effort was being made to insure that the statues would be accepted as valid and living receptacles of the gods' presence in both nations.

tion of the gods' return to Babylon, briefer passages surviving in other texts indicate that the return of the gods appeared as a major theme in at least two other inscriptions: the AsBbF text, for example, includes fragmentary references to priests used for the ceremonies associated with the return, and refers to the slaughter of sheep at regular intervals on the journey;[305] and the AsBbH text describes how the gods assigned the renewing of the statues to Esarhaddon as his fate, and how he brought the statues to Babylon in "joy and rejoicing" and caused them to undergo the mouth-washing and mouth-opening rituals.[306]

The religious and political implications of returning Marduk's statue to Babylon were considerable and were crucial to Esarhaddon's public relations effort. In proposing to return the captured statue of Marduk to the Babylonians, Esarhaddon was offering to restore to them the emblem of their national identity, as well as the statue in which the living spirit of their chief god and heavenly protector was thought to reside. The return of the statue thus promised the Babylonians both the return of prosperity and safety under the protection of a resident patron god, and also the preservation of their national identity despite political assimilation by Assyria. For the benefit of the Assyrians, on the other hand, the AsBbA text described the reconstruction of the statues in a way that implied that the Marduk being returned to Babylon was no longer the head of a rival Babylonian pantheon, but had become, as we have seen, part of the Assyrian pantheon, the god Aššur's son and honored subordinate. The statue of Marduk being returned to the Babylonians had been transformed into a divine emblem of the unity of the two states and a symbol of their proper relationship. It was a brilliant political and religious compromise, represented in concrete and tangible form by the renewed statue itself.

Because the return of the statue was to be the climax of Esarhaddon's efforts to gain support for his efforts to unify the two states, the project of returning the gods was not only presented in the elaborate verbal description of the AsBb texts, whose principal audience was probably the elite of the two states, but also visually to people at every social level in both states through the elaborate procession in which Marduk's statue made its way toward Babylon—in a sense a dramatization of Esarhaddon's policy to unite Assyria and Babylonia peacefully. A procession is a particularly appropriate vehicle

---

[305] The tablet is badly broken, but enough text survives to give Esarhaddon's name and also to mention Ešarra as "the place of my renewing" (IV, 9). As Borger notes, this suggests that the surviving passages were part of a description of the return of the gods, a conclusion strengthened by their similarity to AsBbE.

[306] The surviving passages of AsBbA do not make any clear reference to an anticipated return of the gods (those mentioned as "returned to their places" in rs. l. 41 are almost certainly the lesser gods discussed in that section of the text rather than Marduk and his colleagues); it may be, however, that this was the topic of the later section not included in this excerpt by the ancient copyist.

for the presentation of a controversial policy, since the non-verbal nature of a procession invites neither rational evaluation nor disagreement. Like a Fourth of July parade, it does not demand that participants and observers assent to a particular political policy, but merely invites them to be present— and by being present, to be drawn in.[307] As the statue and its entourage moved slowly south down the river valley, the procession encouraged first Assyrians and then Babylonians to participate in a common activity united around the figure of the god Marduk as they watched the fires being lit, saw the procession pass, and observed the repeated sacrifice of oxen. The procession made Marduk's return, and the Assyrian king's approval of it, dramatically apparent to a wide audience. It was itself a kind of figurative thread, linking the two nations with a line of fires and sacrifices, making the river once again an avenue uniting the two states, no longer the road bringing Assyrian armies to attack Babylonia. Significantly, this thread ran from north to south. Marduk was returning under the patronage of an Assyrian king, and the procession, as it passed by, was an expression of Assyrian dominance as well as of reconciliation and reunion.

The procession returning the gods, presented in several of the "Assur-Babylon" inscriptions as the climax of Esarhaddon's program of reunion with Babylonia, is described there in detail and as a *fait accompli*. Like Esarhaddon's building inscriptions, however, the AsBb inscriptions are proleptic, and the return, with all its pomp, did not actually take place until the first year of Assurbanipal's reign.[308] There is evidence that Esarhaddon actually began the ceremonial return but was forced to bring the statue back to Assyria because of an incident that occurred as the procession reached Babylonian soil. Final planning for the return is reflected in three texts recording omen requests made under Esarhaddon's administration asking the gods' approval for various aspects of these final plans.[309] A letter written to Esarhaddon a short time later (LAS 29) reports the arrival of the grand procession at Labbanat, just north of Babylon, and describes how after its arrival, a certain man had mounted a "strong horse wearing an Ethiopian harness" (plausibly identified by Parpola as the horse drawing the chariot in which Marduk's statue was being transported).[310] The man, who had been promptly seized and arrested, then exclaimed, "The gods Bēl (i.e., Marduk) (and) Ṣar[panītu] (his consort) have sent word to me: Babylon will . . . be the loot of Kurigalzi." While this state-

---

[307] On this point, see the comments of David Kertzer, *Ritual, Politics, and Power*, 13–14 and 67–70.

[308] It is reported in Chr. 1, iv, ll. 34–36 and Chr. 14, ll. 31–37 and in Assurbanipal's inscriptions.

[309] For a discussion of liver omen texts and for the dating of these documents to Esarhaddon's reign, see Appendix I. The omen texts in question are Knudtzon #104 (with its duplicate, #105) and #106. See the comments of Parpola, *Letters*, IIb, pp. 32–35 and Benno Landsberger, *Brief des Bischofs*, 22 ff.

[310] Parpola discusses this letter at length in *Letters*, IIb, pp. 32 ff.

ment may seem enigmatic to us, its implications were evidently both clear and deeply disturbing to the Assyrian officials accompanying the statue. They halted the procession's advance toward Babylon and wrote to the king for instructions. This action, as well as their comment that an informer had later divulged to them that "traitors" (or "law breakers") were waiting farther down the road, suggests that they had understood the incident as an attempted uprising—to rally Babylonians behind the returning statue of their god. Since the statue did not actually return to Babylon until Assurbanipal's reign and is said in Assurbanipal's inscriptions to have been waiting in Aššur in the interim, Esarhaddon evidently decided to return the statue to Assyria to await a more favorable time for its repatriation.

The Labbanat incident, however disturbing it may have seemed at the time, seems to have evoked no general response in Babylonia, and one year later, at the beginning of Assurbanipal's reign, the return of the statues, proudly announced in royal inscriptions, was accomplished without further problems.[311] The return of Marduk's statue, almost certainly welcomed by most Babylonians, was the necessary culmination of Esarhaddon's efforts to win their lasting cooperation, since they were unlikely ever to give full allegiance to a king and nation who continued to hold their god hostage. With Marduk back on Babylonian soil, however, one of the most serious impediments to cooperation with the Assyrians was at last removed. The return of the statue at the beginning of Assurbanipal's reign seems to have been the success that Esarhaddon and his advisers had originally envisioned, helping to inaugurate a long period of Babylonian cooperation with the Assyrian authorities.

The repair and attempted return of Marduk's statue and the elaborate presentation of that project in inscriptions designed for audiences in both Assyria and Babylonia was the final step in Esarhaddon's program to win public support in both Assyria and Babylonia for his controversial effort to unite the two states in a permanent and peaceful union under Assyrian rule.

When he had first come to power, seizing the throne from his warring brothers, his chances of survival—much less of success in implementing a controversial policy—had seemed slim. The Chaldeans were in open revolt against him in Babylonia, the Elamites seemed likely to join them at any moment, and many city leaders in Babylonia appeared ready to lend their support to any promising effort at rebellion. In Assyria, Esarhaddon's political and military base, the new king faced the secret opposition of those supporters of his brothers who had survived the recent war, the resentment of those

---

[311] The statues of Marduk and his entourage were returned to Babylon on the twenty-fourth or twenty-fifth of Ajāru (May 10 or 11—the chronicles vary in the date) of the year 669 (Chr. 1, iv, ll. 34–36; Chr. 14, ll. 35–36; Akītu Chr., ll. 5–8). For references to the statue's return in Assurbanipal's inscriptions, see Streck, *Assurbanipal*, II, p. 396, n. 2.

whose expectations of power and influence had been crushed when Esarhaddon had unexpectedly been selected as heir to the throne over the heads of his elder brothers, and the skepticism of those who had believed his brothers' recent accusations against him. Out of this unpromising beginning, Esarhaddon had managed to forge a relatively successful eleven years of rule.

Perhaps the most striking success of those years was Esarhaddon's pacification of Babylonia, achieved almost entirely without recourse to military force. Suspected rebels were on at least two occasions seized in Babylonia and punished, but the long and bloody campaigns of the Assyrian army in Babylonia that had marked the reigns of Esarhaddon's predecessors came to an end. After the Chaldean rebels fled from the approaching Assyrian army at the beginning of Esarhaddon's reign without ever engaging the Assyrians in battle, no Assyrian military campaigns were waged against Babylonia during all of Esarhaddon's reign, nor were there to be further Assyrian campaigns on Babylonian soil for almost seventeen years after his death.[312]

To achieve this long period of relatively peaceful relations between two states that had been locked in conflict for generations, Esarhaddon used his skills as a diplomat and administrator, but also supported his achievements in those spheres by the development of an extraordinary public relations program designed to strengthen support for his Babylonian policies. Expanding on the conciliatory gestures toward Babylonia of earlier Assyrian kings, Esarhaddon created an extensive and systematic program of public appearances, public statements, and public patronage designed to win acceptance for Assyrian rule in Babylonia.

The first step—and the most visible—was to build. Esarhaddon sponsored construction work on nine temples in Babylonia, beginning with the renowned national cult center Esagila in Babylon itself. Assyrian kings before him had sponsored building projects in Babylonia, but never on this grand scale: from the first year of his reign, Esarhaddon assumed in Babylonia the role of builder king, an essential element in the Babylonian concept of kingship, and did so with a breadth and openhandedness that in time made his friendly intentions toward Babylonia physically evident in cities throughout the country. At the same time, similar building projects were begun across Assyria to reassure the Assyrians of their king's unwavering commitment to their interests despite these attentions to the needs of their recent enemies.

---

[312] Five years after Esarhaddon's death Assurbanipal sent an Assyrian army into Babylonia to stop an Elamite invasion of Babylonia, apparently begun at the joint instigation of the governor of Nippur and the chief of the Gambūlu tribe. The Elamites withdrew, however, at the appearance of the Assyrian army, and were defeated shortly thereafter, at which point the Assyrian army withdrew without further incident. There was no general uprising in Babylonia in support of the Elamites, suggesting that at this point most of Babylonia still accepted Assyrian rule. On this incident, see Brinkman in *Prelude*, 91.

The second step in this program, begun simultaneously, was to present to the Babylonians an image of the king that would underline the ideological message implicit in his building program: that Esarhaddon, a builder king in the best tradition of Babylonian kingship, was in fact an acceptable Babylonian ruler, the embodiment of the essential elements of Babylonian kingship despite his continuing role as king of Assyria. This message was presented in both actions and words. In his first year of reign, the king made a personal appearance in Babylon and enacted the ancient Babylonian royal ritual of "bearing the basket" as part of ground-breaking ceremonies for the restoration of Esagila, the temple of Babylonia's national god Marduk. In the inscriptions commemorating this occasion, the king is described as acting at the command of the Babylonians' own gods, and his personal participation in the rebuilding of the temple is underlined. Moreover, in this and other building inscriptions composed for use in Babylonia, the king revived the use of Babylonian royal titles, not employed in the reign of his predecessor, thus acknowledging both his respect for Babylonian tradition and his intention to permit Babylonia's national identity to survive under Assyrian rule.

In these inscriptions attention is focused on the king, not as an individual, but as a ruler who repeatedly assumes the aspect of a Babylonian king, performing Babylonia's royal ritual, acting as the willing agent of her gods, and using the titles that had long identified Babylonian kings. The texts present Esarhaddon to Babylonians as a suitable embodiment of their national identity and traditions. These texts, I have argued, were not only kept for the future, to commemorate the king's actions, but were also presented orally to contemporary Babylonian audiences, perhaps as speeches at the ground-breaking ceremonies themselves. In this way the texts became effective vehicles for presenting to the Babylonians an image of Esarhaddon as a king worthy of their acceptance and support.

Here again, attentions to Babylonia were balanced by similar attentions to Assyria, where the king also participated in ground-breaking ceremonies at the national temple, and where inscriptions were probably also orally presented to contemporary audiences to present a carefully shaped Assyrian image of the king, providing a counterweight to his actions in Babylonia and to the royal image presented there.

By the middle years of the reign, a new trend begins to be evident in Esarhaddon's public relations program. The degree of acceptance of the king by now evident in both nations, an acceptance strengthened by the military successes of his early years, made it possible for him to begin to encourage both Assyrians and Babylonians to take a further step and acknowledge that their unity lay not only in their rule by a single king, but also in a natural unity based on a long-shared religious and cultural tradition that made them in essence one people, despite their recent bitter relationship. Because of that bitterness, however, the idea of themselves as a single community was likely to encounter resistance in both camps, at least initially, and the inscriptions from the middle years put this idea forward cautiously, implying a community of interests in the introductory titles and epithets of the king, but not in the body of the inscriptions, which retain the local and provincial outlook that was traditional for building inscriptions in both nations.

It was only in the late years of the reign that this changed and expanded national image, an image permitting and in fact encouraging a lasting union of the two states, finally emerged as the main motif of a series of unusual inscriptions prepared for audiences in each of the two states. In these inscriptions projects benefiting each of the two groups were presented with equal emphasis in a single text that addressed Babylonians and Assyrians almost as a single audience, a single community sharing a common interest in projects in both areas.

One reason for this shift in emphasis in the later public relations program, from the earlier focus on the image of the king as a symbol of the unity of the two states to a new focus on a unified national image, may have been the decision to name not one, but two heirs to succeed Esarhaddon on the throne, one king to rule the empire as a whole from Assyria, the other to rule as that king's subordinate in Babylonia. This split meant that after Esarhaddon's death, the Assyrian king would cease to embody so directly the unity of the two states in his own person. Another focus for unity was now required, and the image of nation, rather than that of king, was the one Esarhaddon and his advisers now chose.

The final development in Esarhaddon's public relations program in support of his Babylonian policy appears in these same late texts, as well: the project of restoring the captured statues of Marduk and other Babylonian gods and returning those statues with much fanfare to their now restored temples in Babylonia. The reasons for the Assyrians' choice of this project were two-fold. On the one hand, the return of Marduk was the natural—and necessary—culmination of Esarhaddon's efforts to win the Babylonians' allegiance. Despite the progress Esarhaddon had already made in this regard, the Babylonians were unlikely ever to feel real loyalty toward a king and nation that continued to hold their national gods captive. Marduk's return was necessary to seal their acceptance of Assyrian rule and cement the growing bonds between the two states.

The rehabilitation of Marduk's statue and its return under Assyrian auspices offered to strengthen that bond in a second, more complex, way. Many Assyrians already worshipped Marduk as a god. At least some Assyrians had done so for generations, and the veneration of Marduk in Assyria seemed, particularly after Sargon's patronage of the cult, to be rapidly growing in importance. As a purely religious phenomenon, this growth of the worship of

Marduk in Assyria is not surprising; he was, after all, an appealing deity, a god of light and a revered source of healing and protection from misfortune. Nevertheless, Marduk continued to retain his role as the patron god of Babylon and the Babylonians. It was probably this nationalistic aspect of the god that had produced a recurrent resistance to Marduk's worship in Assyria, particularly evident in the reign of Esarhaddon's father Sennacherib, when military conflicts with Babylonia were intense. If this resistance to Marduk's worship in certain quarters in Assyria could be overcome, the figure of Marduk could make a valuable contribution to Esarhaddon's efforts to draw the two states closer together. As a major god worshipped in both states, Marduk would be a powerful unifying force, a uniquely effective emblem of unity and of divine approval for that unity. Esarhaddon's efforts to return the statue to Babylon under his own patronage seem designed to present Marduk in this light, as a god at once Assyrian and Babylonian, beloved of the Assyrians and supporting their rule at the same time that he continued to care for his own particular people, the Babylonians. In an effort to defuse potential Assyrian resistance to this official encouragement of the cult of Marduk, who after all remained to some extent someone else's patron god, one of Esarhaddon's inscriptions commemorating the restoration of the statue proposed the novel idea that the statue's reconstruction in the temple of Assyria's chief god Aššur represented a kind of rebirth in which Marduk had become the son of Aššur and a permanent—but slightly subordinate—member of the Assyrian pantheon. By this ingenious (and rather audacious) formulation, Marduk was transformed into an emblem of Assyrian-Babylonian unity and at the same time an emblem of Assyria's dominance in that union, one here characterized as reflecting the divine order. This formulation, if accepted, might permit even conservative Assyrians to worship Marduk without further reservations. The restoration and return of Marduk's statue, and the presentation of that project in inscriptions intended for both states as well as in a grand procession, was the final development in Esarhaddon's systematic program to encourage acceptance of his Babylonian policy in both states.

That images, emblems, and figurative action play a significant role in shaping national identities and loyalties is a commonplace of modern political theory; it seems evident from Esarhaddon's public actions and public papers that Esarhaddon and his advisers also understood this principle, at least intuitively, and used it to good advantage. What earlier Assyrian kings had been unable to compel from the Babylonians, Esarhaddon won from them peacefully and by their own consent, doing so in large part by his effective use of figurative aspects of national life as tools to affect political behavior.

Recognizing the importance to Babylonians of preserving a sense of their own national identity, Esarhaddon allied himself to the most powerful foci of that national identity—their king and their god—and made efforts to reshape those images into forces that might encourage the Babylonians to acceptance of Assyrian rule and of closer unity with the Assyrian people. It is perhaps ironic that the Assyrians, a people renowned for their use of military force and their brutality, should have provided us with this model of the effectiveness of the more peaceful tools of government.

Despite their well-earned (and carefully cultivated) reputation as one of the most violently repressive nations of the ancient Near East, the Assyrians were, however, capable at times of a flexibility and sensitivity in government that in the case of Esarhaddon's Babylonian policy proved highly effective. Despite the controversial nature of his policies, he died not by assassination, but from illness, on his way to lead a military campaign against Egypt in 669. The transfer of power to his two sons after his death was carried out peacefully, without any attempt at revolt even in Babylonia, in marked contrast to the situation after the death of his father twelve years earlier.[313] Esarhaddon's successors, Assurbanipal in Assyria and Šamaš-šumu-ukīn in Babylonia, ruled for a further seventeen years without significant outbreaks of resistance in Babylonia, suggesting that Esarhaddon had largely succeeded in creating a climate of opinion in Babylonia that would prove receptive to Assyrian rule even in his absence. It was not until 652, in the seventeenth year of joint rule after Esarhaddon's death, that the mounting rivalry between the two brothers erupted in the ill-fated Babylonian revolt led by Šamaš-šumu-ukīn against Assurbanipal. The war between the two brothers, bitter though it was, should not, I think, be taken as an indication that Esarhaddon's efforts to build acceptance of Assyrian rule in Babylonia had been a failure. Šamaš-šumu-ukīn's revolt, in contrast to earlier Babylonian uprisings, appears to have been in many respects an Assyrian civil war, fueled by Babylonian nationalist feeling, but precipitated in large part by the failure of the two Assyrian rulers to achieve a working relationship.

What is remarkable about the war between the brothers is not that Babylonia had eventually rebelled again, but that it was almost thirty years from the time of Esarhaddon's accession before war between the two states again erupted. Under Esarhaddon's administration, and in the years that followed it, the costly cycle of Babylonian revolts and Assyrian punitive campaigns for a time came to an end, and the image of a united Assyria and Babylonia that Esarhaddon was striving to promote became briefly a reality. The period of peace that Esarhaddon created between these two states stands as a monument to the power of images and to Esarhaddon's effective use of the peaceful arts of government.

---

[313] It should be noted that the smoothness of the transition was encouraged by the action of the dowager queen, Naqi'a, who imposed a second oath of loyalty (ABL 1239+) in support of Assurbanipal's accession at the crucial moment.

Introduction to the Documentary Sources

THE DOCUMENTARY EVIDENCE FROM MESOPOTAMIA
for Esarhaddon's reign is both rich and problematic. This essay is meant to
serve as a brief introduction to this literature, intended particularly for those
not familiar with the genres in common use in Mesopotamia. It provides a
brief introduction to each type of text represented here, a note about where
each individual text is published and finally some comments about any problems each group of texts presents. The essay focuses on Esarhaddon's own inscriptions, since they are the primary source for this study. The exception to
this rule is the Babylonian Chronicles, discussed in the first section of the essay,
which remain the primary source for the chronology of Esarhaddon's reign.
Other sources of documentary evidence for Esarhaddon's reign, including biblical and classical texts, as well as inscriptions of other Assyrian kings, have
been introduced as necessary in the text itself and are therefore not included
here. The dating of the inscriptions is discussed separately, in Appendix II.

The Babylonian Chronicles

The Chronicles are the logical starting point for any study of Esarhaddon
because they provide a dated list of major events in his reign and are the only
source to provide such a comprehensive chronological framework. The
Chronicles have been published in a modern critical edition prepared by
A. Kirk Grayson, *Assyrian and Babylonian Chronicles*, which describes the genre
as a whole and provides a transliteration, translation and commentary for each
chronicle. A typical Babylonian chronicle lists the years of reign of a series
of kings of Babylonia, noting one or two major events that occurred in each
listed year; those kings of Assyria who also ruled Babylonia, such as Esarhaddon, are included. Although a chronicle often records events that occurred
centuries before the copies of the chronicle which we have were written,
comparative studies suggest that the chronicles are relatively accurate chronologically.

Three Babylonian Chronicles deal with the period of Esarhaddon's reign:
Grayson's Chronicle 1, Chronicle 14 (known as the "Esarhaddon Chronicle")
and Chronicle 16 (the "Akitu Chronicle"). Of the three, Chronicle 16 offers
the briefest account. It is a specialized chronicle reporting interruptions in the
annual celebration of the *akītu* festival at Babylon and describing the events
which caused those interruptions—surviving in a single undated copy cover-

ing the period from the reign of Esarhaddon's father Sennacherib in Babylonia (688–681) to the first year of the Babylonian king Nabopolassar (626–605). Its significance for us is its report that the festival was not celebrated during Esarhaddon's reign because the statue of Marduk was in Assyria.

Chronicle 1 and Chronicle 14 are more typical, offering lists of major events in each year of Esarhaddon's reign as seen from a Babylonian perspective. Chronicle 1 survives in three copies, two of them fragmentary and undated, and the third dated to the time of the Persian king Darius I (521–486). It covers the period from the reign of the Babylonian king Nabû-nāṣir (747–734) to that of Esarhaddon's successor in Babylonia, Šamaš-šumu-ukīn (667–648). Chronicle 14, also known as the "Esarhaddon Chronicle," survives in a single undated copy. Although it uses the year-list format typical of the Chronicles, it is unusual in restricting its account to the reign of Esarhaddon and the first few years of his successor. While these two Chronicles offer parallel, sometimes identical, accounts of the reign, suggesting that they drew their information from a common source, Chronicle 14 omits any mention of two major setbacks to Esarhaddon, the sack of Sippar by the Elamites and the disastrous failure of the first Egyptian campaign, substituting for the latter event a minor military success in Babylonia. These differences, and the text's concentration on Esarhaddon's reign, suggest a bias in Chronicle 14 in favor of Esarhaddon, so that the text must be used with some caution.

For the most part, however, the two Chronicles agree, confirming and occasionally supplementing each other's accounts. They offer conflicting information on only two points, both concerning the dates of battles. In reporting the conquest of the land of Šubria in 673/2, Chr. 14 reports that the capital city fell on the 18th of Addāru (Feb./Mar.), the last month of the Assyrian year, while Chr. 1 places that event slightly earlier, in the month Ṭebētu (Dec./Jan.) and adds that booty from the city was sent to Uruk in Kislīmu (Nov./Dec.), that is, almost a year later. This delay in sending the booty seems odd, suggesting an error in the Chr. 1 account here. The two Chronicles also differ in their accounts of Esarhaddon's second Egyptian campaign; Chr. 14 reports a single major battle in Tašrītu (Sept./Oct.), while Chr. 1 reports several battles and places them all earlier, in the month Du'ūzu (June/July). These reports of the Egyptian campaign may not be mutually exclusive, but their differences make it clear that neither Chronicle's account of the campaign can be accepted without further analysis.

In contrast, the two texts agree on two dates which are probably in error: the beheading of the king of Sidon in the month Tašrītu (Sept./Oct.) of 676 and the defeat of the land of Bāzu in that same month. Both events are also reported in Nineveh B7, an inscription dated to the spring of 676, several months before the events even occurred according to both Chronicles' accounts. Israel Eph'al (*The Ancient Arabs*, 54 ff.) has pointed out another possible error which both Chronicles share; both assign the conquest of the town of Arza (a jumping-off place for the desert crossing to Egypt) to the year 679, while Esarhaddon's Nin. A inscription discusses it just after describing the death of the king of Sidon, which probably took place in 676. If the Nin. A inscription is following a roughly chronological plan here, as seems likely, it implies a later date for the seizure of Arza, closer to the beginning of the first campaign to Egypt in 674, for which the capture of Arza would have been a logical first step. It seems likely that on this point the inscription preserves a more accurate record than the two Chronicles.

Despite these minor difficulties, the three Chronicles offer what appear to be accurate, if lamentably brief, chronological accounts of the major events in Esarhaddon's reign as seen from a Babylonian perspective, making them an invaluable source of information not preserved in any other text.

Borger's Edition of Esarhaddon's Royal Inscriptions

Esarhaddon's royal inscriptions, the official public papers of the reign, survive as some seventy-five individual texts, many preserved in multiple copies. All of these texts, which constitute the major contemporary documentary sources for the reign, were collected and republished in an authoritative modern edition prepared by Riekele Borger, *Die Inschriften Asarhaddons Königs von Assyrien*, which provides a transliteration, translation and extensive philological commentary for each inscription. Since 1956, several new texts, fragments and modern copies of texts (some of them recording cuneiform signs or parts of signs which have since been lost as the texts deteriorated) have been published to supplement Borger's edition; these more recently published texts and copies are listed in Appendix III.

Borger's edition (hereafter *Asarh.*) is now acknowledged as the standard edition for most of Esarhaddon's texts. Since, however, it can be confusing to the uninitiated, it requires some introduction. It is helpful, first of all, to understand the system of labeling the inscriptions that Borger adopts, which provides a convenient way to refer to individual texts and groups of texts, and will probably be standard for years to come. Borger assigns each text a name that either reflects the type of text it represents (e.g., monument text or treaty) or, in the case of building inscriptions, reflects the city in which the building project described in the text took place. (It is important to realize that this is not always the city in which the text was discovered; for the provenance of each text, see Appendix IV.) Since there are often several texts describing work in the same city or even on the same project, each distinct text is assigned its own letter, e.g., "Assur A." In addition, each ancient copy of such a text is individually numbered, e.g., "Assur A4."

All the texts to which Borger assigns the same name and letter have been identified by him as essentially identical, with only minor variants. The one exception to this system is the Nineveh palace inscriptions, published as a composite text which Borger calls "Nineveh A–F"; in this case, documents which share the same letter are not necessarily exact duplicates, but are more loosely grouped into "classes" of texts. In some cases these "classes" are made up of duplicate texts, but in other cases the texts included in a single class differ slightly in the material they include (see, for example, Borger's comments on Nin. B on 37–38).

Another possible source of confusion is Borger's decision to publish two large sets of inscriptions, the Nineveh palace inscriptions (Nin. A–F) and the longer Babylon inscriptions (Bab. A–G), as composite texts, an arrangement which facilitates comparison of similar passages in the texts, but which obscures sometimes significant differences in the order of events the texts describe or in the over-all structure of those texts. This is particularly a problem in the case of Nin. B, Nin. C and Bab. G, in which the order of events differs considerably from that of Nin. A and Bab. A, which Borger uses as his main texts.

None of these problems presents any real difficulty, however, so long as the reader is aware of them. A potentially more serious problem in preparing an edition of Esarhaddon's inscriptions was the danger of accidentally creating new "patchwork" texts while attempting to piece together texts which survive only in fragments; a careful review of the original cuneiform editions of these fragmentary texts suggests, however, that Borger has meticulously avoided this pitfall, grouping pieces as parts of a larger text only when there is extensive overlapping in the text preserved on the various fragments. For most major texts, moreover, at least one copy survives in fairly complete form. The result is an edition of commendable accuracy. Borger's publication makes major contributions to our understanding of Esarhaddon's inscriptions and will long remain the definitive edition.

Full-length Building Inscriptions and Brick Inscriptions

Long building inscriptions form the largest single category of Esarhaddon royal inscriptions, including about thirty different texts, some surviving in many copies. These building inscriptions are published in the first section of Borger's *Asarh.* Most of the full-length building inscriptions describe a single large public building project sponsored by the king, usually the construction of a palace and arsenal complex or a temple, or more rarely, a procession street, canal, or other public edifice. The Babylon building inscriptions are a variation on this traditional pattern, describing several projects in that city, rather than restricting themselves to a single building. Building inscriptions were composed in Esarhaddon's reign for projects in both Assyria and Babylonia in a total of eight cities, including Aššur, Babylon, Borsippa, Calaḫ, Nineveh, Nippur, Tarbiṣu, and Uruk. In addition to Esarhaddon's own building inscriptions, Borger publishes one building inscription commissioned by Esarhaddon's mother Naqi'a (K. 2475+, *Asarh.*, 115–116), commemorating her construction of a palace for Esarhaddon in Nineveh. These full-length building inscriptions are usually inscribed on small barrels or prisms of clay, or on clay tablets. Their accounts are echoed by a second group of much briefer inscriptions commemorating the same projects and inscribed or stamped on bricks or stone slabs.

Several of the full-length building inscriptions are of particular interest because they include in their introductions a narrative account of major military and political events of the reign. As in most Assyrian inscriptions, the events included are limited to those in which the king could present himself as ultimately successful. The most detailed of these accounts are preserved in the texts Borger labels Nineveh A–F, the building inscriptions for the Nineveh arsenal and palace complex. In addition, a badly fragmented list of events in the reign introduces Mnm. B, a text inscribed on a stele found at a provincial city in the west. Shorter accounts of events in the reign, in the form of a long list of royal epithets describing the king's achievements, are included in two inscriptions, Calah A and Tarbisu A.

Unlike the royal inscriptions of many of his predecessors, most of Esarhaddon's historical inscriptions present events in geographical groupings rather than in strictly chronological order. Nin. D and Nin. E, however, number military campaigns and present them in chronological order. The fragmentary texts published by Borger at the end of his edition, of which the longest are Frt. A, B, and F, offer fragments of additional accounts of events in the reign; of these, Frt. F, of which a tantalizingly short piece survives, also presents events in a chronological arrangement, numbering each military campaign. The texts known as Babylon A–G also include extensive historical narratives along with their accounts of building activities, but confine themselves largely to the events associated with Babylon's destruction late in Sennacherib's reign and say little about events in the reign of Esarhaddon himself.

Inscriptions Describing Two or More Building Projects

Although most of Esarhaddon's building inscriptions follow the traditional pattern, dealing with only one building project in a single city, a few of his inscriptions take the unusual step of describing projects in more than one city. Several of these describe building projects in the two cities of Aššur and Babylon; these are published by Borger as the "AsBb," or "Assur-Babylon," texts (*Asarh.*, 78 ff.). Two long texts of this type, AsBbA and AsBbE, survive almost intact and describe work on the temples Ešarra and Esagila, in Aššur and Babylon respectively, as well as work on repairing or constructing statues of gods. AsBbE is of particular interest because it includes in its introduction an account (unfortunately broken at the beginning) of Esarhaddon's military successes through the year 671.

A unique text from Esarhaddon's reign, Borger's "Sammeltext" (*Asarh.*, 93 ff.) describes a series of building projects, starting with the rebuilding of the captured Mediterranean city of Sidon as an Assyrian city, "Kār-Esarhaddon," and continuing with brief accounts of building projects and pious donations in cities throughout both Assyria and Babylonia.

Palace Labels on Objects

A series of texts inscribed on various objects identify those objects as belonging to the palaces of Esarhaddon at Nineveh or Calaḫ. The texts are brief, usually consisting only of the name, short titles, and genealogy of the king. Such inscriptions occur on the back of floor slabs (Calah D and Nineveh L), on gaming boards (Nineveh K, under which label Borger also publishes duplicates from Calaḫ), on a vase (Nineveh N) and on a bronze lion weight (Nineveh P). They are published in *Asarh.*, 36 and 69–70.

"Letters to Gods"

The so-called "letter to a god" texts take the form of a detailed report on a single battle or campaign, sometimes cast as a letter to a god or gods. (For a discussion of the characteristics of this genre, see R. Borger, "Gottesbrief," 575–576.) Two Esarhaddon texts appear to be of this type (*Asarh.*, 102–107); although only a small section of the first text (Gbr. I) survives, its extant passages suggest that it originally described the same events as those covered in the much longer second "letter to a god" text (Gbr. II), that is, the successful Assyrian siege of the city of Uppume, capital of the land of Šubria, to the north of Assyria. Both texts are inscribed on tablets found at Nineveh, and Borger, suggesting these were part of the same document, publishes their texts as a single continuous account.

Treaties and Oaths

Copies of several texts recording treaties or oaths of loyalty to Esarhaddon have survived. The first, published by Borger (107 ff.), is an agreement between Esarhaddon and Ba'al of Tyre, inscribed on a tablet found at Nineveh. Two fragmentary documents (Borger's Frt. D [K. 4473] and the text numbered 83–1–18, 386 and described by Borger on p. 120) may also belong to this text, as Borger notes. A more recent edition of the treaty with Ba'al which includes a fragment not known to Borger (Sm. 964) has been published by

Simo Parpola and Kazuko Watanabe, *Neo-Assyrian Treaties and Loyalty Oaths*, 24–27.

The second text usually referred to as a treaty of Esarhaddon is perhaps more accurately characterized as a list of oaths imposed on various vassal city-rulers and chieftains requiring them to support the accession of Esarhaddon's sons Assurbanipal and Šamaš-šumu-ukīn after Esarhaddon's death. The text recording these oaths survives in fragments of what were once nine or more separate documents, each inscribed on a large tablet. These were discovered in a throne room in the temple of Nabû on the citadel of Calaḫ during excavations in 1955. The first edition of the texts is that of D.J. Wiseman, *The Vassal-Treaties of Esarhaddon*. Revised editions have more recently been published by Kazuko Watanabe, *Die adê-Vereidigung anlässlich der Thronfolgeregelung Asarhaddons*, and by Simo Parpola and Kazuko Watanabe, *Neo-Assyrian Treaties*, 28–58. In addition, an Esarhaddon inscription recently published by A. Kirk Grayson ("Akkadian Treaties," 135 ff. and 155 ff.) and now republished in revised form by Parpola and Watanabe *(Treaties, 77–79)* describes what appears to be a more Babylonian version of these oaths. A badly fragmented text, also published by Parpola and Watanabe (59), records an oath of loyalty to Esarhaddon.

Another text recording a formal oath of loyalty to Esarhaddon, first published by Parpola in "Neo-Assyrian Treaties," 170 ff. and 163, and now published in transliteration and translation by Parpola and Watanabe, 22–23, refers to Esarhaddon not as "king," but as "my lord," and probably represents an oath of loyalty requiring support of Esarhaddon when his father should die and he himself claim the throne. It is recorded on a clay tablet found at Nineveh.

Monument Inscriptions

Several long inscriptions of Esarhaddon were inscribed on stelae or on cliff faces, all located outside the Assyrian homeland in the western provinces, and all datable on internal evidence to late in the reign, after the successful campaign against Egypt in 671. They are published in *Asarh.*, 96–102. "Monument A," inscribed on a basalt stele more than 10 feet high, was found at Ja'udi (modern Zincirli) in the Amanus Mountains, capital of the Assyrian vassal state of Sam'al. The stele, in excellent condition, carries both the inscription and a bas-relief, which shows the king facing a series of emblems of gods and holding a horn-shaped object, a mace, and two reins which descend to rings in the noses of two smaller figures, one with Negroid facial features and Egyptian royal insignia who perhaps represents a son of the pharaoh Tarqu, captured during Esarhaddon's second Egyptian campaign, and the other probably representing the Phoenician king Abdi-Milkutti, captured somewhat earlier. (For further discussion, see François Thureau-Dangin, "Tell Aḥmar," pp. 185–205.) The inscription runs across the small figures and the lower body of the king. Two clay tablets provide copies of part of the same text (*Asarh.*, 96). The stele and its provenance are described by the excavator, F. von Luschan, in *Ausgrabungen von Sendschirli*, I (Berlin: 1893), 11–29. A photograph of the stele is published by James B. Pritchard, ed., *The Ancient Near East: An Anthology*, no. 121.

The second monument inscription of Esarhaddon, Mnm. B, inscribed on a large, now fragmented stele of black basalt, was found near the mound of Tell Aḥmar (ancient Til-Barsip), an Assyrian vassal city guarding a major ford across the Euphrates in northern Syria. What remains of its relief is almost identical in design to that of the Zincirli stele, although neither the carving nor the inscription were finished in this case; the modeling of the feet remains uncompleted, and the text breaks off in mid-stream, leaving several blank lines ruled out on the stone but unfilled. A similar stele, uninscribed, was found inside the gatehouse of the city and bears a nearly identical bas-relief. For descriptions of the stelae and their locations, see Thureau-Dangin, "Tell Aḥmar," 185–205.

The third inscribed monument of Esarhaddon, Mnm. C, is one of a series of large rock-cut reliefs left by conquering kings on cliffs at the mouth of the Nahr el-Kelb, just north of Beirut in Lebanon. The relief, badly weathered, depicts a bearded king wearing the Assyrian crown and clothed in an ankle-length tunic. In his left hand he holds a scepter and in his right, a horn or cup. Eight emblems of gods are ranged before his face. The inscription, also badly weathered, runs across the lower body, beginning at waist-level. For a description and photo, see F. Weissbach, *Die Denkmäler und Inschriften an der Mündung des Nahr el-Kelb*, 22–30, and Tf. XI.

A possible fourth Esarhaddon monument inscription was discovered in 1972 by L. Vanden Berghe on a rock face at Shikaft-i Gulgul, a remote location on the western slopes of the Zagros Mountains east of Baghdad. Both inscription and relief are badly weathered, making attribution to Esarhaddon uncertain. For a description and a copy of the inscription, see A. Kirk Grayson and Louis D. Levine, "The Assyrian Relief from Shikaft-I Gulgul," 29–38.

Short Dedicatory Inscriptions

A few short texts are inscribed on objects dedicated to gods. These include Assur H (a dedication to the god Aššur inscribed on a door socket), and Babylon H (a dedication to the god Marduk inscribed on a lapis lazuli cylinder seal depicting a male figure holding lightning bolts). The short brick inscriptions from Babylon (Bab. I–N) and Uruk (Uruk E, F, and G) also belong to the category of short dedicatory inscriptions, although they dedicate buildings and in one case a walkway, rather than small objects. Wilfred G. Lambert has recently published (in "An Eye-stone of Esarhaddon's Queen and other Similar Gems," 65–71) an inscription on an eye-shaped agate which identifies the stone as belonging to Ešarra-ḫamât, one of Esarhaddon's wives. As Lambert notes (70), this also was probably a votive object, with the inscription identifying the donor.

The fragmented inscription found on a decorated strip of bronze recently acquired by the Louvre may also have been a dedicatory inscription, if the strip originally was part of the decoration for an altar or thronebase, as Parrot and Nougayrol suggest. Attribution to Esarhaddon is tentative but plausible. See André Parrot and Jean Nougayrol, "Asarhaddon et Naqi'a sur un Bronze du Louvre (AO 20.185)," *Syria*, 33 (1956), 148–160.

Mortuary Inscriptions

Assur I (*Asarh.*, 10), an inscription carved on a rough and badly broken piece of gypsum found at Aššur, is evidently the remains of a mortuary inscription for the same queen, Ešarra-ḫamât.

Inscribed Seals

Seal impressions found on jar sealings, bullae, and tablets discovered during the excavations at Calah include two inscribed seals of Esarhaddon. These are published by Barbara Parker, "Seals and Seal Impressions from the Nimrud Excavations, 1955–58," 28 and 38. The vassal treaties or oaths of Esarhaddon found at Calah also bear seal impressions. These are not impressions of Esarhaddon's own seal, but rather of the seals of Sennacherib, the god Aššur, and a Middle Assyrian king. For these, see D.J. Wiseman, *The Vassal-Treaties of Esarhaddon*, 13–22 and plates III–VI. (An uninscribed royal seal of Esarhaddon may survive as one of several ancient objects which were made up into a set of jewelry in 1869 for the wife of the first excavator of Calah and Nineveh, Sir Austen Henry Layard. For a description and photo, see R.D. Barnett, "Lady Layard's Jewelry," 172–179 and plate XXIX.)

Amulet Inscriptions

Two ancient copies of inscriptions for neck amulets to be worn by Esarhaddon survive (Borger's 80–7–19, 44, on p. 119, and K. 10220+ K. 10463, p. 118), both on clay tablets.

Documents Presumed Lost

I have not been able to discover the present whereabouts of three documents or sets of documents carrying Esarhaddon inscriptions, if, indeed, they still survive. The first is a set of alabaster slabs found by Layard in a chamber on the mound of Nebi Yunus at Nineveh. He reports that the inscriptions gave the name, titles, and genealogy of Esarhaddon and were identical to those he had found on the backs of bulls and sphinxes in the Southwest Palace

at Calaḫ (A. H. Layard, *Discoveries*, 598; the text is that of Borger's Calah D).
The second missing document, probably found at Uruk, is a cylinder which
Luckenbill describes (*ARAB*, II, p. 279, n. 1) as inscribed with the same text
as Uruk A, with "a large number of variant readings." He reports that the
cylinder survives now only as a cast in the collection of the Haskell Museum
in Chicago, and that the location of the original cylinder is unknown. The
third missing documents are two limestone slabs discovered at Tarbiṣu by
Layard (*Discoveries*, 599). He reports that the text on them described
Esarhaddon's construction of a palace at Tarbiṣu for Assurbanipal. The text
remains unpublished and the location of the slabs themselves unknown.

Letters

In addition to the royal inscriptions, several other types of documents
offer contemporary evidence for the reign. Of these, letters are perhaps the
most numerous and certainly one of the most important. These letters, part
of a collection of almost 3,000 found in the city of Nineveh and dating to
the reigns of Sargon, Esarhaddon and Assurbanipal, were written to Esarhaddon (or in some cases, to his mother) by advisers, officials and various professional consultants; a few letters come from the king himself. They deal particularly with problems of members of the court or royal family, with temple
administration, and with affairs in Babylonia. Addressed simply "to the king,
my lord" and undated, the letters must be assigned to the proper reign and
dated, if possible, on internal evidence alone; Simo Parpola argues persuasively that roughly 80 percent of the Nineveh letters can be dated to
Esarhaddon's reign (*Letters*, IIb, p. XII). As private communications between
the king and his officials and advisers, they provide an invaluable corrective
to the picture which emerges from the king's public papers. Cuneiform copies
of nearly 1,500 of these Nineveh letters of Neo-Assyrian kings were first published by Robert Francis Harper, *Assyrian and Babylonian Letters belonging to the
Kouyunjik Collections of the British Museum, Parts I–XIV*. Although full of errors
and long outdated, this remains the standard cuneiform edition of these texts.
It has now been supplemented by a cuneiform edition of the remaining unpublished Assyrian letters from Nineveh prepared by Simo Parpola, *Cuneiform
Texts from Babylonian Tablets in the British Museum, Part 53: Neo-Assyrian Letters
from the Kuyunjik Collection*, and by a cuneiform edition of the unpublished
Neo-Babylonian letters from Nineveh prepared by Manfried Dietrich, *Cuneiform Texts from Babylonian Tablets in the British Museum, Part 54: Neo-Babylonian
Letters from the Kuyunjik Collection*. See also Dietrich's extensive preliminary
notes, *Welt des Orient*, 4 (1967–68), 61–103 and 183–251; 5 (1969–70), 51–56
and 176–190; and 6 (1970–71), 157–162, as well as his partial translations in
the appendix to his book, *Die Aramäer südbabyloniens in der Sargonidenzeit*

(700–648). See also, however, the critical review by J.A. Brinkman, "Notes on Arameans and Chaldeans in Southern Babylonia in the Early Seventh Century BC," 304–325. Simo Parpola's translations of 345 letters to Esarhaddon and Assurbanipal, *Letters from Assyrian Scholars to the Kings Esarhaddon and Assurbanipal, Part 1: Texts*, AOAT 5/1 and *Part II: Commentary and Appendices*, AOAT 5/2, discusses the formidable difficulties in translation and interpretation which the letters present and describes Parpola's remarkably successful efforts to resolve many of them. In addition to these Nineveh letters, Neo-Assyrian letters have been unearthed in other cities in recent years, but none of significance for the present study.

Economic Texts

Numerous economic texts survive from the reign of Esarhaddon, including records of loans, bills of sale, contracts, and related legal texts. As sources of information on the prosopography and economics of Esarhaddon's period, they provide important background to the present study; they have not, however, played a central role in my discussion, and I will discuss them here only briefly. A collection of Assyrian economic texts from the reign of Esarhaddon, and of other Neo-Assyrian kings as well, was published in a cuneiform edition by Claude H.W. Johns, *Assyrian Deeds and Documents*. An edition of these texts in transliteration and translation was published by J. Kohler and A. Ungnad, *Assyrische Rechtsurkunden*. In addition, a small number of Assyrian economic texts from the reign of Esarhaddon were discovered during British excavations at Calaḫ, beginning in 1949. Economic texts from Babylonia dated to the period of Esarhaddon's reign are listed, with bibliography, by Grant Frame, "Babylonia 689–627 BC: A Political History," in the appendix, Table 1: "Babylonian Economic Texts Dated by the Reign of Esarhaddon." An up-dated list of all dated Babylonian economic texts from this period was published by J.A. Brinkman and D.A. Kennedy, "Documentary Evidence for the Economic Base of Early Neo-Babylonian Society: A Survey of Dated Babylonian Economic Texts, 721–626 BC," 1–90, with the texts dated to Esarhaddon's reign listed on pages 17–20.

Liver Omen Texts

The liver omen texts consist of some hundred clay tablets, each recording a request to the god Šamaš for information about what would happen should the Assyrians undertake a particular project, such as an attack on a certain city, a tax-collecting expedition into the Zagros Mountains, or, in the case of the so-called "Aufstand" texts, the appointment of a particular person to office. The answers to these inquiries were to be indicated by the god through the shapes of the livers of ritually slaughtered sheep, examined and interpreted by experts trained in this type of divination. A large percentage of the extant liver omen texts can be dated to the reign of Esarhaddon, to whom they refer by name and royal title. In the many cases where such passages are broken, references to people and events often link the omen texts to others in which Esarhaddon is named, making it likely that the great majority of the liver omen texts known to us date from Esarhaddon's time. In a few texts, the crown prince Assurbanipal is named as the inquirer, and in one, Klauber's #60, Assurbanipal is named as king. The liver omen texts are published by Jörgen A. Knudtzon, *Assyrische Gebete an den Sonnengott für Staat und königliches Haus aus der Zeit Asarhaddons und Asurbanipals*, and by Ernst Georg Klauber, *Politsch-Religiöse Texte aus der Sargonidenzeit*. Both editions are now outdated, but have not yet been replaced by a more modern edition [see now the edition of Ivan Starr, *Queries to the Sungod: Divination and Politics in Sargonid Assyria*, SAA IV (Helsinki U. Press: Helsinki, 1990)]. For unpublished liver omen queries and reports, see Jussi Aro, "Remarks on the Practice of Extispicy in the Time of Esarhaddon and Assurbanipal," 116.

Reports of Ecstatics

Four unusual texts, which can be dated on internal evidence to Esarhaddon's reign, take the form of collections of statements made by individuals who assert that they are speaking for a deity, often Ištar of Arbela. The messages offer comfort and encouragement to Esarhaddon, or to his mother, and in several cases seem to refer to events in the period of Esarhaddon's difficulties before he managed to take the throne. The texts vary in form and are difficult to translate and to interpret, a problem exacerbated by frequent broken sections in the tablets. The texts are at present available only in scattered and outdated editions. The tablet K. 2401 is published by S. Arthur Strong, "On Some Oracles to Esarhaddon and Assurbanipal," *Sonderabdrucke aus den Beiträgen zur Assyriologie . . .*, Bd. II, 627–643, and by James A. Craig, *Assyrian and Babylonian Religious Texts*, I, pl. 22–25, and corrections. K. 4310 is published by H.C. Rawlinson, *The Cuneiform Inscriptions of Western Asia*, IV, pl. 68 (= second edition, pl. 61), and two other texts, BM 82-5-22, 527 and K. 6259, are published by Stephen H. Langdon, *Tammuz and Ishtar*, pls. II, III and IV. Translations and comments of widely varying reliability are available in these publications as well as in Edgar J. Banks, "Eight Oracular Responses to Esarhaddon," 267–77; A. Delattre, "The Oracles Given in Favour of Esarhaddon," 25–31; Friedrich Schmidtke, *Asarhaddons Statthalterschaft in Babylonien*, 115–121; André Parrot and Jean Nougayrol, "Asarhaddon et Naqi'a sur un Bronze du Louvre," 158, n. 6; Robert Biggs, "Oracles Concerning Esarhaddon," *ANET*, II, 169; and Manfred Weippert, "Assyrische Prophetien der Zeit Asarhaddons und Assurbanipals," 71–115.

"Religio-Political" Texts

Several texts discussed in the final chapter, in particular the "Sin of Sargon" and the so-called "Ordeal of Marduk" texts, are at once religious and political in their implications. Space precludes a full analysis of their complexities, but the problems they present are discussed briefly in the text where they are significant for the argument.

Conclusion

Even from this brief survey, it is apparent that the documentary evidence for Esarhaddon's reign includes a wide variety of texts, many of them still not well understood—an embarrassment of riches. Even with the extensive work done on Esarhaddon texts in recent years, it will be some time before reliable modern editions are available for all of them, and even longer before we will have untangled some of the more vexing problems the texts present. The recent publications of major text groups from Esarhaddon's reign by Borger, Parpola, Dietrich, Watanabe and Wiseman, however, make it possible for us to begin at last a reevaluation of Esarhaddon's reign and of the Assyrian empire in its final years of power.

The Dating of the Inscriptions

TO TRACE THE CHANGES IN ESARHADDON'S BABYLONIAN policy over time, we must first establish the date of each of his inscriptions, so far as the evidence permits. The simplest place to begin is with the inscriptions that were dated by the scribes who copied them. Nineteen of the copies of Esarhaddon's various building inscriptions and three copies of his vassal treaties conclude with year-dates which are still intact (month and date, if included, are noted in parentheses):

Dated Esarhaddon Inscriptions

680: Bab. G (Ajāru); Bab. A1; Bab. C2; Bab. E3
679: Ass. A4 (Simānu, day broken)
678: (none)
677: Nin. G (Ulūlu 20)
676: Nin. B7 (Ajāru 22); Klch. A8 (Abu 21); Klch. A9 (Ulūlu 10); Klch. A10 (Ulūlu 10); Klch. A14
675: (none)
674: (none)
673: Nin. A1 (Addāru); Nin. A26 (Addāru); Nin. A2, Nin. A16 and Nin. A31 (Pēt-bābi)
672: Nin. A28 (Nisannu); Klch. A7 (Ajāru 18); Trb. A (Ajāru 18); Klch. A1 (Abu 5); VT 36C (Ajāru 16); VT 54B and 54F (Ajāru 18)

One additional copy of the Nin. A inscription is said to be dated, but has not yet been published, nor has its date been reported (Lambert and Millard, *Catalogue*, 25). In addition, several inscriptions not included in the list have partially broken dates in which only the month survives; Assur A1 is dated only by day and month (19th[?] of Du'ūzu).

The modern (Julian calendar) equivalents of the Assyrian months in the list above are as follows: Nisannu, Mar./Apr.; Ajāru, Apr./May; Simānu, May/Jun.; Abu, Jul./Aug.; Ulūlu, Aug./Sept. For a discussion of the problems involved in converting Assyrian dates to Julian dates and for a table for converting dates in the reign of Esarhaddon, see Parpola, *Letters*, IIb, Appendix A: Assyrian Chronology 681–648 BC. The month Pēt-bābi was not commonly used in Assyrian dating, and its Julian calendar equivalent is uncertain. Parpola (*Letters*, IIb, 186–187) notes that it refers in letters to at least two different months. In Esarhaddon's Bab. A, B, and C (Ep. 13), however, it is mentioned in a passage describing astronomical events which occurred over a brief period of time, probably in the space of two months, the first of which is named as Simānu, making Pēt-bābi, the second month in this passage, equivalent in this case to Du'ūzu, or June/July.

Since the events reported in the dated inscriptions are consistent with the dates assigned to those texts by their scribes, and since there would seem to be little reason for scribes to have falsified the dates (except perhaps in the special case of the Babylon inscriptions, which are discussed below), the dates in the list above can probably be accepted as reasonably accurate.

The dated Babylon inscriptions, however, pose a special problem. In dating them, Esarhaddon's scribes used a Babylonian dating formula, written with the logograms MU.SAG.NAM.LUGAL.LA, literally meaning, "year of the beginning of kingship." This dating formula was used in Babylonian inscriptions as the term for the accession year of a king, the period between his predecessor's death and his own formal installation as king at the beginning of the following year, which fell in mid-March.

Esarhaddon's full-length Babylon inscriptions (Borger's Babylon A–G texts), however, were almost certainly not written in his accession year, despite the use of this dating formula on several of them. This is particularly clear in the case of Babylon G, which is dated to the month Ajāru (April–May) of the MU.SAG.NAM.LUGAL.LA, a month not included in Esarhaddon's brief accession "year," which began with his father's death in the month Ṭebētu (Dec.–Jan.), almost at the end of the Assyrian year, and long after Ajāru had passed.

Tadmor argues that the other three dated Babylon texts were not written in the accession year, either, and suggests that the dating formula used in the Esarhaddon Babylon inscriptions had no chronological validity. He begins by pointing out (in *Assyrian Royal Inscriptions: New Horizons*, 13–25, esp. p. 22) a repeating pattern in Mesopotamian royal inscriptions, in which events which can be shown to have occurred at a later date are nevertheless attributed to the first year of a king's reign, a device which Tadmor suggests was intended to enhance the king's image as an energetic and successful ruler from the outset. Tadmor suggests that the Babylon texts of Esarhaddon which have accession year dates are an example of this pattern, pointing out (following Cogan in *History, Historiography and Interpretation*, 85–87) that at least one of these inscriptions, Babylon C, refers to the return of plundered gods from Elam, an event which the Babylonian Chronicles date to Esarhaddon's seventh year of reign, 674. It seems clear that Babylon C, like Babylon G, cannot be dated to the accession year, despite its MU.SAG.NAM.LUGAL.LA formula. Tadmor therefore argues that all four dated Babylon texts were employing the accession-year dating formula as a rhetorical device to enhance the king's image, rather than as an indication of actual date.

Practical considerations make it very likely in any case that none of the texts, including the four dated ones, were written in Esarhaddon's accession year. The Babylonian Chronicles report that Esarhaddon took some time to gain control of Assyria after his father's death, not ending the civil war and ascending the throne until the eighteenth (or perhaps the twenty-eighth) of Addāru (Feb.–Mar.), so that he actually held full control of Assyria for no more than the last twelve days of his accession year. It seems most unlikely that the publication of a building inscription, even as laconic and preliminary an inscription as Babylon G, would have taken place in this brief period.

Since it is clear that the Babylon inscriptions' accession year dates cannot be taken at face value, it seems best to disregard them, at least initially, and approach the problem of dating the Babylon A–G inscriptions by examining them for other evidence of the period or periods in which they were written. In the case of Babylon C, as we saw, its reference in Ep. 36 to the return of gods' statues requires a date of 674 or later, despite the MU.SAG.NAM. LUGAL.LA date on one copy of the text. The detailed description the text offers of the final stages of building and outfitting the temple of Babylon (Ep. 33) adds additional corroboration to this relatively late date, since it suggests that the text was written to commemorate a fairly advanced stage in the building project. Babylon F, although badly fragmented and with no date surviving, contains the same description of the events of 674, and should thus be assigned a similar date, sometime late in the reign. Babylon E, although it does not mention the return of gods' statues in 674, does include a more succinct but similar account of the final outfitting of the temple as that of Babylon C (Ep. 33), suggesting that it, too, was composed at about the same time, as the temple refurbishing project neared completion, probably in 674 or later—again, despite the accession year date on one copy of this text.

In contrast, an examination of the events described in Babylon A (one copy of which has the accession year date) and Babylon B (undated) suggests that they are probably both genuinely early texts, since both of them focus on the planning and foundation-laying stages of the project, and unlike Babylon C, E, and F, offer only cursory accounts of the later stages of the temple's reconstruction, perhaps not fully planned at the point when Babylon A and B were composed. Although both texts were probably written early in the reign, their dates of composition must be placed after October of 680 because both include an account (Ep. 13) of movements of the planet Jupiter which occurred at that time (Parpola, private communication, 24 February 1977).

Babylon D, like Babylon A and B, focuses on preparations for the reconstruction of temple and city, and like those texts, deals with the actual rebuilding of the temple and city in a cursory fashion. This focus on preliminaries suggests that Babylon D also should be dated to the first two or three years of the reign. This early date for all three texts rests on the hypothesis that the rebuilding of Babylon was actually begun, or at the very least, announced, in the first two or three years of the reign, which seems likely, since there were clear advantages to Esarhaddon in making some visible progress on the project as early in the reign as possible, and little advantage in delaying a project that was central to his conciliatory Babylonian policy.

Although five of the inscriptions, Babylon A, B, C, D and E, refer to a year of brickmaking preceding the actual building (Ep. 22), this is of dubious value as chronological evidence; the phrase (which also appears in Esarhaddon's account of rebuilding the Aššur temple in Aššur [Assur A, iv 41–v 1–2]) should probably be understood in all six texts as a literary *topos* echoing the description in the Enūma eliš myth (vi, 60) of the first construction of the temple Esagila by the gods.

The dating of Babylon G is a special case to which we must now return. Unlike the other dated Babylon inscriptions, Babylon G uses not only the formula MU.SAG.NAM.LUGAL.LA, but specifies a month as well, the month Ajāru, as if in this case the scribe were using the accession year phrase as a genuine indicator of date, rather than as a rhetorical device. The Babylon G inscription appears to be the earliest account of Babylon's reconstruction, offering the briefest description of actual building and focusing its attention on the preliminary task of draining the still partially flooded city; a date in the accession year, 681, is not possible, however, because the month Ajāru is included in the text's date, as we saw earlier. Parpola offers a plausible solution to the puzzle, suggesting (in David Owen and Kazuko Watanabe, "Eine Neubabylonische Gartenkaufurkunde," 37–38) that Esarhaddon's Assyrian scribes, although adopting a Babylonian dating formula here, were using it unconventionally; he suggests that MU.SAG.NAM.LUGAL.LA did not mean "accession year" in these inscriptions, in the Babylonian fashion, but was instead used in its literal sense to mean "first year of kingship," referring to Esarhaddon's first full year as king, the year 680—a date which fits the evidence admirably.

To summarize, Esarhaddon's Babylon texts seem to cluster in two periods. The first group of texts was written at the very beginning of the reign, with Babylon G composed in the second month of 680, Babylon D written shortly thereafter, perhaps in the same year, and Babylon A and B following in the first two or three years of the reign. The second group of texts, consisting of Babylon C, E and F, was composed several years afterwards when the project of rebuilding the temple and city was approaching completion, in 674 or shortly thereafter. Since none of the texts refer to the appointment of a crown prince for Babylon, a major event that one would expect to have been mentioned had it already taken place, it seems likely that all of the Babylon A–G texts were composed before 672 at the latest, when the appointment of the crown princes occurred. (Cogan, in Tadmor and Weinfeld, ed., *History, Historiography and Interpretation*, 85–87, has independently dated the Babylon inscriptions using the same principle of analyzing the detail with which each text describes the various stages of building; he comes to similar conclusions but posits a more even distribution of inscriptions throughout the years from 680 to 674.)

Aside from the problematic accession year dates on Babylon inscriptions, the dates on Esarhaddon's inscriptions should probably be accepted as reliable. Many of the remaining inscriptions, although undated, can be assigned approximate dates on internal evidence by linking references in the texts to datable events in the reign. The dated list of events in Esarhaddon's reign in the various Babylonian Chronicles, together with the date of Esarhaddon's vassal treaties, provides us with a basic chronological framework for dating these texts, summarized below:

681/80: 20 Ṭebētu (Dec.-Jan.), Sennacherib murdered. 2 Addāru (Feb.–Mar.), uprising in Assyria ends. 18 (or 28) Addāru, Esarhaddon enters Nineveh, takes throne.

680/79: Uprising in Babylonia led by Nabû-zēr-kitti-līšir collapses. Ulūlu (Aug.–Sept.), gods' statues returned to Dēr and Dūr-Šarrukīn.

679/78: Arza is taken. Slaughter of Cimmerians.

678/77: Governor of Nippur and Šamaš-ibni of Bīt-Dakkūri executed in Assyria.

677/76: Sidon captured and sacked.

676/75: Bāzu captured. King of Sidon beheaded.

675/74: Elamite raid on Sippar. Assyria fights in Meliddu. Another governor of Nippur and a chief of Bīt-Dakkūri deported to Assyria, executed (?).

674/73: Assyria defeated in Egypt. Ištar and gods of Akkad returned from Elam.

673/72: King's wife dies. Šubria sacked by Assyria.

672/71: Assurbanipal and Šamaš-šuma-ukīn proclaimed heirs to thrones of Assyria and Babylonia.

671/70: Assyria conquers Egypt.

670/69: Assyrian officials put to death.

669/68: Esarhaddon dies enroute to Egypt. Assurbanipal becomes king of Assyria. Marduk returned to Babylon.

Using this information, we can draw up the following list of Esarhaddon inscriptions arranged in chronological order. The evidence for dating each text is indicated in parentheses. Texts of somewhat uncertain date are preceded by a question mark.

681/80: ?Nin. J (Esar. as heir apparent, thus before death of Senn. in Jan., 680)

680: Bab. G (dated, Ajāru)

680 or shortly after:
  Bab. A (early stages of work on Esagila, but after Jupiter omens of late Oct., 680)
  Babylon B (early work on Esagila; same period)
  Babylon D (early work on Esagila; same period)

679: Ass. A (dated, day x, Simānu)

678: (dated but still unpublished entry inscriptions for Nebi Yunus palace)

677: Nin. G (dated, Ulūlu 20)
677 or after:
  Ass. D (Sidon)
  Nin. D (Sidon; possibly as late as 671, room for ref. to Egypt success)
  ?Nin. H (if eponym is Abi-râmu, as Borger proposes)
676: Nin. B7 (dated, Ajāru 22)
  Klch. A8 (dated, Abu 21)
  Klch. A9 and Klch. A10 (dated, Ulūlu 10)
  Klch. A14 (dated; no month)
676 or after:
  Nin. C (ref. to Bāzu; bef. 671, since no ref. to Egypt)
675: (none)
674 or later:
  Bab. C (Ep. 36, return of gods from Elam)
  Bab. F (same)
  ?Bab. E (no Ep. 36, but similar to Bab. C refs. to completion of Esagila)
673: ?Ass. I (after death of a queen)
  Nin. A2 (dated, Pēt-bābi [here Jun.–Jul.])
  Nin. A16 (dated, Pēt-bābi)
  Nin. A1 (dated, Addāru)
  Nin. A26 (dated, Addāru)
673 or later:
  Gbr. (Šubria)
  Treaty with Ba'al (after defeat of Sidon in 677, but not mentioned in Nin. B [676];
    first mention in Nin. A [673])
672: Nin. A28 (dated, Nisannu)
  Vassal Treaties (dated, Ajāru 16 and 18)
  Klch. A7 (dated, Ajāru 18)
  Trb. A (dated, Ajāru 18)
  Klch. A1 (dated, Abu 5)
672 or later:
  Ass. E (Assurbanipal as heir)
  Nin. F (Assurbanipal as heir)
  ?AsBbG (Šamaš-šumu-ukīn given to Marduk to strengthen acceptance as heir in
    Bab.? Priests installed in completed temple [Esagila?])
671 or later:
  Ass. H (E. as overlord of Egypt)
  Klch. D (E. as overlord of Egypt)
  Nin. E (conquest of Egypt described)
  Nin. P (inscribed on vase identified as booty from Egypt)
  Trb. B (E. as overlord of Egypt)
  AsBbA (E. as overlord of Egypt, obv. 28–9)
  AsBbE (conquest of Egypt, obv. 8–9)
  Smlt (booty from Egypt, obv. 25 and 28)
  Mnm. A (E. as overlord of Egypt, obv. 16)

?Mnm. B (strong similarity to Mnm. A)

Mnm. C (E. as overlord of Egypt, ll. 5–6)

Frt. F (describes army's journey to Egypt)

?AsBbF (describes procession returning Marduk's statue; 1st datable ref. in AsBbE
 [671 or later])

?AsBbH (describes procession returning Marduk: see above)

These are the inscriptions to which years can be assigned with some degree of confidence. We can also draw more tentative conclusions about the period of composition of some of the remaining inscriptions. It is possible to assign tentative dates to Uruk A–G and to Nippur A, for example, since the texts are closely related and the reconstruction of the Uruk temple described in the Uruk texts almost certainly occurred before the return of the statue of the god Uṣur-amatsa to that temple, first mentioned in AsBbA (671 or later). Since neither the statue's return nor the repair of the temple are mentioned in the long historical summary of Nin. B (earliest exemplar dated 676), where some reference to the project might reasonably be expected, we can probably place the composition of all the Uruk texts between 676 and not long after 671. Since Nippur A is virtually identical to Uruk A, it seems likely that it was composed at roughly the same time. In both cases, the several inscriptions commemorating the temple rebuilding were probably composed over a span of time, each new composition marking the beginning or completion of a different stage of the work. There is no clear indication, however, of the order in which the various parts of the project were undertaken, and hence no indication of the order in which the various texts were composed.

If we add to our chronological framework information derived from an analysis of certain letters from Esarhaddon's reign, it is possible to propose a date for Brs. A as well. This date is, however, somewhat more conjectural than dates resting on material derived from the Babylonian Chronicles because the dating depends on conclusions drawn from arguments linking several letters and from deductions about the relationship of those letters to the reconstruction of the temple of Gula at Borsippa, which Brs. A commemorates but which is never explicitly mentioned in any of these letters. Parpola argues plausibly in his commentary on the letters that LAS 57, 58, 276 and 281 all describe the construction of a tiara for the god Nabû (judging from LAS 281, the god Nabû of Borsippa, whose affairs are discussed at length there). References in the four letters to the crown prince and to booty from Egypt place them in the time period between 672 and 670, as Parpola argues. Since the tiara they discuss was probably a gift for Nabû intended to accompany the reopening of the refurbished temple, the dates of the letters suggest that the Borsippa temple project was at least planned in detail and probably already underway by 672 or a little later. The Brs. A inscription commemorating the project can thus be tentatively assigned to that period.

No firm conclusion can be drawn about the date of composition of Frags. A–D, however, despite datable events mentioned in them, because we have no way to establish the final cut-off point for their reports of events. Frag. A, for example, mentions a series of events which occurred in the period from late 681 to about 677, but it might well have reported on later events in the concluding sections of the text, which are now completely broken away.

In addition to the royal inscriptions, many of the letters from Esarhaddon's reign are datable. In *Letters*, IIb Parpola presents the often intricate network of decisions involved in his dating of many of the letters that he assigns to Esarhaddon's reign. I have for the most part followed his dating here; in the few cases where my conclusions differ from his, my reasons for proposing a different date are presented in the footnote accompanying the discussion. Dated economic texts and legal texts from Esarhaddon's reign offer additional information about his years of rule but have for the most part not proven significant for my discussion here. In the few cases where they are mentioned, their dating is dealt with in the text or accompanying footnotes.

Texts Published after Borger's Edition

SINCE BORGER'S EDITION OF THE ESARHADDON INSCRIP-tions appeared in 1956, several more ancient examplars of the texts published there (some largely intact, some surviving only as fragments) have been identified and published, and several previously unknown Esarhaddon inscriptions have been discovered in the course of excavations at Nippur, Nineveh, and Calaḫ and during research in museum collections. In addition, a number of fragments have been identified as missing parts of previously known Esarhaddon texts and joined to them, in some cases significantly expanding our understanding of those documents. This appendix is intended as a supplement to Borger's edition, providing a list of the new texts, fragments, and joins, together with a brief note about where each text has been published or described. To save space, the references are in abbreviated form; for complete citations, see the bibliography. The list of new material follows the order of text groups in Borger's edition; new documents have been assigned labels and numbers following Borger's system of labeling. Joined texts are marked with a "+" sign.

After the publication of some of the new texts, Borger published revised editions incorporating the new material that had by then become available. These were published in three articles: "Die Inschriften Asarhaddons (AfO Beiheft 9), Nachträge und Verbesserungen," *AfO*, 18 (1957–8): 113–118; "Der Neue Asarhaddon-Text AfO 18, S. 314 ff.," *AfO*, 19 (1959–60): 148; and "Zu den Asarhaddon-Texten aus Babel," *BiOr*, 21 (1964): 143–148. Some time later, improved copies of several Esarhaddon Babylon inscriptions in the British Museum, prepared years earlier by T. Pinches, were at last published as part of the volume *CT*, 44 (London: 1963); the Esarhaddon texts published there include Bab. A1 (#3), Bab. C1 (#4), Bab. C2 (#5), Bab. E1 (#6), Bab. E2 (#7), Bab. E3 (#8), and Bab. F (#9). Of these, only the text completing Bab. C (#5, part 1) had been unknown to Borger.

List of New Materials

Assur A6: VAT 9642, unpubl. clay tablet, text = III 32–IV 22 and V 40–VI 13; variants and descript., Borger, *AfO*, 18 (1957–8): 113.

Assur J: Assur 21506e (Photo Ass. 6554); photo only survives; 17 ll., on building of Ešarra by Esar.; translit. and transla., Borger, *AfO*, 18 (1957–8): 113–114.

Babylon A4: BM 60032; parts of 7 faces of solid octagonal prism; Millard, *AfO*, 24 (1973): 117.

Babylon A5: BM 132294; top and 4 faces, solid octagonal prism; Millard, *AfO*, 24 (1973): 117–118. (Now joined to Babylon C1: see below, p. 186).

Babylon A6: BM 30153; 4 cols. from top of octag. prism; Cogan, *AfO*, 31 (1984): 75 (no copy or translit.).

Babylon B2: BM 82-3-23, 55; frag. from 1 face of clay tablet, 12 ll. ; Millard, *AfO*, 24 (1973): 119 and pl. 14.

Babylon C2+: BM 78221; frag. of prism; joins Borger's Babylon C2 (BM 78222) in col. iv; starts with Ep. 1 and continues for 4 cols.; cuneiform copy by Pinches, *CT* 44, no. 5.

Babylon E3+: AO 7736; frag. of hexag. prism; joins at base of Bab. E3, completing cols. i, iii, iv, v, and vi; first-year date; Nougayrol, *AfO*, 18 (1957–8): 314–318.

Babylon E4: BM 42668; ½ of solid hexag. prism; Millard, *AfO*, 24 (1973): 118 and pl. 13.

Babylon E5: BM 34899 (Sp. 2,411); prism; C.B.F. Walker, *CT* 51, no. 78 (cited in Brinkman, *JAOS*, 103, p. 38).

Kalach A7: ND 11308; hollow barrel cyl.; dated; Hulin, *Iraq*, 24 (1962): 116–118.

Kalach A8–11: ND 7097–ND7100; 4 clay cyls.; in quarters of the *rab ekalli*, Ft. Shalmaneser, Nimrud; variously dated; Millard, *Iraq*, 23 (1961): 176–178.

Kalach A12: ND 5404a+b+c; 3 small frags. of 1 cyl.; citadel at Nimrud; Wiseman, *Iraq*, 26 (1964): 122 and pl. xxvii.

Kalach A13: ND 9902; cyl. frag.; in fill above floor of room NE2 in Ft. Shalmaneser, Nimrud; unpubl.; described by Mallowan, *Nimrud*, II, p. 638, n. 8.

Kalach A14: ND 9903; cyl. frag.; found near ND 9902 (above); dated to 676; unpubl.; ref. Mallowan, *Nimrud*, II, p. 638, n. 8.

Kalach E1–3: ND 4313–ND 4315; 3 frags. from 2 or 3 cyls.; describe work on Nabû and Tašmētum shrine; Nabû temple complex, Nimrud; Wiseman, *Iraq*, 26 (1964): 122–123 and pl. xxvii.

Kalach F: 2 copies of gateway inscrip.; on stones of outer wall flanking postern gate RI, s.w. corner of Ft. Shalmaneser, Nimrud; unpubl.; photo in J.E. Reade, in *Fifty Years*, John Curtis, ed. (London: 1983), fig. 78, p. 105; descrip. by Mallowan, *Nimrud*, II, pp. 466–67.

Kalach Brick Inscriptions: see Nin. M, below.

Nineveh A25: 1932-12-10, 378 = BM 123435; prism, part of base and 2 faces; unpubl.; ref. Lambert and Millard, *Cat.*, 25.

Nineveh A26: BM 127872+127975+134488+138195; prism, dated 673; Cogan, *AfO*, 31 (1984): 72.

Nineveh A27: BM 138184; small prism frag., ca. 20 ll. of text; described by Cogan, *AfO*, 31 (1984): 72.

Nineveh A28: BM 127879 = 1929-10-12, 535; prism frag., part of base and 2 faces; dated; unpubl.; ref. Lambert and Millard, *Cat.*, 35.

Nineveh A29: BM 127951 = 1929-10-12, 607; prism, parts of 2 faces; unpubl.; ref. Lambert and Millard, *Cat.*, 40.

Nineveh A30: BM 128068 = 1929-10-12, 724; prism, flake from one face; unpubl.; ref. Lambert and Millard, *Cat.*, 46.

Nineveh A31: BM 128221+128222+128232; join of small frags.; Cogan, *AfO*, 31 (1984): 72–73.

Nineveh A2 + A11: joined by Cogan, *AfO*, 31 (1984): 73.

Nineveh A32: Join of BM 128269+128279+128289. Cogan, *AfO*, 31 (1984): 73.

Nineveh A34: BM 128322 = 1932-12-10, 579; prism, part of two faces; unpubl.; Lambert and Millard, *Cat.*, 61.

Nineveh A35: BM 134468 = 1932-12-12, 463; prism, part of top and one face; unpubl.; ref. Lambert and Millard, *Cat.*, 70.

Nineveh B7: Complete prism; dated 676; found in mud-brick platform, Esar. palace, n. corner of Nebi Yunus; publ. by A. Heidel and A.L. Oppenheim, *Sumer*, 12 (1956): 9–37, and pls. 1–12; for variants, see Borger, *Asarh.*, "Nachträge," 125.

Nineveh B4 + B5: joined by Cogan, *AfO*, 31 (1984): 73.

Nineveh D2: 1932-12-12, 460 = BM 134465; octag. prism, part of base and 3 faces; unpubl.; ref., Lambert and Millard, *Cat.*, 70.

Possible Nineveh D/E text: frag. of 8-sided prism, parts of 2 long cols. with wide lines; Wiener Museum für Völkerkunde; publ., Borger, *AfO*, 18 (1957–58): 114–115.

Nineveh I: Join of cyl. frag. 1902-5-10, 6 to Nin. I1, restoring almost half of the inscrip.; photos, translit. and transla., Cogan, *AfO*, 31 (1984): 73–75.

Nineveh M: Two more copies, on bricks, found at Nimrud; Walker, *Brick Inscrips.*, 69, no. 33, and p. 125.

Nineveh O: Brick inscrip. from Nineveh. Walker, *Brick Inscrips.*, 126.

Nippur A or B: 9NT9; frag. of barrel cyl.; G. Buccellati and R.D. Biggs, AS, 17 (Chicago: 1969), no. 30, p. 13, and p. 35., no. 30.

Nippur A and B: 10 frags. of inscribed barrel cyls., found in excavations at Nippur; published as part of a composite text by A. Goetze, *JCS*, 17 (1963): 119–131, with copies.

Nippur B: 12N43; new cyl. frag. of Nippur B; found at Nippur; confirms Nippur A and B as separate texts; Civil, *RA*, 68 (1974): 94.

Tarbisu D: 2 copies, on bricks from Nineveh; Walker, *Brick Inscrips.*, 126.

Uruk text: perhaps Esar., originally publ. as earlier text; (Falkenstein, *LKU*, no. 46) partial transla. and commentary by Borger, *AfO*, 18 (1957–58): 116–117.

Shikaft-i Gulgul Inscrip.: perhaps Esar.; inscribed on cliff face, in Zagros Mts. on the southwestern slopes of the Kabir Kuh; Grayson and Levine, *Iranica Antiqua*, 11 (1975): 29–38.

Text related to Gbr. and to 2nd Eg. campaign: K. 3082; descrip. by Labat, *Annuaire*, 1973/4, 65–67.

Vassal Treaties: Frags. of several treaties regulating succession: found in Ft. Shalmaneser, Nimrud; Wiseman, *Vassal-Treaties.*

Accession Treaty of Esarhaddon: 3 frags. of one tablet fr. Nineveh; Esar. named as "lord" rather than king; Parpola, *JCS*, 39 (1987): 170 ff. and 163.

Oath of Loyalty to Esarhaddon: Bu 91-5-9, 22; small frag. of left half of clay tablet; Parpola, *JCS*, 39 (1987): 174 f.

Inscription related to Esar.'s Vassal Treaties: 2 frags. of a 2-col. clay tablet; probly. from Sippar; Grayson, *JCS*, 39 (1987): 135 ff. and 155 ff.; join proposed by Parpola and Watanabe, SAA II, p. 77.

Eye-stone Inscription: on carved agate; inscrip. of Esar.'s wife; Lambert, *RA*, 63 (1969): 65–71.

Esarhaddon Seal Impressions from Calaḫ: Barbara Parker, *Iraq*, 24 (1962): 28 and 38.

Egyptian Statues from Esarhaddon's Palace, Nineveh: 3 life-sized statues of pharaoh Taharka, from room near entrance to Esarh. palace, Nebi Yunus; 2 with hieroglyphic inscrip.; see Weidner, *AfO*, 17 (1956): 228; transla., W.K. Simpson, *Sumer*, 10 (1954): 193–194 and *Sumer*, 11 (1955): 111–116.

Inscribed Bronze Plaque: AO 20.185; purchased, no provenance; bas-relief of Assyrian king and woman with name "Naqi'a" on shoulder; inscrip. similar to part of AsBbH and AsBbE; probly. Esarh.; Parrot and Nougayrol, *Syria*, 33 (1956): 147–160.

Texts related to Egyptian Campaign of Esarh.: K. 3082; 79-7-8, 196; 80-7-19, 15; and 91-5-9, 18; descrip., Labat, *Annuaire*, 1973/4, 65–66.

Document List with Provenance and Description

IT IS OFTEN HELPFUL TO KNOW SOMETHING ABOUT THE object on which a text was inscribed or the place where it was discovered, but physical descriptions of texts and information about their place of discovery are not always readily accessible. Borger's notes on the inscriptions included in *Asarh.*, for example, do not consistently describe the physical appearance of texts or record their provenance, making it necessary to search through earlier publications for whatever information they may offer. This appendix is intended to supplement the notes and comments on each group of Esarhaddon's inscriptions in Borger's edition by providing a list giving the provenance of each copy of Esarhaddon's royal inscriptions and a description of the object on which that copy of the text was inscribed; the list includes all of the Esarhaddon inscriptions published by Borger (except those he indicates are of doubtful attribution to Esarhaddon), as well as the royal inscription and treaty texts of Esarhaddon (and of his wife and mother) published since Borger's edition.

The list is based on published information, supplemented in some cases by information provided to me from the records of the British Museum by Julian E. Reade and from the files of the Royal Inscriptions of Mesopotamia project by Louis D. Levine. To both of them, my heartfelt thanks. ("JER" and "LDL" in the entries below refer to their informal reports in letters to me; I have tried to record their information faithfully, but any errors and confusions that may have crept in are my own.) Reade comments that the provenances he reports are based on British Museum departmental records without reference to the contents of the texts and should be treated with some reservation. The reader should be aware that I have not had the opportunity to verify the published descriptions of the texts through personal examination. (The one exception is the Esarhaddon inscriptions held by Yale University, which I was able to examine personally, thanks to the courtesy of the Yale Babylonian Collection and its curator, William W. Hallo.)

The sources of my information are noted in brief form in parentheses after each entry; see the bibliography for complete citations. "B." refers to Borger's edition of the Esarhaddon inscriptions, *Die Inschriften Asarhaddons, Königs von Assyrien*, *AfO* Beiheft 9 (Graz: 1956). "Bezold, *Cat.*" refers to Carl Bezold,

Catalogue of the Cuneiform Tablets in the Kouyunjik Collection of the British Museum (London, 1889–1899); "King, *Cat.*" to L.W. King, *Catalogue of the Cuneiform Tablets in the Kouyunjik Collection, etc.: Supplement* (London, 1914); and "Lambert and Millard, *Cat.*" to W.G. Lambert and A.R. Millard, *Catalogue of the Cuneiform Tablets in the Kouyunjik Collection, etc.: Second Supplement* (London, 1968). In cases where published accounts supplement one another or appear contradictory, I have recorded the information offered by each (in the case of texts recorded as found in the area of the palace of Assurnasirpal II at Nineveh, located between the Nabû and Ištar temples, it is not the location in which the tablets were discovered that is debated, but the existence of such a palace in that area).

Texts are listed in the order in which they appear in Borger's *Asarh.* and with the identifying labels Borger assigns them there; new texts not known at the time of Borger's edition, and new examples of texts published earlier by Borger, are marked with a star and assigned a name and number in accordance with Borger's system. Information about where each text was originally published can be found in the notes preceding each text group in Borger's edition or, for texts published after Borger's edition, in the list of texts which appears here in Appendix III.

Each entry begins with the name assigned the text by Borger. Texts comprised of fragments now recognized as parts of a single copy of a particular text are marked by a "+" to indicate a join. A description of the object on which the text is inscribed appears to the right of its name, along with any comments about the text, such as whether a photo taken at the time of its excavation is available in museum collections. Below the text's name is a list of each of the pieces of which the text is comprised, identified by the object's museum inventory number, or, failing that, its excavation number or museum acquisition number. Any additional identifying numbers for that piece are listed to its right along with information about where the piece was discovered. Merkes, Kasr, and Sahn are sections of the ruins of Babylon, and Hillah is the city nearest those ruins. The comment "no prov." means that I have found no information about the place where the piece was discovered.

A few of the conventions used in the list may require explanation. See the list below for the characteristic pattern of each museum's acquisition and inventory numbers. British Museum inventory numbers in some cases also provide clues to when, where or how a particular object was acquired. An object identified by a British Museum registration number in the form 88-5-12, 14, for example, is the fourteenth object formally acquisitioned by the British Museum on (or in some cases, before!) the 12th of May, 1888. Objects whose identification number begins with the letter "K" are part of a group of objects belonging to the British Museum, most (but not all) of which were discovered at Kuyunjik, one of the two groups of ruins which together comprise the remains of ancient Nineveh. Initials introducing British Museum registration numbers refer in some cases to the purchaser of the tablet (e.g., "Bu." refers to purchases made by E.A. Wallis Budge on behalf of the British Museum) and in other cases to the archeologist in charge of the excavation during which the object in question was discovered (e.g., "TM" identifies objects discovered during the Nineveh excavations conducted by Thompson and Mallowan). These notations are helpful indicators of probable provenance, but have sometimes proven to be inaccurate and should be used with caution. Some texts are further identified by a number assigned the text by its excavators at the time of its discovery; identifying numbers beginning with "ND," for example, were assigned to texts excavated at Nimrud (ancient Calah).

The following is a key to conventions and abbreviations used in the museum numbers and excavation numbers of Esarhaddon inscriptions:

a. Texts in the British Museum, London

BM	British Museum
Bu	Budge
DT	Daily Telegraph
K	Kuyunjik (part of ruins of Nineveh)
Ki	King
Rm	Rassam
Sm	Smith
Sp	Spartoli
TM	Thompson and Mallowan

(Tablets given a registration date only, such as 80-10-14, 23, are also British Museum texts.)

b. Excavation Numbers

Assur	Texts excavated at Aššur
ND	Texts excavated at Nimrud (Calah)
Uruk	Texts excavated at Uruk
inv.	Inventory list, Babylon excavations
N-T	Texts excavated at Nippur

c. Friedrich-Schiller-Universität, Jena

HS	Frau Professor Hilprecht-Sammlung

d. Iraq Museum, Baghdad

IM	Iraq Museum

e. Musée d'Art et d'Histoire, Geneva

MAH	Musée d'Art et d'Histoire

f. Musée du Louvre, Paris

AO	Département des Antiquités Orientales

g. Museum of the Ancient Orient, Istanbul

Ist.	Istanbul

h. Oriental Institute, U. of Chicago, Chicago

Oriental Institute

i. University Museum, U. of Pennsylvania, Philadelphia
    CBS   Catalogue of the Babylonian Section
j. Staatliche Museen, Berlin
    VA   Vorderasiatisches Museum
    VAT   Vorderasiatische Abteilung Tontafel
k. Yale University Library, New Haven, Connecticut
    NBC   Nies Babylonian Collection
    YBC   Yale Babylonian Collection
    Peabody Peabody Museum, Yale University

The provenance and description list below reflects the course of my own investigations and is far from exhaustive; I hope its publication will neverthe-less make research on Esarhaddon's reign easier for others and will encourage them to fill in the gaps. I would be grateful to hear of additions and corrections.

List of Texts with Description and Provenance

Assur A1+   Part of an 8-sided prism (*KAH* II, p. 82); Date, 19th(?) Du'ūzu (B., p. 6).
    VA10130   No prov.
    VA8411   Assur, outer corner of inner wall, at fA10V (*KAH* II, #126, p. 109).
    UM32-22-5   No prov.

Assur A2+   Piece of clay tablet (B., p. 1); Photo=Ph. 5665/66 (B., p. 1); Istanbul Mu. (LDL).
    Assur 18231a+b Assur, at iD51, s. gateway Assur temple enclosure, in paving (B., p. 1 and Andrae, *Wieder. Assur*, city plan).

Assur A3   Prism fragment (*ARAB* II, p. 271).
    VA7513   Assur 1783; Assur (*KAH* I, no. 51); s. part of forecourt, Assur temple, in group of prisms and cylinders (Pedersen, II, p. 13, n. 9).

Assur A4   Frag., 8-sided prism (*KAH* II, p. 82, #127); dated Simānu, (day broken), 679 (B., p. 6).
    VA7504   Assur 986; Assur, "nordl. Prothyse," (*KAH* II, no. 127, p. 109); Assur temple forecourt, s. part, in group of prisms and cylinders (Pedersen, II, p. 13, n. 9).

Assur A5   Prism frag., photo Assur 2019/20, Istanbul Mu. (B., p. 1; LDL).
    VA8428   Assur 8814; Assur, at dA6II ["Neuer Palast" area] (B., p. 1).

*Assur A6   Clay tablet (Borger, *AfO*, 18, p. 113).
    VAT 9642   No prov.; possible join to VAT 11095 (Borger, *HKL*, II, p. 18).

Assur B   Clay tablet (*KAH* II, no. 125, pp. 80–81); or, clay cylinder (Pedersen, II, p. 13, n. 9); Photo: Ass. 172 (Pedersen, II, p. 13, n. 9).
    VAT 7511   Ass. 943; Assur, in temple, at gE5I (*KAH* II, p. 109, no. 125).

Assur C+	Join by Borger, in Lambert, *Ad bene*, p. 158; clay tablet, probably 6 cols., remains of 4 extant, late Ass. script (Lambert, p. 159).
K.6048	Nineveh? (K. number).
K.8323	Nineveh? (K. number).
Assur D	On 2 alabaster vases, booty from Phoenicia (Andrae, *Wieder. Assur.*, p. 159).
——	Assur, palace of Assurnasirpal II (Andrae, *Wieder. Assur*, p. 159).
Assur E	Stone blocks in wall (Andrae, *Fest.*, pp. 177–179); photo BM 113864 (Borger, *HKL*, II, p. 18).
——	Assur, on blocks of wall identified by excavators as part of *muslālu* (Andrae, *Fest.*, pp. 177–79).
Assur F1	Piece of lapis lazuli (*ARAB* II, p. 278 and *KAH* I, no. 53).
——	Assur (*KAH* I, no. 53).
Assur F2	Onyx amulet (*ARAB* II, p. 278 and *KAH* I, no. 54).
——	Assur (*KAH* I, no. 54).
Assur F3	Small stone tablet with projection (handle?) at top (Gadd, *CT* 36, p. 8).
BM 113864	1919-7-12, 613; Assur? (JER).
Assur F4	
——	No prov., no description.
Assur G	Limestone blocks (Andrae, *Fest.*, p. 177).
——	Assur, in wall identified by excavator as *muslālu* (Andrae, *Fest.*, p. 177).
Assur H	Door socket stone (see drawing, Nassouhi, *MAOG*, III, p. 20).
——	No prov.
Assur I	Irregular piece unsmoothed gypsum (Nassouhi, *MAOG*, III 1–2, p. 21).
Inv. 7864	Assur (Nassouhi, *MAOG* III 1–2, p. 21).
*Assur J	No description; Photo Ass. 6554.
——	21506e; Assur, at iC6III in fill on floor of House N3 (family of chief singers) with ca. 92 unbaked clay tablets (Borger, *AfO*, 18, pp. 113–114; Pedersen, II, p. 37).
Babylon A1+	7-sided prism (JER); symbols stamped into top and bottom (*CT* 44, pl. IV); dated to first year of Esar. (B., p. 29).
BM 78223	No prov. (originally in private hands).
Bu. 88-5-12, 77	Hillah (B. Mu. records, Budge's handwriting: JER).
Bu. 88-5-12, 78	Hillah (B. Mu. records, Budge's handwriting: JER).
Babylon A2	Grayish 6-sided prism, lines 48 mm. long , Ass. script (Boissier, *RA*, 30, p. 73).
MAH 15877	No prov.

Babylon A3   Prism frag.; photos show 2 sides (LDL); Assur 8000; Photo Ph.
                          2019/20 (LDL; B., p. 10).

VA 8420   Assur (B., p. 10).

*Babylon A4   Solid 8-sided prism, 7 faces preserved in part (Millard, *AfO*, 24,
                          p. 117).

BM 60032   82-7-14, 4442. Sippar (JER).

[Babylon A5 (BM 132294) now joined to Bab. C1; see below.]

*Babylon A6   Top of 8-sided prism, badly weathered, 4 cols. preserved, Bab.
                          script (Cogan, *AfO*, 31 [1984], p. 75).

BM 30153   No prov. Probably acquired by B. Mu. before 1870 (JER).

Babylon B1a (+? b)   Frags. of clay tablet, clear Ass. script (Bezold, *Cat.*, p. 50 and
                          638).

K. 192   Possible join, (B., p. 10). Nineveh? (K. nos.).
K. 4513(+?)

*Babylon B2   12-line frag. from one face of clay tablet (Millard, *AfO*, 24, p. 119
                          and pl. 14). Cited by Borger as Babylon H in *HKL*, II, p. 18,
                          and by Brinkman as Babylon "H" (*JAOS*, 103, p. 38) to sep-
                          arate it from Borger's original Babylon H (B., p. 29; see Baby-
                          lon H, below.) Could also be frag. of a Bab. G text instead.

BM 82-3-23, 55   Kuyunjik (JER).

Babylon C1+   Part of 6-sided prism (see copy, Meissner and Rost, *BA* III,
                          pp. 335–337). BM 132294 was Borger's Bab. A5. For possible
                          join of third piece, see forthcoming article by I.L. Finkel (JER).

BM 78224   Bu. 88-5-12, 79. Hillah (B. Mu. records, in Budge's hand: JER).
BM 132294   1958-4-12, 28 (JER).
———(+?)   Sotheby, lot 83, 17–18 July, 1985; in private hands; possible join,
                          see I.L. Finkel, forthcoming (JER).

*Babylon C2+   10-sided prism (JER); dated "first year" of Esar. (B., p. 29).
Bm 78221   Bu. 88-5-12, 74. Hillah (B. Mu. records, not in Budge's hand: JER).
BM 78222   Bu. 88-5-12, 75+76. Hillah (B. Mu. records, in Budge's hand: JER).

Babylon AC   Fragment of 8-sided prism (Legrain, *PBS*, XIII, no. 10, p. 46).
CBS 1526   No prov.

Babylon D   4-sided black stone (IR 49); of basalt (*ARAB* II, p. 242); more
                          probably black limestone (JER); symbols carved on top (*ARAB*,
                          II, p. 242, n. 2).

BM 91027   60-12-1, 1 (B., p. 10). Nineveh (I R 49).

Babylon E1+   7 (or possibly 8) –sided prism (JER); archaizing Bab. script (JER).
BM78225   Bu. 88-5-12, 80 (B., p. 10). Hillah (B. Mu. records, in Budge's
                          hand: JER).

———   Fragment of prism; in Hirayama Coll., Kamakura, Japan; prob-
                          able join (Tsukimoto, *ARRIM*, 8, pp. 63–69).

Babylon E2	6-sided prism (JER).
BM 78248	Bu. 88-5-12, 103 (B., p. 10). Hillah (B. Mu. records, in Budge's hand: JER).
Babylon E3+	6-sided prism; join; dated to "first year" of Esar. (Nougayrol, *AfO*, 18, 314 ff.).
BM 78246	Bu. 88-5-12, 101; Hillah (B. Mu. records, in Budge's hand: JER).
A07736	No prov.; Louvre (Nougayrol).
***Babylon E4**	Half of a solid 6-sided prism; a more nearly Assyrian script than E3 (Millard, *AfO*, 24, p. 118 and pl. 13).
BM 42668	81-7-1, 430. No prov. (Millard, p. 118).
***Babylon E5**	———
BM 34899	Sp. 2, 411; Babylon? (Brinkman, *JAOS*, 103, p. 38, citing Walker, *CT* 51, 78).
Babylon F	10-sided(?) prism (JER); symbols stamped on end (illus., *CT* 44, pl. IV, no. 3).
BM 78247	Bu. 88-5-12, 102; Hillah (B. Mu. records, not in Budge's hand: JER).
***Babylon G+**	5-sided prism (King, *Cat.*, pp. 7–8); dated Ajāru, "first year" of Esar. (B., p. 29).
BM 98972	Ki. 1904-10-9, 1; Nineveh; 4¾″ h. (King, *Cat.*, pp. 7–8).
BM 122617	1930-5-8, 6; or, 1929-10-17, 6. (JER). Nineveh, 1929, 200 yards west of the Ninlil gate (Lambert and Millard, *Cat.*, p. 13).
BM 127846	1929-10-12, 502. Physical join to BM 122617. All three are parts of the same prism, 3 faces preserved, but no physical join possible to BM 98972 (Millard, *AfO*, 24, p. 118).
Babylon H	Lapis lazuli cylinder seal with incised figure of bearded male holding lightning bolts (Koldewey, *Tempel.*, pp. 45–46 and 48).
———	Babylon, among treasures in basket buried under floor of Parthian-period building beside Esagila (Koldewey, *Tempel.*, pp. 45–46 and p. 48).
Babylon I1	Square brick, intact; 10-line stamped inscription; Abklatsch no. 871 (Wetzel and Weissbach, *Hauptheil.*, p. 38 and Koldewey, *MDOG*, 7, p. 22).
Inv. #8084	Babylon, in Esagila, in entryway to main enclosure (Wetzel and Weissbach, *Hauptheil.*, p. 86).
Babylon I2	Square brick, intact, 10-line stamped inscription (Wetzel and Weissbach, *Hauptheil.*, p. 38 and Koldewey, *MDOG*, 7, p. 22).
Inv. #41183	Babylon. Sahn south, at ai34 (Wetzel and Weissbach, *Hauptheil.*, p. 86).
Babylon I3	Brick, broken, 1st 3 lines of 10-line stamped inscription (Wetzel and Weissbach, *Hauptheil.*, p. 38 and Koldewey, *MDOG*, 7, p. 22).
———	Babylon (Wetzel and Weissbach, p. 38).

Babylon I(?)	Brick, text unpubl., describes *tallaktu* (Wetzel and Weissbach, *Hauptheil.*, pp. 9–10).
——	Babylon, Esagila, Room 12 paving (Wetzel and Weissbach, pp. 9–10).
Babylon I or K(?)	Brick fragment (Wetzel and Weissbach, *Hauptheil.*, p. 86).
Inv. #41472	Photo 3283, I, Babylon, on Kasr (Wetzel and Weissbach, p. 86).
Babylon J1	Square brick, stamped (Wetzel and Weissbach, *Hauptheil.*, p. 38).
Inv. #39840	Abklatsch no. 1813, Babylon, Sahn east, in gateway IV to Etemenanki enclosure, at as20 (Wetzel and Weissbach, p. 86).
Babylon J2	Square brick, stamped (Wetzel and Weissbach, *Hauptheil.*, p. 38).
Inv. #41099	Babylon, Sahn south, at ad38 (Wetzel and Weissbach, p. 86).
Babylon J3	Square brick, stamped (Wetzel and Weissbach, *Hauptheil.*, p. 38).
Inv. #46408	Babylon, Merkes, in brick pillar on "Ziggurat-Street" (Wetzel and Weissbach, p. 86, and O. Reuther, *Innenstadt*, pp. 70 ff.).
Babylon K1–9	All bricks: 3 with 3-line stamped inscription; 4 with 9-line stamped inscription; 1 with 10-line stamped inscription; 1 with no description (Wetzel and Weissbach, *Hauptheil.*, p. 38 f., c, d, and e). Found at Babylon, at locations noted below (Wetzel and Weissbach, *Hauptheil.*, p. 86, inventory list).
K1=Inv. #44638	Kasr, on surface.
K2=Inv. #41230	Sahn south, at at33, inside Etemenanki enclosure (plan 5).
K3=Inv. #41054	Sahn south, at ad38.
K4=Inv. #32167	Kasr, at K21.
K5=Inv. #46402	Merkes, brick pillar, layer 31.
K6=Inv. #46403	Merkes, brick pillar, layer 37.
K7=Inv. #46405	Merkes, brick pillar, layer 37.
K8=Inv. #46406	Merkes, brick pillar, layer 37.
K9=Inv. #46404	Merkes, brick pillar, layer 34.
Babylon L	Square brick with stamped inscription (Wetzel and Weissbach, *Hauptheil.*, p. 38 f.).
Inv. #46407	Babylon, Merkes, brick pillar, layer 37 (Wetzel and Weissbach, p. 86).
Babylon M	Brick, handwritten inscription (Wetzel and Weissbach, *Hauptheil.*, pp. 38 f. and 86).
Inv. #46374	Babylon, Merkes, layer 37 of brick pillar (Wetzel and Weissbach, p. 86).
Babylon N1	Brick, handwritten inscription (Wetzel and Weissbach, *Hauptheil.*, p. 39).
Inv. #15316	Babylon, Ninurta temple, s. gate to court (Wetzel and Weissbach, p. 86).

Babylon N2	Baked brick, handwritten inscription (Wetzel and Weissbach, *Hauptheil.*, p. 39).
Inv. #41419	Babylon, Sahn north at aq 15 (Wetzel and Weissbach, p. 86); re-used in brick water run-off channel in late renewal of n. wall of Etemenanki enclosure (Wetzel and Weissbach, p. 16 and Wetzel, *MDOG*, 44, pp. 20 ff.).
Babylon N3	Brick, handwritten inscription (Wetzel and Weissbach, *Hauptheil.*, p. 39).
Inv. #46410	Babylon, Merkes, layer 37 in brick pillar (Wetzel and Weissbach, p. 86).
Babylon N4	Brick, handwritten inscription (Wetzel and Weissbach, *Hauptheil.*, p. 39).
Inv. #46435	Babylon, Merkes, layer 37 in brick pillar (Wetzel and Weissbach, p. 86).
Babylon N5	Brick, handwritten inscription (Wetzel and Weissbach, *Hauptheil.*, p. 39).
Inv. #46436	Babylon, Merkes, layer 37 in brick pillar (Wetzel and Weissbach, p. 86).
Babylon X	Brick with unspecified Esar. inscription (Wetzel and Weissbach, *Hauptheil.*, p. 86, inventory list).
Inv. #8050	Babylon, Esagila entryway (Wetzel and Weissbach, p. 86).
Borsippa A	Fragment of small cylinder, badly broken (*ARAB* I, p. 297, there attributed to Shalmaneser V).
K. 3845	Nineveh? (K. no.).
Kalach A1	Well-preserved cylinder, dated Abu 5, 672 (Wiseman, *Iraq*, 14, p. 54).
ND 1126	Calaḫ. Found by ploughman ca. 1 mi. w. of tell, near e. bank of Tigris (Wiseman, p. 54); "brought to us by Shaikh Abdullah of Nimrud," almost certainly discovered under floor of house in old village of Nimrud where it had been reburied in modern times (Mallowan, *Nimrud*, II, p. 638, n. 8).
Kalach A2–6	No description, unpublished (B., p. 32).
A2=K. 1643	Nineveh? (K. no.).
A3=K. 1653	Nineveh? (K. no.).
A4=K. 1656	Nineveh? (K. no.).
A5=K. 1657	Nineveh? (K. no.).
A6=K. 1659	Nineveh? (K. no.).
*Kalach A7	Hollow barrel cylinder, dated Ajāru 18, 672 (Hulin, *Iraq*, 24, pp. 116–118).
ND 11308	Calaḫ, at Nimrud Spring, just outside s. wall of town at s.e. corner (Hulin, pp. 116–118); in debris along s. wall of Ft. Shalmaneser (Mallowan, *Nimrud*, II, p. 638, n. 8).

*Kalach A8–11   Fragments of 4 baked clay cylinders (Mallowan, *Nimrud*, II, p. 421), all but one dated to 676 (see below) and all found at Calaḫ, at various points in rooms SE1, 2, 10 and 11, and quarters of the *rab ekalli* (Millard, *Iraq*, 23, pp. 176–8 and Mallowan, *Nimrud*, II, p. 421).

A8=ND 7100   Dated Abu 21, 676 (Millard, p. 176).

A9=ND 7097   Dated Ulūlu 10, 676 (Millard, p. 176).

A10=ND 7098   Dated Ulūlu 10, 676 (Millard, p. 176).

A11=ND 7099   Date missing (Millard, p. 176).

*Kalach A12   3 fragments of one cylinder (Wiseman, *Iraq*, 26, p. 122).

ND 5404a+b+c   Calaḫ, in the citadel (Wiseman, p. 122).

*Kalach A13   Fragment of cylinder (Mallowan, *Nimrud*, II, p. 638, n. 8).

ND 9902   Calaḫ, Ft. Shalmaneser, in fill above floor of NE2 (Mallowan, p. 638, n. 8; Oates, *Iraq*, 23, p. 12).

*Kalach A14   Cylinder fragment, dated 676 (Mallowan, *Nimrud*, II, p. 638, n. 8).

ND 9903   Calaḫ, near Kalach A13 (above) (Mallowan, p. 638, n. 8).

Kalach B   Fragment of clay cylinder, 2⅛″ l., segmental arch 1½″, chord 1⅜″, remains of 7 lines, clear Ass. script (Bezold, *Cat.*, p. 325).

K. 1652   Nineveh? (K. no.).

Kalach C   On front and back of a stone slab fallen into interior of tunnel, originally part of the tunnel's stone lining (B., p. 35; Layard, *Nin.*, I, pp. 80–81 and II, pp. 199–200).

———   Near Calaḫ, in tunnel running e.-w. through rock bluff on n. bank Great Zab River, opposite modern Quwair. Tunnel leads to rock-cut channel going to s.e. corner of outer walls of Calaḫ (D. Oates, *Studies*, p. 46).

Kalach D1–6   All from Calaḫ: on back of a slab (*ARAB* II, p. 286); on a brick (Meissner-Rost, BA III, p. 206); on bulls and sphinxes in S.W. Palace (Layard, *Disc.*, p. 598; JER).

*Kalach E1   Cylinder fragment, 5×7 cm. (Wiseman, *Iraq*, 26, pp. 122–123 and pl. 27).

ND 4313   Calaḫ, Nabû and Tašmētum temple on citadel, above pavement, in n.w. corner of SEB XI, at depth of 2.4 m., with ND 4312 (Wiseman, p. 122, n. 17).

*Kalach E2   Cylinder fragment, 7×10 cm. (Wiseman, *Iraq*, 26, pp. 122–123 and pl. 27).

ND 4314   Calaḫ, on floor of SEB XIII (Wiseman, p. 122, n. 17).

*Kalach E3   Cylinder fragment (Wiseman, *Iraq*, 26, pp. 122–123 and pl. 27).

ND 4315   Calaḫ, on pavement by s. door of Tašmētum shrine (Wiseman, p. 122, n. 17).

*Kalach F1–2	On stones flanking the postern gate (J.E. Reade in *Fifty Years*, ed. John Curtis, p. 105 and fig. 78).
——	Calaḫ, inscribed on each side of postern gate RI, s.w. corner of Ft. Shalmaneser (Reade in Curtis, p. 105 and fig. 78).
Nineveh A1	Complete 6-sided prism (Thompson, *PEA*, p. 7); dated Addāru, 673 (B., p. 64).
BM 121005	Th. 1929-10-12, 1; Nineveh, at House SH on the flats in the fields below the Kuyunjik mound, within the city walls (Thompson, *Iraq*, 7, p. 96 and *PEA*, p. 7).
Nineveh A2+	Lower half and fragments of a six-sided clay prism (Bezold, *Cat.*, p. 1690 and p. 328); dated Pēt-bābi, 673 (B., p. 64). Join by Cogan, *AfO*, 31, p. 73.
48-11-4, 315	
K. 1667	Nineveh? (K. no.). Clearly written Assyrian characters (Bezold, *Cat.*, p. 328).
K. 6387	Nineveh? (K. no.) (K. 1667 + K. 6387 were formerly listed as an independent text, Borger's Nin. 11. Previous join of these 2 fragments to Nin. A25 was in error: Cogan, p. 72).
Nineveh A3	No description.
——	Susa, in Elam (Scheil, *Prisme S*, p. 28).
Nineveh A4	No description.
——	Susa, in Elam (Scheil, *Prisme S*, p. 28).
Nineveh A5	6-sided prism (Scheil, *Prisme S*, photo, p. 2).
A16962 and 16963	Nineveh, found in unofficial digging, bought by Scheil's brother. Exact location or mound unknown (Scheil, p. 2). Oriental Institute, Chicago.
Nineveh A6	Parts of at least 2 clay prisms (B., p. 37; copies in Hirschberg, *Studien*, pls. 1–5).
VA 3458–64	No prov.; Staatliche Museen, Berlin (Hirschberg, p. 17).
Nineveh A7	("Zurich prism"); clay prism, in collections of U. Zürich (Boissier, *RA*, 30, pp. 71–72; Hirschberg, *Studien*, p. 17 and copy, pl. 6); dated "month of the god MAḪ," year broken, ". . . in the year of . . . its booty" (B., p. 64).
——	Bought by Tisserant in Mesopotamia (Boissier, pp. 71–72).
Nineveh A8	Fragment of a prism, part of one face (Lambert and Millard, *Cat.*, p. 3).
BM 121007	1929-10-12, 3. Nineveh, House SH (Thompson, *Iraq*, 7, p. 96).
Nineveh A9+	Prism (Lambert and Millard, *Cat.*, p. 35 and 72, and Cogan, *AfO*, 31, p. 73); join by Cogan (p. 73).
BM 127875	1929-10-12, 531. Nineveh (Lambert and Millard, *Cat.*, p. 35).
BM 134489	TM 1931-2, 6; 1932-12-12, 484. Nineveh, S.W. Pal. of Senn. [?] (Lambert and Millard, *Cat.*, p. 72); House SH [?] (Thompson, *Iraq*, 7, p. 96).

Nineveh A10   No description.
TM 1931–2, 18   Nineveh (Thompson, *Iraq*, 7, p. 105).

[Nineveh A11 has been joined to Nin. A2.]

Nineveh A12   Fragment of upper part of a prism (Bezold, *Cat.*, p. 1655).
Rm. 2, 184   No prov.

Nineveh A13   Fragment of upper part of a prism (Bezold, *Cat.*, p. 1672).
Rm. 2, 384   No prov.

Nineveh A14   6-sided prism (JER).
BM 99043   1904-10-9, 72. Nineveh, Kuyunjik (JER).

Nineveh A15   6-sided prism (JER).
BM 99044   1904-10-9, 73. Nineveh, Kuyunjik (JER).

Nineveh A16   No description; dated Pêt-bābi, 673 (B., p. 64).
VA 3826   No prov.

Nineveh A17   No description.
VA 3827   No prov.

Nineveh A18   No description.
VA 3829   No prov.

Nineveh A19   Prism (LDL).
VA 8425   Assur 14549. Assur, at hE9I, on small mound in e. section of city,
                    near remains of a small section of wall, no major building
                    nearby (B., p. 37, and Andrae, *Wieder. Assur*, city plan).

Nineveh A20–24   Fragments (no further description) (B., p. 37).
A 16917   Oriental Institute, Chicago. No prov. (B., p. 37).
A 16925–8   Oriental Institute, Chicago. No prov. (B., p. 37).

*Nineveh A25   Part of base and two faces of clay prism (Lambert and Millard,
                    Cat., p. 25); no join to Nin. A2, as previously argued (Cogan
                    AfO, 31, p. 72, n. 4); date still unpublished (Lambert and Millard,
                    p. 25).
BM 123435   1932-12-10, 378. Nineveh, in the Chol (term both for the flat
                    area within the curve of the river and the outer city walls, and
                    for area of dumps from early excavation) (Lambert and Millard,
                    Cat., p. 25).

*Nineveh A26+   Join, Cogan (*AfO*, 31, p. 72); prism; dated Addāru, 673 (Cogan,
                    p. 72).
BM 127872   1929-10-12, 528. Nineveh, in House SH, prism, part of 2 faces
                    (Lambert and Millard, *Cat.*, p. 35).
BM 127975   1929-10-12, 631. Nineveh, prism, part of 2 faces (Lambert and
                    Millard, *Cat.*, p. 41).
BM 134488   1932-12-12, 483. Nineveh, prism, part of 1 face (Lambert and
                    Millard, *Cat.*, p. 72).

BM 138195	Part of a prism; no prov., but part of a group of texts with many joins to texts excavated by Thompson at Nineveh (Cogan, *AfO*, 31, p. 72).
*Nineveh A27	Prism fragment (Cogan, *AfO*, 31, p. 72).
BM 138184	Nineveh, part of same group of British Museum texts as BM 138195; see comment above (Cogan, p. 72).
*Nineveh A28	Prism, part of base and 2 faces, dated Nisannu, 672 (Lambert and Millard, *Cat.*, p. 35).
BM 127879	1929-10-12, 535. Nineveh, Ištar temple, at N (Lambert and Millard, p. 35).
*Nineveh A29	Prism, parts of 2 faces (Lambert and Millard, *Cat.*, p. 40).
BM 127951	1929-10-12, 607. Nineveh (Lambert and Millard, p. 40).
*Nineveh A30	Prism, flake from one face (Lambert and Millard, *Cat.*, p. 46).
BM 128068	1929-10-12, 724. Nineveh (Lambert and Millard, p. 46).
*Nineveh A31+	Prism. Joined by Cogan (*AfO*, 31, p. 73). Dated Pēt-bābi, 673 (Lambert and Millard, *Cat.*, p. 56).
BM 128221	1932-12-10, 478. Nineveh, prism, part of base and 4 faces (Lambert and Millard, *Cat.*, p. 55).
BM 128222	1932-12-10, 479. Nineveh, prism, part of 3 faces (Lambert and Millard, p. 55).
BM 128232	1932-12-10, 489. Nineveh, at House SH, trench II, prism, part of base and 2 faces (Lambert and Millard, p. 56).
*Nineveh A32+	First three fragments joined by Cogan (*AfO*, 31, p. 73). Possible additional join to BM 128243 (Lambert and Millard, *Cat.*, p. 57).
BM 128289	1932-12-10, 546. Nineveh, prism, part of 2 faces (Lambert and Millard, p. 59).
BM 128269	1932-12-10, 526. Nineveh, prism, part of 1 face (Lambert and Millard, p. 58).
BM 128279	Nineveh; join (Lambert and Millard, p. 58).
BM 128243	1932-12-10, 500. Prism, part of 1 face; join not certain. (Lambert and Millard, p. 57).
*Nineveh A33	Prism, part of one face (Lambert and Millard, *Cat.*, p. 58).
BM 128274	1932-12-10, 531. Nineveh (Lambert and Millard, p. 58).
*Nineveh A34	Prism, part of two faces (Lambert and Millard, *Cat.*, p. 61).
BM 128322	1932-12-10, 579. Nineveh (Lambert and Millard, p. 61).
*Nineveh A35	Prism, part of top and one face (Lambert and Millard, *Cat.*, p. 70).
BM 134468	1932-12-12, 463. Nineveh (Lambert and Millard, p. 70).
Nineveh B1	6-sided prism with lengthwise hole (Bezold, *Cat.*, p. 1689; Budge, *By Nile*, II, p. 26; and Layard, *Nineveh and Its Remains*, II, p. 186).
48-10-31, 2	Nineveh; Nebi Yunus? Bought by Layard from a family living on Nebi Yunus who were using it as a candlestick (Budge, *By Nile*, II, p. 26; Layard, *Nineveh and Its Remains*, II, p. 186).

Nineveh B2	Fragment of a clay prism (Scheil, *RA*, 18, p. 3).
——	Bought by Eugène Tisserant in Mesopotamia (Scheil, *RA*, 18, p. 3).
Nineveh B3+	6-sided clay prism, 1 col. missing (Stephens, YOS, IX, p. 18).
YBC 2297	No prov.; Yale Babylonian Collec.
Peabody 6970	No prov.; small fragment, joining 14 lines of col. ii and adding fragments of 4 of col. iii; owned by Peabody Mu. of Natural History, Yale U., on loan to Yale Babylonian Collec., Yale U. (Beckman, *ARRIM*, 6, pp. 3–4).
Nineveh B4 + **Nineveh B5**	Joined by Cogan (*AfO*, 31, p. 73); 6-sided prism (JER; Bezold, *Cat.*, p. 1092 and p. 1699).
K. 10490	Probably Nineveh (Kuyunjik) (JER).
79-7-8, 8	
Nineveh B6	Fragment from middle of a prism (Bezold, *Cat.*, p. 1904).
83-1-18, 601	Nineveh. From S.W. Palace (JER).
*Nineveh B7	6-sided prism, nearly complete, 30 cm. × 14 cm., dated to Ajāru 22, 676 (Heidel and Oppenheim, *Sumer*, 12, p. 9).
——	Nineveh, Nebi Yunus mound, 15 m. below surface in mud-brick terrace of Esarhaddon palace, n. corner of mound (E. Weidner, *AfO*, 17, p. 228 and *AfO*, 18, p. 177; Naji al Asil in Heidel and Oppenheim, p. 9).
Nineveh C+	Parts of a six-sided prism (JER; Bezold, *Cat.*, p. 938, p. 330, and p. 1919); joins by Borger (B., p. 38); Dated Abu 18, year broken (B., p. 64).
K. 8542	Nineveh? (K. no.).
BM 91029	K. 1679. Nineveh ? (K. no.).
Bu. 89-4-26, 29	Join (B., p. 38).
Nineveh D1	Prism (Thompson, *Iraq*, 7, p. 95). Probably 6-sided (B., p. 38).
TM 1931–2, 4	Nineveh, at KK6, by n.e. doorway of Nabû temple (Thompson, p. 95); or, in Ištar temple, at sq. KK (Lambert and Millard, *Cat.*, p. 70).
*Nineveh D2	8-sided prism, part of base and 3 faces (Lambert and Millard, *Cat.*, p. 70).
BM 134465	1932-12-12, 460. Nineveh (Lambert and Millard, p. 70).
Nineveh E	8-sided prism (JER); piece from middle of prism (Bezold, *Cat.*, p. 1730).
80-7-19, 15	Nineveh, S.W. Palace (JER).
*Nineveh D or E?	Frag. of 8-sided prism, parts of 2 cols.; the "Wiener Mu. frag." (Borger, *AfO*, 18, pp. 114–115).
——	No prov.
Nineveh F	8-sided prism (JER; Bezold, *Cat.*, p. 1828).
82-5-22, 13	Nineveh, Kuyunjik (JER).

Nineveh G+	Join by Borger (B., p. 66); solid clay barrel cylinder (Thompson, *Iraq*, 7, p. 96 f.; Lambert and Millard, *Cat.*, p. 13); dated Ulūlu 20, 677 (B., p. 67).
BM 122619	1930-5-8, 8 (JER). Nineveh, 15′ below surface at G, ca. 50′ from Sargon's Well, near Ištar temple (Thompson, *Iraq*, 7, pp. 96 ff.); in "palace of Assurnasirpal II" at Sq. G (Lambert and Millard, *Cat.*, p. 13).
K. 1658	Nineveh? (K. no.).
Nineveh H1	Clay barrel cylinder frag. (JER).
BM 99082	1904-10-9, 111. Nineveh (JER).
Nineveh H2+	Fragment of cylinder, total 3⅝″ l., 2–2¼″ w. (Bezold, *Cat.*, p. 471).
K. 2742	Nineveh? (K. no.).
K. 2743	Nineveh? (K. no.).
Nineveh H3	Fragment of cylinder, part of right end (Lambert and Millard, *Cat.*, p. 5).
BM 121032	1929-10-12, 28. Nineveh (Thompson, *Iraq*, 7, p. 109).
Nineveh I1+	Barrel cylinder fragment (photo, Cogan, *AfO*, 31, pp. 73–75); joined by Cogan (*AfO*, 31, p. 73).
1902-5-10, 6	No prov.
BM 120066	1928-7-16, 66. No prov.
Nineveh I2	Solid barrel cylinder fragment, 19 ll. (Lambert and Millard, *Cat.*, p. 13).
BM 122618	1930-5-8, 7 (Cogan, *AfO*, 31, p. 73). Nineveh, beside fragment of wall ca. 10′ from inner edge of libn platform of Nabû temple, near Sargon's Well (Thompson, *Iraq*, 7, p. 96); in "palace of Assurnasirpal," sq. D, chamber IX (Lambert and Millard, *Cat.*, p. 13).
Nineveh J(+?)	Barrel cylinder (Lambert and Millard, *Cat.*, p. 69).
BM 134446	1932-12-12, 441; TM 1931–2, 24. Fragment of barrel cylinder, right end (Lambert and Millard, *Cat.*, p. 69); Nineveh, in House SH (Thompson, *Iraq*, 7, pp. 85 and 96).
BM 127964	1929-10-12, 620. Fragment of barrel cylinder, 8 lines (Lambert and Millard, *Cat.*, p. 40); possible join suggested by Borger (noted in Lambert and Millard, *Cat.*, p. 40).
Nineveh K	On game-boards (B., p. 69).
——	Found at Nineveh and Calaḫ (B., p. 69).
Nineveh L	On a brick (Meissner and Rost, *BA* III, p. 202); on back of slabs (Bezold, *Cat.*, p. 2235).
——	The brick is from Nineveh, Nebi Yunus (Meissner and Rost, *BA*, III, p. 202); no prov. given for slabs.
Nineveh M1	Brick (Meissner and Rost, *BA*, III, p. 204).
48-11-4, 29	Nineveh, Nebi Yunus mound (Meissner and Rost, p. 204); no. only listed (Bezold, *Cat.*, p. 1952).

Nineveh M2–3	Two bricks (Walker, *Brick*, pp. 69 and 125).
——	Calaḫ (Walker, *Brick*, p. 69, no. 33; unclear if Nin. M1 duplicate from Calaḫ is one of these or a 3rd brick: B., p. 69, par. 33).
Nineveh N	Alabaster vase (Meissner and Rost, *BA*, III, p. 204).
——	Nineveh, Kuyunjik (Meissner and Rost, p. 204).
Nineveh O	Brick (Walker, *Brick*, p. 126).
——	Nineveh (Walker, p. 126).
Nineveh P	Bronze lion weight (Meissner and Rost, *BA*, III, p. 202).
——	No prov.; Istanbul Mu. (Meissner and Rost, p. 202).
Nineveh Q	Frag. of alabaster bowl (Thompson, *Arch.*, 79, p. 121, no. 48 [not no. 49, as in B., p. 70] and pl. 63, no. 39, 4).
——	Nineveh, Nabû temple, w. of central courtyard (Thompson, p. 121).
Nineveh R	No description.
——	No prov.
Nippur A1	Fragment from right edge of barrel cylinder, ca. 8 cm. at widest point (F. Steele, *JAOS*, 70, p. 69).
1N 142	(Given as 1N-T142 in Goetze, *JCS*, 17, p. 119). Nippur, in Achaemenian-level debris near Achaemenian well in "Tablet Hill" mound (Steele, p. 69).
Nippur A2	Fragment of barrel cylinder (Steele, *JAOS*, 70, p. 69).
L29-634	No prov.; University Mu., Phila. (Steele, p. 69).
Nippur A3	Fragment of barrel cylinder (Steele, *JAOS*, 70, p. 69).
L29-637	No prov.; University Mu., Phila. (Steele, p. 69).
Nippur A4	Very small fragment of barrel cylinder (Steele, *JAOS*, 70, p. 69).
L29-635	No prov.; University Mu., Phila. (Steele, p. 69).
*Nippur A5	Barrel cylinder fragment (Goetze, *JCS*, 17, p. 119).
6N-T1046	Nippur, Inanna temple area(?) (Goetze, p. 119); Istanbul Mu. (Goetze, p. 119).
*Nippur A6	Barrel cylinder, 3 ll. fragment (Goetze, *JCS*, 17, p. 119).
6N-T1045	Nippur, Inanna temple area(?); Amer. School of Oriental Research (Goetze, p. 119).
*Nippur A7	5 fragments, ca. half of a baked clay barrel cylinder (Buccellati and Biggs, AS, 17, p. 4; Goetze, *JCS*, 17, p. 119, and copy, p. 4).
8N-T2	IM 66885. Nippur, at SB 78 in fill below Level II (Buccellati and Biggs, AS, 17, p. 4).
*Nippur A8	Barrel cylinder fragment, left part (Goetze, *JCS*, 17, p. 119).
6N-T1043	Nippur, Inanna temple area(?) (Goetze, p. 119).
*Nippur A9	Barrel cylinder fragment, right part (Goetze, *JCS*, 17, p. 119).
5N-T476	Nippur, Inanna temple area(?) (Goetze, p. 119).

*Nippur A10	Baked clay cylinder fragment, toward right end (Buccellati and Biggs, AS, 17, p. 4; Goetze, *JCS*, 17, p. 119 and copy, p. 127).
8N-T3	A32262. Nippur, at SL, Levels VI/VII (Buccellati and Biggs, p. 4).
*Nippur A11	Barrel cylinder fragment (Goetze, *JCS*, 17, p. 119).
4N-T76	Nippur, Inanna temple area(?) (Goetze, p. 119).
*Nippur A12	Barrel cylinder fragment, left part (Goetze, *JCS*, 17, p. 119).
4N-T75	Nippur, Inanna temple area(?); Amer. School Oriental Research (Goetze, p. 119).
*Nippur A13	Barrel cylinder frag., center part (Goetze, *JCS*, 17, p. 119); clay, good condition (YBC files); creamy golden clay, clear Ass. script, ruled in broad sections (personal inspection).
NBC 11323	5N-T564. Nippur, Inanna temple area(?) (Goetze, p. 119); Yale Babylonian Collec. (YBC files).
*Nippur A14	Barrel cylinder fragment, about half a barrel (Goetze, *JCS*, 17, p. 119); clay, good condition (YBC files); light tan clay, beautifully clear Ass. script, ruled (personal inspection).
NBC 10653	6N-T1044. Nippur, Inanna temple area(?); Yale Babylonian Collec. (Goetze, p. 119).
Nippur B1	Fragment, no further description (B., p. 70).
CBS 2350	No prov.; Univ. Mu., Phila. (B., p. 70).
Nippur B2	Fragment of barrel cylinder, toward left end (Goetze, *JCS*, 17, p. 119).
H-S 1956	No prov.; Hilprecht Sammlung, Jena (B., p. 70).
*Nippur B3	Fragment of barrel cylinder (Civil, *RA*, 68, p. 94).
12N43	Nippur, near n.w. wall of Parthian fortress enclosure (Civil, p. 94; J. Knudstad, *Sumer*, 22, pp. 111 ff.).
*Nippur A or B?	Cylinder fragment (Buccellati and Biggs, AS, 17, p. 13).
IM 70310	9 NT 9. Nippur, surface (Buccellati and Biggs, p. 13).
Nippur C	Brick (Goetze, *JCS*, 17, p. 119).
———	5NT702. Nippur, n. gate of Inanna temple (Goetze, p. 119).
Nippur D	Brick (M. Civil, *RA*, 68, p. 94).
———	No prov.
Tarbisu A+	Small barrel cylinder (Nassouhi, *MAOG*, III, 1–2, p. 22); photos Ass. 238/39, 241/42; dated Ajāru 18, 672 (B., p. 72).
IST. 6703	Ass. 1588+1757a+b. Aššur, near temple Eḫursagkurra (Wiseman, *Iraq*, 14, p. 55; Nassouhi, p. 22); in s. part of forecourt, Aššur temple, with other prisms and cylinders (Pedersen, II, p. 13, n. 9).
Tarbisu B	Brick (Meissner and Rost, *BA* III, p. 204).
———	No prov.
Tarbisu C	Brick (Meissner and Rost, *BA* III, p. 204).
———	No prov.

*Tarbisu D1–2   Two bricks (Meissner and Rost, *BA*, III, p. 204; Walker, *Bricks*, p. 126).

——   Tarbiṣu (Walker, p. 126; labeled "Assyrian Basement, no. 118" and "Nimroud Gallery, no. 756" in Bezold, *Cat.*, p. 2235).

Uruk A1   Complete cylinder, 41 ll. (Meissner and Rost, *BA*, III, p. 351 ff., and *ARAB* II, p. 279).

81-6-7, 209   No prov.

·Uruk A2   Small fragment of left half of a cylinder, 1⅜" long, 9 ll., Babyl. script (Meissner and Rost, *BA*, III, p. 353; Bezold, *Cat.*, p. 783).

K. 6386   No prov.

Uruk A3   Barrel cylinder (Nies and Keiser, BIN, II, no. 28); solid tan clay cylinder, unbroken, one pick-mark in center, lightly lined, signs lightly incised and somewhat worn away (personal examination).

NBC 2510   No prov.; purchased by Nies (Nies and Keiser, nr. 28).

Uruk A4   Clay barrel cylinder, ¾ preserved, 14 cm. × 7 cm., Neo. Bab. script (Stephens, YOS, IX, no. 137); yellowish clay, unbaked; clear, moderately deep signs; ruled; in 2 pieces, joined to make full height, base diam. 6 cm. (personal examination).

NBC 6055   No prov. (YBC files).

Uruk B1   Clay barrel cylinder, Ass. script (Clay, YOS, I, p. 56 + copy, pl. XXVII); intact; sharply incised signs, clear and deep, ruled; 11½ cm. h., base diam. 4 cm. (personal examination).

YBC 2147   Uruk (Clay, p. 56).

Uruk B2   Barrel cylinder frag. (Nies and Keiser, BIN, II, no. 27); broken on one side and part of bottom; clay uneven dark grey, with splotches of cream color remaining, bottom blackened as if burnt, ruled in broad lines, large clear signs, preserved h., 13.5 cm. (personal examination).

NBC 2509   No prov. (YBC files).

Uruk B3   Cylinder (Schott in Jordan, *APAW*, 1929, 7, pp. 48 ff. and pp. 57 f., no. 23).

Uruk #856   Uruk (Schott, pp. 57 ff.).

Uruk C1   Barrel cylinder, 15 cm. h. (Thureau-Dangin, *RA*, 11, p. 96).

——   Uruk (Thureau-Dangin, p. 96).

Uruk C2   Small, single-columned cylinder, dark brown clay, neat hand (Gadd, *CT* 36, p. 8).

BM 113204   No prov.

Uruk C3   Cylinder fragment, handwritten (Schott in Jordan, *APAW*, 1929, pp. 48 ff. and p. 58, no. 24).

#4098   Uruk at Pe XIV5, by n.w. court wall of Sargon (Schott, pp. 48 ff.).

Uruk D   Clay barrel cylinder, 11.3 cm. x 6 cm., Assyr. script (Clay, YOS, I, pl. 56, no. 40).

——   Uruk (Clay, no. 40).

Uruk E1	Stamped clay brick, 33.5 × 6.5–7 cm. (Schott in Jordan, *APAW*, 1929, 7, p. 57).
Uruk #942	Uruk, Stadtgebiet, at QbXV4 (Schott, p. 57).
Uruk E2	Stamped clay brick, 33.5 × 6.5–7 cm. (Schott in Jordan, *APAW*, 1929, 7, p. 57).
Uruk #3764	Uruk, Stadtgebiet, at QdXV4, in refuse (Schott, p. 57).
Uruk E3	Stamped clay brick, 33.5 × 6.5–7 cm. (Schott in Jordan, *APAW*, 1929, 7, p. 57).
Uruk #3885	Uruk, Eanna area (Schott, p. 57).
Uruk E4	Stamped clay brick, 33.5 × 6.5–7 cm. (Schott, *APAW*, 1929, 7, p. 57).
Uruk #4238	Uruk, in refuse, Innin-temple (Schott, p. 57).
Uruk F	Stamped brick, 4 ll. inscrip. (Schott in Jordan, *APAW*, 1929, 7, p. 57).
Uruk #4496	Uruk, at QdXIV 5 (Schott, p. 57).
Uruk G	No description.
——	No prov.
AsBbA1+	Clay tablet (JER); overall 8¼″ h. × 5⅝″ w.; 52+ 56+ 2 ll. (Bezold, *Cat.*).
K. 2801	Tablet fragment, probably from Nineveh (Kuyunjik) (JER).
K. 3053	Tablet fragment, probably from Nineveh (Kuyunjik) (JER).
DT 252	Tablet fragment, probably from Nineveh (Kuyunjik) (JER).
AsBbA2+	Clay tablet (JER).
K. 221	Probably S.W. Palace, Nineveh, Kuyunjik (JER).
K. 2669	Probably S.W. Palace, Nineveh, Kuyunjik (JER).
AsBbB	Upper part of rev. of tablet, 2½″ × 1⅛″ (Bezold, *Cat.*, p. 667).
K. 4845	Nineveh? (K. no.).
AsBbC	Fragment from middle of tablet, 2³⁄₁₆″ × 1¼″ (Bezold, *Cat.*, p. 1462; JER).
Sm 1089	Nineveh (JER).
AsBbD	Fragment of terra cotta cylinder, 1⅝″, ruled into sections, very clear Assyr. script (Bezold, *Cat.*, p. 325).
K. 1654	Nineveh? (K. no.).
AsBbE	Tablet of bluish alabaster, 5 cm. thick (*MDOG*, 26, p. 41 f.; and Messerschmidt, *KAH* I, nr. 75, pp. 69–70 and p. XIII); photo Ass. 378–381, 404 (LDL).
ES6262	Assur #3916. Aššur, in group of rooms at s.w. side of great court, Aššur temple, in uppermost layers of rubble from collapsed clay-brick walls, at hC4I (Messerschmidt, *KAH* I, p. XIII); with some 200 baked clay tablets, some alabaster tablets and inscribed stone objects, in n.w. part of s.w. courtyard, Aššur temple (Pedersen, II, p. 12); Istanbul Mu. (LDL).

AsBbF	Upper part of tablet, 3¾″ × 3½″ (Bezold, *Cat.*, p. 880).
K. 7862	Nineveh? (Kuyunjik number).
AsBbG	Lower part of tablet, 2⅞″ × 2¾″ (Bezold, *Cat.*, p. 711).
K. 5382b	Nineveh? (Kuyunjik number).
AsBbH	Fragment of left half of tablet, 2⅞″ × 1⅝″ (Bezold, *Cat.*, p. 1461).
Sm. 1079	No prov.
K. 2388	(Borger, *Asarh.*, p. 92); upper part of tablet, 3⅞″ × 2¼″ (Bezold, *Cat.*, p. 438).
K. 2388	Nineveh? (Kuyunjik number).
Sammeltext 1	Right half of tablet, 7″ × 2¾″ (Bezold, *Cat.*, p. 468).
K. 2711	Nineveh? (Kuyunjik number).
Sammeltext 2	Frag. from middle of tablet, 2¼″ × 2″ (Bezold, *Cat.*, p. 636).
K. 4487	Nineveh? (Kuyunjik number).
Monument A1	Basalt stele, 10′6¾″ h., with bas-relief of king and 2 prisoners (Von Luschan, *Ausgrabungen*, I, pp. 30 ff.; photo, Pritchard, *The Ancient Near East*, #121; descrip., App. I).
———	Zincirli, in the small court within the outer city gate, fallen beside its heavy stone base (Von Luschan, I, pp. 11 ff. and 30 ff.).
Monument A2	Tablet fragment, mid-section, 1⅝″ × 1⅛″ (Bezold, *Cat.*, p. 1328).
K. 13649	Nineveh? (Kuyunjik number).
Monument A3+	Tablet fragments (Bezold, *Cat.*, pp. 1567 and 1817).
DT 299	No prov.
82-3-23, 39	No prov.
Monument B	Bottom section of large black basalt stele with unfinished bas-relief showing king and 2 prisoners (Thureau-Dangin, *Syria*, 10, pp. 185–205; descrip., App. I).
———	Til-Barsip, in fragments, near the tell (Thureau-Dangin, pp. 185–205).
Monument C	On cliff-face, inscribed across figure of king (F. Weissbach, *Denkmaler . . . Nahr el-Kelb*, pp. 27 ff.; for descrip, see App. I).
———	Mouth of Nahr el-Kelb, north of Beirut, Lebanon (Weissbach, pp. 27 ff.).
Gottesbrief 1	Tablet, partly broken, upper part (Winckler, *AOF*, I, p. 530 f.; Labat, *Annuaire*, 1973/4, p. 66).
K. 7599	Nineveh? (Kuyunjik number).
Gottesbrief 2+	Tablet, upper part and fragment (Bezold, *Cat.*, p. 481 and 1029).
K. 2852	Nineveh? (Kuyunjik number).
K. 9662	Nineveh? (Kuyunjik number).
***"Wiener fragment"**	Fragment of 8-sided prism, text of right col. parallel to Gbr. (Borger, *AfO*, 18, pp. 114 ff.).
———	No prov.; Wiener Museum für Völkerkunde.

Treaty, **Ba'al of Tyre+**	Tablet fragments (Bezold, *Cat.*, pp. 539, 633, and 1074).
K. 3500	Nineveh? (Kuyunjik numbers).
K. 4444	Nineveh? (Kuyunjik numbers).
K. 10235	Nineveh? (Kuyunjik numbers).
Frt. A	Tablet fragment, right half (Bezold, *Cat.*, p. 464).
K. 2671	Nineveh? (Kuyunjik number).
Frt. B	Tablet fragment, lower part (Bezold, *Cat.*, p. 935).
K. 8523	Nineveh? (Kuyunjik number).
Frt. C	Tablet fragment (Bezold, *Cat.*, p. 1486).
Sm 1421	No prov.
Frt. D	Tablet, upper part of 1 side (Bezold, *Cat.*, p. 635); may be part of Treaty with Ba'al (B., p. 111).
K. 4473	Nineveh? (Kuyunjik number).
Frt. E	Tablet, lower part of right half (Bezold, *Cat.*, p. 1894).
83-1-18, 483	No prov.
Frt. F+	Tablet fragments (Bezold, *Cat.*, p. 501).
K. 3082	Nineveh? (Kuyunjik number).
K. 3086	Nineveh? (Kuyunjik number).
Sm 2027	Nineveh? (Kuyunjik number).
Frt. G	Tablet fragment, mid-section (Bezold, *Cat.*, p. 1716).
79-7-8, 196	No prov.
Frt. H	Tablet fragment (Bezold, *Cat.*, p. 1334).
K. 13721	Nineveh? (Kuyunjik number).
Frt. I+	Tablet fragment (Bezold, *Cat.*, p. 505).
K. 3127	Nineveh? (Kuyunjik number).
K. 4435	Nineveh? (Kuyunjik number).
Frt. J	Fragment, middle of clay prism, 3¼" (Bezold, *Cat.* p. 1948).
Bu 91-5-9, 218	No prov.
Frt. K	Fragment, middle of clay cylinder, division lines (Bezold, *Cat.*, p. 1941).
Bu 91-5-9, 134	No prov.
Frt. L	Tablet fragment, mid-section (Bezold, *Cat.*, p. 1601).
Rm 284	No prov.
Frt. M	Tablet fragment, mid-section (Bezold, *Cat.*, p. 1912).
83-1-18, 836	No prov.
*Frt. N?	Fragment of 1-col. tablet, small script; possible Esar. text related to return of Marduk (Lambert, in *Ad bene . . .*, pp. 158–71).
K. 13383	Nineveh? (Kuyunjik no.).

Naqi'a Prism 1+   2 fragments from middle of 6-sided prism (Bezold, *Cat.*, p. 471
                         and 1617); Borger join (B., p. 115).

   K. 2745   Nineveh? (Kuyunjik no.).

   Rm 494   Nineveh? (Kuyunjik no.).

Naqi'a Prism 2   Fragment of prism, mid-section, 2⅜″ h., parts of 2 cols. (Bezold,
                         Cat., p. 1768).

   81-2-4, 173   No prov.

K. 7943   Fragment, upper part of tablet, archaising script imitating Su-
                         merian linear inscriptions (Bezold, *Cat.*, p. 884 and B., p. 117
                         [labeled only by no.]).

   K. 7943   Nineveh? (Kuyunjik no.).

K. 10057   Tablet fragment, mid-section (Bezold, *Cat.*, p. 1060).

   K. 10057   Nineveh? (Kuyunjik no.).

K. 10220 +   Upper part and right-hand corner of tablet (Bezold, *Cat.*, pp.
K. 10463   1073 and 1090).

   K. 10220   Nineveh? (Kuyunjik no.).

   K. 10463   Nineveh? (Kuyunjik no.).

K. 13733   Fragment of tablet, mid-section (Bezold, *Cat.*, p. 1335).

   K. 13733   Nineveh? (Kuyunjik no.).

K. 13753   Fragment of tablet, mid-section (Bezold, *Cat.*, p. 1336).

   K. 13753   Nineveh? (Kuyunjik no.).

DT 82   Fragment of tablet, mid-section (Bezold, *Cat.*, p. 1549).

   DT 82   No prov.

80-7-19, 44   Tablet, upper half (Bezold, *Cat.*, p. 1732); badly salt-encrusted,
                         now cleaned and much more legible (B., p. 119).

   80-7-19, 44   No prov.

Lion's Head Inscr.   On a lion's head; Ass. script (B., p. 121).

   BM 91678   Sippar (B., p. 121).

*Vassal treaties   9 or more large clay tablets, much broken; ND 4327, recon-
                         structed, measures 45.8 × 30 cms. (D.J. Wiseman, *Iraq*, 20
                         [1958], part 1, p. 1, n. 6; pls. 1–53).

   ND 4327   IM64188. And duplicates, comprised of ca. 350 fragments
                         (grouped as separate texts and listed in Watanabe, BaM, 3, pp.
                         47–54); Calaḫ, in building at s.e. corner of acropolis, just n. of
                         temple of Nabû, in n.w. corner of throneroom SEB2 near dais,
                         in doorway of anteroom NTS3, and in south doorway of SEB2
                         and in the adjoining courtyard (Wiseman, p. 1); just north of
                         Nabû sanctuary and within the Ezida Temple precincts, in debris
                         and ash on floor of throneroom, in doorway of anteroom NTS3,
                         and in s. doorway of SEB2 and in the adjacent courtyard (Mal-
                         lowan, *Nimrud*, I, pp. 241 ff.).

*Treaty inscrip.+	Fragments of 2-col. clay tablet (Parpola and Watanabe, p. l).
BM 50666	Probably from Sippar (Parpola and Watanabe, p. l).
50857	Probably from Sippar (Parpola and Watanabe, p. l).
53678	Probably from Sippar (Parpola and Watanabe, p. l).
53728	Probably from Sippar (Parpola and Watanabe, p. l).
51098	Probably from Sippar (join not direct) (Parpola and Watanabe, p. l).
*Accession Treaty+	3 fragments of one tablet, no direct join (Parpola and Watanabe, p. xlvii).
83-1-18, 420	Nineveh (Parpola and Watanabe, p. xlvii).
83-1-18, 493	Nineveh (Parpola and Watanabe, p. xlvii).
Bu 91-5-9, 131	Nineveh (Parpola and Watanabe, p. xlvii).
*Loyalty Oath	Tiny fragment, left half clay tablet (Parpola and Watanabe, p. xlviii).
Bu 91-5-9, 22	Nineveh (Parpola and Watanabe, p. xlviii).
*Plaque Inscrip.	Inscribed bronze plaque fragment with bas-relief of king and woman with "Naqi'a" inscribed on shoulder (Parrot and Nougayrol, *Syria*, 33, pp. 147–160).
AO 20.185	No prov.
Eye-stone Inscrip. of Ešarhamat	Agate carved to resemble an eye (Lambert, *RA*, 63, pp. 65–71).
Ashmolean 197.1483	No prov.

Bibliography

AHMED, SAMI. *Southern Mesopotamia in the Time of Ashurbanipal.* Studies in Ancient History, 2. The Hague and Paris: Mouton, 1968.

ANDRAE, WALTER. "Aus den Berichten aus Assur." *MDOG*, 26 (1905): 19–64.

———. "Aus den Berichten W. Andraes." *MDOG*, 33 (1906–07): 11–23.

———. *Der Anu-Adad-Tempel in Assur.* WVDOG, 10. Leipzig: J.C. Hinrichs, 1909.

———. *Die Festungswerke von Assur.* 2 vols. WVDOG, 23. Leipzig: J.C. Hinrichs, 1913.

———. *Das Wiedererstandene Assur.* Sendschrift der Deutschen Orient-Gesellschaft, 9. Leipzig: J.C. Hinrichs, 1938.

ARO, JUSSI. "Remarks on the Practice of Extispicy in the Time of Esarhaddon and Assurbanipal." *La divination en Mésopotamie ancienne et dans les régions voisines.* Compte rendu de la 14e Rencontre Assyriologique Internationale, Strasbourg, 1966. Paris: Presses Universitaires de France, 1966. Pp. 109–117.

ASIL, NAJI AL-. "Editorial Notes: The Assyrian Palace at Nebi Yunis." *Sumer*, 10 (1954): 110–111.

———. "Recent Archeological Activity in Iraq." *Sumer*, 12 (1956): 3–7.

AYNARD, JEANNE-MARIE. Review of R. Borger, *Die Inschriften Asarhaddons*. *Bibliotheca Orientalis*, 14 (1957): 81–83.

———. *Le Prisme du Louvre AO 19.939.* Paris: Honoré Champion, 1957.

BANKS, E.J. "Eight Oracular Responses to Esarhaddon." *AJSL*, 14 (1897–98): 267–277.

BARNETT, R.D. *Assyrian Palace Reliefs and their Influence on the Sculptures of Babylonia and Assyria.* London: Batchworth Press, 1960.

———. "Lady Layard's Jewelry." *Archaeology in the Levant: Essays for Kathleen Kenyon.* Ed. Roger Moorey and Peter Parr. Warminster, England: Aris and Phillips, 1978. Pp. 172–179.

BARNETT, R.D., AND MARGARETE FALKNER. *The Sculptures of Aššur-naṣir-apli II (883–859 BC), Tiglath-Pileser III (745–727 BC), Esarhaddon (681–669 BC) from the Central and South-west Palaces at Nimrud.* London: British Museum, 1962.

BASMACHI, F. "Quelques considérations à propos des statues de Taharqa, trouvées dans les ruines du Palais d'Esarhaddon." *Sumer*, 11 (1955): 149–153.

BAUER, THEO. "Review of R.C. Thompson, *The Prisms of Esarhaddon and of Ashurbanipal*; Bruno Meissner, *Neue Nachrichten über die Ermordung Sanheribs und die Nachfolge Asarhaddons*, and Hans Hirshberg, *Studien zur Geschichte Esarhaddons.*" *ZA*, 42 (1934): 170–184.

BECKMAN, GARY. "A Join-piece to the Esarhaddon Prism YOS 9.76." *Annual Review of the Royal Inscriptions of Mesopotamia Project*, 6 (1988): 3–4.

BEZOLD, CARL. *Catalogue of the Cuneiform Tablets in the Kouyunjik Collection of the British Museum.* 5 vols. London: British Museum, 1889–99.

BIGGS, ROBERT D. "Oracles Concerning Esarhaddon." *The Ancient Near East: Supplementary Texts and Pictures Relating to the Old Testament*. Ed. James B. Pritchard. Princeton: Princeton U. Press, 1969. P. 169.

BING, J.D. "A History of Cilicia during the Assyrian Period." Diss., U. of Indiana. Bloomington, Ind.: 1969.

―――. "A Further Note on Cynda/*Kundi*." *Historia*, 22 (1973): 346–350.

BÖHL, FRANZ MARIUS THEODOR DE LIAGRE. "Der Zeitalter der Sargoniden nach Briefen aus dem königlichen Archiv zu Nineve." *Opera Minora: Studies en Bijdragen op Assyriologisch en Oudtestamentisch Terrein*. Gronigen and Djakarta: J.B. Walters, 1953.

BOISSIER, ALFRED. "Prisme d'Asarhaddon à l'Université de Zürich." *Babyloniaca*, 9 (1926): 27–28.

―――. "Notes Assyriologiques II: A) Asarhaddon." *RA*, 30 (1933): 71–78.

BORGER, RYKLE (also Riekele). *Die Inschriften Asarhaddons, Königs von Assyrien*. (*AfO*, Beiheft 9) Graz: 1956.

―――. "Gottesbrief." *Reallexikon der Assyriologie und vorderasiatischen Archäologie*, III. Ed. Ernst Weidner and Wolfram von Soden. Berlin: Walter de Gruyter, 1957 ff. Pp. 575–576.

―――. "Die Inschriften Asarhaddons (AfO Beiheft 9)." *AfO*, 18 (1957–8): 113–118.

―――. "Der Neue Asarhaddon-Text AfO 18, S. 324 ff." *AfO*, 19 (1959–60): 148.

―――. "Zu den Asarhaddon-Verträgen aus Nimrud." *ZA*, 54 (1961): 171–196.

―――. "Zu den Asarhaddon-Verträgen aus Nimrud: Nachtrag." *ZA*, 56 (1963): 261.

―――. *Einleitung in die assyrischen Königsinschriften*, I. Handbuch der Orientalistik, Abt. I, Ergänzungsband 5. Leiden and Köln: E.J. Brill, 1964.

―――. "Zu den Asarhaddon-Texten aus Babel." *BiOr*, 21 (1964): 143–148.

BOTTÉRO, J. "Le Substitut royal et son sort en Mésopotamie ancienne." *Akkadica*, 9 (1978): 2–24.

BRINKMAN, JOHN A. "Merodach-Baladan II." *Studies Presented to A. Leo Oppenheim*. Ed. R.D. Biggs and J.A. Brinkman. Chicago: Oriental Institute, 1964. Pp. 6–53.

―――. "Ur: 721–605 BC." *Orientalia* (n.s.), 34 (1965): 241–258.

―――. "Elamite Military Aid to Merodach-Baladan." *JNES*, 24 (1965): 161–166.

―――. *A Political History of Post-Kassite Babylonia 1158–722 BC*. Analecta Orientalia, 43. Rome: Pontifical Biblical Institute, 1968.

―――. "Ur: The Kassite Period and the Period of the Assyrian Kings." *Orientalia* (n.s.), 38 (1969): 310–348.

―――. "Sennacherib's Babylonian Problem: An Interpretation." *JCS*, 25 (1973): 89–95.

―――. "The Early Neo-Babylonian Monarchy." *Le Palais et la royauté (archéologie et civilisation)*. Compte rendu de la 19e Rencontre Assyriologique Internationale, Paris, 1971. Ed. Paul Garelli. Paris: Geuthner, 1974. Pp. 409–415.

―――. "The Monarchy in the Time of the Kassite Dynasty." *Le Palais et la royauté (archéologie et civilization)*. Compte rendu de la 19e Rencontre Assyriologique International, Paris, 1971. Ed. Paul Garelli. Paris: Geuthner, 1974. Pp. 395–408.

―――. "Notes on Arameans and Chaldeans in Southern Babylonia in the Early Seventh Century BC." *Orientalia* (n.s.), 46 (1977): 304–325.

―――. "Babylonia Under the Assyrian Empire, 745–627 BC." *Power and Propaganda: A*

Symposium on Ancient Empires. Ed. Mogens T. Larsen. Mesopotamia, 7. Copenhagen: Akademisk Forlag, 1979. Pp. 223–250.

————. "Babylonia c. 1000–748 BC." *The Cambridge Ancient History, v. III, pt. 1: The Prehistory of the Balkans; and the Middle East and the Aegean World, Tenth to Eighth Centuries BC*. Ed. John Boardman, I.E.S. Edwards, N.G.L. Hammond, E. Sollberger. 2nd ed. Cambridge and London: Cambridge U. Press, 1982. Pp. 282–313.

————. "Through a Glass Darkly: Esarhaddon's Retrospects on the Downfall of Babylon." *JAOS*, 103 (1983): 35–42.

————. *Prelude to Empire: Babylonian Society and Politics, 747–626 BC*. Occasional Publications of the Babylonian Fund, 7. Philadelphia: The University Museum, 1984.

BRINKMAN, JOHN A., AND D.A. KENNEDY. "Documentary Evidence for the Economic Base of Early Neo-Babylonian Society: A Survey of Dated Babylonian Economic Texts, 721–626 BC." *JCS*, 35 (1983): 1–90.

BUCCELLATI, GIORGIO AND ROBERT D. BIGGS. *Cuneiform Texts from Nippur: The Eighth and Ninth Seasons*. Assyriological Studies, 17. Chicago: U. of Chicago, 1969.

BUDGE, E.A. WALLIS. *The History of Esarhaddon, Son of Sennacherib, King of Assyria, BC 681–668*. London: Trubner, 1881.

————. *A Guide to the Babylonian and Assyrian Antiquities*. 2nd ed., rev. London: British Museum, 1908.

————. *By Nile and Tigris: A Narrative of Journeys in Egypt and Mesopotamia on Behalf of the British Museum between the Years 1886 and 1913*. 2 vols. London: John Murray, 1920.

BURSTEIN, STANLEY MAYER. *The* Babyloniaca *of Berossus*. Sources from the Ancient Near East, 1/5. Malibu, Calif.: Undena, 1978.

CARTER, ELIZABETH AND MATTHEW W. STOLPER. *Elam: Surveys of Political History and Archaeology*. U. of California Publications, Near Eastern Studies, 25. Berkeley, Los Angeles and London: U. of California Press, 1984.

CASSIN, ELENA. *Fischer Weltgeschichte, Band III*. Ed. Elena Cassin, Jean Bottéro, and Jean Vercoutter. Frankfurt: Fischer Taschenbuch, 1966. P. 81.

CIVIL, MIGUEL. "Note sur les inscriptions d'Asarhaddon à Nippur." *RA*, 68 (1974): 94.

CLAY, ALBERT T. *Miscellaneous Inscriptions in the Yale Babylonian Collection*. Yale Oriental Series, 1. New Haven: Yale U. Press, 1915.

COGAN, MORTON (also, Mordechai). *Imperialism and Religion: Assyria, Judah and Israel in the Eighth and Seventh Centuries BCE*. Society of Biblical Literature Monograph No. 19. Missoula, Montana: Society of Biblical Literature, 1974.

————. "Omens and Ideology in the Babylon Inscriptions of Esarhaddon." *History, Historiography and Interpretation*. Ed. H. Tadmor and M. Weinfeld. Jerusalem: Magnes, 1983. Pp. 76–87.

————. "New Additions to the Corpus of Esarhaddon Historical Inscriptions." *AfO*, 31 (1984): 72–75.

CRAIG, JAMES A. *Assyrian and Babylonian Religious Texts, Being Prayers, Oracles, Hymns, etc., Copied from the Original Tablets Preserved in the British Museum and Autographed by James A. Craig*. 2 vols. Assyriologische Bibliothek, Bd. XIII. Leipzig: J.C. Hinrichs, 1895–97.

CRAWFORD, VAUGHN E. "Nippur, the Holy City." *Archaeology*, 12 (1959): 74–83.

DELATTRE, A. "The Oracles Given in Favour of Esarhaddon." *The Babylonian and Oriental Record*, 3 (1889): 25–31.

DELLER, KARLHEINZ. "The Neo-Assyrian Epigraphical Remains of Nimrud." *Orientalia* (n.s.), 35 (1966): 179–194.

———. "Die Briefe des Adad-šumu-uṣur." *Lišān Mitḫurti: Festschrift Wolfram von Soden* Ed. W. Röllig, with assistance of M. Dietrich. AOAT, 1. Neukirchen-Vluyn: Butzon and Bercker Kevelaer, 1969. Pp. 45–64.

DEUTSCH, KARL. *Nationalism and Social Communication: An Inquiry into the Foundations of Nationality.* New York: The Technology Press of M.I.T. and John Wiley, 1953, and London: Chapman and Hall, 1953.

DIAKONOFF, I.M. "A Babylonian Political Pamphlet from about 700 BC." *Studies in Honor of Benno Landsberger on His Seventy-fifth Birthday, April 21, 1965.* Ed. H. Güterbock and Th. Jacobsen. Chicago: U. of Chicago, 1965. Pp. 343–349.

DIETRICH, MANFRIED. "Neue Quellen zur Geschichte Babyloniens (I) (Ein Vorbericht)." *Die Welt des Orients,* 4 (1967–68): 61–103.

———. "Neue Quellen zur Geschichte Babyloniens (II) (Ein Vorbericht)." *Die Welt des Orients,* 4 (1967–68): 183–251.

———. "Neue Quellen zur Geschichte Babyloniens (II—Indizes)." *Die Welt des Orients,* 5 (1969–70): 51–56.

———. "Neue Quellen zur Geschichte Babyloniens (III): Die Briefe des Truppenkommandanten ᵈBēl-ibni aus dem Meerland (Ein Vorbericht)." *Die Welt des Orients,* 5 (1969–70): 176–190.

———. *Die Aramäer südbabyloniens in der Sargonidenzeit (700–648).* AOAT, 7. Neukirchen-Vluyn: Butzon and Bercker Kevelaer and Neukirchener Verlag des Erziehungsvereins, 1970.

———. "Neue Quellen zur Geschichte Babyloniens (IV): Die Urkunden der Jahre 700 bis 651 aus dem Archiv des Urukäers Nabû-ušallim." *Die Welt des Orients,* 6 (1970–71): 157–162.

———. *Cuneiform Texts from Babylonian Tablets in the British Museum, Part 54: Neo-Babylonian Letters from the Kuyunjik Collection.* London: British Museum, 1979.

DOUGHERTY, RAYMOND P. "Cuneiform Parallels to Solomon's Provisioning System." *Annual of the American School of Oriental Research,* 5 (1925): 23–65.

DRIEL, G. VAN. *The Cult of Aššur.* Assen, The Netherlands: Van Gorcum, 1969.

EBELING, ERICH. *Keilschrifttexte aus Assur religiösen Inhalts,* I. WVDOG, 34. Leipzig: J.C. Hinrichs, 1923.

———. "Esabad." *Reallexikon der Assyriologie und vorderasiatischen Archäologie,* II. Ed. Erich Ebeling and Bruno Meissner. Berlin and Leipzig: Walter de Gruyter, 1938.

———. "Ešeriga." *Reallexikon der Assyriologie und vorderasiatischen Archäologie,* II. Ed. Erich Ebeling and Bruno Meissner. Berlin and Leipzig: Walter de Gruyter, 1938.

EDWARDS, I.E.S. [Letter of 1 March, 1955, about a bronze statuette from the Esarhaddon palace at Nebi Yunus, written to Dr. Naji al Asil] in "News and Correspondence." *Sumer,* 11 (1955), p. 129.

EL AMIN, MAHMUD. "Die Reliefs mit Beischriften von Sargon II. in Dûr-Sarrukîn." *Sumer,* 10 (1954): 23–42.

ELLIS, RICHARD. *Foundation Deposits in Ancient Mesopotamia.* New Haven and London: Yale U. Press, 1968.

EPH'AL, ISRAEL. "'Arabs' in Babylonia in the 8th c. BC." *JAOS*, 94 (1974): 108–115.

———. *The Ancient Arabs: Nomads on the Borders of the Fertile Crescent, 9th–5th Centuries BC.* Jerusalem: Magnes Press, and Leiden: E.J. Brill, 1982.

FALES, F.M. AND G.B. LANFRANCHI. "ABL 1237: The Role of the Cimmerians in a Letter to Esarhaddon." *East and West* (n.s.), 31 (1981): 9–33.

FALKENSTEIN, ADAM. *Literarische Keilschrifttexte aus Uruk.* Berlin: Staatliche Museen zu Berlin, Vorderasiatische Abteilung, 1931.

FECHT, GERHARD. "Die Schlacht bei 'Ša-amelie' (Asarhaddon-Chronik)." *Mitteilungen des Deutschen Archäologischen Instituts, Abteilung Kairo*, 16 (1958): 116–119.

FRAME, GRANT. "Babylonia 689–627 BC: A Political History." Unpublished diss., U. of Chicago. June, 1981.

———. "The 'First Families' of Borsippa during the Early Neo-Babylonian Period." *JCS*, 36 (1984): 67–80.

FRANKFORT, HENRI. *The Art and Architecture of the Ancient Orient.* 2nd ed. Baltimore, Md.: Penguin, 1969.

FRANKFORT, HENRI, H.-G. FRANKFORT, JOHN WILSON, AND THORKILD JACOBSEN. *Before Philosophy: The Intellectual Adventure of Ancient Man.* 1946; rpt. Baltimore: Penguin, 1954.

FRYMER-KENSKY, TIKVA. "The Tribulations of Marduk: The So-called 'Marduk Ordeal Text.'" *JAOS*, 103 (1983): 131–141.

GADD, C.J. *Cuneiform Texts from Babylonian Tablets in the British Museum, etc., Part 36.* London: British Museum, 1921.

———. "Inscribed Barrel Cylinder of Marduk-apla-iddina II." *Iraq*, 15 (1953): 123–134.

GALTER, HANNES D. "Die Bautätigkeit Sanheribs am Aššurtempel." *Orientalia*, 53 (1984): 433–441.

GARDNER, ERNST ARTHUR. *A Handbook of Greek Sculpture.* London: Macmillan, 1897.

GARELLI, PAUL. "Les Sujets du roi d'Assyrie." *La Voix de l'opposition en Mésopotamie.* Ed. André Finet. Bruxelles: Institut des Hautes Études de Belgique, 1973. Pp. 189–213.

———. "L'État et la légitimité royale sous l'empire assyrien." *Power and Propaganda: A Symposium on Ancient Empires.* Ed. Mogens Trolle Larsen. Mesopotamia, 7. Copenhagen: Akademisk Forlag, 1979. Pp. 319–328.

———. "La Conception de la royauté en Assyrie." *Assyrian Royal Inscriptions: New Horizons in Literary, Ideological, and Historical Analysis.* Ed. F.M. Fales. Rome: Istituto per Oriente, 1981. Pp. 1–12.

———. "The Achievement of Tiglath-Pileser III: Novelty or Continuity?" *Ah, Assyria . . . : Studies in Assyrian History and Ancient Near Eastern Historiography Presented to Hayim Tadmor.* Ed. Mordechai Cogan and Israel Eph'al. Scripta Hierosolymitana, 33. Jerusalem: Magnes Press, Hebrew U., 1991. Pp. 46–51.

GERARDI, PAMELA. "Assurbanipal's Elamite Campaigns: A Literary and Political Study." Diss., U. of Pennsylvania, 1987.

GIBSON, M. "Kiš." *Reallexikon der Assyriologie und Vorderasiatischen Archäologie*, V. Ed. D.O. Edzard. Berlin and New York: Walter de Gruyter, 1976–80. Pp. 613–620.

GOETZE, ALBRECHT. "Esarhaddon's Inscriptions from the Inanna Temple in Nippur." *JCS*, 17 (1963): 119–131.

———. "An Inscription of Simbar-Šīḫu." *JCS*, 19 (1965): 121–135.

GRAYSON, A. KIRK. "Problematical Battles in Mesopotamian History." *Studies in Honor of Benno Landsberger on his Seventy-fifth Birthday*. Ed. H. Güterbock and T. Jacobsen. Assyriological Studies, 16. Chicago: U. of Chicago Press, 1965. Pp. 337–342.

——. *Assyrian and Babylonian Chronicles*. Texts from Cuneiform Sources, V. Locust Valley, N.Y.: J.J. Augustin, 1975.

——. "Assyrian Royal Inscriptions: Literary Characteristics." *Assyrian Royal Inscriptions: New Horizons in Literary, Ideological, and Historical Analysis*. Ed. F.M. Fales. Rome: Istituto per l'Oriente, 1981. Pp. 35–47.

——. "Assyria and Babylonia." *Orientalia* (n.s.), 49 (1980): 140–194.

——. "Akkadian Treaties of the Seventh Century BC." *JCS*, 39 (1987): 127–160.

GRAYSON, A. KIRK, AND LOUIS D. LEVINE. "The Assyrian Relief from Shikaft-I Gulgul." *Iranica Antiqua*, 11 (1975): 29–38.

GREENFIELD, JONAS C. "Babylonian-Aramaic Relationship." *Mesopotamien und seine Nachbarn*. Ed. Hans-Jörg Nissen and Johannes Renger. Berliner Beiträge zum vorderen Orient, 1. Berlin: Dietrich Reimer, 1982. Pp. 471–482.

HAINES, RICHARD C. "A Report of the Excavations at Nippur during 1960–1961." *Sumer*, 17 (1961): 67–70.

HALL, H.R. "The Assyrians in Egypt." *Cambridge Ancient History*, III. Ed. J.B. Bury, S.A. Cook, and F.E. Adcock. Cambridge, Eng.: Cambridge U. Press, 1929. Pp. 280–283.

HALLO, WILLIAM W. *Early Mesopotamian Royal Titles: A Philologic and Historical Analysis*. American Oriental Series, 43. New Haven: American Oriental Society, 1957.

——. "From Qarqar to Carchemish: Assyria and Israel in the Light of New Discoveries." *Biblical Archeologist*, 23 (1960): 34–61.

——. "The Royal Inscriptions of Ur: A Typology." *Hebrew Union College Annual*, 33 (1962): 1–43.

——. "The House of Ur-Meme." *JNES*, 31 (1972): 87–95.

——. "The Royal Correspondence of Larsa: I. A Sumerian Prototype for the Prayer of Hezekiah?" *The Kramer Anniversary Volume: Cuneiform Studies in Honor of Samuel Noah Kramer*. Ed. Barry L. Eichler, with Jane W. Heimerdinger and Åke W. Sjöberg. Alter Orient und Altes Testament, 25. Neukirchen-Vluyn: Butzon and Berker Kevelaer, 1976. Pp. 209–224.

——. "The Expansion of Cuneiform Literature." *Proceedings of the American Academy for Jewish Research*, 46–47 (1979–80): 307–322.

——. "Letters, Prayers and Letter-Prayers." *Proceedings of the Seventh World Congress of Jewish Studies, Jerusalem, 1981*. Jerusalem: Perry Foundation for Biblical Research, World Union of Jewish Studies, 1981. Pp. 17–27.

——. "Sumerian Historiography." *History, Historiography and Interpretation*. Ed. H. Tadmor and M. Weinfeld. Jerusalem: Magnes, 1983. Pp. 9–20.

——. "Dating the Mesopotamian Past: The Concept of Eras from Sargon to Nabonassar." *Bulletin of the Society for Mesopotamian Studies* (Sept., 1983): 7–18.

HALLO, WILLIAM W., AND WILLIAM KELLY SIMPSON. *The Ancient Near East: A History*. New York: Harcourt, Brace, Jovanovich, 1971.

HARPER, ROBERT FRANCIS. *Assyrian and Babylonian Letters Belonging to the Kouyunjik Collections of the British Museum*. 14 parts. London and Chicago: U. of Chicago and Luzac and Co., 1892–1914.

HEIDEL, ALEXANDER. *The Babylonian Genesis: The Story of Creation*. 2nd ed., 1951; rpt. Chicago and London: U. of Chicago, 1974.

HEIDEL, ALEXANDER, AND A. LEO OPPENHEIM. "A New Hexagonal Prism of Esarhaddon (676 BC)." *Sumer*, 12 (1956): 9–37 and plates 1–12.

HIRSCHBERG, HANS. *Studien zur Geschichte Esarhaddons König von Assyrien (681–669)*. Diss., Friedrich-Wilhelm Universität, 1932. Berlin: Hermann Eschenhagen, 1932.

HOFFNER, HARRY A. "Propaganda and Political Justification in Hittite Historiography." *Unity and Diversity*. Ed. Hans Goedicke and J.J.M. Roberts. Baltimore: Johns Hopkins U. Press, 1975. Pp. 49–64.

HULIN, P. "Another Esarhaddon Cylinder from Nimrud." *Iraq*, 24 (1962): 116–118.

HUNT, ROBERT C. "The Role of Bureaucracy in the Provisioning of Cities: A Framework for Analysis of the Ancient Near East." *The Organization of Power: Aspects of Bureaucracy in the Ancient Near East*. Ed. McGuire Gibson and R.D. Biggs. Studies in Ancient Oriental Civilization, 46. Chicago: Oriental Institute of the U. of Chicago, 1987. Pp. 161–192.

ISHIDA, TOMOO. "The Succession Narrative and Esarhaddon's Apology: A Comparison." *Ah, Assyria . . .: Studies in Assyrian History and Ancient Near Eastern Historiography presented to Hayim Tadmor*. Ed. Mordechai Cogan and Israel Eph'al. Scripta Hierosolymitana, 33. Jerusalem: Magnes Press, Hebrew U., 1991. Pp. 46–51.

JACOBSEN, THORKILD. *Toward the Image of Tammuz and Other Essays on Mesopotamian History and Culture*. Ed. William L. Moran. Cambridge, Mass.: Harvard U. Press, 1970.

———. *The Treasures of Darkness: A History of Mesopotamian Religion*. New Haven and London: Yale U. Press, 1976.

———. "Ur-Nanshe's Diorite Plaque." *Orientalia* (n.s.), 54 (1985): 65–72.

JASTROW, MORRIS. *Bildermappe zur Religion babyloniens und assyriens*. Giessen: Töpelmann, 1912.

JOHNS, CLAUDE H.W. *Assyrian Deeds and Documents Recording the Transfer of Property, Including the So-Called Private Contracts, Legal Decisions and Proclamations, Preserved in the Kouyunjik Collections of the British Museum, Chiefly of the 7th Century BC*. 4 vols. Cambridge: 1898, 1901, 1901, and 1923.

JORDAN, JULIUS. *Uruk-Warka nach den Ausgrabungen durch die Deutsche Orient-Gesellschaft*. WVDOG, 51. Leipzig: J.C. Hinrichs, 1928.

KERTZER, DAVID I. *Ritual, Politics, and Power*. New Haven and London: Yale U. Press, 1988.

KING, LEONARD W. *Cuneiform Texts from Babylonian Tablets in the British Museum, etc., Part 13*. London: British Museum, 1901.

———. *Babylonian Boundary-Stones and Memorial-Tablets in the British Museum*. 2 vols. London: British Museum, 1912.

———. *Catalogue of the Cuneiform Tablets in the Kouyunjik Collection of the British Museum: Supplement*. London: British Museum, 1914.

———. *Cuneiform Texts from Babylonian Tablets in the British Museum, etc., Part 34*. London: British Museum, 1914.

KINNIER WILSON, J.V. *The Nimrud Wine Lists: A Study of the Men and Administration at the Assyrian Capital in the Eighth Century, BC*. London: British School of Archaeology in Iraq, 1972.

KLAUBER, ERNST GEORG. *Politisch-religiöse Texte aus der Sargonidenzeit*. Leipzig: Eduard Pfeiffer, 1913.

KNUDSTAD, JAMES E. "A Report on the 1964–1965 Excavations at Nippur." *Sumer*, 22 (1966): 111–114.

KNUDTZON, JÖRGEN ALEXANDER. *Assyrische Gebete an den Sonnengott für Staat und königliches Haus aus der Zeit Asarhaddons und Asurbanipals.* 2 vols. Leipzig: Eduard Pfeiffer, 1893.

KOHLER, J. AND A. UNGNAD. *Assyrische Rechtsurkunden.* Leipzig: Eduard Pfeiffer, 1913.

KOLDEWEY, ROBERT. *Das wieder erstehende Babylon: Die bisherigen Ergebnisse der Deutschen Ausgrabungen.* Leipzig: J.C. Hinrichs, 1913.

———. *Die Tempel von Babylon und Borsippa.* WVDOG, 15. 1st ed., 1911; rpt. Osnabruck: Otto Zeller, 1972.

KRAELING, E.A. "The Death of Sennacherib." *JAOS*, 53 (1933): 335–346.

KRAMER, SAMUEL NOAH. *The Sumerians: Their History, Culture, and Character.* Chicago and London: U. of Chicago Press, 1963.

KÜMMEL, HANS MARTIN. *Familie, Beruf und Amt im spätbabylonischen Uruk: Prosopographische Untersuchungen zu Berufsgruppen des 6. Jahrhunderts v. Chr. in Uruk.* Abhandlungen der Deutschen Orient-Gesellschaft, 20. Berlin: Mann, 1979.

LABAT, RENÉ. "Le Sort des substituts royaux en Assyrie au temps des Sargonides." *RA*, 40 (1945–6): 123–142.

———. "Asarhaddon et la ville de Zaqqap." *RA*, 53 (1959): 113–118.

———. "Das Assyrische Reich unter den Sargoniden." *Fischer Weltgeschichte (Band 4), Die Altorientalische Reiche, III: Die Erste Halfte des 1. Jahrtausends.* Ed. Elena Cassin, Jean Bottéro, and Jean Vercoutter. Frankfurt am Main: Fischer Bucherei GmbH, 1967. Pp. 68–93.

———. "Rapports sur les conférences: Assyrien." *Annuaire, École Pratique des Hautes Études, IVe Section: Sciences historiques et philologiques*, (1973–74). Pp. 65–68.

———. "Un Prince éclairé: Assurbanipal." *Académie des Inscriptions et Belles-Lettres. Comptes rendus des séances de l'année 1972.* Paris: 1973. Pp. 670 ff.

LACKENBACHER, SYLVIE. *Le roi bâtisseur: les récits de construction assyriens des origines à Teglat-phalasar III.* Études assyriologiques, Cahier 11. Paris: Éditions Recherche sur les civilisations, 1982.

LAMBERT, WILFRED G. "A Part of the Ritual for the Substitute King." *AfO*, 18 (1957–58): 109–112.

———. "Divine Love Lyrics from Babylon." *Journal of Semitic Studies*, 4 (1959): 1–15.

———. "The Ritual for the Substitute King—a New Fragment." *AfO*, 19 (1959–60): 119.

———. *Babylonian Wisdom Literature.* Oxford: Clarendon Press, 1960.

———. "The Great Battle of the Mesopotamian Religious Year: The Conflict in the Akītu House." *Iraq*, 25 (1963): 189–190.

———. "The Reign of Nebuchadnezzar I: A Turning Point in the History of Ancient Mesopotamian Religion." *The Seed of Wisdom: Essays in Honour of T.J. Meek.* Ed. W.S. McCullough. Toronto: U. of Toronto Press, 1964. Pp. 3–13.

———. *Enūma Eliš: The Babylonian Epic of Creation. The Cuneiform Text.* Oxford: Clarendon Press, 1966.

———. "An Eye-stone of Esarhaddon's Queen and other Similar Gems." *RA*, 63 (1969): 65–67.

———. "The Seed of Kingship." *Le Palais et la royauté (archéologie et civilisation).* Ed. Paul

Garelli. Compte rendu de la XIXe Rencontre Assyriologique Internationale. Paris: Geuthner, 1974. Pp. 427–440.

———. "The Historical Development of the Mesopotamian Pantheon: A Study in Sophisticated Polytheism." *Unity and Diversity.* Ed. Hans Goedicke and J.J.M. Roberts. Baltimore and London: Johns Hopkins U. Press, 1975. Pp. 191–192.

———. "The God Aššur." *Iraq,* 45 (1983): 82–86.

———. "Esarhaddon's Attempt to Return Marduk to Babylon." *Ad bene et fideliter seminandum: Festgabe für Karlheinz Deller zum 21. Februar 1987.* Ed. Gerlinde Mauer and Ursula Magen. AOAT, 220. Neukirchen-Vluyn: Butzon und Bercker Kevelaer, 1987.

LAMBERT, WILFRED G., AND A.R. MILLARD. *Catalogue of the Cuneiform Tablets in the Kouyunjik Collection of the British Museum: Second Supplement.* London: British Museum, 1968.

LANDSBERGER, BENNO. *Brief des Bischofs von Esagila an König Asarhaddon.* Mededeelingen der Koninklijke Nedeerlands Akademie van Wetenschappen, afd. Letterkunde, Nieuwe Reeks, Deel 28, No. 6. Amsterdam: N.V. Noord-Hollandische Uitgevers Maatschappij, 1965.

LANDSBERGER, BENNO, AND TH. BAUER. "Nachträge zu dem Artikel betr. Asarhaddon, Assurbanipal usw., o.S. 61 ff." *ZA,* 37 (1926–27): 215–222.

———. "Zu neuveröffentlichten Geschichtsquellen der Zeit von Asarhaddon bis Nabonid." *ZA,* 37 (1926–27): 61–98.

LANGDON, STEPHEN. *Die neubabylonischen Königsinschriften.* Vorderasiatische Bibliothek, 4. Leipzig: J.C. Hinrichs, 1912.

———. *Tammuz and Ishtar: A Monograph upon Babylonian Religion and Theology Containing Extensive Extracts from the Tammuz Liturgies and All of the Arbela Oracles.* Oxford: Oxford U. Press, 1914. Pp. 130–141 and plates II–IV.

———. *Excavations at Kish: The Herbert Weld (for the University of Oxford) and Field Museum of Natural History (Chicago) Expedition to Mesopotamia, I.* Paris: Paul Geuthner, 1924.

LAYARD, AUSTEN HENRY. *Discoveries in the Ruins of Nineveh and Babylon, with Travels in Armenia, Kurdistan and the Desert: Being the Result of a Second Expedition Undertaken for the Trustees of the British Museum.* London: John Murray, 1853.

———. *Nineveh and its Remains.* 6th ed., 1854; rpt. and abridged by H.W.F. Saggs. London: Praeger, 1969.

LEGRAIN, LEON. *Historical Fragments.* Publications of the Babylonian Section, v. 13. Philadelphia: The University Museum, 1922.

LEICHTY, ERLE. "Esarhaddon's 'Letter to the Gods.'" *Ah, Assyria . . .: Studies in Assyrian History and Ancient Near Eastern Historiography Presented to Hayim Tadmor.* Ed. Mordechai Cogan and Israel Eph'al. Scripta Hierosolymitana, 33. Jerusalem: Magnes Press, Hebrew U., 1991. Pp. 46–51.

LEHMANN, C.F. *Šamaššumukín, König von Babylonien, 668–648 v. Chr.: Inschriftliches Materiel über der Beginn seiner Regierung.* Leipzig: J.C. Hinrichs, 1892.

LENZEN, HEINRICH J. "The Ningišzida Temple Built by Marduk-apla-iddina II at Uruk (Warka)." *Iraq,* 19 (1957): 146–150.

LENZEN, HEINRICH J., ET AL. *Vorläufiger Bericht über die von dem Deutschen Archäologischen Institut und der Deutschen Orient-Gesellschaft aus Mitteln der Deutschen Forschungsgemeinschaft unternommenen Ausgrabungen in Uruk-Warka Winter 1959/60.* Berlin: Gebr. Mann, 1962.

LEVINE, LOUIS D. *Geographical Studies in the Neo-Assyrian Zagros.* Toronto: The Royal Ontario Museum, and London: The British Institute of Persian Studies, 1974. Reprinted from *Iran*, 11 (1973): 1–27, and *Iran*, 12 (1974): 99–124.

———. "Sennacherib's Southern Front: 704–689 BC." *JCS*, 34 (1982): 28–58.

———. "Preliminary Remarks on the Historical Inscriptions of Sennacherib." *History, Historiography and Interpretation.* Ed. Hayim Tadmor and Moshe Weinfeld. Jerusalem: Magnes, 1983. Pp. 58–75.

LEWY, HILDEGARD. "Nitokris-Naqî'a*." *JNES*, 11 (1952): 264–286.

LIE, A.G. *The Inscriptions of Sargon II, King of Assyria, Part I: The Annals. Transliterated and Translated with Notes.* Paris: Paul Geuthner, 1929.

LINDENBERGER, JAMES M. *The Aramaic Proverbs of Ahiqar.* Baltimore: Johns Hopkins U. Press, 1983.

LIVERANI, MARIO. "The Ideology of the Assyrian Empire." *Power and Propaganda: A Symposium on Ancient Empires.* Ed. Mogens Trolle Larsen. Copenhagen: Akademisk Forlag, 1979. Pp. 297–317.

LIVINGSTONE, ALASDAIR. *Court Poetry and Literary Miscellanea.* State Archives of Assyria, III. Helsinki: Helsinki U. Press, 1989.

LUCKENBILL, DANIEL DAVID. "The Ashur Version of the Seven Tablets of Creation." *American Journal of Semitic Languages and Literatures*, 38 (1921–22): 12–35.

———. *The Annals of Sennacherib.* Oriental Institute Publications, II. Chicago: U. of Chicago Press, 1924.

———. "The Black Stone of Esarhaddon." *AJSL*, 41 (1925): 165–173.

———. *Ancient Records of Assyria and Babylonia* 1st ed., 1927; rpt. New York: Greenwood Press, 1968.

LUSCHAN, FELIX VON, ed. *Ausgrabungen in Sendschirli*, I. Mitteilungen aus den orientalischen Sammlungen, 11. Berlin: W. Spemann, 1893.

LYON, DAVID G. *Keilschrifttexte Sargon's Königs von Assyrien (722–705 v. Chr.) nach den Originalen neu herausgegeben, umschrieben, ubersetzt und erklärt.* Assyriologische Bibliothek, 5. Leipzig: J.C. Hinrichs, 1883.

MACHINIST, PETER. "Literature as Politics: The Tukulti-Ninurta Epic and the Bible." *Catholic Biblical Quarterly*, 38 (1976): 455–482.

MALLOWAN, M.E.L. "Ivories from the Throne-room of King Esarhaddon." *The Illustrated London News*, 28 Jan. 1956, pp. 128–131.

———. "The Excavations at Nimrud (Kalḫu), 1955." *Iraq*, 18 (1956): 1–21.

———. *Nimrud and Its Remains.* 3 vols. London: Collins, 1966.

McCARTHY, DENNIS J. *Treaty and Covenant: A Study in Form in the Ancient Oriental Documents and in the Old Testament.* Analecta Biblica, 21. Rome: Pontifical Biblical Institute, 1963.

MEIER, GERHARD. "Ein Brief des assyrischen Gelehrten Balasi." *Orientalia* (n. s.), 8 (1939): 306–308.

MEISSNER, BRUNO. *Könige Babyloniens und Assyriens: Charakterbilder aus der altorientalischen Geschichte.* Leipzig: Quelle and Meyer, [1926].

———. "Neue Nachrichten über die Ermordung Sanheribs und die Nachfolge Asarhaddons." *Sitzungsberichte der Preussischen Akademie der Wissenschaften, Phil.-Hist. Klasse*, 1932. Pp. 250–263.

———. "Wo Befand sich Asarhaddon zur Zeit der Ermordung Sanheribs?" *Analecta Orientalia*, 12 (1935): 232–234.

MEISSNER, BRUNO, AND P. ROST. "Die Bauinschriften Asarhaddons." *Beiträge zur Assyriologie und Semitischen Sprachwissenschaft*, Bd. 3. Leipzig: 1898. Pp. 189–362.

———, ed. *Die Bauinschriften Sanheribs*. Leipzig: Eduard Pfeiffer, 1893.

MESSERSCHMIDT, LEOPOLD. *Keilschrifttexte aus Assur historischen Inhalts, Erstes Heft*. WVDOG, 16. Leipzig: 1911.

MILLARD, A. R. "Esarhaddon Cylinder Fragments from Ft. Shalmaneser, Nimrud." *Iraq*, 23 (1961): 176–178.

———. "Some Esarhaddon Fragments Relating to the Restoration of Babylon." *AfO*, 24 (1973): 117–119 and plates XIII and XIV.

———. "Assyrians and Arameans." *Iraq*, 45 (1983): 101–108.

MULLO-WEIR, CECIL J. "The Return of Marduk to Babylon with Shamashshumukin." *Journal of the Royal Asiatic Society of Great Britain and Ireland* (1929): 553–555.

NA'AMAN, NADAV. "Sennacherib's 'Letter to God' on his Campaign to Judah." *Bulletin of the American Schools of Oriental Research*, 214 (1974): 25–39.

NASSOUHI, ESSAD. "Textes divers relatifs à l'histoire d'Assyrie." *Mitteilungen der Altorientalischen Gesellschaft*, 3 (1927): 18–22.

NEUGEBAUER, P.V. AND O. HILLER. *Spezialler Kanon der Mondfinsternisse*. Astronomische Abhandlungen, Ergänzungsheft zu den Astronomischen Nachrichten, Bd. 9, no. 2, S.B. 3. Kiel: 1934.

NIES, JAMES B. AND CLARENCE E. KEISER. *Historical, Religious and Economic Texts and Antiquities*. Babylonian Inscriptions in the Collection of James B. Nies, II. New Haven: Yale U. Press, 1920.

NÖLDEKE, ARNOLD, ET AL. *Achter Vorläufiger Bericht über die von der Deutschen Forschungsgemeinschaft in Uruk-Warka unternommenen Ausgrabungen*. Berlin: Akademie der Wissenschaften, 1937.

NOUGAYROL, JEAN. "Nouveau fragment de prisme d'Asarhaddon relatant la restauration de Babylone." *AfO*, 18 (1958): 314–318.

OATES, DAVID. "The Excavations at Nimrud (Kalḫu), 1960." *Iraq*, 23 (1961): 1–14.

———. *Studies in the Ancient History of Northern Iraq*. London: Oxford U. Press, 1968.

OATES, JOAN. *Babylon*. London: Thames and Hudson, 1979.

OLMSTEAD, ALBERT TEN EYCK. *Assyrian Historiography: A Source Study*. U. of Missouri Studies, Social Sciences Series, III/1. Columbia, Mo.: U. of Missouri, 1916.

———. *History of Assyria*. Chicago: U. of Chicago Press, 1923.

OPPENHEIM, A. LEO. "The City of Aššur in 714 BC." *JNES*, 19 (1960): 133–147.

———. *Ancient Mesopotamia: Portrait of a Dead Civilization*. Chicago and London: U. of Chicago Press, 1964.

———. "A Note on the Scribes in Mesopotamia." *Studies in Honor of Benno Landsberger on his Seventy-fifth Birthday*. Ed. Hans Güterbock and Thorkild Jacobsen. Assyriological Studies, 16. Chicago: U. of Chicago Press, 1965. Pp. 253–256.

———. "Divination and Celestial Observation in the Last Assyrian Empire." *Centaurus*, 14 (1969): 97–135.

———. "Neo-Assyrian and Neo-Babylonian Empires." *Propaganda and Communication in*

World History, I: The Symbolic Instrument in Early Times. Ed. Harold D. Lasswell, Daniel Lerner, and Hans Speier. Honolulu: U. Press of Hawaii, 1979. Pp. 111–144.

OPPENHEIM, A. LEO., JOHN A. BRINKMAN, ET AL., ed. *The Assyrian Dictionary of the Oriental Institute of the University of Chicago.* Chicago, Ill.: The Oriental Institute, and Glück-stadt, Germany: J.J. Augustin, 1956–.

OPPOLZER, THEODOR VON. *Canon of Eclipses.* Trans. Owen Gingerich. Trans. and rpt. of *Canon der Finsternisse* (Wien: 1887). New York: Dover, 1962.

OTTO, EBERHARD. "Ninive." *AfO,* 18 (1957–58): 177–178.

OWEN, DAVID I. AND KAZUKO WATANABE. "Eine Neubabylonische Gartenkaufurkunde mit Flüchen aus dem Akzessionsjahr Asarhaddons." *Oriens Antiquus,* 22 (1983): 37–48.

PALLIS, SVEND AAGE. *The Babylonian Akîtu Festival.* Det. Kgl. Danske Vrdenskabernes Selskab., Historisk-filologiske Meddelelser, XII, 1. Copenhagen: Andr. Fred. Host, 1926.

PARKER, BARBARA. "Seals and Seal Impressions from the Nimrud Excavations, 1955–58." *Iraq,* 24 (1962): 26–40.

PARKER, RICHARD AND WALDO DUBBERSTEIN. *Babylonian Chronology 626 BC–AD 75.* Providence, R.I.: Boston U. Press, 1956.

PARPOLA, SIMO. *Neo-Assyrian Toponyms.* AOAT, 6. Neukirchen-Vluyn: Butzon und Bercker, 1970.

———. *Letters from Assyrian Scholars to the Kings Esarhaddon and Assurbanipal. Part I: Texts,* and *Part II: Commentary and Appendices.* Alter Orient und Altes Testament, 5/1 and 5/2. Neukirchen-Vluyn: Butzon und Bercker Kevelaer, 1970 and 1983.

———. *Letters from Assyrian Scholars to the Kings Esarhaddon and Assurbanipal. Part IIA: Introduction and Appendixes.* Diss., Helsinki U. Neukirchen-Vluyn: Kevelaer, 1971.

———. "A Letter from Šamaš-šumu-ukīn to Esarhaddon." *Iraq,* 34 (1972): 21–34.

———. Unpublished comments on dating an astronomical omen and on the professional probity of omen interpreters. Private correspondence, 24 Feb. 1977.

———. *Cuneiform Texts from Babylonian Tablets in the British Museum, Part 53.* London: British Museum, 1979.

———. "The Murderer of Sennacherib." *Death in Mesopotamia.* Ed. Bendt Alster. Mesopotamia, 8. Copenhagen: Akademisk Forlag, 1980. Pp. 171–182.

———. "Assyrian Royal Inscriptions and Neo-Assyrian Letters." *Assyrian Royal Inscriptions: New Horizons in Literary, Ideological, and Historical Analysis.* Ed. F.M. Fales. Rome: Istituto per l'Oriente, 1981. Pp. 117–141.

———. Unpublished notes toward a revised edition of "The Sin of Sargon." Private correspondence, July, 1985.

———. "The Royal Archives of Nineveh." *Cuneiform Archives and Libraries.* Compte rendu de la 30e Rencontre Assyriologique Internationale, Leiden, 1983. Ed. Klaas R. Veenhof. Leiden: Nederlands Historisch-Archaeologisch Institut te Istanbul, 1986. Pp. 223–236.

———. "Neo-Assyrian Treaties from the Royal Archives of Nineveh." *JCS,* 39 (1987): 161–189.

PARPOLA, SIMO, AND KAZUKO WATANABE, with ill. ed. by Julian Reade. *Neo-Assyrian Treaties and Loyalty Oaths.* State Archives of Assyria, II. Helsinki: Helsinki U. Press, 1988.

PARROT, ANDRÉ AND JEAN NOUGAYROL. "Asarhaddon et Naqi'a sur un Bronze du Louvre (AO 20.185)." *Syria*, 33 (1956): 147–160.

PEDERSEN, OLAF. *Archives and Libraries in the City of Assur: A Survey of the Material from the German Excavations.* 2 vols. Studia Semitica Upsaliensia, 6. Uppsala: 1985.

PETTINATO, G. "I Rapporti Politici di Tiro con L'Assiria alla Luce del 'Trattato tra Asarhaddon e Baal.'" *Rivista di Studi Fenici*, III/2 (1975): 145–160.

PINCHES, TH. G. *Cuneiform Texts from Babylonian Tablets in the British Museum, Part 44: Miscellaneous Texts.* London: British Museum, 1963.

POSTGATE, J.N. "Royal Exercise of Justice under the Assyrian Empire." *Le Palais et la royauté (archéologie et civilisation).* Compte rendu de la 19e Rencontre Assyriologique Internationale, Paris, 1971. Ed. Paul Garelli. Paris: Geuthner, 1974.

———. *Taxation and Conscription in the Assyrian Empire.* Studia Pohl: Series Major, 3. Rome: Biblical Institute Press, 1974.

———. "The Economic Structure of the Assyrian Empire." *Power and Propaganda: A Symposium on Ancient Empires.* Ed. Mogens Trolle Larsen. Mesopotamia, 7. Copenhagen: Akademisk Forlag, 1979. Pp. 193–221.

POSTGATE, J.N., AND J. E. READE. "Kalḫu." *RLA*, V. Ed. Dietz Otto Edzard. Berlin and New York: Walter de Gruyter, 1976–80. Pp. 303–323.

PRITCHARD, JAMES B. *Ancient Near Eastern Texts Relating to the Old Testament.* 2nd ed. Princeton: Princeton U. Press, 1955.

———. *The Ancient Near East: An Anthology.* Princeton: Princeton U. Press, 1958.

———. *The Ancient Near East: Supplementary Texts and Pictures Relating to the Old Testament.* Princeton: Princeton U. Press, 1969.

PURSER, L.C. "Canephorus." *A Dictionary of Greek and Roman Antiquities*, I. Ed. William Smith, William Wayte, and G.E. Marindin. 2 vols. 3rd edition. London: John Murray, 1890. P. 354.

RASSAM, HORMUZD. *Asshur and the Land of Nimrod, Being an Account of the Discoveries Made in the Ancient Ruins of Nineveh, Asshur, Sepharvaim, Calah, Babylon, Borsippa, Cuthah, and Van, etc.* Cincinnati and New York: Curts and Jenning, and Eaton and Mains, 1897.

RAWLINSON, HENRY C. *The Cuneiform Inscriptions of Western Asia, Vol. I: A Selection from the Historical Inscriptions of Chaldea, Assyria, and Babylonia.* London: Harrison and Sons, 1861.

———. *The Cuneiform Inscriptions of Western Asia, Vol. III: A Selection from the Miscellaneous Inscriptions of Assyria.* London: R.E. Bowler, 1870.

———. *The Cuneiform Inscriptions of Western Asia, Vol. IV: A Selection from the Miscellaneous Inscriptions of Assyria.* London: R.E. Bowler, 1875.

READE, JULIAN E. "Sources for Sennacherib: The Prisms." *JCS*, 27 (1975): 189–196.

———. "Shikaft-i Gulgul: Its Date and Symbolism." *Iranica Antiqua*, 12 (1977): 33–44 and plates I–IV.

———. "Ideology and Propaganda in Assyrian Art." *Power and Propaganda: A Symposium on Ancient Empires.* Ed. Mogens Trolle Larsen. Mesopotamia, 7. Copenhagen: Akademisk Forlag, 1979. Pp. 329–343.

———. "Nimrud." *Fifty Years of Mesopotamian Discovery.* Ed. John Curtis. London: British School of Archaeology in Iraq, 1982. Pp. 99–112, and plates 7a–8b.

————. "Archaeology and the Kuyunjik Archives." *Cuneiform Archives and Libraries.* Compte rendu de la 30e Rencontre Assyriologique Internationale, Leiden, 1983. Ed. Klaas R. Veenhof. Leiden: Nederlands Historisch-Archaeologish Institut te Istanbul, 1986. Pp. 213–222.

————. "Rassam's Excavations at Borsippa and Kutha, 1879–82." *Iraq,* 48 (1986): 105–116 and pls. xiii–xix.

READE, JULIAN E., AND C.B.F. WALKER. "Some Neo-Assyrian Royal Inscriptions." *AfO,* 28 (1981–82): 113–122.

REUTHER, OSCAR. *Die Innenstadt von Babylon (Merkes).* 2 vols. WVDOG, 47. Leipzig: J.C. Hinrichs, 1926.

ROGERS, ROBERT W. *Haverford College Studies,* 2. Haverford: Haverford College, 1889.

ROST, PAUL. *Die Keilschrifttexte Tiglat-Pilesers III.* 2 vols. Leipzig: Eduard Pfeiffer, 1893.

ROUX, GEORGES. *Ancient Iraq.* Harmondsworth, Middlesex, Eng.: 1964, rpt. 1966.

SAN NICOLÒ, MARIANO. *Beiträge zu einer Prosopographie neubabylonischer Beamten der Zivil-und Tempelverwaltung.* Sitzungsberichte der Bayerischen Akademie der Wissenschaften, Phil.-Hist. Klasse, 1941, Bd. II, H. 2. Munich: 1941.

————. *Babylonische Rechtsurkunden des Ausgehenden 8. und 7. Jahrhunderts v. Chr.,* I. Abhandlungen der Bayerischen Akademie der Wissenschaften, Phil.-Hist. Kl., neue folge, vol. 34. Munich: 1951.

SASSON, JACK. *English-Akkadian Analytical Index to the Chicago Assyrian Dictionary: Part 1.* Chapel Hill, N.C.: U. of North Carolina, 1973.

SCHAUMBERGER, JOHANN AND ALBERT SCHOTT. "Die Konjunktion von Mars und Saturn im Frühjahr 669 v. Chr. nach Thompson, Reports Nr. 88 und anderem Texten." *ZA,* 44 (1938): 271–289.

SCHAWE, JOSEF. Review of Hans Hirschberg, *Studien zur Geschichte Esarhaddons. AfO,* 9 (1933–34): 55–60.

SCHEIL, V. *Le Prisme S d'Assarhaddon, roi d'Assyrie 681–668.* Bibliothèque de l'École des Hautes Études, IVe Section, 208. Paris: Honoré Champion, 1914.

————. "Catalogue de la Collection Eugène Tissérant." *RA,* 18 (1921): 1–33.

SCHMIDT, JÜRGEN, ET AL. *XXVI and XXVII vorläufiger Bericht über die von dem Deutschen Archäologischen Institut und der Deutschen Orient-Gesellschaft aus Mitteln der Deutschen Forschungsgemeinschaft unternommenen Ausgrabungen in Uruk-Warka (1968 and 1969)* Berlin: Mann, 1972.

————, ed. *Uruk-Warka. Vorläufiger Bericht über die von dem Deutschen Archäologischen Institut aus Mitteln der Deutschen Forschungsgemeinschaft unternommenen Ausgrabungen in Uruk-Warka.* Berlin: Mann, 1970.

SCHMIDTKE, FRIEDRICH. *Asarhaddons Statthalterschaft in Babylonien und seine Thronbesteigung in Assyrien 681 v. Chr.* Altorientalische Texte und Untersuchungen, I/2. Leiden: E.J. Brill, 1916.

SCHOCH, CARL. "Astronomical and Calendrical Tables," in *The Venus Tablets of Ammizaduga* by Stephen Langdon and J.K. Fotheringham. London: Oxford U. Press, 1928. Pp. 94–109 and I–XVI.

SCHOTT, ALBERT. "Die inschriftlichen Quellen zur Geschichte Eannas." In Julius Jordan, ed., "Ausgrabungen in Uruk-Warka 1928–29." *Abhandlungen der Preussischen Akademie der Wissenschaften,* 1929, Phil.-Hist Kl., no. 7, pp. 46–67.

SCHOTT, ALBERT, AND JOHANN SCHAUMBERGER. "Vier Briefe Mâr-Ištars an Asarhaddon uber Himmelserscheinungen der Jahre 670/668." *ZA*, 47 (1941–42): 89–130.

SCHRAMM, WOLFGANG. *Einleitung in die assyrischen Königsinschriften. Zweiter Teil: 934–722 v. Chr.* Handbuch der Orientalistik, Abt. 1: Der nahe und der mittlere Osten, Ergänzungsband 5, Abschnitt 1. Leiden and Köln: E.J. Brill, 1973.

SCHROEDER, OTTO. *Keilschrifttexte aus Assur historischen Inhalts*, II. WVDOG, 37. Leipzig: J.C. Hinrichs, 1922.

SEUX, M.-J. *Épithètes royales akkadiennes et sumériennes.* Paris: Letouzey et Ane, 1967.

SIMPSON, WILLIAM KELLY. "The Pharaoh Taharqa" in "News and Correspondence." *Sumer*, 10 (1954): 193–194.

———. Letter in "News and Correspondence." *Sumer*, 11 (1955): 131–132.

SMITH, GEORGE. "Egyptian Campaigns of Esarhaddon and Aššur-bani-pal." *Zeitschrift für ägyptische Sprache und Altertumskunde* (1868): 93–99 and 113–122.

SMITH, SIDNEY. *The First Campaign of Sennacherib, King of Assyria, BC 705–681.* London: Luzac, 1921.

———. "Sennacherib and Esarhaddon." *The Cambridge Ancient History, Vol. III: The Assyrian Empire.* Cambridge: Cambridge U. Press, 1929. Pp. 61–87.

SODEN, WOLFRAM VON. "Assarhaddon—Überheblichkeit und Angst." *Herrscher im alten Orient.* Verständliche Wissenschaft, Bd. 54. Berlin, Göttingen, and Heidelberg: Springer-Verlag, 1954. Pp. 118–126.

———. "Gibt es ein Zeugnis dafür, dass die Babylonier an die Wiederauferstehung Marduks geglaubt haben?" *ZA*, 51 (1955): 130–166.

———. "Beiträge zum Verständnis der neuassyrischen Briefe über Ersatzkönigsriten." *Festschrift für Victor Christian.* Ed. Kurt Schubert, with Johannes Botterweck and Johann Knobloch. Vorderasiatische Studien. Wien: 1956. Pp. 100–109.

———. "Ein neues Brückstück des assyrischen Kommentars zum Marduk-Ordal." *ZA*, 52 (1956): 223–234.

———, ed. *Akkadisches Handwörterbuch unter Benutzung des lexikalischen Nachlasses von Bruno Meissner (1868–1947).* Wiesbaden: Otto Harrasowitz, 1965–81.

SOLLBERGER, EDMOND AND JEAN-ROBERT KUPPER. *Inscriptions royales sumériennes et akkadiennes.* Paris: Éditions du Cerf, 1971.

SOMMERFELD, WALTER. *Der Aufsteig Marduks: Die Stellung Marduks in der babylonischen Religion des zweiten Jahrtausends v. Chr.* AOAT, 213. Neukirchen-Vluyn: Verlag Butzon und Bercker Kevelaer and Neukirchener Verlag, 1982.

SPALINGER, ANTHONY. "Esarhaddon and Egypt: An Analysis of the First Invasion of Egypt." *Orientalia* (n.s.), 43 (1974): 295–326.

———. "The Foreign Policy of Egypt Preceding the Assyrian Conquest." *Chronique d'Égypte*, 53 (1978): 22–47.

SPEK, R.J. VAN DER. "The Assyrian Royal Rock Inscription from Shikaft-i Gulgul." *Iranica Antiqua*, 12 (1977): 45–47.

STAHLMAN, WILLIAM D. AND OWEN GINGERICH. *Solar and Planetary Longitudes for Years –2500 to +2000 by 10-Day Intervals.* Madison, Wis.: U. of Wisconsin Press, 1963.

STEELE, FRANCIS RUE. "Esarhaddon Building Inscription from Nippur." *JCS*, 70 (1950): 69–72.

———. "The University Museum Esarhaddon Prism." *JAOS*, 71 (1951): 1 ff.

STEINER, RICHARD AND CHARLES F. NIMS. "Ashurbanipal and Shamash-Shum-Ukin: A Tale of Two Brothers from the Aramaic Text in Demotic Script." *Revue Biblique*, 92 (1985): 58–81.

STEPHENS, FERRIS J. *Votive and Historical Texts from Babylonia and Assyria*. Yale Oriental Series, 9. New Haven: Yale U. Press, 1937.

STRASSMAIER, JOHANN N. "Einige kleinere babylonische Keilschrifttexte aus dem Britischen Museum." *Actes du huitième Congrès international des Orientalistes, tenu en 1889 à Stockholm et à Christiana. Deuxième Partie.* Leiden: E.J. Brill, 1893. Section IB, pp. 279–283 and plates 1–35.

STRECK, MAXIMILIAN. *Assurbanipal und die letzen assyrischen Könige bis zum untergange Nineveh's.* 3 vols. Vorderasiatische Bibliothek, 7. Leipzig: J.C. Hinrichs, 1916.

STRONG, S. ARTHUR. "On Some Oracles to Esarhaddon and Asurbanipal." *Sonderabdruck aus den Beiträgen zur Assyriologie und vergleichenden semitischen Sprachwissenschaft*, Bd. II. Leipzig: J.C. Hinrichs, 1893. Pp. 627–643.

TADMOR, HAYIM. "The 'Sin of Sargon'." *Eretz Israel*, 5 (1958), p. 93 (Eng. summary) and pp. 150–163 (Hebrew) and table 3.

———. "Philistia under Assyrian Rule." *Biblical Archeologist*, 29 (1966): 86–102.

———. "History and Ideology in the Assyrian Royal Inscriptions." *Assyrian Royal Inscriptions: New Horizons in Literary, Ideological and Historical Analysis.* Ed. F.M. Fales. Rome: Istituto per l'Oriente, 1981. Pp. 13–33.

———. "The Aramaization of Assyria: Aspects of Western Impact." *Mesopotamien und seine Nachbarn.* Ed. Hans-Jörg Nissen and Johannes Renger. Berliner Beiträge zum Vorderen Orient, Bd. 1. Berlin: Dietrich Riemer, 1982. Pp. 449–470.

———. "Autobiographical Apology in the Royal Assyrian Literature." *History, Historiography and Interpretation.* Ed. H. Tadmor and M. Weinfeld. Jerusalem: Magnes, 1984. Pp. 36–57.

TADMOR, HAYIM, BENNO LANDSBERGER, AND SIMO PARPOLA. "The Sin of Sargon and Sennacherib's Last Will." *State Archives of Assyria Bulletin*, 3 (1989): 3–52.

THOMPSON, R. CAMPBELL. *The Reports of the Magicians and Astrologers of Nineveh and Babylon in the British Museum.* 2 vols. London: Luzac, 1900.

———. *The Prisms of Esarhaddon and Ashurbanipal found at Nineveh, 1927–8.* London: Oxford U. Press, 1931.

———. "Notes to My Prisms of Esarhaddon." *Annals of Archaeology and Anthropology*, 20 (1933): 126 ff.

———. "A Selection from the Cuneiform Historical Texts from Nineveh (1927–32)." *Iraq*, 7 (1940): 85–131.

THOMPSON, R. CAMPBELL, AND R. W. HUTCHINSON. *A Century of Exploration at Nineveh.* London: Luzac, 1929.

———. "XII. The Excavations on the Temple of Nabû at Nineveh." *Archaeologia*, 79 (1929): 103–148.

THUREAU-DANGIN, FRANÇOIS. *Les Cylindres de Goudea: Transcription, traduction, commentaire, grammaire et lexique, Part 1: Transcription et traduction.* Paris: Ernest Leroux, 1905.

———. *Une Rélation de la huitième campagne de Sargon (714 av. J.C.).* Paris: Paul Geuthner, 1912.

———. "Notes assyriologiques, XXVI. Un Barillet d'Asarhaddon." *RA*, 11 (1914): 96–101.

———. "Tell Aḥmar." *Syria*, 10 (1929): 185–205.

TSUKIMOTO, AKIO. "A New Esarhaddon Prism Fragment Concerning the Restoration of Babylon." *Annual Review of the Royal Inscriptions of Mesopotamia Project*, 8 (1990): 63–69.

TUMAN, V.S. "Astronomical Dating of Esarhaddon's Stela." *Griffith Observer*, 51 (1987): 10–19.

TURNER, GEOFFREY. "Tell Nebi Yūnus: The *Ekal Māšarti* of Nineveh." *Iraq*, 32 (1970): 68–85.

UNGER, ECKHARD. *Die Stele des Bel-Harran-Beli-Usser; ein Denkmal der Zeit Salmanassars IV.* Publicationen der Kaiserlich Osmanischen Museen, III. Constantinople: Ahmed Ihsan, 1917.

———. "Akkad." *Reallexikon der Assyriologie*, I. Ed. Erich Ebeling and Bruno Meissner. Berlin and Leipzig: Walter de Gruyter, 1928.

———. "Aššur." *Reallexikon der Assyriologie*, I. Ed. Erich Ebeling and Bruno Meissner. Berlin and Leipzig: Walter de Gruyter, 1928. P. 188.

———. "Babylon." *Reallexikon der Assyriologie*, I. Ed. Erich Ebeling and Bruno Meissner. Berlin and Leipzig: Walter de Gruyter, 1928. Pp. 330–369.

———. "Borsippa." *Reallexikon der Assyriologie*, I. Ed. Erich Ebeling and Bruno Meissner. Berlin and Leipzig: Walter de Gruyter, 1928. Pp. 402–429.

UNGNAD, ARTHUR. "Der Ort der Ermordung Sanheribs." *ZA*, 35 (1923–24): 50–51.

———. "Eponymen." *Reallexikon der Assyriologie*, II. Ed. Erich Ebeling and Bruno Meissner. Berlin and Leipzig: Walter de Gruyter, 1938. P. 414.

VAN BUREN, ELIZABETH DOUGLAS. *Foundation Figurines and Offerings.* Berlin: Hans Schoetz, 1931.

VIEYRA, M. "Notes d'histoire." *RA*, 54 (1960): 41–42.

VIKENTIEV, VLADIMIR. "Quelques considérations à propos des statues de Taharqa trouvées dans les ruines du palais d'Esarhaddon." *Sumer*, 11 (1955): 111–116.

WALKER, C.B.F. *Cuneiform Brick Inscriptions in The British Museum; The Ashmolean Museum, Oxford; The City of Birmingham Museums and Art Gallery; The City of Bristol Museum and Art Gallery.* London: British Museum, 1981.

WALL-ROMANA, CHRISTOPHE. "An Areal Location of Agade." *JNES*, 49 (1990): 205–245.

WALTERS, STANLEY. *Water for Larsa: An Old Babylonian Archive Dealing With Irrigation.* Yale Near Eastern Researches, 4. New Haven and London: Yale U. Press, 1970.

WALZER, MICHAEL. "On the Role of Symbolism in Political Thought." *Political Science Quarterly*, 82 (1967): 191–205.

WATANABE, KAZUKO. *Die adê-Vereidigung anlässlich der Thronfolgeregelung Asarhaddons.* Baghdader Mitteilungen, Beiheft 3. Berlin: Gebr. Mann, 1987.

WATERMAN, LEROY. *Royal Correspondence of the Assyrian Empire Translated into English, with a Transliteration of the Text and a Commentary.* 4 parts. University of Michigan Studies, Humanistic Series, Vols. XVII–XX. Ann Arbor, Michigan: U. of Michigan Press, 1930–36.

WEIDNER, ERNST W. *Handbuch der babylonischen Astronomie, I: Der Babylonische Fixsternhimmel.* Assyriologische Bibliothek, 23. Leipzig: J.C. Hinrichs, 1915.

———. "Assurbânipal in Assur." *AfO*, 13 (1939–41): 204–218.

———. "Hochverrat gegen Asarhaddon." *AfO*, 17 (1954): 5–9.

———. "Ninive." *AfO*, 17 (1954–56): 228.

———. "Ninive." *AfO*, 18 (1957–58): 177.

WEIHER, E. VON. "Ḫanigalbat." *Reallexikon der Assyriologie*, IV. Ed. D.O. Edzard. Berlin and Leipzig: Walter de Gruyter, 1972–75. Pp. 105–107.

WEINFELD, MOSHE. "Justice and Righteousness in Ancient Israel against the Background of 'Social Reforms' in the Ancient Near East." *Mesopotamien und seine Nachbarn*. Ed. Hans-Jörg Nissen and Johannes Renger. Berliner Beiträge zum Vordern Orient, Bd. 1. Berlin: Dietrich Riemer, 1982. Pp. 491–520.

WEIPPERT, MANFRED. "Assyrische Prophetien der Zeit Asarhaddons und Assurbanipals." *Assyrian Royal Inscriptions: New Horizons in Literary, Ideological, and Historical Analysis*. Ed. F.M. Fales. Rome: Istituto per l'Oriente, 1981. Pp. 71–115.

WEISSBACH, F. *Die Denkmäler und Inschriften an der Mündung des Nahr el-Kelb*. Wissenschaftliche Veröffentlichung des Deutsch-Turkischen Denkmalschutz-Kommandos, 6. Berlin and Leipzig: Walter de Gruyter, 1922.

———. "Der assyrische Name von Qal'at al-'Aris." *ZA*, 38 (1928): 108–110.

———. "Aššurahiddin." *Reallexikon der Assyriologie*, I. Ed. Erich Ebeling and Bruno Meissner. Berlin and Leipzig: Walter de Gruyter, 1932. Pp. 198–203.

———. "Babylonien." *Reallexikon der Assyriologie*, I. Ed. Erich Ebeling and Bruno Meissner. Berlin and Leipzig: Walter de Gruyter, 1932. Pp. 369–384.

WETZEL, FRIEDRICH. *Die Stadtmauern von Babylon*. WVDOG, 48. Leipzig: J.C. Hinrichs, 1930.

WETZEL, FRIEDRICH, AND F.H. WEISSBACH. *Das Hauptheiligtum des Marduk in Babylon, Esagila und Etemenanki*. WVDOG, 59. Leipzig: J.C. Hinrichs, 1938.

WILCKE, CLAUS. "Die Anfänge der akkadischen Epen." *ZA*, 67 (1977): 153–216.

WINCKLER, HUGO, with copies by Ludwig Abel. *Die Keilschrifttexte Sargons nach den papierabklatschen und originalen neu herausgegeben*. 2 vols. Leipzig: Eduard Pfeiffer, 1889.

———. "Supria." *Altorientalische Forschungen*, II. Leipzig: Eduard Pfeiffer, 1893–97.

WINTER, IRENE. "Royal Rhetoric and the Development of Historical Narrative in Neo-Assyrian Reliefs." *Studies in Visual Communications*, 7 (1981): 2–38.

———. "The Program of the Throne room of Assurnasirpal II." *Essays in Near Eastern Art and Archaeology in Honor of C.K. Wilkinson*. Ed. P.O. Harper and H. Pittman. New York: Metropolitan Museum, 1983.

WISEMAN, D.J. "An Esarhaddon Cylinder from Nimrud." *Iraq*, 14 (1952): 54–60.

———. *The Vassal Treaties of Esarhaddon*. *Iraq*, 20 (1958), part 1. Rpt., London: British School of Archaeology in Iraq, 1958.

———. "Fragments of Historical Texts from Nimrud." *Iraq*, 26 (1964): 118–124 and plates xxv–xxvii.

———. "Murder in Mesopotamia." *Iraq*, 36 (1974): 249–260.

ZEISSL, HELENE VON. *Äthiopen und Assyrer in Ägypten: Beiträge zur Geschichte der Ägyptischen "Spätzeit."* Ägyptologische Forschungen, 14. Glückstadt and Hamburg: J.J. Augustin, 1944.

ZIMMERN, HEINRICH. "Zum Babylonischen Neujahrsfest." *Berichte über die Verhandlungen der Königlich Sächsischen Gesellschaft der Wissenschaften*, Phil.-Hist. Kl., Bd. 58. Leipzig: Teubner, 1906.

———. "Zum Babylonischen Neujahrsfest, Zweiter Beitrag." *Berichte über die Verhandlungen der Königlich Sächischen Gesellschaft der Wissenschaften*, Phil.-Hist. Kl., Bd. 70/5. Leipzig: Teubner, 1918.

Index

Material in the footnotes has been included in the index and is listed according to the page on which it appears. As a convenience, Appendix I has also been indexed. Akkadian words are shown in italics, except for proper names, and both Akkadian words and names are alphabetized without regard to their diacritical marks, e.g., words beginning with Š and words beginning with S are listed together, without differentiation.

THE MIDDLE EAST

Showing Places Mentioned in the Text

ELAM   Ancient Country or Region
•   Ancient City
Nippur Ancient City with Modern/Classical Name
Babylon
•   Ancient City of Uncertain Location
Labbanat
○   Modern City
Baghdad
IRAQ   Modern Country
------ Modern Border
        Modern Border
        Swamp

Scale: 1:4,700,000

0   50   100   MILES
0   50   100   150   KILOMETERS

Lambert Conformal Conic Projection
Standard Parallels 33°20' and 38°40'

Mediterranean Sea

TURKEY
AMANUS MTS
KUMMUHU
HANIGALBAT
ŠUBRIA
URARTU
MANNEA
IRAN
ZAGROS MOUNTAINS
ELAM

Tarbisu
Dur-Sarrukin
Mosul
Nineveh
Calah (Nimrud)
Ekallate
Assur
Arbela
Zab
Little Zab
Tigris
Samarra
ASSYRIA
Zahiru
Labbanat
Der
Diyala
Baghdad
Sippar-anunit
Ur-Kungabzu
Sippar
Kutha
Babylon
Kish
Borsippa
Dilbat
Nippur
Isin
Umma
Uruk
Larsa
Lagash
Sa-amile
 Larak
Ur
Eridu
Kisik
BABYLONIA
SEA LAND

Hursag-kalamma
Susa

Euphrates
Habur
Til-Barsib
Harrān
SYRIA
SYRIAN DESERT
Damascus
Nahr el-Keb
LEBANON
Tyre
Sidon
Jerusalem
ISRAEL
JORDAN
SAUDI ARABIA
IRAQ

KUWAIT
Persian Gulf

Caspian Sea

www.ingramcontent.com/pod-product-compliance
Lightning Source LLC
Chambersburg PA
CBHW080923100426
42812CB00007B/2352